REPAIR MY HOUSE

REPAIR MY HOUSE

Becoming a "Kindom" Catholic

MICHAEL H. CROSBY

ORBIS BOOKS

Maryknoll, New York 10545

Founded in 1970, Orbis Books endeavors to publish works that enlighten the mind, nourish the spirit, and challenge the conscience. The publishing arm of the Maryknoll Fathers and Brothers, Orbis seeks to explore the global dimensions of the Christian faith and mission, to invite dialogue with diverse cultures and religious traditions, and to serve the cause of reconciliation and peace. The books published reflect the views of their authors and do not represent the official position of the Maryknoll Society. To learn more about Maryknoll and Orbis Books, please visit our website at www.maryknollsociety.org.

Copyright © 2012 by Michael H. Crosby
Published by Orbis Books, Box 302, Maryknoll, NY 10545-0302.
All rights reserved.

Nihil Obstat:
Rev. Francis Dombrowski, OFMCap., STL
   Provincial Censor of Books
   November 7, 2011
Very Rev. John Celichowski, OFMCap.
   Provincial Minister
   Province of St. Joseph of the Capuchin Order
   December 12, 2011

Manufactured in the United States of America

Library of Congress Cataloging-in-Publication Data

Crosby, Michael, 1940-
   Repair my house : becoming a "kindom" Catholic / Michael H. Crosby.
      p. cm.
   Includes bibliographical references (p.   ) and index.
   ISBN 978-1-57075-953-6 (pbk.); eISBN 978-1-60833-114-7
      1. Church renewal—Catholic Church. 2. Catholic Church—History—21st century.
I. Title.

   BX1746.C695   2011
   262'.02—dc23
                                                            2011044901

Contents

Introduction

The Roman Catholic Church, at least in the West, is in crisis. In his September 2011 trip to his native Germany, Pope Benedict XVI repeated this recurring theme of his pontificate: "The real crisis facing the Church in the western world is a crisis of faith." He then pointed to the key way this crisis must be addressed: "If we do not find a way of genuinely renewing our faith [in God], all structural reform will remain ineffective."[1] While I completely agree that the underlying "crisis facing the Church in the western world" is a crisis of faith, I believe that one of the key reasons for this crisis is the functioning of the historically determined structures of the Catholic Church itself and the fact that these structures do not reflect the organization within the Godhead we know to be triune. I believe the Pope himself intimated as much when he said in the same speech: "We have more than enough by way of structure but not enough by way of Spirit." Again, while agreeing with the Pope, the evidence reviewed in this book will suggest that the crisis of faith in the church of the West is not about faith in the Spirit as much as it is about lack of faith in the institutional church itself.

The main evidence supporting such a statement cannot be linked directly with past clerical sexual abuse of children or the allegations of episcopal cover-ups connected to it. Rather, the crisis is deeper. On the one hand, it involves a precipitous drop in church membership and, on the other, the ever-declining influence of its clerical leaders. What began decades ago in the Pope's native Germany and other parts of Western Europe has found its patterns replicated in Ireland and the United Kingdom, Australia and New Zealand, and, more recently, in English-speaking Canada and the United States. While church leaders have pointed fingers at the people in the pews and the "isms" they claim are eroding their faith (especially relativism,[2] individualism,[3] and secularism[4]), an examination of the hard data yields a more subtle causation pointing to the church's form of governance itself and the "isms" this reveals.

This book probes the data that reflects this phenomenon of declining allegiance to the teachings of church leaders[5] and the hemorrhaging of participation in the church. It will then show that much of this decline reflects a decline of meaning in the "official" church for more and more Catholics. The data will suggest that any repair of the *institutional* model of the Roman Catholic Church demands a return to the core message of Jesus' proclamation of the kingdom of God, by which I mean the gospel of the rule of trinitarian connectedness that must be in evidence at all levels of life, including the governance of the church. This will demand a new way of being Catholic.

This book discusses the above notions in three parts: (1) The impact of the various forms of contemporary atheism on Catholicism and the parallel crisis in the Roman Catholic Church; (2) the need to understand this crisis in apocalyptic terms in a way that invites a return to the core evangelical message of Jesus Christ; and (3) the need to develop a revitalized way of being "Catholic" that entails a form of contemporary discipline that is grounded in a clear cosmology that is Christ centered, consciously aware, deeply connected and connecting, contemplative in its core, compassionate in its witness, and communal in its bonding.

Catholicism and Apocalypse: Tradition Eclipsing Scripture

For the 2011 Los Angeles Religious Education Congress in Anaheim, California, I decided to investigate and address the challenges of the "new atheists." The more I read their arguments (despite their often polemical way of framing them), the more I realized they could not be easily dismissed. Along with my research on their writings, I began to examine other data behind the huge decline in the number of practicing Catholics in the economically developed countries. The data revealed an even more serious matter. While the theoretical challenges of the "new atheists" cannot be dismissed with *ad hominem* arguments, an even greater challenge lies in the fact that in such countries, "former" Catholics now number approximately 100 million or more persons.[6] Besides these two challenges, an examination of the worldview of many Catholics who still practice the faith reveals few appreciable differences between their politics and lifestyle and those of the mainstream. This raises the question as to whether such Catholics are more grounded in the god of Americanism or capitalism than in the God of Jesus Christ.

One cannot honestly examine such data without concluding that a crisis of huge proportion faces the institutional Roman Catholic Church today. This does not refer to its mystical foundation. Nor does it call into question its creed or its sacraments. It also does not impugn the sincerity of its leaders themselves. Rather, it revolves around secondary issues that have become primary with church leaders to the point that these differences have become virtually equated with doctrine. The result of such a conflation is found in the promotion of a "remnant but right" form of Catholicism. This "leaner but cleaner" way of being "Catholic" echoes patterns associated with the church prior to the Second Vatican Council, a model of church that the dominant clerical leaders in the present church seem to want to restore (including such features as greater separation between the role of clergy and laity during Mass, more

Latin or Latin-based prayers, the emphasis on kneelers and fasting, reservation of the Blessed Sacrament near the main altar, and so forth). I will argue that such apparent priorities are much more historically determined than divinely ordained. Furthermore, when such practices are stressed, an imbalance between tradition and scripture results to the point that many church leaders know canon law better than divine revelation. The resulting imbalance finds the tradition trumping the scriptures. And we know what the scriptures say Jesus thought about that (see Mark 7:1-23; Matt. 15:1-20)!

Actual data showing the dramatic decline in membership in the Catholic Church in the last decade in places like the United States (among non-Hispanics) reveals little or no link to arguments based on "isms" like relativism, despite declarations by church authorities. Rather, they flow from an increasing sense of the *irrelevance* of historically determined, culturally conditioned ecclesiastical patterns of thinking, speaking, and acting that reveal a structure in serious need of repair. These patterns reveal the "structural sins" of Roman Catholicism.

To say that structural sin has found its way into the existing institutional form of the Roman Church does not imply that any specific individuals have consciously created these sinful patterns. Rather, they reflect culturally derived patterns that may have had a purpose at one time, but which are now experienced as sinful human dynamics, which must be challenged and repaired if structural conversion is to occur in our church. In this I find support for my thinking in Pope John Paul II's own understanding of how history often moves in ways that result in "structural" or "institutional" sin. His insight is especially helpful when we examine how these human dynamics are all too evident in the scandals that have been revealed in our church. He wrote:

> If the present situation can be attributed to difficulties of various kinds, it is not out of place to speak of "structures of sin," which . . . are rooted in personal sin and thus always linked to the concrete acts of individuals who introduce these structures, consolidate them, and make them difficult to remove. And thus they grow stronger, spread, and become the source of other sins, and so influence people's behavior. "Sin" and "structures of sin" are categories which are seldom applied to the situation of the contemporary world. However, one cannot easily gain a profound understanding of the reality that confronts us unless we give a name to the root of the evils which afflict us.[7]

Admitting how such an insight by the Pope applies to one's own "family" (i.e., the Roman Catholic Church) is not easy. However, once we make the necessary distinction between the mystical, divine organism called the Body of Christ from the human, organizational patterns that have arisen from history, such a distinction is not only desirable, but absolutely necessary. This demands a willingness to apply the insight of Pope John Paul II to dynamics in our own church. Overly ideological forms of what will be called "Culture I Catholicism" may seem justifiable with an appeal to some layers of tradition, but will fall short when such beliefs are critiqued from the lens of good biblical theology, as well as unbiased historical analysis.

With these insights from my LAREC talk, I prepared for another talk to the leadership group of the women's and men's religious congregations in Ireland (CORI) during the height of the then-daily news items related to allegations of child abuse by priests and religious, along with related exposés of episcopal cover-ups. This led to another realization: that the crisis we face is one of an apocalyptic nature. I use the term apocalypse to mean the end of something that no longer gives life, an ending that is accompanied by a call to renewal and return to the ultimate source of life.

This made me realize that being in apocalyptic times invites us to consider how the challenge of the Spirit to the Church of Ephesus might apply to us as we face the contemporary crisis of the "church in the West." Whereas the Ephesian Christians were accused of having abandoned their "first love" (Rev. 2:4), so we might be accused by the same Spirit of having abandoned the very gospel message of the historical Jesus: the proclamation of what he called "the Kingdom of God," which I will be retranslating as "the rule or governance of trinitarian relatedness and structuring."

Jesus' Gospel of the Kingdom of God: Reclaiming the Metaphor of "House"

A third talk at Maryknoll helped to further the thoughts I will be sharing in this book. Robert Ellsberg, publisher at Orbis Books, the publishing arm of Maryknoll, had asked me to speak on the topic "Science and Spirituality: Can They Meet?" In that talk I refrained from much discussion based on the physical sciences (which are not my field). Instead, I showed that one of the social sciences—economics—offers us a significant lens to help us understand what theologians for centuries have called the Economic Trinity, and how the whole "economy of salvation" involves being "saved from" dynamics that do not reflect the pattern of God's way of being Trinity. Since very different dynamics of relationality and participative indwelling have come to be revealed throughout creation, they all must be evident in human relationships and human institutions, especially the church.

Since "economy" means the "ordering of the house," I will argue that the metaphor of "house" must be retrieved as the underlying, archetypal, and architectural model for the whole created order. I will show how Jesus' proclamation of the rule or governance (the Kingdom) of God demands that we work to bring about a trinitarian form of rule or governance on earth as it is expressed in heaven. From this perspective I will argue that a truly *evangelical asceticism* in the church must motivate all of us to find our rightful vocation and place in the "economy of salvation" in a way that will bring about the rule of trinitarian relatedness at every level of our world, especially if we are to go into that world to proclaim the gospel message. In this proclamation of trinitarian order, the "whole world" will be invited to return to its source, to more clearly mirror its Maker.

Given the above, I will argue that if the church is to witness to the trinitarian God, the Roman Church itself must be trinitarian at every level—from the lives of every baptized member right up to its internal structures—in a way that brings about ever greater equality, mutuality, and participation. If it does not do this, it will show itself to be "outside" the authentic faith of the true church. Furthermore, I will argue, to the degree that its ecclesiastical structures and patterns do not reflect trinitarian relationships and dynamics, to that degree they will be, de facto, untrinitarian; as such they will be "outside" the reign or governance of the trinitarian God in a way that reflects the "sin of the world." Such an understanding of reality demands that everyone who calls him- or herself "Catholic" must hear the call of conversion in order to help move the institutional church from any sinful structures and patterns to grace-filled ones.

Needless to say, just as happened to Jesus and, true to his prophecy, any contemporary followers proclaiming this "gospel" can expect from our own religious authorities and their adherents the same persecution promised by Jesus to those who willingly embrace the discipline of being his disciples. Finally, I will suggest that the heart of an evangelical asceticism of discipleship inherent in Jesus' invitation "to follow" in his footsteps invites us to a new way or *dao* of the Kingdom (or "the Kindom"): a contemporary way of be[com]ing his disciples.

The *Dao* of Being a "Kindom" Catholic:
Seven Contemporary Sacramentals

As I brought together my ideas for this book, it became increasingly clear to me that, while what will be called Culture I Catholicism involves a clear set of meanings that are embodied in rituals and rubrics reflecting its priorities, the same cannot be said of the more liberal "Culture II" form of being Catholic.[8] Given the fact that there must be a *cultural* form of Catholicism that is *countercultural,* this lack begs for the creation of contemporary Catholic rituals and practices that will flourish in the twenty-first century as a "Catholic *dao*" or discipline that challenges its adherents to patterns of behavior that help give them their own more nuanced definition of faith.

I borrow the word *dao* from the Chinese spiritual classic the *Dao De Ching* by Lao-Tse. The *dao* refers to a "way" of being in tune with the principles of balance and harmony that underlie reality. The Catholic *dao* I envision will be quite different from the organizational dynamics to which Culture I Catholicism often appears to be wedded. Rather, grounded in the best of tradition and scripture, it outlines a new way to be a "practicing" Catholic that will accompany and even enhance the regular practice of the sacraments. This will involve embracing a new "Catholic Story" that is grounded in what we know from science about the physical world. Embodied in "Seven Cs," it will offer key elements of the practice of a Catholicism worthy of the future. This way of being a contemporary *Catholic* will be more cosmic, Christic, conscious, connected, contemplative, and compassionate. All this will be done in a way of discipleship that is also communitarian.

The past years have been marked by an uneasy relationship between bishops and theologians in the United States. Constructive criticism in the Catholic Church involves honest dialogue arising from a solid understanding of what "authentic" and "official" church teaching involves, as well as what has always defined the heart of Catholic moral theology: a rightly formed conscience. I would hope such foundational principles of Catholic teaching and morality might guide readers of all persuasions as they ponder the points I make here. I hope that the approach I use here will invite lively debate on solidly grounded and meaningful ways to truly build up our church. I trust that this repair of our church will reflect at every level of its life the Trinity into which we have been baptized and in whose dynamics we have been divinely chosen to live, move, and have our being.

Many of the ideas expressed here were originally offered in the above-mentioned talks. Encouraged by Robert Ellsberg to organize these ideas into a book, I decided to bring them together for the regular retreat that I had been preaching during Holy Week at Holy Spirit Retreat Center in Encino, California. Toward the end of the retreat, I received an affirmation for this approach from one of the participants, Nancy Snooks. Breaking the silence of the retreat she approached me and said, "I have figured out why you are saying the kind of things you have been sharing in your conferences." "You have?" I asked. "Yes; you are a Franciscan and you are just being faithful to who you must be as a Franciscan." "What do you mean?" I asked. "Your charism in the church is to repair it. And that's what I think you are trying to do. You are a 'repairer of the church.'" I was and remain humbled by her insight.

Francis of Assisi heard words from the cross in the abandoned Church of San Damiano: "Francis, go repair my house; you can see it is falling into ruin." Interpreting the words literally, he set out to fix up physically the dilapidated church with bricks and mortar. However, he soon realized that the "repair" of the church envisioned for him demanded a new way of evangelical living that was not evident in the institutional church. This new way of living the gospel as an alternative community *within* the sinful structures of the Catholic Church (which were part of the "world" he said he was called "to leave") came to him, he said, from divine inspiration.[9]

Unlike my approach in this book, Francis did not expose and critique the *unevangelical* (and, therefore, the *untrinitarian*) ways the Roman Church had been ordering its institutional life. Rather, he offered a compelling and nonviolent alternative to its worldly ways with a vision of the gospel for his followers centered around the Trinity.[10] Thus, whether in the evangelical rejection of all clerical titles for his friars or in a form of obedience based not on a dominating hierarchy but on becoming "subject to all in the same house,"[11] Francis's "repair" of the *house* of the Crucified One involved a reclaiming of what I believe it means to be truly "Catholic."

It is my hope that I will prove faithful to his admonition to us, his followers, that we always "be, live, and speak as Catholics."[12] While my approach in this book may differ from the unthreatening, charismatic way of Francis's understanding of being "Catholic," I do hope and pray that the way of being Catholic I outline for our age might have as its *goal* the same one that he intended for his age: to make the Gospel of the Way of Life of the Trinity something so apparent in our personal, communal, and institutional behavior that it becomes transformative for our lives and our world.

* * *

I want to give special thanks to those who helped me in the editing of this book: Jack Augenstein, Emily John, Joseph Juknialis, Howard Ebert, Charlotte Prather, Ken Smits, and Suzanne Tamiesie. Most especially I am indebted to Robert Ellsberg for asking me to write this kind of a book and for his patient and thorough editing of it.

CATHOLICISM AND APOCALPYSE

Tradition Eclipsing Scripture

The transition from the charismatic, organic form of church found in the Acts of the Apostles and the Letters of Paul to the one familiar to readers of the daily press today has been dramatic. At least in the West, what was once a thriving and formidable force in the world has become just one more institution that has lost credibility with its members and the wider public.

The chapters in Part I address the question of how this happened. Many problems in the Roman Catholic Church involve consequences deriving from historically conditioned ways in which it has evolved from a movement grounded in a mystical experience and understanding of its identity (as the Body of Christ) to an entity overly identified with the Vatican, its episcopal representatives, and their clerical appointees throughout the world. This institutional form of church represents what many people were taught to believe in; many still refer to it when they ask: "What does *the church* say about . . . ?"

Just as Tip O'Neill said that "all politics is local," so the main experience of "church" for most practicing Catholics takes place at the local level, the parish. This book does not address this reality as it is experienced by the average practicing Catholic. Often, this local church can be quite important, even serving as the primary community for many Catholics. Important reasons for membership in such parishes involve liturgies with relevant preaching, good music, a sense of welcome, and an experience of community. Often it includes a good school and religious education programs attractive to the young. This form of parish, found mainly in areas with younger white families, new ethnic communities, or in racially mixed neighborhoods, thankfully still serves as the norm of "church" for millions of Catholics. This influential local church, often found in Hispanic neighborhoods, is not the subject of this book.

Instead, the church in need of reform that I will be discussing in this book involves the "curial" and "clerical" way church leaders—from the Vatican to the local chancery to an increasing number of parishes—are too often seen by the people in the pews as isolated from their daily lives and concerns. The result is a church that too often seems defined more by orthodoxy (correct belief—but often adherence to what are really secondary teachings) rather than orthopraxy (belief in action) regarding the core message of Jesus Christ as found in the Gospels. Recalling two contemporary sayings, we too often see in Roman Catholicism a replacement of "What would Jesus do?" with "What does the church say?" regarding right practice and morality. The consequence of this involves the second part of the title for Part I: "Tradition Eclipsing Scripture."

This imbalance between tradition and scripture in the Roman Catholic Church became clear to me at a gathering of the priests of the Archdiocese of Los Angeles, June 10-14, 2002. I had been asked to talk on "church" as part of the priests' mandated continuing education. When I accepted the welcome invitation and the topic, neither the coordinators nor I knew that this same week would be the occasion for the U.S. Conference of Catholic Bishops to meet in Dallas. Their gathering occurred in the midst of the second phase of the large-scale scandal in the United States regarding allegations of clerical child abuse,[1] coupled with parallel allegations of episcopal cover-ups. The bishops met to find ways to address and remedy the abuse of children, only to be challenged for not discussing their own failures related to the scandals.

After being greeted by Cardinal Mahoney, who then went to Dallas, we began our days together in Los Angeles. Almost from the beginning it became obvious to everyone that a small group of young priests were resistant to virtually everything I said. The fact that these priests always sat with one another and made not-too-hushed remarks to one another during my presentations was very obvious. Yet, nobody challenged their behavior.

After a full day of this, to his credit, one of the priests raised a hand. When I acknowledged him, he said: "We are very upset with what you are saying," he declared. "Why," I asked? In effect, he answered: "The Roman Catholic Church is defined by two pillars: scripture and tradition. Ever since you began your talks, all we are hearing from you is the scriptural foundation of the church. You are not giving equal time to the importance of tradition. We do not think you are giving a balanced presentation." The gauntlet was thrown down.

What I attribute to a moment of divine inspiration led me to respond: "Your argument is valid and well taken. The Roman Catholic Church is defined by its two fonts of scripture and tradition. You are also correct in saying that you have only heard from me what the scriptures say about the meaning of 'church.' However, I don't think we should forget about what the bishops of this nation are talking about in Dallas as we talk about church during these days."

I then created a chart on the board based on my elaboration of the famous "Models of the Church" by the Jesuit-made-Cardinal, Avery Dulles (whose expanded edition included the church as a "Community of Disciples").[2] Then

I added the notion of the church as "family," which came from the African Synod. Finally I offered my own model of church as being in "exile" with its adherents unable to find a place to rest their heads.

Even though Avery Dulles offered no real scriptural basis for his six models, I suggested a Gospel passage or two that might show how each of the eight ecclesial models had some kind of a christological basis. I also showed what core emphasis might flow from such a model. I outlined the models using the following chart:

TRADITION ECLIPSING SCRIPTURE IN THE ROMAN CATHOLIC CHURCH

Models/Images of the Church

For the sake of your tradition you nullify the Word of God
(Mark 7:13; Matthew 15:3)

Model of the Church	*Gospel Basis: Christology*	*Application: Ecclesiology*
Institution	Matthew 16:17-19	Stress on Petrine primacy
Mystical communion	Matthew 18:18-20	Stress on Christ's continued presence
Sacrament	John's notion of sign(s)	Stress on sign as action
Herald	Matthew 28:16-20	Stress on preaching
Servant	Luke 4:16-21; Matthew 25:31-46	Stress on poor and justice
Community of disciples	The call to discipleship in all the Gospels	Stress on Jesus connection
Family (from African Synod)	Matthew 12:46-50	Stress on sister-/brotherhood
Exile	Matthew 8:20; Luke 9:58	Stress on pilgrim and stranger

I then located the scriptural foundation for each of the eight models of church in the gospel "story" of Jesus, arguing that it is from this story that we derive both our Christology and ecclesiology. Then I responded directly to the young priest and said, "If you look at all eight models of the church, only one has been interpreted in a way that has created the problems we are facing in the Catholic Church today and which the bishops are addressing in Dallas. The crisis they face didn't arise from considering the church as a communion or community of disciples or even as a family with various dysfunctions. They didn't come from viewing the church as herald or servant. They have arisen from misinterpretations around only one type: the *institutional* model of church."

I continued: "Furthermore, the problems that created this crisis have resulted in large part from that historically and culturally conditioned approach to 'tradition' that permitted the abuse of power, whose consequences and victims we are now facing. It is the fruit of faulty and selective interpretations of scripture regarding the church as institution." I noted that this interpretation reinforcing the tradition is something that has been drilled into our heads as Catholics to the degree that tradition has come to eclipse the scriptures. (What I didn't say then would have been even more to the point: Jesus' own challenge to *his religious leaders* arose from the fact that their closed system could not recognize him as the fulfillment of the scriptures. I also didn't say that these same dynamics are being played out with an interpretation of the scriptures by clerics in our church that reinforces the tradition of male, celibate supremacy at the expense of a better balance between the two models of church revealed by Matthew 16 and 18, as well as between scripture and tradition). Consequently, Matthean scripture scholar Donald Senior, a member of the Pontifical Biblical Commission, has said that Jesus' "judgment on past generations of Israel's leaders" can also be applied to "false leadership in the Christian community"[3] of any day.

I continued: "Everyone in this room knows full well what our tradition has told us and is telling us about what it means to be part of the institution called the Roman Catholic Church. So, with your permission, I will continue to stress the other pillar of our church that has been eclipsed by tradition, namely the scriptural underpinnings of the church in which we believe and to which we belong."

I don't know if I convinced them. However, I do know, from the results of our days together, that neither they nor anybody else questioned the fact that many of the problems in our Catholic Church have resulted from an ideological misreading of the Matthew 16 text ("You are Peter and upon this Rock I will build my church"). The result has been the creation of a Petrine model of church that has become overly institutionalized and patriarchal. The chapters in the first part of this book address this issue at greater length.

Before we outline the crisis and challenges we face, I want to be clear that this book will not be attacking any leader in the Catholic Church. It will not call into question the authority they have been given. Nor will I raise questions about their integrity as human beings or critique their sincerity. Indeed, I think that someday some of them may experience their own kind of Pauline conversion and recognize, as he did, that they acted in ignorance in their zeal to preserve "their" church (1 Tim. 1:13).

Because church leaders are exercising their power in a closed institution, they are unable to perceive the exact nature of how they are perpetuating the dynamics that have influenced the downward spiral we continue to experience. When they consider the constitutive nature of the church as an institution, many are convinced that the teaching power they have received at ordination makes them the sole authoritative voice in the church. While they do have the grace of office, and, to that degree have been divinely anointed, some seem to forget that this grace also is exercised by men with human natures. Precisely because grace builds on nature, the human expression of their divinely authorized power can always suffer possible negative consequences of bias. This creates blinders that can do a great amount of harm,[4] just as clear vision can do a great amount of good.

As I was finishing this book, I read a *Harvard Business Review* article about insights related to executive decision making. Its opening paragraph caught my eye: "Thanks to a slew of popular new books, many executives today realize how biases can distort reasoning in business. *Confirmation bias*, for instance, leads people to ignore evidence that contradicts their preconceived notions. *Anchoring* causes them to weigh one piece of information too heavily in making decisions; *loss aversion* makes them too cautious."[5] The article stated that data also show that simple awareness of these biases does little to improve the quality of decision-making at either the individual or institutional level. Such change can only happen by balancing this kind of awareness with a genuine effort to change such biases. Their conclusion regarding executives in general "demands" what Pope Benedict XVI has called a "change in mindset" in how decision-making is exercised in the institutional church.[6] "The real challenge for executives . . . is the need to build awareness that even highly experienced, superbly competent, and well-intentioned managers are fallible. Organizations need to realize that a disciplined decision-making process, not individual genius, is the key to a sound strategy. And they will have to create a culture of open debate in which such processes can flourish."[7]

The relevance of these remarks to the situation of the church will become clear in the following chapters.

1

UNDERSTANDING THE VARIOUS FORMS OF ATHEISM

The Challenge to Catholicism

Every year I look forward to an invitation to speak at the Los Angeles Religious Education Congress in Anaheim, California. With the participation of 30,000 adults representing every imaginable racial and ethnic group, the Congress and the opportunity to watch the people, talk to the vendors, listen to other speakers and attend the liturgies give my pride in being Catholic its annual booster shot. In 2009 I received an invitation to give two workshops. As always, I was asked to speak on justice, so I decided to talk on "Matthew's Justice at the Heart of Jesus' Subversive Prayer, the 'Our Father.'"[1] But because I was intrigued by the challenges from the "new atheists," I decided I'd like to read their books and talk about my conclusions. The title for my talk became "God for Those Who Think They Don't Need God."

Little did I know what I had bargained for.

When I first thought about talking on "God" (including the "non-God" of the atheists), I immediately thought of courses I had taken on the sociology and anthropology of religion and my subsequent readings on the psychology of religion. These considered the origin of religion as based in the human response to mystery, the unknown, or to basic needs. I wanted to address (and debunk) the notion of a "god" who speaks primarily to human limitations and inadequacies. I had begun to think that any god worthy of being called "Total Love" must place no conditions or expectations on those receiving that love. I had concluded that a God defined by love will not make demands, only gentle urgings and invitations that honor our freedom.

I also had come to believe that only when God makes no demands on us, except the "demand" of our wholehearted love, will we be able to develop a spirituality that honors such a believable God. Only when we decide freely to worship a God who does not demand worship, will we be able to celebrate the absolute transcendence and immanence of that God in, among, and around us.

7

This made me conclude that only when we freely believe in a God not based on need[2] but from a desire to be consciously and intimately connected to this God can this God be believable.

Only when we find a God who makes us free not to believe will that God be worthy of our belief. Such a God, Vladimir Lossky wrote, stands "power-less before human freedom."[3] Only when we can believe in a "powerless" God whose way of relating to us is defined not by any form of control or obliga-tion but only by unconditioned love will that God be believable. Only when that love includes freedom from divine judgment will our reciprocal love be grounded in love rather than fear (1 John 4:18). Only when the will of God revolves around free and wholehearted love on our part will we be able to develop a spirituality that honors who God truly is. Only when we freely decide to bow before a God who does not demand our obeisance will that God be worthy of authentic worship. Only when we come to believe in a God who approaches us saying, "Behold I stand at your door and knock" (Rev. 3:20), knowing we may or may not decide to respond, is such a God worthy of being invited in. And, as a corollary, only when we find a religion that promotes belief in such a God will its own leaders not base their authority on dictates but on the strength of their arguments that generate respect, trust, and obedience from consciences that are fully free and faithfully formed.[4]

I knew the God I was coming to believe in did not set forth full answers to life's deepest questions. But I wanted to address these and other questions raised for centuries about life and death, suffering and loss, how we know and don't know and how we decide to believe or not believe. Deeper than this, I myself was seeking a God that could be understandable to non-believers even if not embraceable. I wanted a God who made sense in the midst of sense-lessness.

The more I read the arguments of the "four horsemen" of the contemporary atheists (Christopher Hitchens, Richard Dawkins, Daniel Dennett, and Sam Harris), the more I found that *their* god not only did a disservice to the God of my personal beliefs; it was a misnomer. Their god was not the personal, loving force that has come to make more and more sense to me. Instead they were locked into a notion of "god" that I had stopped believing in long ago. Further-more, it made a caricature of many things attributed to the God of Catholicism as well as the God represented in the other two main religions that also bear the brunt of their critiques: Islam and Mormonism.

At the core of their arguments are conclusions about the origin of the uni-verse that simply do not include or allow room for belief in God. Furthermore, they simply reject any notion of an ultimate "how" (much less an ultimate "why") this universe has come to be. None of them have made a blanket dec-laration, like Stephen Hawking, that "philosophy is dead" (because it "has not kept up with modern developments in science, particularly physics"[5]).

The "how" and "why" questions around creation have not gone away. These philosophical questions about the ultimate source or cause of everything will remain. They will have greater force if they can be addressed more credibly through parallel theological and pastoral representations of God that reflect an understanding of what we know from "modern developments in science."

Given the challenges raised by science, a spiritual question arises as well: Will we choose to live more honestly and with greater integrity when we move from religious myths about God that are increasingly unbelievable to an understanding of God that makes sense? It is precisely this God, Pope Benedict XVI said to a group of scientists June 30, 2011, who cannot be "an object of human experimentation" or observed by scientific data. Rather, as with the Pope, the only God I can now believe in is not an object but a subject. Richard Rohr would say that such a "God becomes more a verb than a noun, more a process than a conclusion, more an experience than a dogma, more a personal relationship than an idea."[6] When I probe this God more fully, I find One who has been manifest in ways that a quantum worldview does not deny but actually helps to illuminate.

As I studied the arguments of the new atheists (not always framed in constructive or charitable ways), I found myself often agreeing with some of their points. Furthermore, I also knew any counter-argument would be useless because, from what I read and heard about their debates with "believers," even at places like Notre Dame University, the conclusion was almost always the same. No matter who the believing debate partner might be the atheists in those debates invariably won on debating points.

The more I investigated their militant form of atheism, I came to realize that atheism comes in three types. First we have the "avowed or theoretical atheists." Then we have the "de facto or practical atheists," especially among those baptized Catholics (and others from the mainline denominations of Christians) who have left their original faiths but have not replaced these with any other kind of observable practice. The third group of atheists includes believers who practice their faith, often religiously. However their faith is ultimately grounded in the god of the culture rather than the God of Jesus Christ. They have become acculturated in such a way that there is no appreciable difference between their way of living and that of the wider, secular, society. These are the ones who are more "American" than "Catholic."

In this chapter I will examine the dynamics involved in these three groups.

The Avowed Atheists

The morning of my afternoon session on "God for Those Who Think They Don't Need God" at the L.A. Congress, I attended a talk by the popular theologian Robert Barron, "Thomas Aquinas and Why the Atheists Are Right."[7]

Despite his somewhat truncated analysis of the positions of the avowed atheists, something Father Barron said helped me bring together some of the points I wanted to make later that day. He summarized the main arguments of the atheists against religion in four categories: (1) The representatives of religion are fundamentalist in their interpretation of the scriptures; (2) they are overly identified with religiously sanctioned violence; (3) they are wedded to an entrenched, historically generated and unscientific worldview; and, finally, (4) they are (without recognizing and/or acknowledging it), child abusers.

Although Father Barron did not develop a response to what he said were the key arguments against religion, they need to be addressed non-defensively, especially regarding their (non)applicability to Catholicism. Unfortunately, I have found, their arguments do contain some points that ring true.

On the first argument by the theoretical atheists regarding religions being fundamentalist and selective in their interpretation of Scripture, I find a prime example of this in Catholicism and will elaborate on it in Chapter 2. There I will show how our present form of institutional Catholicism reveals a dynamic wherein tradition has eclipsed the scriptures to reveal a clerical understanding of church that has become overly dogmatic and fundamentalist. The result has been a violation of good scriptural exegesis in favor of an ideologically based model of church. This has led to a hierarchical and patriarchal model of church (said to be based on Matt. 16:17-19) that effectively excludes the parallel communitarian model of church articulated in Matthew 18:17-20.

When I examine the second point about how the Roman Catholic Church might be overly identified with forms of religiously sanctioned violence, I find much evidence from the past as well as the present. Probably the greatest evidence of this is found in the Crusades. Here we find the "God wills it" sermons by the likes of Bernard of Clairvaux[8] (which, thankfully, were not embraced by the likes of Francis of Assisi). But there is a subtle way we choose not to talk about those violent passages in the Hebrew Scriptures and even in the New Testament , where Jesus talks about God's wrath, berates his opponents, and uses violent language to dismiss the requests of those considered "other." In my mind, the greatest form of present-day religiously sanctioned violence comes from applying to the "official" church the words of the U.S. bishops themselves with regard to domestic violence. In their document *When I Call for Help*, they define violence as "any kind of behavior" that one uses "to control an intimate partner through fear and intimidation."[9] Broadening this definition to the institutional model of Catholicism controlled by the Vatican and the bishops, it is clear that fear and intimidation rule the dynamics of the official church at every level, including the dynamics within the various bodies of the Vatican and the bishops themselves. They also say "violence against women, inside or outside the home" can *never* be justified; any form of violence "is sinful."[10]

When it comes to the third concern the atheists have about religion, we find it writ large in many parts of Catholicism, namely, the unscientific basis for many of its beliefs. While popes have been better at accepting the facts of science about the universe and creation,[11] neither they nor many bishops and priests have been able to move the average church-going Catholic from perceptions and practices of Catholicism that still represent what Michael Dodd calls a "flat-earth Christianity."[12] This does not mean they literally believe that the earth is flat but that people's religiosity and religious practices still function as though it is.

The charges regarding religiously sanctioned child abuse represents something even more than the terrible, decades-long revelations of sexual abuse of children by clerics in the church. While, at its organizational level, the Roman Church has never sanctioned such behavior, it has been accused of having put its own interests ahead of its offending priests and, especially, ahead of the interests of the children who were placed in the care of such priests and other religious leaders.

The clearest link I have found between the mentality of individual clerical child abusers and the mentality of church officials whose primary concerns have always been the preservation of the clerical system is that of Fran Ferder, FSPA, and John Heagle in their article "The Inner Workings of a Hierarchy with a Sex Offender Mentality." From their "psychological evaluations of dozens of clergy sex abusers" and "their style of cognitive processing" for over more than twenty-five years, they have concluded that the same dynamics are replicated "in the responses of church officials from the cathedrals of the United States to the basilicas of Rome." Probably nowhere have we seen it evidenced more clearly than in the debate between Dublin and the Vatican in the latter's response to Dublin's allegations of Vatican failures in its awareness of clerical child abuse in Ireland. Ferder and Heagle write:

> We are not suggesting that church leaders are sex offenders. But we must name a tragic reality: Many of them think or respond the way sex offenders do when confronted with clergy sex abuse and its cover-up. They deny, defend and blame. They minimize and cover up. They become outraged when their abysmal handling of abuse cases is exposed. Most egregious of all, they display appalling deficits in empathy for victims. They turn to categorizing crimes when all people want is a heartfelt pastoral response from their leaders.[13]

As serious as the above may be, at a deeper theological level, the form of child abuse that is too often actually promoted has been part of our mindset for centuries. This refers to the soteriology (salvation story) that it was "God the Father's will that Jesus, His only Son, die on the cross in order to save us from our sins." In other words, God the Father willed that Jesus be killed as *the way* God decided could be the *only way* to bring about atonement for humanity's sins. This is child abuse, by any definition. It is just less violent to say that God willed Jesus to die than to say God wanted Jesus to be killed. Interpreted literally, this would make God at least complicit in child abuse, the murder of "His own Son," for in Catholic theology to will the sin to occur is to be guilty of it as much as the one who makes it happen. Furthermore, for such a killing, God would have to have willed that those doing the killing violate God's own revelation as found in the Fifth Commandment, "Thou shalt not kill." Again, God would be guilty of breaking God's own commandment.

I am happy to belong to the Franciscan tradition for many reasons, but one of them involves the rejection of such a "theological" notion. Indeed, Blessed John Duns Scotus taught that God, being unconditioned by anything (or anyone) but love, could only "come to earth" for one reason: to manifest that love. Therefore the reason for the incarnation was not the sin of humans but God's love. The death of Jesus was the inevitable consequence of that love, but *never* willed by God. None of the "theoretical atheists" really examine in any depth the theological issue of "God"; indeed they are not theologians and their main enemy is the way religions present God. Such a god, we have seen, is not worthy of our belief. However, having affirmed this key point of departure from their positions, I do find very helpful the taxonomy of "a spectrum of probabilities . . . about the existence of God" that Richard Dawkins places "between two extremes of opposite certainty." He writes in his 2008 best-seller, *The God Delusion,* "The spectrum is continuous, but it can be represented by the following seven milestones along the way." He outlines these seven categories on a continuum of belief/disbelief:

1. 100 percent theist: doesn't believe; knows God exists.
2. De facto theist: Not certain, but certainly believes in God's existence.
3. > 50 percent: Technically agnostic but leaning to theism.
4. 50/50: A/theism equally possible/probable.
5. < 50 percent: Has questions and/or doubts about God's existence but not very many.
6. De facto atheist: Has [been given] no compelling reason to believe in a God.
7. Strong atheist: the one who clearly knows there is no god.

Dawkins places himself in the sixth place on his continuum.[14] Having argued in the first part of his book that "God almost certainly doesn't exist,"[15] he moves to spend the rest of his book arguing against those who say that, even if God might not exist, there still is a place for religion. He summarizes these "roles" for religion and then proceeds to attack their credibility, often with hard facts, including data that show atheists are just as moral as people who self-identify as "religious": "Doesn't religion have a lot going for it? Isn't it consoling? Doesn't it motivate people to do good? If it weren't for religion, how would we know what is good? Why, in any case, be so hostile? Why, if it is false, does every culture in the world have religion? True or false, religion is ubiquitous, so where does it come from?"[16]

For his part, the title of Christopher Hitchens's book says it all: *God Is Not Great: How Religion Poisons Everything*. His main objects of derision are theocratic regimes and organized religion itself. He summarizes his key arguments about "man-made religion" in "at least three provisional conclusions": The first is that religion and the churches have evolved historically. As such they are human, not divine. The second is that ethics and morality are quite independent of faith, and exist quite well without it. The third is that religion—because it claims a special divine exemption for its practices and beliefs—is not just amoral but immoral, especially because of its connection to violence.

Among the "four horsemen," I find Daniel Dennett the most difficult to understand. I noted with interest his insistence that we should distinguish between a "Moslem Child" and "Catholic Child" and say more clearly, a "Child of Moslems" or a "Child of Catholics." He also argues that all children should be taught not just the "Three Rs" but a fourth "R": reading, writing, and 'rithmetic but also religion. But the way this religion is taught must not be limited to just one group but include the teachings of all the major religions. In this way children might come to make more informed decisions regarding their embrace and practice of a specific religion.

The fourth of the Horsemen is the neuroscientist Sam Harris. Rather than just attacking religion like the others, he probes more deeply the nature of belief and faith as the underpinnings of religion, even as he seeks to undermine them. For him a "belief is a lever that, once pulled, moves almost everything else in a person's life." He explains: "Are you a scientist? A liberal? A racist? These are merely species of belief in action. Your beliefs define your vision of the world; they dictate your behavior; they determine your emotional responses to other human beings."[17]

For Harris, faith represents "belief in, and life orientation toward, certain historical and metaphysical propositions."[18] These, in turn, are reinforced by religion, which promotes propositions and dogmas as truths that must be believed as a matter of faith. He concludes, "the fact that religious beliefs have a great influence on human life says nothing at all about their validity."[19] Following this logic he rejects those forms of religious belief that have no validity in the scientific world.

I will return to this argument. But now I want to turn to the other two kinds of atheists: former Catholics who have become "practical atheists" and the present Catholics for whom the trinitarian God revealed in the person and teachings of Jesus Christ makes no appreciable difference in their lives.

The Practical Atheists

Compelling data indicates Roman Catholicism in the United States is hemorrhaging members at an unprecedented rate, especially among "emerging adults." This can be found in Gallup Polls used by Leisa Anslinger in her *Turning Hearts to Christ: Engaging People in a Lifetime of Faith*,[20] the 2007-2008 findings of the National Survey of Youth and Religion,[21] the 2008 and 2009 studies from the Pew Forum on Religion & Public Life, and a book on the state of religion in the United States by Robert D. Putnam and David E. Campbell.[22] The Pew data and Putnam/Campbell book, in turn, echo the 2006 findings of the General Social Surveys, many of which have been used by Christian Smith and his colleagues at the University of Notre Dame.[23] Such studies have generated reviews from a wide range of Catholic writers, including Cathleen Kaveny,[24] Thomas Reese, SJ,[25] and Peter Steinfels.[26]

In an overview of U.S. religious affiliation, the Pew study reported that 78.4 percent defined themselves as Christians; 1.7 percent as Jews; Buddhists, Muslims and Hindus as less than 1 percent; while atheists numbered 1.6 percent, agnostics accounted for 2.4 percent, and 12.1 percent as "nothing in particular." Such low numbers related to atheists and agnostics indicate that any "threat" coming from their influence is minimal, especially when compared to the challenge from other data (below) showing the rapid decline of membership in the Catholic Church.

While the overall number of Catholics in the United States has remained steady—about 25 percent of all adults—it was sustained only by continued waves of Latino immigration. In 2008 one in three U.S. Catholics was Latino. The Pew survey found that "the Roman Catholic Church, which estimates its U.S. membership at 67 million, has lost more adherents than any other denomination." Responding to such data, Archbishop Timothy Dolan told a Catholic News Agency interviewer in 2009, "It scares the life out of me when I find out that the second most identifiable religious grouping on the religious landscape of the United States are people who say, 'I used to be Catholic.'"

While nearly one in three U.S. adults were raised in the Catholic Church, less than one in four who were baptized in the Catholic Church now describe themselves as Catholic.[27] While 2.6 percent of people in the United States have become Catholics, 10 percent of people in the United States consider themselves former Catholics. That is why the Roman Catholic Church "has experienced the greatest net losses as a result of affiliation changes."[28] For almost every person joining the Catholic Church, four have left. Whereas nearly one in three U.S. adults was raised in the Catholic Church, less than 25 percent now describe themselves as Catholic. Data from the 2007-2008 National Study of Youth and Religion show that, along with Judaism, Catholicism has lost more of the critical "emerging adults" (ages 18-23) than any other denomination.[29] I think it is important to realize that these are the ones formed to be Catholic in the generation of Pope John Paul II.

Among all those who have left the Catholic Church, half no longer identify with any church; the others have joined a Protestant church. Most often this Protestant church is "evangelical." The sentiment of one of these "former" Catholics (who even entered our Capuchin novitiate but soon left) is summarized in the rationale for leaving that he gave me: "I now belong to a 'Bible-believing' church." He also made it clear that he was worried about my salvation, especially because he did not think, as a Catholic, I could have a personal relationship with Jesus Christ (as he understood John 3:16).

This material, reviewed on the Vatican news service Zenit, told much the same story, especially the "growing number of young people [who] are renouncing any religion at all in the last decade." Reflecting the "fluidity of allegiances" to their parents' religion, just less than two-thirds of young people still participate in the church of their parents. The Vatican's news service noted that, among white Catholics, "just over 60% have left the Church, with an almost equal division between those who have lapsed and rarely take part in any church activity, and those who have switched religion." A clear result of this dramatic shift has been "an increased polarization, with more people who are either highly religious or resolutely secular, and fewer in the middle."[30] Furthermore, among those who are unaffiliated, the data do not support the oft-repeated statement about today's younger generation: "they may not be religious, but they are spiritual." To this Christian Smith and Patricia Snell say that "a solid majority of emerging adults simply are not that interested in matters religious or spiritual."[31] While they may be "open" to spirituality, their seeking it is minimal. Indeed, they show that "only for quite a small minority of emerging adults are spiritual seeking and practicing lives that are spiritual-but-not-religious on the priority list."[32]

The Pew data make it clear that the reasons for the disaffection of so many Catholics involve neither issues considered liberal (abortion, same-sex issues, birth control) nor conservative (loss of the Latin in liturgy, male dominance in the church, ritual insistence). Even more, contrary to commonly held assumptions, the data also show that (dis)agreement about dogmas and doctrines do not register as significant factors for those who leave the church (nor among those tens of millions who still practice the faith). Rather, among those who have left the church, the main reasons point to the dynamics of organizational patterns that simply do not meet their "spiritual needs."

Something happened in the lives of such people that led them to desire more than required religious observance. Their need for meaning has not been addressed. Thus, more than 80 percent of the once-Catholic respondents who joined a Protestant denomination did so, they said, because they found meaning in its religious dynamics and worship patterns. This echoes another key finding of the study which showed that the trend in shifts among those leaving denominations like Catholicism also involved movement "towards more personal religion," such as that found in the more evangelical churches, many of which are the mega-churches in our major cities.

This realization came to me several years ago when I visited Metrobrook, one of various satellite communities of Milwaukee's megachurch, Elmbrook. I have always been interested in religious movements and the increase and decrease of membership in religious institutions, so I decided one Sunday (December 10, 2006) to visit Metrobrook.

The members gathered in the auditorium of the local technical college. There I met various couples who had stopped believing in the God of Catholicism. Instead, using their words, they had come to be deeply committed to the God of Jesus Christ in ways they had never experienced before.

What I experienced was so powerful that I returned home and wrote a letter of concern to Pope Benedict XVI, which I make public now because I received only a four-line response to it from a Vatican monsignor informing me, "The Holy Father has received your letter and he has asked me to thank you. He appreciates the concerns which prompted you to share your thoughts with him." He added that "His Holiness will pray for the success of your pastoral ministry." This was accompanied by the pope's "Apostolic Blessing."[33]

In my letter to the pope I wrote:

> Today, I decided I would "go to church" incognito at the newly founded non-denominational church three blocks from our parish at St. Benedict's: "Metrobrook." In my row, while singing Christmas Carols (on the Second Sunday of Advent!), I asked people on my left and right: "How long have you been coming to Metrobrook?" After each told me, I asked: "What denomination did you come from?" Both groups of husbands and wives said: "The Catholic Church." After the service, a woman came to me saying she had heard I was "new to Metrobrook." She invited me to brunch. At the restaurant, I discovered that they too had been Catholics. All I encountered today were "cultural Catholics"; now they were committed, enthusiastic Christians. This led to this letter.
>
> Something is not working in our church with people like this. One can't say that they are relativists or secularists. Rather they have found in this "church" a primary community to which they actually com-

mit their lives, unlike so many Roman Catholics. They are joyful and energized. And, as you can see from my invitation to join the couple for lunch, they are always ready to evangelize!

From here I strongly urged the Pope to use his influence on the conferences of bishops in the United States and elsewhere to study this phenomenon that is being replicated around the United States. I wrote,

> Our bishops have not publicized any study that asks why the largest group of Christians [outside the Catholic Church] in the U.S.A. is inactive Catholics or why so many cultural Catholics like those today go to such churches. Why has no study been made? Why does it appear that our church leaders stress issues and externals that too often fall on deaf ears (if they are heard in the first place), when tens of millions of Latin Americans "leave" the Roman Church—only to commit themselves to be actively engaged as evangelicals and Pentecostals? Could it be that the sin involved is the intransigency of the institutional church and its leaders who seem locked in a tradition-based model of church that is increasingly clericalized, closed and irrelevant to peoples' search for God?[34]

The questions I asked of Pope Benedict XVI in 2006 were raised more forcefully by Thomas Reese, SJ, in a 2011 article summarizing the main findings of a later Pew Center poll. Among the "many lessons that we can learn from the Pew data," he wrote, we can focus on three:

> First, those who are leaving the church for Protestant churches are more interested in spiritual nourishment than doctrinal issues.... While the hierarchy worries about literal translations of the Latin text, people are longing for liturgies that touch the heart and emotions. More creativity with the liturgy is needed, and that means more flexibility must be allowed....
>
> Second, . . . that Catholics are leaving to join evangelical churches because of the church teaching on the Bible is a disgrace. Too few homilists explain the scriptures to their people. Few Catholics read the Bible. . . . The church needs to acknowledge that understanding the Bible is more important than memorizing the catechism. . . .
>
> Finally, the Pew data show that two-thirds of Catholics who become Protestants do so before they reach the age of 24. . . . Programs and liturgies that cater to their needs must take precedence over the complaints of fuddy-duddies and rubrical purists.[35]

Turning to the other 50 percent of Catholics who have left the Catholic Church, we find that most don't practice anything; they have become indifferent or atheists de facto. Furthermore, one hears less and less the refrain from parents that "they may not be religious, but they are very spiritual." Instead, it seems, their separation from official Catholicism (which often was perceived to identify its ways with God's ways) resulted in their being indifferent to any evident relationship with God. The result has created a situation wherein their children have become de facto unbelievers or, as the title for this section states: practical atheists. In effect, the reality (or possibility) of God makes no effective difference in their lives. And, as I learned at a dinner party in Spain with medical professionals—all of whom were cultural Catholics, the more the secularism of "the West" takes over, the less such people even feel any need to call on God (or the priests of the Catholic Church), even when they face tragedy, including death. If they do ask for a funeral at a Catholic church, it is not for religious but for cultural reasons.

The phenomenon of religious indifference was perceived more than twenty years ago by the Jesuit Michael J. Buckley in a *Theological Studies* article, "Experience and Culture: A Point of Departure for American Atheism." He wrote, "The resultant indifference is not so much a deliberate act, as a set of arguments that terminates in the denial of the existence of God." Rather, he concludes, "The denial of the existence of God today is much more cultural drift and distance."[36]

Like the theoretical atheists, this group no longer evidences a "need for God" nor does their behavior indicate any observable interest in or search for God.

The Catholics Who Have Become Acculturated to the "Gods" of the Nation

When considering the notion of "God," data also show that, at least in the United States, people have many different ideas about what they mean by "God." This fact is especially important to realize for us preachers when we consider the God-image people in the pews use to filter our God-talk. While 90 percent of people in the United States say they believe in God, surveys of U.S. adults between 2006 and 2008 revealed four different images of God around which we orbit. Besides the 5 percent defining themselves atheist or agnostic, 28 percent believed in an "authoritative God," 21 percent believed in a "critical God" engendering fear, 24 percent viewed God as "distant," while 22 percent believed in a benevolent God.[37] So which God do we preach?

This fact leads into a segue to the third section of this chapter, which addresses the phenomenon of those who say they believe in God and practice their faith but whose basic allegiance to God is overlaid by the twin national gods of Americanism and consumerism. This is shown in their virtual disconnect from and unresponsiveness to the core gospel message of Jesus Christ about bringing "good news to the poor." Instead, they represent those Catholics who, in the days of the Cold War, labeled others concerned about peace and justice as being "Communist" or "promoters of class warfare." Today, they are found among those who might accuse a priest of being a Democrat if he talks too much about the ever-widening disparity between the rich and the poor, or our evangelical responsibility to be concerned about the hungry and destitute (see Matt. 25:31-46). Their fears about such anti-market thoughts will be reinforced if priests preach about the parishioners' responsibility to redress the structural and systemic underpinnings associated with an unfettered "free" market that may be making such disparities ever greater.

The last time the United States had such a gap between its richest and poorest citizens was in 1929 when the richest 1 percent had 18.4 percent of the national income. Commenting on this ever-increasing disparity, a 2010 editorial in *The Economist* stated, "There was not a single year between 1952 and 1986 in which the richest 1% of American households earned more than a tenth of national income. Yet after rising steadily since the mid-1980s, reckon Thomas Piketty and Emmanuel Saez, two economists, in 2007 the income share of the richest 1% reached a staggering 18.3%."[38] Around the same time the *Wall Street Journal*, noting that the highest paid workers earned 364 percent more than the lowest paid workers, said "U.S. wage inequality keeps hitting new records."[39]

Most Americans find a disconnect between capitalism and Christianity. For Democrats 53 percent (vs. 26) agree they are incompatible. Among Republicans, only 37 percent (vs. 46) find them at odds. Those with annual household incomes of $100,000 are more likely to agree with the compatibility of capitalism and Christianity than those earning $30,000 or less (exactly half: from 46 percent to 23 percent).[40] Furthermore, while data show citizens of the United States consistently desire a more egalitarian society, the same data show that they are unwilling to support efforts to bring this about.

A main reason people do not really want to challenge the prevailing dynamics that favor the rich is that a high percentage of citizens believe that they might someday achieve the "American Dream" and be in that top 1 percent. What David Brooks, the conservative columnist for the *New York Times*, wrote over a decade ago is still evident in the way the Horatio Alger story has infected the American psyche. He noted,

> The most telling polling result from the 2000 election was from a *Time* magazine survey that asked people if they are in the top 1 percent of earners. Nineteen percent of Americans say they are in the richest 1 percent and a further 20 percent expect to be someday. So right away you have 39 percent of Americans who thought that when [during the

2000 election] Mr. Gore savaged a plan that favored the top 1 percent, he was taking a direct shot at them.

It's not hard to see why they think this way. Americans live in a culture of abundance. They have always had a sense that great opportunities lie just over the horizon, in the next valley, with the next job or the next big thing. None of us is really poor; we're just pre-rich.[41]

In such a "wealthy" country as ours, despite the gaps noted above, it's also easier to be psychically numbed to the gap between the rich and poor in the economically developing nations as well. In a nation where the majority of people can choose where they might eat each evening, it is hard to believe that one in six people in the world—more than 1 billion—go hungry, receiving fewer than 1,800 calories a day. This gets compounded by the almost universally held myth that "the United States is the most generous nation in the world." Because of its size it might give the most to development assistance ($27.8 billion in 2008), but this represents less than a half of a percent of its national income, much less than many other "developed" nations.

Joined at the hip to the god of free-market capitalism is the idea of "American exceptionalism."[42] Because the average Catholic citizen also worships between the pillars holding up this altar, it is hard to truly preach the gospel about the detrimental impact of our lifestyle on people who are poor and marginalized.

Not long ago, David Gelernter, a conservative Republican, wrote a stirring defense of the "religion" of "Americanism." While his insights seem *unbelievable* to me, to "true believers" they are dogma:

> Anti-Americanism has blossomed frantically in recent years. [It encompasses] the supposed evils of America and Americanism in general. In its passionate and unreasoning intensity, anti-Americanism resembles a religion—or a caricature of a religion. And this fact tells us something about Americanism itself.
>
> By Americanism I mean the set of beliefs that are thought to constitute America's essence and to set it apart; the beliefs that make Americans positive that their nation is superior to all others—morally superior, closer to God.[43]

What are the consequences of this kind of Catholic worship at the altar of the nation's twin gods of materialism and Americanism? Without recalling Jesus' challenge about the inability to serve God and Mammon, one need go no further to see its contemporary consequences than an article in the Jesuit weekly *America* by John DiIulio. This former appointee of President George W. Bush in charge of faith-based initiatives wrote,

Catholics' post-1960 march into the all-American political and cultural mainstream has come at a price. . . . On nearly every public policy issue on which there is good national polling data—from immigration to environmental protection, the death penalty to welfare spending and myriad other issues—Catholics as a group come as close as any religious denomination does to mirroring what most Americans believe.

He then concludes with a question that has challenged me and should challenge every other priest and preacher in the U.S. Catholic Church: "Have American Catholics been folded so completely into the nation's political and cultural mainstream that they can no longer be its political salt and cultural light, or so divided among themselves that they can never speak truth to power in one faith-filled voice? I pray not, but I fear so."[44]

Ever since my failure as a young parish priest (1968-1973) to reconcile black and white Catholics torn apart by issues around property values and white flight, I have long held to the assumption that today's cultural Catholics in the United States are more formed by the twin gods of our nation than the trinitarian God revealed in Jesus Christ. While Catholics such as those described above might honor this God with their lips, their hearts, their voting, and their lifestyles demonstrate where their ultimate loyalty and worship rest. This unfortunate and challenging fact is echoed in the words of Alan Jacobs, who often writes in the *Wall Street Journal's* "Houses of Worship" column. In one such column discussing the arguments of the avowed atheists writing about religion's lack of impact on the culture, he declared,

> When people say that they are acting out of religious conviction, I tend to be skeptical; I tend to wonder whether they're not acting as I usually do, out of motives and impulses over which I could paint a thin religious veneer but which are really not religious at all.

Then he gets to the heart of the argument by honestly admitting:

> The books I read, the food I eat, the music I listen to, my hobbies and interests, the thoughts that occupy my mind throughout the greater part of everyday—these are, if truth be told, far less indebted to my Christianity than to my status as a middle-aged, middle-class American man.[45]

For him and for many others among us, the culture has trumped the cult.

Imbalance in Church Governance
Based on a Misuse of Scripture[*]

In March 2003, Yale University's Catholic Center sponsored a conference titled "Governance, Accountability, and the Future of the Church."[1] In his key-note address, Donald Wuerl, then Bishop of Pittsburgh and now Archbishop-Cardinal of Washington, DC, stressed the need to distinguish between divine "givens" and human contingencies in the Catholic Church. In his official response, *New York Times* religion columnist Peter Steinfels agreed, with a res-ervation. He noted that some assumptions related to divine "givens" regarding church governance need to be critiqued to make sure that their development in the historical tradition does not reveal an origin more human than divine.[2] This chapter addresses a key "given" that needs such a nuance from a deeper examination of the notion of "church" in Matthew's Gospel.

Among all the four Gospels, only Matthew's Gospel uses the word "church" (*ekklēsia*). The word is found a total of three times in two different places. For centuries Catholic tradition has viewed unquestionably (and uncritically) Mat-thew 16:17-19 as a "divine given." In this text about "the church," Jesus gives Peter the keys of the Kingdom of heaven along with the power to bind (*deō*) and loose (*lyō*). The text about the giving of the keys and the power to bind and loose does not specifically equate the keys *with* the power of binding and loosing. Still, as Catholic tradition evolved, Catholics were taught that these three lines justify a certain form of governance in the *ekklēsia* with little or no mention of the only other time "*ekklēsia*" is used in Matthew: 18:17-20. Here the Greek shows that the same power of binding and loosing given Peter is present in the local community as well; furthermore, both texts reveal, the divine authority of the "heavenly father" stands behind both the Petrine and the communal expressions of power (Matt. 16:17; 18:19).[3]

---

[*] An expanded version of this chapter can be found in Michael H. Crosby, "Rethinking a Key Biblical Text and Catholic Church Governance," *Biblical Theology Bulletin* 35, no. 1 (Spring 2008), 37-43.

When one asks why the one text would be given so much stress while the other remains virtually unacknowledged, the answer seems to involve some ideological need regarding the former text that might be compromised by a more nuanced balance with the other. I don't think the imbalance has been intentional; however, the consequence has been the continued justification for a form of church governance that stresses the hierarchical and more central-ized organization of the church to the exclusion of the more communal and local model.

One time I was asked to give reflections on the scriptural notions of "church" in a large archdiocese in the western part of the United States. When I noted the virtual silence about what I call "the church of Matthew 18" and the forms of absoluteness connected to "the church of Matthew 16," especially in the last hundred years, one of the priests yelled out: "Why are you against the Pope?" I was dumbfounded. After taking a deep breath and saying a quick prayer, I could only respond, "I don't think I'm against the Pope. All I'm saying is that we need a better balance between the 'church of Matthew 16' and the 'church of Matthew 18.'"

In order to understand how both passages even came to be found in Mat-thew's Gospel, we need to study them from the approach proffered by the Pontifical Biblical Commission (PBC), especially in its 1992 document, "The Interpretation of the Bible in the Church" (IBC).

The Appropriate Use of the Bible in the Church

The IBC (with a preface by the then-Cardinal Joseph Ratzinger) was written "to attend to the criticisms and the complaints as also to the hopes and aspira-tions" about biblical issues, "to assess the possibilities opened up by the new methods and approaches and, finally, to try to determine more precisely the direction which best corresponds to the mission of exegesis in the Catholic Church."[4] The document covers four main areas: methods and approaches for understanding, questions of hermeneutics (i.e., interpretation or meaning of the scripture), characteristics of Catholic interpretation, ending with the proper interpretation of the Bible in the life of the church.

"Characteristics of Catholic Interpretation" highlights a consideration of the text within its historical and literary context. It states that one cannot understand the meaning of a text *without understanding its original context.* The IBC rejects the notion that any study of a text can occur "without start-ing from a 'pre-understanding' of one type or another." This involves pre-conceived ideas that might not be sufficiently critiqued. It says that Catholic hermeneutics always involves some kind of "pre-understanding that holds closely together modern scientific methods of interpretation combined with the religious tradition emanating from Israel and from the Christian community." This creates the possibility that a specifically "Catholic" pre-understanding can pose unforeseen problems (especially, I would say, when a text like Matt. 16:17-19 is interpreted): "All pre-understanding, however, brings dangers with it. As regards Catholic exegesis, the risk is that of attributing to biblical texts a meaning that they do not contain but which is a product of a later development within the tradition. The exegete must beware of such a danger."[5] Unless this danger is addressed in a way that frees subsequent interpretation from such blinding assumptions, it is quite likely that a snowball effect might take place. The result will occur wherein the text will be interpreted by the tradition in a way that reflects a lack of any critical examination of the text itself. It also can unwittingly be used for ideological purposes.

The Context for Matthew 16:17-19
in Light of the Two Source Tradition

The IBC proffers the historical-critical method as "the indispensable method for the scientific study of the meaning of ancient texts."[6] This approach, approved by then-Cardinal Joseph Ratzinger, has also been endorsed by the now Pope Benedict XVI in his recent books on Jesus.[7] While acknowledging that some challenge the "two source" hypothesis—which posits the composition of the Gospels of Matthew and Luke arising from "on the one hand, the Gospel of Mark and, on the other, a collection of the sayings of Jesus (called Q, from the German word *Quelle*, meaning "source)"—the IBC states, "In their essential features, these two hypotheses retain their prominence in scientific exegesis today."[8]

A couple of years ago I had an extended conversation with a bishop regarding the biblical notion of "church." In the midst of our dialogue, having been told by him that he is a "successor to the apostles," I asked him: "Bishop, from where in the scriptures do you find the basis for your power as a bishop?" Rather than pointing to the texts about the "apostles" in Matthew 10:1-4 (to whom Jesus gives his *authority* [*exousia*] to preach and heal), or Matthew 18:16-20 (where the Risen One gave *exousia* to the "eleven" to teach), the bishop said, "Matthew 16." He and I both knew the text that he was referencing. At this I responded, "Bishop, may I give an exegesis of this text?" When he agreed, I outlined its relationship to its original source in Mark and parallel in Luke, as below.

Mark 8:27-30	*Luke 9:18-21*	*Matthew 16:13-20*
Jesus went on with his disciples to the villages of Caesarea Philippi; and on the way he asked his disciples, "Who do people say that I am?" And they answered him, "John the Baptist; and others, Elijah; and still others, one of the prophets." He asked them, "But who do you say that I am?" Peter answered him, "You are the Messiah."	Once when Jesus was praying alone, with only the disciples near him, he asked them, "Who do the crowds say that I am?" They answered, "John the Baptist; but others, Elijah; and still others, that one of the ancient prophets has arisen." He said to them, "But who do you say that I am?" Peter answered, "The Messiah of God."	Now when Jesus came into the district of Caesarea Philippi, he asked his disciples, "Who do people say that the Son of Man is?" And they said, "Some say John the Baptist, but others Elijah, and still others Jeremiah or one of the prophets." He said to them, "But who do you say that I am?" Simon Peter answered, "You are the Messiah, the Son of the living God." And Jesus answered him, "Blessed are you, Simon son of John! For flesh and blood has not revealed this to you, but my Father in heaven. And I tell you, you are Peter, and on this rock I will build my church, and the gates of Hades will not prevail against it. I will give you the keys of the kingdom of heaven, and whatever you bind on earth will be bound in heaven, and whatever you loose on earth will be loosed in heaven."
And he sternly ordered them not to tell anyone about him.	He sternly ordered and commanded them not to tell anyone.	Then he sternly ordered the disciples not to tell anyone that he was the Messiah.

Without the benefit of the chart, I responded to the bishop by saying something like, "Following the two-source theory, the three texts are quite consistent in their context: Mark and Matthew have Jesus at Caesarea Philippi; Luke says he was praying. All portray Jesus asking his disciples how people interpret his identity. Upon hearing the list of various prophets being named, Jesus directly asks them the same question: 'But who do you say that I am?' (Matt. 16:15; Mark 8:29; Luke 9:20a). In response, all texts record Peter's 'confession' of faith, though each of the three expresses the profession with different nuances."

I then said to the bishop that, while Mark and Luke immediately follow Peter's confession of faith in Jesus as "the Christ" with the text that has Jesus charging them "not to tell anyone," Matthew (who also ends with the same warning "to tell no one that he was the Christ" [Matt. 16:20]) departs from his Markan source by adding three key verses.

I noted that fidelity to the two-source theory indicates that these three verses be clearly seen as a Matthean addition. Consequently, the three sentences cannot be said to have their origin in any actual words of the historical Jesus. Lest the bishop be concerned about my "lack of faith," I immediately added, "Of course I believe these texts because they are part of divine revelation." At the same time I added, "However, Bishop, they cannot be said to have been given us by the historical Jesus." To this he had no response, especially knowing that the PBC's document to which I referred had a preface by the one who is now named the "Successor to Peter."

Aware of the depth of the ideological and theological biases that insist on the traditional, unbalanced interpretation that continues the imbalance in our church's governance, I then asked, "Bishop, if this was so essential for the life of the church, why does only Matthew and not his Markan source (nor Lukan parallel) include the text? If Jesus was insistent that this way of 'binding and loosing' was to be so critical for the structuring of the church, why does only Matthew 16 mention it?" Again, the bishop had no response to my question.

Matthew's unique placement of the three lines invites us to probe not only a rationale for their inclusion but why the tradition came to use these three verses as a warrant for a certain form of exclusive governance in the church. This probe is necessary, given the statement of the IBC about the dangers of embracing a fundamentalist approach to the text: "In what concerns the Gospels, fundamentalism does not take into account the development of the Gospel tradition, but naively confuses the final stage of this tradition (what the evangelists have written) with the initial (the words and deeds of the historical Jesus)."[9] Following the IBC in this redaction, these three sentences are not "dominical" (from "the Lord") but Matthean in their authorship (but still are divinely inspired). The IBC theory makes it clear that the reason for their

Matthean placement must have involved dynamics impacting the later community of Matthew. However, because such interpretation does not acknowledge how history has come to select the Matthew 16 text without its parallel "binding and loosing" text in Matthew 18 the result is a clear "Catholic pre-understanding" related to the three lines.

Consequently, an unawareness or unwillingness to acknowledge a "Catholic pre-understanding" of the text can lead to certain scripturally unwarranted assumptions about authority in the church, such as that noted earlier by Cardinal Donald Wuerl. In this sense one can apply to the insistent advocates of a strictly Matthew 16:17-19 interpretation of the text in Catholicism the same label of "fundamentalism" attributed to those called "John 3:16 Protestant fundamentalists" who justify their understanding of salvation from this text alone without considering other important passages.

According to the IBC, interpreting a text in a fundamentalist way "starts from the principle that the Bible, being the word of God, inspired and free from error, should be read and interpreted literally in all its details." Such a "literal interpretation" of the scriptures, it states, can become "naively literalist" when it excludes "every effort at understanding the Bible" in a way "that takes account of its historical origins and development." Such an approach also is opposed to "the use of the historical-critical method, as indeed to the use of any other scientific method for the interpretation of Scripture."[10]

The IBC affirms fundamentalism's "right to insist on the divine inspiration of the Bible, the inerrancy of the word of God and other biblical truths" that are core to its basic approach to biblical interpretation. However, it states that such a fundamentalist approach can become ideological when it demands "an unshakable adherence to rigid doctrinal points of view and imposes, as the only source of teaching for Christian life and salvation, a reading of the Bible which rejects all questioning and any kind of critical research."[11]

When I had shared my exegesis of Matthew 16 with the bishop, I asked: "Bishop, may I ask you another question?" When he agreed, I said, "Bishop, Matthew is the only Gospel that mentions the word *ekklēsia*. The word is used a total of three times in two different places. Do you know the other time it appears?" "No I don't," was his honest reply. "It's in Matthew 18:17-20," I said.

It is to that text we now turn. In so doing we will discover its inseparable connection to Matthew 16.

The Context for Matthew 18:17-20
in Light of the Two-Source Tradition

Both Matthew 16:17-19 and 18:17-20 are unique to this Gospel—a strong indication they were both written to reflect dynamics occurring in the Matthean

Matthew 16:13-20

Now when Jesus came into the district of Caesarea Philippi, he asked his disciples,
"Who do people say that the Son of Man is?" And they said, "Some say John the Baptist, but others Elijah, and still others Jeremiah or one of the prophets." He said to them, "But who do you say that I am?" Simon Peter answered, "You are the Messiah, the Son of the living God."
And Jesus answered him,
"Blessed are you, Simon son of John! Flesh and blood has not revealed this to you, but my Father in heaven. And I tell you, you are Peter, and on this rock I will build my church (*ekklēsia*), and the gates of Hades will not prevail against it. I will give you the keys of the kingdom of heaven, and

whatever you bind on earth will be bound in heaven, and whatever you loose on earth will be loosed in heaven" (*ho ean dēsēs epi tēs gēs estai dedemenon en tois ouranois, kai ho ean lysēs epi tēs gēs estai lelymenon en tois ouranois*).
Then he sternly ordered the disciples not tell anyone that he was the Messiah.

Matthew 18:15-20

If another member of the community sins against you, go and point out the fault when the two of you are alone. If the member listens to you, you have regained that one. But if you are not listened to, take one or two others along with you, so that every word may be confirmed by the evidence of two or three witnesses.

If the member refuses to listen to them, tell it to the church (*ekklēsia*); and if the offender refuses to listen even to the church (*ekklēsia*), let such a one be to you as a Gentile and a tax collector. Truly (*Amēn*) I tell you, whatever you bind on earth will be bound in heaven and whatever you loose on earth will be loosed in heaven" (*hosa ean dēsēte epi tēs gēs estai dedemena en ouranō, kai hosa ean lysēte epi tēs gēs estai lelymena en ouranō*).
Again, truly (*amēn*) I tell you, if two of you agree on earth about anything you ask, it will be done for you by my Father in heaven. For where two or three are gathered in my name, I am there among them.

---

house churches more than being attributable to any indisputable words of the historical Jesus. The Greek makes it clear that the power to bind and loose singularly given to Peter in Matthew 16:19 (albeit with the keys) is equally given to the local community in Matthew 18:18 (when two or three gather in Jesus' name [i.e., in his presence and power]). In interpreting the two texts on "church" in Matthew, John Meier writes, "For Matthew, church leadership does not swallow up the authority of believers acting as one body. Thus Matthew can assign to the local church in 18:18 the power to bind and loose which is given to Peter in 16:19."[12]

Given the parallels between the texts, one can rightly ask, Is there *any* difference between the power to bind and loose given Peter in Matthew 16 and that given the community in Matthew 18? Is there a Petrine way of exercising the power to bind and loose in the *ekklēsia* and a communal way of exercising the power to bind and loose in the *ekklēsia*? The answer to both questions must be "yes." Both texts must be considered as equal in their power to bind and loose. They differ insofar as Peter receives "the keys to the kingdom" in Matthew 16 rather than the community in Matthew 18. At the same time, the community in Matthew 18 receives the promise of Christ's abiding presence in their binding and loosing in a way that is not given Peter in Matthew 16.

In a deeper probe of the parallels and differences between the texts, a current member of the PBC, Donald Senior, CP, writes,

> Peter's role as foundation rock brings with it new authority, and once again, the evangelist uses biblical and Jewish imagery to convey this. The disciple is given "the keys of the kingdom" a probable reference to Isaiah 22:22, where Eliakim is made prime minister of Judah in place of the faithless Shebna. Eliakim is given "the key of the House of David . . . should he open, no one shall close, should he close, no one shall open." And Peter too shall have such powers. He has the discretion of "binding" and "loosing," Jewish legal terms that referred either to the power of interpreting the obligations of the Law or to the power of excommunicating from the synagogue. It is not clear which of these is being conferred on Peter here (note that similar powers are given to the *community* in 18:18).[13]

Biblical scholars will always debate what the power of the keys means regarding jurisdiction in the church (or if such can even be deduced from the text). However, to equate the transmission of the keys with a kind of unilateral authority given to Peter and, from this, extend this power to an absolute authority of the pope over bishops, the bishops over priests, and the pastors over the people, invites all who promote this sole interpretation of the text not only to ask about their possible ideological reasons for doing so, but to heed another IBC caveat: "No single interpretation can exhaust the meaning of the whole, which is a symphony of many voices. Thus the interpretation of one particular text has to avoid seeking to dominate at the expense of others."[14] In other words, when it comes to "governance" in the Roman Catholic Church, the two entities receiving the power to bind and loose must be balanced: one recognizing the unique role of the keys in the Petrine "office" in the church as such, and the other given to the local church which also has been promised (by two "amens") the abiding presence of the "I am" to ratify its decisions.

While Senior says it is "not clear" whether the binding and loosing in Matthew 16 refers to Peter's "power of interpreting the obligations of the Law or to the power of excommunicating from the synagogue," which would reflect Judaic instances of how an indefinite kind of power would be worked out in historical circumstances, it seems clear from Matthew 18 that a case can be made for the power of excommunication being given the community[15] in a way not evident in the Matthew 16 text.

Whether the understanding of this text reflects Jesus' example of communicating forgiveness rather than excommunicating is open to different interpretations (although, from Peter's protestation on how many times forgiveness is necessary toward repeat offenders [Matt. 18:21] and Jesus' response [Matt. 18:22]), I think that those arguing for *never* closing anyone off might have better grounds. However, it is clear that, if the communal binding and loosing in the church of Matthew 18 is obstructed or denied in order to promote the Petrine office and its defined prerogatives, one can ask whether Christ's abiding presence will be found in the church of Matthew 16. Similarly, when any local church tries to function as a power source independent of Peter and the keys, its participation in the wider church likewise will be compromised. Rather than either/or, power and governance in the church should be a matter of both/and.

Matthew 16:17-19 and Catholic Fundamentalism: The Subversion of the Tradition

I would like to conclude this chapter with one further probe as to why such fundamentalism might be so persistent around the Matthean 16:17-19 text, despite concerns we have discussed related to this approach raised by the PBC itself. As noted earlier, this approach reveals a fundamentalist "way of presenting these truths [that] is rooted in an ideology which is not biblical, whatever the proponents of this approach might say. For it demands an unshakable adherence to rigid doctrinal points of view and imposes, as the only source of teaching for Christian life and salvation, a reading of the Bible that rejects all questioning and any kind of critical research."[16]

This insight of the IBC is critical to recall, especially when confronted by those who challenge what "proponents of this approach might say" that would suggest a "Catholic" pre-understanding or ideological bias. This insight also deserves recollection when universally recognized Matthean exegete, Ulrich Luz, reminds us that such a selective interpretation might actually undermine the institutional church's credibility. This occurs because the "Roman interpretation of Matt. 16:18 has too often been a self-legitimating of the rulers of the church. . . ." He concludes with a warning: "History also shows that an institution that uses such kinds of secondary biblical legitimateness for its dominant positions carries its own history as a heavy burden."[17]

If "to approach the text apart from its context is a pretext for a proof text," it is clear that, in many circles identified with what the next chapter will discuss as "Culture I Catholicism," Matthew 16:17-19 has evolved to become *the* "Catholic proof text." However, if our Roman Catholic ecclesiology is to rest on the twin pillars of scripture and tradition, to ground and promote its governance and accountability on such a selective and fundamentalist interpretation of this one text represents both intellectual dishonesty and scriptural errancy. Furthermore, to justify such an interpretation with an ideological appeal to an ever-entrenched tradition of male, patriarchal authority in the church makes those Catholics who insist on its dominical foundation no more scripturally honest than their evangelical equivalents who do the same when they limit the concept of salvation to texts such as John 3:16 or John 14:6 to the exclusion of other texts such as John 6:53-54.

The only rationale as to why this would continue, given biblical scholarship today, rests on the conclusion that Catholic tradition has been used ideologically here to nullify or at least compromise the Word of God. As James Hanvey shows so well in his "Tradition as Subversion," "tradition can become ideology when the hermeneutics of power within a community determines our understanding of tradition."[18] Such ideologies, he concludes, "represent totalizing visions that claim the right to adjudicate on what may or may not pass as truth."[19]

In conclusion, it is necessary, as Cardinal Donald Wuerl would declare, that we distinguish between "divine givens" and their "human exigencies." However, following Peter Steinfels, it is equally imperative that we also recognize that the received tradition—in this case the interpretation of Matthew 16:17-19 as an assumed divine given regarding ecclesiastical governance and accountability—demands greater biblical accuracy and historical integrity. By placing Matthew 16:17-19 in contrast to its Markan context and paralleling it with Matthew 18:16-20, it can be hoped a more balanced form of governance in the Roman Church will begin to be acknowledged and reestablished in ways that will have both dimensions of "church" be more authentic and accountable to each other.

3 ————————————————————————————

Catholicism's Crisis as Organizational

Finding New Meaning in the Mystical

The previous chapter discussed the two dimensions of the use of the word *ekklēsia* in Matthew's Gospel. It noted that the stress on Matthew 16:17-19 by the male clerical leaders in the church to the virtual exclusion of the power to bind and loose given to the community in Matthew 18:17-20 has created serious tensions over the governing structure and dynamics in the contemporary Catholic Church. Until those differences are acknowledged, addressed, and resolved toward the balance articulated in the First Gospel, conflicts in our church will never be resolved. Furthermore, until the unequal power dynamics involved in these two ways of being "church" become more balanced, we will continue to have abuses of power identified with those leaders in the "church of Matthew 16."

I have already discussed those abuses of power in the institutional model of the church that represent addictive and abusive dynamics,[1] so I will not repeat them here. However, their overpowering destructive dynamics cannot be discounted as key factors in the resulting crisis of meaning in the institutional model of the church that will be developed in this chapter. Just one theological implication of this fact is attested by the second article in a trilogy on "Hope and the Church" which I read in *Theological Studies* while writing this book. It was entitled "Post-Traumatic Ecclesiology and the Restoration of Hope."[2]

As noted, rather than making a simplistic link identifying the current crisis in the Roman Church of the West with issues related to abuse, the thrust of this chapter revolves around the report of the 63rd annual convention of the Catholic Theological Society of America (2008). Its theme was "Generations" and the Catholic Church. The findings presented, which are updated every triennium (the latest being 2011), offer powerful reading for anyone in the church, but especially its leadership. This includes everyone from the local parish priest to the hierarchy in the U.S. Catholic Church to Vatican officials, including the pope. These findings were more recently confirmed, with a bevy of excellent supporting data, by Pierre Hegy in his *Wake Up, Lazarus! On Catholic Renewal.*[3]

In his opening remarks to the CTSA, the Purdue University sociologist James D. Davidson noted that four age groups constitute adult U.S. Catholics.[4] The first is my cohort: those born in or before 1940; we constitute 17 percent of all Catholics (and, we will see, are the most church-going). Those born between 1941 and 1960 he called the Vatican II generation; it numbers one-third of all Catholics. The years 1961 to 1982 gave rise to the "post-Vatican II" Catholics, with 40 percent of the Catholic population. The "millennial generation includes people who have been born since 1983. They are about 8 percent of adult Catholics."[5]

Data showed all four cohorts in basic agreement regarding key dogmas that have traditionally defined Catholic faith-matters (Trinity, the Incarnation, the resurrection, Christ's real presence in the sacraments, Mary's role as Mother of God, and concern for the poor). However, beyond this commonality (which is critical when one considers that the core of the Catholic faith is found in the Nicene and Apostles' Creeds and the sacraments), other, more historically developed and culturally conditioned factors delineated the four cohorts, which he divided into "Culture I Catholics" and "Culture II Catholics."[6] The basic differences between the two groups went from "seeing the Church as a hierarchical institution to seeing it as the People of God; from an emphasis on ordination to an emphasis on baptism; from laypeople passively complying with church teachings to laypeople taking more responsibility for their own faith; and from seeing the world as a place to be avoided to seeing it as a place [in which] we should participate."[7] Recalling the discussion of the last chapter, broadly speaking, Culture I Catholics would be defined quite exclusively by the "church of Matthew 16" while Culture II Catholics would identify more with the "church of Matthew 18." The goal of a good ecclesiology in theory and practice rests in a balance between the two.

Before discussing Davidson's data, I want to repeat that both Culture I and Culture II Catholics agree on the fundamental dogmas found in our Creeds and the officially defined doctrines. So the purported differences we hear so much about *within the church* do not arise from issues around the substance of our faith. Nonetheless, these lesser differences can be magnified out of proportion. This happens, Robert Putnam and David Campbell say, when "religious" people view their stance as representative of "the truth." This can lead them to be less tolerant of views that clash with their own.[8] This dynamic of advocating "pure religion" plays out in the wider arena as well. Its adherents, according to the French social theorist Olivier Roy, will be effectively disengaged in the public square except in those forms that evidence "a display of religious 'purity,' or of reconstructed traditions."[9] When such groups take a restorationist approach by simply transposing the religious accoutrements that expressed the sense of the sacred of one era and apply them *carte blanche* to another era thinking to endow such practices with "a new mantra," instead it evokes some kind of "magical effect." In the name of engagement with the culture for its transformation, it actually isolates itself from the possibility of such transformation.[10] Finally, ideologically to cling exclusively to either a Culture I or Culture II Catholicism is to deny the power of the Spirit of God, who continually reminds us, within the core beliefs that will not and should not change, "Behold, I make all things new" (Rev. 21:5).

The church that is too exclusively defined by the historically and culturally derived dynamics of a Culture I Catholicism and a Matthew 16 church, that insists on male governance as God's will, must be balanced with a model of hierarchy that reflects what is becoming increasingly clearer from research about nature and its laws (i.e., natural law). Rather than a "dominator hierarchy," what is called a "natural hierarchy" is an order of increasing wholeness, such as subatomic particles to atoms to cells to organisms. The whole of one becomes part of the whole of the next. In other words, Ken Wilber notes, "natural hierarchies are composed of holons."[11] This kind of hierarchy is really a holarchy wherein each part is in the wider whole and the whole is in each and every part. Within this *natural way* of social organization all hierarchy is at the service of the holarchy. The old order of dominating hierarchy has given way to a hierarchy that truly reflects natural law. Such, I believe, is a contemporary way of structuring Paul's conviction that "we, though many, are one body in Christ, and individually members one of another" (Rom. 12:5).

In Catholicism, when the sources of our secondary disagreements are examined more thoroughly and honestly, the differences involved invariably have to do with dynamics addressed in the last chapter: proper governance in the church. Since governance involves authority and all authority involves some form of power, an overriding, but seldom acknowledged, point of division between Culture I and Culture II Catholics involves different notions about power.[12] This power will be of a more dominating and domineering type or it will be more collaborative and collegial. Consequently, such power involves the question of who will have ultimate authority in the church: only men who are clerics or a more inclusive representation of the baptized that acknowledges the gifts of both the church of Matthew 16 and the church of Matthew 18.

When I consider my own position on issues noted above by Davidson, I have made quite clear my opposition to abortion. However, when I examine the only two key points where I differ from Culture I Catholics and am thus simply defined by some of them as outside "the faith," the issues involve the role of women in the church and artificial birth control for married couples.

And, while these involve the exercise of the magisterium in the church, it cannot be denied that the way they have been interpreted by one dimension of the magisterium to the exclusion of the other ultimately involves the issue of governance and power in the church, including *who has the power* to do such defining.

If the only real theological differences in our church, at least for people like me, involve the two issues of the full equality of women in the church and the right of married couples to determine how they will be conscientiously open to bring children into our world, why is there such polarization around them? This becomes especially troublesome when there remains much debate regarding the question of the "reception" of such papal declarations within the whole church. Only when the churches of Matthew 16 and 18 agree on such matters of faith can they be considered binding. Until then, there will be differences; however these two differences should not be the basis for one group excluding the other from the title "Catholic." To this effect, the Second Vatican Council peritus Joseph Ratzinger wrote, "Criticism of papal declarations will be possible and necessary to the degree that they do not correspond with Scripture and the Creed, that is, with the belief of the church. Where there is neither unanimity in the church nor clear testimony of the sources, then no binding decision is possible; if one is formally made, then its preconditions are lacking, and therefore the question of its legitimacy must be raised."[13]

The power issue at the heart of disagreement around the issues of birth control and women priests becomes clearer when we consider the debates at the highest levels in the Vatican that dealt with birth control at the time of the initial establishment and later expansion of the Papal Birth Control Commission (1962-1966) by Pope Paul VI. The rejection of the "Majority Report" that led to the publication of *Humanae Vitae* (1968) did not ultimately result from theological or moral arguments around the nature of sexual reproduction in marriage. Rather, they revolved around the "Minority Report's" core argument: a change in the "official teaching" regarding birth control would call into question the basic authority of the "official teachers." The ultimate reason thus had little or nothing to do with good theology or morals regarding sexual reproduction among married people, but rather the preservation of the male, celibate, clerical system of power and governance in the church.

Next, considering the official teaching of male clerics defining issues around women's "place" in the church, an honest discussion on the issue is virtually impossible because of the blinders on those involved. The environment of the flat-earth, culturally conditioned first-century Mediterranean world that influenced the decision making of the historical Jesus and limited his leadership group to men only is invoked as justified in an ongoing way. The best way to understand this limited worldview is by seeing its dynamics worked out today in many parts of the Islamic world where male clerics issue theological *fatwas* that reinforce male domination over women.[14] However, in "the West," which seems to be the model of culture advocated by Pope Benedict XVI,[15] full equality between men and women is the law almost everywhere except the more monarchical Roman Church. Consequently, in various letters to the pope (both as Cardinal Ratzinger and as Supreme Pontiff), I have argued why it is time to change. In one of these letters I wrote:

> Such a teaching overlooks the role of the context (wherein women and children "did not count") that influenced Jesus' actions; it demeans the power of the Risen Christ (the basis of all sacramental life in the church) as the one in whom there can be no Jew nor Gentile, slave nor free, woman nor man, and belies the nature of the non-exclusive trinitarian God, the source of all grace bestowed equally to all. Our church teaches the Trinity must ground all human relationships, including our church, but the Trinity is a community of full equals sharing power, roles and functions equally.
>
> You have also reiterated, as Pope, the teaching that "the church has not been given the power" to ordain women. This seems to belie Matthew 28:16-20 as well as the fact that "the church" was never given the power to limit priesthood in the Latin Church to celibates in a way that restricts the pool of sincere men and women for priesthood and the laity for capable and equipped ministers.[16]

The fact that the same Spirit-power of Jesus Christ articulated by Paul in Galatians (regarding the breakdown of culturally received structures that separated from power Jews from Gentiles, slaves from free men, and women from men) led the church of the Acts of the Apostles to break the cultural bonds that separated Jew and Gentile. It could also be argued that purely cultural constructs kept the official church virtually silent for centuries regarding the inherent social sin associated with slavery (with some of its leading religious orders actually owning slaves). With the issue of full equality for women now recognized as God-given, it seems it is time for that final barrier to be broken in our church. If all are "one in Christ," the governance structures in the church should reflect this. When the "church of Matthew 16" issues decrees on women and reproduction that are "not received" by the "church of Matthew 18" it is time that the dynamics around these two issues be revisited. As indicated in the previous chapter, such an approach to the scriptures begs for less ideology and greater integrity in our tradition.

Returning to the material shared at the CTSA in 2008, I believe Davidson's taxonomy is critical when we consider the differences between Culture I and Culture II Catholics, especially when the data show both groups united in believing the core elements that have always defined membership in the Catholic Church. It is the secondary elements that define the differences.

Grounded in these different stresses, the grid below delineates further key elements that define the Culture I and Culture II poles of Catholicism.[17] These seem to bear out the characteristics of the people constituting those religious stances found by Davidson and others. Believing they are self-explanatory, I simply share the grid here, without further comment, except to say that I also believe these two poles on the "continuum of Catholicism" mirror the core dynamics of another grid I will share in Part III related to the two basically different ways we understand the nature and action of God.

TWO POLES ON THE CONTINUUM OF HOW CATHOLICS VIEW CHURCH

CULTURE I	CULTURE II
The Church of Matthew 16	*The Church of Matthew 18*
Scriptural stress on highlighting male authorities: Matt. 16:17-19; 10:1-4; 28:16-20	Scriptural stress on highlighting Holy Spirit: Luke 4:18-19; Acts 2:1-4, 17-21; Rom. 12:3-8; 1 Cor. 12
The Roman Catholic Church established as an organization established by Jesus Christ	The Roman Catholic Church as part of the wider organism called the Mystical Body of Christ
Popular notion of the church as a "what" that can result in an "us" and "them" way of thinking	Popular notion of the church as a "we" that views all as equal members
Institutional model of church highlighted: "the church's children" under the pope (and Vatican), bishops, and priests. Ordination dominates	Community-of-disciples model of church highlighted: the baptized and their leaders as co-responsible. Baptism dominates
Structures linked to "flat-earth" understanding of the universe: stress on hierarchy that is patriarchal	Structures linked to evolutionary view of universe: stress on hierarchy at service of holarchy[18]
Magisterium identified primarily with papal pronouncements; secondarily with episcopal statements	Magisterium indentified with collegiality wherein unanimity exists among hierarchy, the people, and theologians
Obedience as submission of mind and intellect to what the above magisterium says	Obedience as respectful service of all to the common good
Eucharist primarily identified with the action of the clerically ordained who determine how lay people will participate	Eucharist as source and summit of the life of the whole church being celebrated, with the priests presiding, by the whole people

Unfortunately, rather than seeing the above construct as involving *two poles* within which Catholics might find their particular religious expressions, *polarities* too often result. Thus, the question raised by Pope Benedict XVI regarding divisions among the Christian churches can be applied with even greater force regarding polarities within the Catholic Church: "If Christians present themselves disunited, moreover, often in opposition, will the proclamation of Christ as the only savior of the world and our peace be credible to a world that does not know Christ or that has distanced itself from him, or that appears indifferent to the Gospel?"[19] It seems that Pope Benedict also recognizes the long-term futility of the existing polarities around governance in the church that separate the power of binding and loosing between the churches of Matthew 16 and 18. Calling for a "change in mindset" that will bring about a greater balance between the power and responsibility invested in both, he said that this new mentality was the task of everyone in the church—"from the Pope to the most recently baptized child." He said that we all need to realize that our communion with one another demands that lay people "must no longer be viewed as 'collaborators' of the clergy but truly recognized as 'co-responsible' for the Church's being and action."[20] Because we are not yet experiencing in Catholicism this kind of unity and co-responsibility being articulated by Pope Benedict XVI, we need to probe the reasons why.

The theological and pastoral implications of the model Davidson created to describe Culture I and Culture II Catholics seem to reflect dynamics that represent a deeper ecological construct in the human psyche itself. More and more data seem to be showing that we somehow, by nature or nurture (or, probably, by a combination of both), develop two basic worldviews that encapsulate the constructs that get expressed in our different moral attitudes and stances. Hugh Heclo notes in his book *On Thinking Institutionally* that these constructs are deeply woven into the personal and collective identity of the individuals and groups who practice them.[21] These, in turn, impact our economic and political viewpoints as well as our religious way of thinking. I also believe, by extension, they impact our understanding of God and what we humans divine to be God's will. From these we create institutions that reflect those values.

More specific to our point, in the mid-1990s, University of California (Berkeley) linguist George Lakoff discovered from examining peoples' verbal patterns two basically different worldviews. These were echoed in differing moral viewpoints regarding the way we order our lives, starting with our family life. He called these differing social constructs the "Strict Father model" and the "Nurturant Parent model." Lakoff's cultural models resonate with similar studies revealing differing worldviews, including a wide range of either "individualist" or "communitarian" as well as "hierarchical" or "egalitarian" outlooks. As he finds these forms descriptive of differing approaches to Christianity,[22] so I find them reflective of the two poles of Culture II and Culture I Catholicism.

Such data also show that, if people are not aware of the lens through which they particularly see the world, it can easily skew any data coming from science that might contradict that worldview and adversely affect their decision making. The consequence will be a filtering of all opposing data about anything according to people's pre-existing worldview, including the consequent beliefs related to God and "God's will" that this entails. In other words, people of such a kind of faith respond to scientific evidence in ways that justify their preexisting beliefs.[23] This resistance to change, even when confronted with facts that undermine one's previously held convictions, is not done out of ill-will as much as from unrecognized fears, especially for people in leadership in an organization like the Roman Church. This fact was made clear to me by a Catholic psychotherapist with whom I was discussing some of the contents of this book. He said,

> Regarding "change" [whether the Catholic Church or any church], it is always difficult for those in power to make changes to tradition even in the event that current tradition isn't aligned with Jesus' teachings. Remember that faith is what Søren Kierkegaard would refer to as a subjective truth, and these subjective truths inform who we are. To change a subjective truth is to change a part of who we are, and for a faith-based institution such as the Catholic Church, making changes to tradition can destabilize the base that supports their followers' faith. Whether right or wrong, care is given to not shake this foundation.[24]

Keeping in mind this faith-based rationale for understanding why there is such resistance in the Roman Church to change externals having little to do with the faith itself, we can return to Lakoff's model. Here we find two poles applicable beyond religion to the wider world insofar as we view our nation as a family (i.e., "homeland" security) with the government as parent. It also applies to our economic theories insofar as we talk about problems in it demanding "cleaning the house." In the same vein, I would add, we see the church as a "family" with differing approaches as to how it is to be governed: by the "Strict [Holy] Father" in the Vatican or by a more dialogical nurturance, of what we've seen by solely a Matthew 16 approach or one that balances the churches of Matthew 16 and 18. In describing the two moral stances of each position he writes,

> Strict Father morality assigns highest priorities to such things as moral strength (the self-control and self-discipline to stand up to external

and internal evils), respect for and obedience to authority, the setting
and following of strict guidelines and behavioral norms, and so on. . . .
    Nurturant parent morality has a different set of priorities. Moral
nurturance requires empathy for others and the helping of those who
need help. To help others, one must take care of oneself and nurture
social ties. And one must be happy and fulfilled in oneself, or one will
have little empathy for others.[25]

One of the problems in the contemporary culture that vitiates against a
healthy model of either stance occurs with partisanship, polarization, and ideological (and theological) purity. Here, normal core orientations are amalgam-
ated into a collective "group think." These dynamics pit not only one person
against another but one group against the other. They are further calcified and
become ideological when the leaders are chosen, ultimately, on the basis of
loyalty to one position in contrast to the other. Hence, the ease with which
either an adherent of a Matthew 16 or a Matthew 18 worldview can dismiss
the other as "no longer Catholic." This dynamic is reinforced in a climate of
unacknowledged and unrecognized abuse and victimization. Thus, we see the
outcry by representatives of the Matthew 16 worldview when the Irish prime
minister identified the dynamics of the hierarchical and patriarchal church,
with its central offices in the Vatican, as representing "the dysfunction, dis-
connection, elitism—and the narcissism—that dominate the culture of the
Vatican to this day."[26]
    Within such environments it becomes very difficult to lead a truly spiritual
life. Janet Ruffing pointed out this fact in a keynote address at the 2011 Assembly of Spiritual Directors International. She stated that we are now witnessing
the "not uncommon rise of profoundly narcissistic personalities to positions
of authority that treat the least display of criticism or independence as intoler-
able and then require the elimination of the offending person from the situation." She noted that it need not happen in the same way: "Sometimes this is
done psychologically; sometimes it is done physically."[27] Such destructive and
annihilating dynamics arise not so much from good theology but authoritative ideology as well as cultural constructs. The violence involved can be quite
detrimental to the integrity of individual, group, and organizational life and
spirituality itself.
    As the chart above noted, Culture I and Culture II Catholicism represent
two poles on a continuum; ideally the truly "catholic" Catholic would have an
anchor in one theological stance without rejecting key elements of the other.
To make any one stance the "only" stance, given our understanding of scriptural fundamentalism, could be hugely detrimental not only to dialogue; it
could easily indicate one has become ideological—rigid and authoritarian—
in one's stance toward life.

I discovered how easy it is to label a person as Culture I or Culture II (or by other terminology such as "traditionalist" or "liberal") or to be given such labels by others when I was speaking with a bishop whom I had known for quite some time. I had referred to myself as a "liberal" Catholic. "Mike," he said, "how can you say you are liberal; you are against abortion." "Well," I said, "I guess I'm a liberal who's against abortion!"

Even though there is always a tendency to polarize around our mental and moral constructs, Lakoff has demonstrated that such stances generally are not monolithic. "There will not be a single conservative or liberal worldview to fit all conservatives or all liberals," he writes. "Conservativism and liberalism are radical categories. They have, I believe, central models and variations on those models. I take as my goal the description of the central models and the descriptions of the major variations on those central models."[28]

Having said this, perhaps because of my Franciscan background, I find Lakoff's model and its echoes in Culture I and Culture II Catholicism manifested in a key choice made by Francis of Assisi in his attempt to "repair" the house of the church. This involves the way he made a clear break from the "Strict Father" model of life represented by his abusive father, Pietro Bernadone, to that of the Nurturant Parent model of the Trinity when he disrobed before Bishop Guido of Assisi. In this act of stark nakedness he not only declared his rejection of the dominating and patriarchal example of organizing life in his culture that was given by his father; he indicated his willingness to embark on another way of relating that would not be defined by violence. This has been memorialized in his famous words: "Until now I have called Pietro di Bernadone my father. But . . . from now on I will only say 'Our Father who art in heaven,' and not 'My father, Pietro di Bernadone.'" He further indicated his rejection of the "Strict Father" model for the "Nurturant Parent" he found in his heavenly Father when he felt called to embrace the life of the gospel and to make its evangelical ways the rule of his Order. Thus, in his Earlier Rule he not only quoted the Matthean passage about not calling anyone on earth "Father";[29] he made this theology performative by never referring to himself as "Father Francis" but "Brother Francis" and by insisting on a more motherly, nurturing way of relating among the brothers.[30] Furthermore, when he did articulate what he meant by God as "Father," he immediately linked it to the other members of the Trinity.[31]

Having said this, Francis made it clear that his way of life was to take place within the dominant institutional model of the church of his day. The observance of this evangelical way of living "the Holy Gospel of Our Lord Jesus Christ" by himself and his followers for all time was always to take place under the authority of the popes of "the Roman Church."[32] Nonetheless, while he never said it directly, his writings make clear that the more nurturing and

familial way of the Order was to serve as a nonviolent alternative to the hierarchical and patriarchal structures of the Roman Church. Consequently, I find
in his understanding of the "evangelical life" a much deeper identification with
what we see exhibited by Culture II Catholicism than with the dominance and
dominating ways of Culture I Catholicism.

Returning to Davidson's interpretation of the data shared at the CTSA,
within these two groupings he pointed to three key demographics that showed
the marked differences between them: (1) "the cultural orientation of the institutional church"; (2) "differences in the status of American Catholics"; and (3)
"differences in church leaders' control over the laity."[33] The first refers more
specifically to the issues above which define Culture I and Culture II Catholicism. The second involves status arising from U.S. Catholics' economic level
and sense of "belonging" in the wider society. The third addresses the actual
influence of the church's clerical leaders over the decision making of Catholics
in the pews.

Regarding the first cohort of us born in or before 1940, the institutional
church was Culture I; our status in the society was lower class; we were outside the mainstream culture. The church leaders' control over the laity was
high. I experienced this at every level in my family life and by belonging to
St. Patrick's Church in Fond du Lac, Wisconsin. For those of the next generation (1941-1960), Culture II Catholicism became more dominant than
Culture I thinking; Catholics became middle class economically and found
themselves half inside and half outside the mainstream culture. The influence
of the leaders over the laity was middling. After Vatican II, things shifted significantly for Catholics. The institutional dynamics of the church changed so
that, during this period, there was a virtual equation of Culture I and Culture
II priorities; Catholics had become upper middle class. However, by now, the
influence of the leaders on the laity was low. With the millennials, a major shift
in effective ecclesiology took place. At least in terms of the institutional form
of Catholicism, Culture I Catholicism reclaimed its dominance over Culture
II Catholicism; meanwhile Catholics maintained their economic and cultural
role of being upper middle class. However, even though the "official" theology
had reverted to a Culture I model, the leaders' influence over the lives of the
laity continued to remain low. The data showed a continual shrinkage in "official" Catholic affiliation and loyalty. Consequently, Davidson's statistics show
clearly that the influence of the leaders in institutional Catholicism is quite
limited. This becomes even clearer (along with the significant consequences
of this change) when one studies the result of what each of the four cohorts
thought about (1) what it meant to be a "Good Catholic"; (2) whether they
would ever "leave the church"; and (3) where they found the locus of authority
in their lives.

In surveys taken every three years up to 2011, a consistently increasing number of respondents say they can be a good Catholic without obeying official church teaching on divorce and remarriage. Similar patterns are found in those who said they "would never leave the church." While my cohort has 69 percent agreeing they would never leave the church, the number drops to 35 percent among the millennials. (Other data also show that, unless we find a way to offer something viable to this group, the numbers "leaving" the church will keep increasing.[34]) Finally, considering the "locus of moral authority," besides questions around birth control, homosexual behavior, sex outside of marriage, remarriage without an annulment, a question was asked about who has the "final say" regarding abortion. The results are almost unbelievable.

Among my cohort one-third believe church leaders have the final say on abortion; the Vatican II cohort have 30 percent believing so. The post-Vatican II cohort has 21 percent believing such authority trumps personal conscience, while none among the millennials agree that church leaders have the final say regarding the locus of their moral authority: it rests in their own consciences.[35] My first reaction to this final piece of data was incredulity because I was thinking of the small number of evangelical Catholics among millennials who embrace a Culture I model of church. However, the more I thought of this, the more I concluded that (1) their numbers may be truly insignificant or (2) they know even Catholic teaching says that the *ultimate locus* of moral authority is the informed conscience of the Catholic. Hopefully these have been well-formed, including the influence of "official" church teaching and officials in the church.

Though the popes and the U.S. bishops as a body have offered a range of constructive teachings on issues from immigration to the rights of workers, their words on these subjects get eclipsed when the average Catholic reads only about the financial consequences of past clerical sins around pedophilia and continued allegations of cover-ups at the highest levels of the church. It is not surprising that the Catholic News Service in 2010 noted that the approval rating for the U.S. Catholic bishops fell dramatically from 62 percent in 2008 to 45 percent in 2010. Clearly this shows the inability of the bishops to get Catholics to find their messages relevant and their governance effective.[36]

Given such data, the future does not bode well for the influence of official leaders of the Roman Catholic Church, especially over a generation of Catholic school graduates who may have been very well catechized but poorly evangelized.[37] The leaders have insisted on orthodoxy and right teaching when the people need to encounter the person of Jesus Christ. It is the contrast between a "what," to which they have little allegiance, versus a "who" to whom they are attracted and committed. John C. Haughey, SJ, articulated the difference well in a seminal article appearing in *America* in 2004:

Many non-Catholic Christian students, especially those whose backgrounds are Lutheran or evangelical, are not shy about making personal faith statements in my theology classes at Loyola University Chicago. Faith statements made in a classroom are pure gold for a teacher of theology, because they legitimize conversations that go beyond theology to the convictions in the hearts of the students.

Catholic students, on the other hand, are very slow to make faith statements or statements about a personal relationship with Christ, even though Pope John Paul II has insisted that a personal, even intimate relationship with Christ should be the aim of our programs of catechesis in the church. This has led me to ask an uncomfortable question: have Catholic students been catechized into what one might call Church-ianity, whereas many of our non-Catholic Christian students are in a religious condition of Christ-ianity?[38]

When the "church" is experienced as a "what" rather than a "who" and when faith is equated with a person's agreement to "what" is taught rather than to "Who" is the Teacher, it is not surprising that Haughey would have such an experience with young people still defining themselves as Catholic. This makes anyone wonder how long such a commitment will last for them. Indeed, the data show that it often will be short lived.

Uncovering a Key Source of the Crisis

During the pontificate of Pope John Paul II and into that of his successor, Pope Benedict XVI, one became accustomed to hearing blame for the church's problems on such philosophically laden "isms" as secularism and relativism. Who can forget the pre-conclave sermon of then-Cardinal Joseph Ratzinger wherein he reflected on the passage from Ephesians 4: 7, 11-16, that "we must no longer be children, tossed to and fro and blown about by every wind of doctrine. . . ." This led him to talk about the "many winds of doctrine" that reflected "ideological currents" that were "tossed from one extreme to the other: from Marxism to liberalism to libertinism; from collectivism to radical individualism; from atheism to a vague religious mysticism; from agnosticism to syncretism, etc." From here, reflecting his concern about the church in the West (contra the reality of the church in Africa) he spoke of how the "dictatorship of relativism" seems to dominate. In contrast to this, Cardinal Ratzinger rightly called for an adult kind of faith "profoundly rooted in friendship with Christ" in a Pauline way whose practice would bring "about truth in charity."[39]

The pope's insight that the aim of faith formation is spiritual adulthood is lofty (as well as necessary). However, when faith formation meets the bureaucratic apparatus established to make it happen, one can only ask if the very system of organized Catholicism is not meant to keep the "faithful" in the status of children rather than of mature adults in their personal faith. This situation has powerful consequences that must be addressed, and that seem to be registering on the radar screen of Pope Benedict XVI. While he has continued to speak about the "dictatorship of relativism" as a core cause for the crisis of the church in the West, at other times during his pontificate he has seemed less certain about the causes, as well as the cures, for the "dying" of what he named "the so-called great churches" in places like Europe and Australia. Indeed, he admitted in 2005 that he himself had no "recipe for a rapid change."[40] This notion was echoed in 2011 by one of the scholars chosen to address the Ratzinger Schulkreis at Castel Gandolfo while Pope Benedict XVI was present. Otto Neubauer said that the "most adult, mature and old Church" [i.e., the church in "the West"] must become free from her own limitations.[41]

When a bishop or cardinal raises questions about the way the church has been organized or operates, he is often retired, such as Bishop Geoffrey Robinson or Bishop Francis A. Quinn. The latter said, "An overarching crisis in today's church is a crisis of faith; not faith in God, not faith in Jesus Christ, but a crisis of faith in the institutional church."[42] Such statements have been few and far between and rarely expressed by more influential clerics, save for the possibility of the controversial Diarmuid Martin of Dublin. However, with more and more data showing the hemorrhaging of members in countries such as the United States, Canada, Ireland, and Australia and more and more revelations of abuse of authority in the scandal of pedophilia in the church, it has become virtually impossible to "blame the victim."

Increasing data shows that the problem may also have a key source in the system itself. This realization reached its apogee when Enda Kenny, the practicing Catholic *Taoiseach* (prime minister) of Ireland, along with its parliament, "criticized the Vatican, rather than local church leaders, over the 17 years of pedophile-priest scandals in Ireland." In remarks covered by the Vatican News Service (Zenit), he said that "the church's leaders had repeatedly sought to defend their institutions at the expense of children, and to 'parse and analyze' every revelation of a church cover-up 'with the gimlet eye of a canon lawyer.'"[43]

In the United States, upon his election to be chair of the United States Conference of Catholic Bishops, Archbishop Timothy Dolan himself suggested the possibility of problems related to the operational structure of Catholicism. In an interview with the *New York Times* he talked about the need for the bishops' conference to confront "internal problems like the 'sobering study' showing that one-third of Americans born and baptized Catholic have left the church. 'The bishops are saying we need to make sure our house is in order as a church. We need to recover our vigor . . . Then we can be of better service to the world and to our culture.'"[44] The same intimation of the need to consider issues related to the institution, rather than limiting the finger pointing to the people in the pews, came from the head of the Australian bishops' Pastoral Research Office: "When we asked people why they stopped going to church … they said they stopped because they can't find relevance; they can't see a connection between the church's agenda and their own agenda, they disagree with certain church teachings."[45]

Archbishop Diarmuid Martin of Dublin, among members of the Catholic hierarchy, has probably highlighted better than anyone else a key source of the crisis in the organization of Catholicism. He continually points to the issue of institutional power and, in particular, one particular misuse of power in the form of a "culture of clericalism" that has had such pervasive power in the organizational dynamics of Catholicism.[46] In a 2011 speech covered by Zenit, he said that this "narrow culture of clericalism has to be eliminated" if the Catholic Church in Ireland is to have a viable future for the next generations of its people. But this will not be easy, he added: "It did not come out of nowhere and so we have to address its roots from the time of seminary training onwards."[47] In another discussion of clericalism, speaking of the unspeakable abuses of authority exposed in the Catholic Church of Ireland (and applicable wherever such abuse occurred), he said: "The culture of clericalism has to be analyzed and addressed. Were there factors of a clerical culture which somehow facilitated disastrous abusive behaviour to continue for so long? Was it just through bad decisions by bishops or superiors? Was there knowledge of behaviour which should have given rise to concern and which went unaddressed?"[48]

Finally, in what might be an indication of his realization that the "crisis of the church in the West" might not rest alone on the people in the pews, Pope Benedict XVI himself indicated that it may also have a source connected to the way he and they were being perceived. In a talk to a gathering of the cardinals in the Vatican where he reflected on issues facing the church, especially upon the allegations of sexual abuse of children by priests in many countries in Europe, using the word "our," the pope said: "We must ask ourselves what was wrong in our proclamation, in our whole way of living the Christian life, to allow such a thing to happen."[49]

The Crisis of Faith as a Crisis of Meaning in Culturally Conditioned Catholicism

The cultural accretions in the overly centralized, Vatican-oriented Catholic Church, coupled with the abuse of authority by some of its top officials (accompanied by their stress on issues that do not touch the lives of the people in the pews or, in the case of the pressure of the Vatican on bishops' conferences regarding the new Roman Missal, which has touched the lives of the people in the pews), have contributed to a serious crisis of faith. However, upon further examination, this crisis of faith points to an even deeper malaise: the crisis of meaning. In effect, the official form of Catholicism has not just led to the loss of faith for millions of its members. For many of these "former Catholics" they have lost faith in God because the "god" they were given—represented by an organizational model identified with a male-only, celibate clerical way of being "the church"—has become unbelievable. Thus, their loss of faith in institutional Catholicism has contributed to jeopardizing their faith in God because of the many ways its leaders have identified *their* ways with God's ways and their decrees as God's will and the historical organization with the organism.

One of my favorite authors examining the nature of faith, especially in young people, is Sharon Daloz Parks. In 1990, I took a class that featured her thought. One particular insight has remained with me ever since. She wrote,

> If we are to recover a more adequate understanding of human faith in the context of present cultural experience, we must be clear . . . we are speaking of something quite other than belief in its dominant contemporary usage. . . . Though faith has become a problematic, the importance of "meaning" has not. Modern people can more easily recognize that the seeking and defending of meaning pervades all of human life.[50]

What Parks is saying is that what my generation hears as "a loss of faith" in Catholicism for an ever-increasing number of people indicates that its organizational practices just no longer "mean anything." In my one-sided correspondence with church officials noting my concerns about the future of Catholicism in the United States and "the West," I continually talk about the problem not being one of relativism so much as (ir)relevance. If relevance deals with meaning and meaning is another word for faith, the faith these leaders promote—from their rituals to their seminaries—is irrelevant and meaningless. To this degree any lack of faith should weigh more heavily on their consciences than on the consciences of the people who "lose their faith."

In one of my letters to Pope Benedict XVI,[51] I shared my concerns about what was happening to the church both he and I love. Aware that some believe in a "leaner but cleaner" kind of Catholicism wherein the disagreements do not refer to dogmas and doctrines as much as to issues around governance and power as well as rubrics and rituals, I wrote,

> Catholics who believe the . . . stress on rituals and regulations represents "the church" may be having their way and may give you financial and personal support. You and they may think this reflects the "pure" church. And those who do not endorse so many of these ways to be "essential" to what it means to be "Catholic" are easily labeled

"outside" the true faith. . . . Clearly, something is wrong in our evangelization. I am unwilling to point a finger at the people in the pews;
increasingly I think it is coming from the other end: the leaders of our
institution, their almost obsession with returning to "tradition" [i.e.,
Roman rituals]. . . .

These points have been stated much better by Drew Christiansen, editor-in-
chief of *America* magazine. In a 2010 article he talked about the teaching authority of the bishops that has become compromised because of their abuse of that
authority—not so much in their official teaching as in their practice. The consequence, he wrote (quoting Cardinal Newman), is that such abuse of the pastoral
office among the "educated classes" will end in "indifference," while, among the
less educated, it will end in more "superstition." He wrote, "When the teaching
office leans excessively on its authority, it mistakes commanding for teaching."[52]
The result often will be conflicts in, among, and around the statements of episcopal authorities or, as we have seen, increasing indifference to them.

This phenomenon became overwhelmingly clear to me during a conversation I had with a bishop who was noted for his abusive ways with priests and
people in his diocese. During our conversation he kept saying, "My priests
don't respect my authority." When I heard this more than a couple of times,
I said, "Bishop, may I say something?" When he affirmed my request, I said,
"Bishop, I have heard you say various times, 'My priests don't respect my
authority.' Can I respond to that?" When he said I could, I said, "Bishop, I have
written a book on power. In it I define power as 'the ability to influence' and
authority as the 'ability to elicit respect, trust and obedience' from others.[53] So,
Bishop, if you say your 'priests don't *respect* your authority, the problem can't be
with the priests. Rather the problem would have to be in the way you are exercising your authority."[54] Rather than use his authority to dominate, the bishop
would have been much more effective had he acted on the data that show that
people give authority to leaders they genuinely like.[55]

The consequence of such questionable (if not actually abusive) uses of
authority by bishops often differs depending on whether one is a Culture I
or Culture II Catholic. Christiansen writes, "The Left no longer listens to the
bishops, and the Right only listens to learn whether the bishops are saying
what they want said."[56] The ultimate consequence, clearly, is a hierarchy whose
official teaching makes little difference to both Culture I and Culture II Catholics. It also belies a deeper crisis: the crisis in the very authority of the bishops;
they have lost their credibility.

When we look at the resulting "crisis of faith" being experienced in Catholicism, the "exact nature" of the crisis (to use "Twelve-Step" language) points
to something much deeper than the abuse of children by priests and even the
abuse of their authority by bishops. It reveals the reality that, except for those

people whose psychological constitution or limited understanding of Catholic tradition consigns them to Culture I Catholicism, the underlying crisis in Catholicism is cultural and even systemic. At the same time it exposes a parallel consequence of the crisis. While it is clear what a Culture I Catholicism should look like, the fact that Culture II Catholicism has not sufficiently made itself "Catholic" shows the need for its adherents to find new and meaningful symbols, rituals, and patterns within the best of the tradition that invite another way to be authentically Catholic. (This will be discussed in Part III.)

Two of the best interpreters of what "culture" means, in my estimation, are Clifford Geertz and Ann Swidler. They have parallel explanations of culture that highlight the notion of "meaning" front and center. I juxtapose them here.

Clifford Geertz on Culture	*Ann Swidler on Culture*
Historically transmitted pattern of meanings embodied in symbols, a system of inherited conceptions expressed in symbolic forms by means of which [wo]men communicate, perpetuate, and develop their knowledge about and attitudes towards life.	Symbolic vehicles of meaning, including beliefs, ritual practices, art forms, and ceremonies, as well as informal cultural practices such as language, gossip, stories and rituals of daily life.

It seems clear from their definitions that the notion of "meaning" is at the core of culture. Closely connected are symbols and patterns of behavior that give evidence of shared meaning. In this sense I sympathize with those Culture I Catholics who fear that a movement to the theology of Culture II Catholicism might lead to chaos instead of clarity regarding a new model of meaning. But such fear does not justify remaining locked into something that is jeopardizing the faith of ever-increasing numbers. In this I am heartened by the words of Pope John Paul II about the need for purification in all cultures: "Since culture is a human creation, and is therefore marked by sin, it too needs to be 'healed, and ennobled, and perfected.'"[57]

When data show the "crisis" in Western Catholicism (as in Western Europe, the United States, Canada, and Australia) has little to do with differences about our core dogmas as professed in our creedal statements, one must look to other sources for the problem. From my reading of the data, many of our divisions or differences ultimately result from a stress on correct Vatican or episcopal teaching rather than right practice, and a unilateral exercise of authority that does not promote a balance of power in the church. Well can it be said of this culturally derived model of church that it evokes Jesus' response (himself quoting Isaiah) regarding the dynamics he experienced in the cultural form of religion of his time: "For the sake of your tradition, you have made void the word of God. You hypocrites! Well did Isaiah prophesy of you, when he said: 'This people honors me with their lips, but their heart is far from me; in vain do they worship me, teaching as doctrines the precepts of men'" (Matt. 15:6-9; Mark 7:6-7).

This is the pattern we now experience way too often in the institutional model of the church. It fits well the insight of Langdon Gilkey about any culture:

> Culture is the locus of the social institutions that pass on systemic injustice; it was culture's information system that perpetuated and justified slavery, and also class, gender and racial domination. Culture is also the locus of the mores and morals that encourage, defend and justify those unjust (and cruel) institutions. Culture is the site of ideology, whether religious or secular, which incites, increases, and excuses, in fact justifies through its myths and rituals, these injustices.[58]

A key result of this pattern is the environment of "Catholicism" that has come to dominate the Culture I model of the church. There is a deep contradiction between its mystical, organic identity that is living and adapting (like any open model) and its organizational identity that is becoming increasingly closed and no longer open to its originating power. When this humanly derived, culturally conditioned institutional model becomes *the only way* to "be church," crisis cannot be far behind. Describing a crisis as "a rapidly deteriorating situation that if left untended will lead to disaster in the near future," Ilia Delio notes, "A crisis can either terminate a system or signal a new one. In closed systems a crisis functions like a sharp pain; it indicates something wrong in the system or that the system has been disrupted. In open systems a crisis functions like a strange attractor" that pulls "the system into new patterns of behavior over time."[59]

Putting it another way, when the leaders of an organization recognize that its human members are basically organisms containing energy and that their energy is being energized or entropied (i.e., drained), they need to find ways to ensure, as Tony Schwartz, founder of Starbucks, says, "that people have full tanks of energy. This is one of the big variables that will determine which organizations thrive in the next 10 or 20 years."[60]

If leaders will not allow and enable this to happen, they will find themselves presiding over organizations that will become increasingly closed, and when systems close, they begin to die. The classical thermodynamics theory of entropy sets in.[61] The more entropy in the system, the less the system will change; the more closed the system is, the less able it is to exist within its wider environment in a way that empowers it to grow and evolve into something ever new. The consequence of such dynamics, for an ever-increasing number of people, especially the young (the future of the church) is meaninglessness and, for the leaders, a greater awareness of its being in crisis.

4 _____

Finding a New Model of Meaning

The Need for a New Catholic Myth

The root word for "meaning" (as well as "meaninglessness") is the Greek word *muein*. In adapting the insights of one of the pre-eminent sociologists of religion, Max Weber, to our discussion,[1] we find that charismatic figures arise within an environment of meaninglessness, in which they preach and embody a new, hope-filled and energizing kind of meaning that draws disciples. This leads to the formation of a new way of life for those disciples who, in turn, upon the death of the founder, gradually "routinize" the charism in such a way that the institutional patterns that arise from the tradition gradually eclipse the original vision and mission. This gives rise to more meaninglessness and the need to have a "refounding." It is the story of religious movements over and over again.[2]

At the core of every refounding lies a power in the refounding person or persons that offers something beyond simple repair of cosmetic cracks in the façade. There is a rebirth that springs from the way that person or persons grasp the power (*archē*) of the original mystery. An example of this would be Francis of Assisi's grasp of Jesus' proclamation of the "Kingdom of God" and how this "gospel" became the way he not only became faithful to the mandate to "repair my house," but actually brought about a new way of being church within the wider church. He experienced and gave expression to the "mystery" of the Kingdom of God.

Essential for the refounding of our church is a reclaiming of the original sense of mystery that created the kind of *meaning* that has the power to bring about a new birth from an organization in crisis. As for Francis, he said that his grasp of the mystery of the "Kingdom of God" that he called "living the gospel" came from divine inspiration. Mystery involves the way the divine meets the human, offering the hope of a transformative rebirth. To some this mystery or "secret" (or "sense of the plan") is given; to others it is not (see Matt. 13:11). As we will see in Chapter 6, at the heart of the experience of this mystery that

51

gives new meaning to one's life and mission is the most basic mystery of our faith: the mystery of the Holy Trinity. Encountering the One-in-Threeness at the core of our being brings about a sense of our connectedness to that same presence at the core of everything else. Its experience at the depth of our being inspires expression. While at first this is expressed as a person or group's spirituality, it gradually becomes institutionalized as religion. This leads ultimately to enough meaninglessness that a rebirth of meaning and mystery is needed. The cycle of institutional dying and rebirth through a reclaiming of the original mystery continues. In effect, the life cycle of the church, indeed of all created reality, is defined by the pattern of the Trinity.

This process of reclaiming meaning by a personal grasp and powerful proclamation of the mystery or "secret" meaning within institutional impasse or anomie (meaninglessness) can be transformative. Stephen V. Doughty has articulated some of the results in his compelling article "Mystery *and* Institutional Rebirth." He notes that if we examine the dynamics "closely, we see how they work to break barriers, unite enemies, draw all creation into one, even lift the veil of death and introduce us to a Jesus who will transform us and about whom we shall forever have more to learn. If we root ourselves in these mysteries, we plainly live from a new reality. Through them, God's eternity and a whole new way of being are breaking in."[3]

Returning to our original reflection on *muein,* we find it is not only the root word for meaning and meaninglessness, as well as mystery; it serves as the root of other words involving religion. Among these are mythic, mysterious, and mystify. The myth or mythology represents a people's deepest-felt understanding of the sacred. These images involve some basic elementary ideas (about the sacred or focus of ultimate concern) that reveal archetypes found in the collective unconscious. When myth is identified with the collective unconscious , it can create a bond of meaning that brings people together. Rather than providing just one meaning, a genuine myth should have many layers of meaning, inviting those who believe in it to probe ever more profoundly.

Unfortunately, as Thomas Berry has written, "we have lost the interpretative patterns of our existence" that come to us in our myths. He explains:

> Myths are narratives that indicate the meaning of the human mode of being as well as the meaning of the universe itself. Our critical faculties, committed to the analytical processes of the rational mind, have destroyed the naiveté of ancient beliefs in favor of critical reflection and pragmatic realism. As the excitement of the new realism has diminished, we find ourselves encompassed by a world without meaning. . . . The world of the sacred presented so forcefully in ancient myth and symbol no longer provides the atmosphere in which we can breathe humanly. Thus the suffocation of contemporary humans in

consumerism and the excitement over the instant communication of the trivial.[4]

Realizing that the language of myth often speaks in metaphors, Joseph Campbell writes as follows in his classic book *The Inner Reaches of Outer Space: Metaphor as Myth and as Religion*: "As the imagery of a dream is metaphorical of the psychology of its dreamer, that of a mythology is metaphorical of the psychological posture of the people to whom it pertains."[5] Unlike a simile that makes a comparison ("he is built like an ox" or "she moves like a swan"), a metaphor identifies one reality with another ("he is an ox" or "she is a swan"). Metaphor comes from two Greek words, *meta* (remaining with) and *phorein* (to carry). It involves how one "moves from" (carries) one way of understanding to another. Such metaphors lead to a deeper meaning about the way another is who that one is.

We have seen, in Chapter 1, that the core arguments of the "new atheists" have little to do with the existence of God as God but much more to do with aberrations and contradictions associated with the "god" of religion. These are the "gods" and religious myths and beliefs that stand outside of or are actually opposed to science and observable facts. As Joan Chittister says, in her characteristic turn of phrase, "We want science, which deals with matter, to explain God to us. We want religion, which deals with the spirit, to be an authority on the biological nature of life. In the end, we make a thing of God and a god of science."[6] The consequence of the inability of religion to make sense from a scientific perspective will be, especially for those seeking some connection, the rise of meaninglessness.

This leads people like me to try to uncover new meaning for our faith, especially when we see so clearly that the crisis of faith in Western Catholicism—especially for people born after 1960—involves a crisis in meaning that arises *ad extra* regarding what we know from science and *ad intra* regarding the organizational dynamics of the hierarchical church itself. As we will see in Part II, a retrieval of meaning grounded in the heart of whom we understand God to be and the message of this God revealed in Jesus Christ will be based on reclaiming the core belief or *mythos* that we come to know as "Trinity" and the "gospel of the Kingdom of God" (i.e., Trinity). This myth of the Trinity will be further revealed from the metaphor of "house."

While the core myth of our faith regarding the Trinity might not be scientifically provable, we should try to frame it so it is not scientifically questionable. This effort will involve a retrieval of the metaphor of house that finds the Economic Trinity revealed at the deepest level of creation as well as the source and summit of the economy of salvation. When the myth of the Trinity and the metaphor of house come together, we can find renewed energy and meaning.

The stimulus for the move in this direction came to me when I read the millennial edition of the *Wall Street Journal*, January 1, 2000. In this unique, two-section, Saturday edition, the *WSJ* sought out experts in various fields, asking them to draw on their academic or professional background to describe their prognostications for the future. The one that intrigued me most was an interview with Edward O. Wilson. He won the Pulitzer Prize for his 1978 book, *On Human Nature,* as well as for a later one, *The Ants* (1990). His specialty is the social nature of individuals at all levels of life.

In the interview, which took place in Wilson's office in the Museum of Comparative Zoology at Harvard University, the *WSJ* writer asked him, "You wrote some years ago in 'On Human Nature' that the 'predisposition to religious belief is the most complex and powerful force in the human mind.' How can religion possibly survive what science is doing?"[7]

The question raised by the *Wall Street Journal* writer reflects the ongoing discussion about the relationship between religion and science. However, before addressing Wilson's response, I think it is important to approach the question from its historical underpinnings as has been so-well outlined by Karen Armstrong in her writings.

In her discussions about science and religion, Armstrong distinguishes between the *logos* of science and the *mythos* of religion. She writes, "In most pre-modern cultures, there were two recognized ways of thinking, speaking, and acquiring knowledge. The Greeks called them *mythos* and *logos*. Both were essential and neither was considered superior to the other; they were not in conflict but complementary. Each had its own sphere of competence, and it was considered unwise to mix the two."[8] Questions able to be answered within the domain of human reason involve the realm of *logos*. On the other hand, *mythos*, the domain of religion, addresses issues of "why" and, especially, "who" that lay beyond the purview of science. In today's language, we might call *mythos* the realm of the sacred and *logos* the domain of the secular. The sphere of *logos* involved the area of reason and what might be observable; *mythos* addressed issues beyond that to concerns that helped people address life's unanswered and ever-unanswerable questions.

Myth provides the tools we use to get at the truths beyond the truth of *logos*. According to Armstrong, *mythos* always has been meant "to help us live creatively, peacefully, and even joyously with realities for which there were no easy explanations and problems that we could not solve: mortality, pain, grief, despair, and outrage at the injustice and cruelty of life."[9] Through myth people connect to the unseen and still-to-be defined powers at the heart of the universe. If taken as literally or historically verifiable or true, myths lose their sacred sense and become treated as secular and the basis of argumentation and provability rather than serving as the basis of a sense of awe and wonderment.

Primitive people knew a myth was a myth; a way of helping them interpret what lay beyond the observable and categorically organized. Armstrong argues that a key problem with contemporary religion arises when
the myth—what primitive people accepted to be a way to understand life's
unanswerable questions—becomes a fact. As a syndicated columnist in
diocesan newspapers once said to me (apart from the audience to whom I
was speaking, so that he would not be heard), "Isn't it amazing how we take
what everyone once knew to be a myth, make it a fact, and then create a creed
and institution built on this. It becomes a religion based on myth." When
this *mythos*-becomes-*logos* happens, the *mythos* has lost its purpose and the
logos becomes delusional. At this, the insight of Joseph Campbell (who was
concerned about the way some religions equate what were once known to
be spiritual metaphors with historical facts) becomes even more evident:
"the leftover residue of such myths tends to support survival of institutions
crafted from and for the past, instead of nurturing greater wholeness and a
sense for the global common good in people living within those institutions
today."[10]

Too often, contemporary people, unlike those in pre-modern societies,
have come to eclipse the *mythos* with the *logos* which then becomes the "only"
path to reliable truth. The result has been the creation of a serious imbalance
in our lives and relationships, to say nothing of our commitment to the truths
that lie beyond "the truth." Armstrong writes, "A myth was never intended
as an accurate account of a historical event; it was *something that had in some
sense happened once but that also happens all the time.*" This is where the original
notion of "meaning" that once reflected the core meaning of "myth" must be
understood as something that is more associated with the mystical dimension
of life than the historical basis of life.

Building on these notions, and agreeing with Armstrong that "we live in
a society of scientific *logos*, and myth has fallen into disrepute,"[11] I think it
important here to put these ideas into the following chart (see page 56). It outlines the assumptions that lay behind the question posed to E.O. Wilson by the
Wall Street Journal reporter.

The issue raised by the *Wall Street Journal* reporter addresses the critical
nexus between religion and science: How can religion, which has arisen from
and is sustained by the *muein* of the "myth," prevail against what Karen Armstrong calls the "*logos*" or the logic that one gets from scientific facts? More
specifically, how can the whole worldview or meaning system undergirding
the religious stance survive in the face of what science is making quite abundantly clear? How can the beliefs of a faith-based approach to life sustain the
daily doses of facts which come non-stop from science?

ASSUMPTIONS BEHIND QUESTION

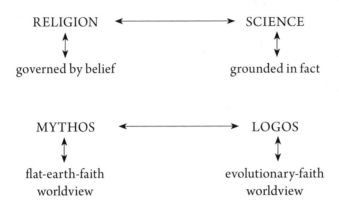

MEANING MAKING

A large part, if not the very core, of our contemporary scientific worldview is now constituted by the general theory of quantum mechanics. It says that the quantum is the basic unit of energy and that all matter is energy massed. In addition to almost all of physics and the whole of chemistry, the theory has been extended to much of biology, electronics, and nuclear physics, as well as to a large part of astrophysics and cosmology. While the theory holds its own mystique, quantum theory is the mathematical theory that describes the sub-atomic world.[12] This notion of quantum theory lies behind the question of the *Wall Street Journal*'s question and Wilson's subsequent response about the way "the world really works."

The response of Wilson has remained with me ever since; indeed I have memorized its last line:

> Make no mistake about it: The expansion of human knowledge with science and technology, especially neuroscience, genetics and evolu-tion, renders traditional religious belief less and less tenable, more and more difficult to justify and argue logically. The more we understand from science about the way the world really works, all the way from subatomic particles up to the mind and on to the cosmos, the more difficult it is to base spirituality on our ancient mythologies.

Note that Wilson did not conclude, "the more difficult it is to base *religion* on our ancient mythologies"; he said: "the more difficult it is to base *spirituality* on our ancient mythologies." It would seem that Wilson understands how hard it is for religions to extricate themselves from the violations they have done to the *mythos* by giving the impression it is historical and/or provable. The only remedy, then, would be to reclaim the heart of spirituality.

In Wilson's response, two key words—religion and spirituality—need deeper probing. Since Wilson does not say what he means by those terms, I think it best if I share my meaning. My meaning is colored by a dynamic I use when I work with people to distinguish between the two words. First, I ask my audiences to think of an "experience of religion" that they have had in their lives. Since most people in my audiences are Catholic, images immediately are shared: saying the rosary; first communion or confession; genuflecting before the Blessed Sacrament, and so forth. Then I ask them to describe their first "religious experience." No such readiness is evident; no hands shoot up as occurs when I ask people to describe their first "experience of religion." The reluctance to share comes from peoples' unawareness of religious experience itself or because the dynamics of one's religious experience (or what Sam Harris also calls mysticism or spirituality) are much more interior and personal.

Moving beyond the various definitions found in dictionaries of religion (from *re-ligare*: to "bind back" to the source, the *archē*), in a way that makes something re-connected and/or more whole, I mean the experience of the organizational, culturally determined form of individuals' commonly accepted beliefs and practices, oftentimes associated with the rules, rituals, and ways of an "official" religion (such as those that have been associated with Catholicism). Having studied the academic field of *spirituality* from Sandra Schneiders, IHM, I would not even try to offer a definition of the elements of spirituality that would be covered in one of her courses.[13] Rather, adapting her definition, I define spirituality in general as "the experience of some transcendent power that becomes the ultimate grounding in a person's life which leads that person to translate (express) that experience in behaviors synchronous with that experience; ideally this takes place in solidarity with others sharing the experience and expression." This involves an internal dimension (the experience of the transcendent), an external dimension (one's consequent behavior molded by that experience), and gets its support in a community of like-minded people.

Applying this understanding of spirituality in general to what I will be outlining as "Catholic spirituality," and given the fact that Pope Benedict XVI says that the church "originates in the trinitarian God,"[14] I would define such "Catholic spirituality" as "the experience of the Trinity that becomes the ultimate grounding in a Catholic's life which leads that person to work to bring about at every level of the world relationships that reflect that trinitarian experience through participation in the Catholic Faith." As will become ever clearer, the issue will not be so much the experiential or even the expressive dimension of the definition; it will be how one can bring about this kind of trinitarian spirituality within the dominant form of Catholicism. It is my con-

tention that the pattern of Jesus Christ and the Gospel of the Rule of trinitarian connectedness that he proclaimed (at least as we understand it now) must
be the consoling force when one faces rejection from representatives of the
"official" religion: "If they have persecuted me, they will persecute you" for
fidelity to the Word (John 15:20; see Matt. 5:11-14; 10:16-20).

Returning to Wilson, I think his distinction between the mythologies that
too often have become the ethos of religion, including Culture I Catholicism,
and the *mythos* of spirituality makes utter sense. When religion has become a
closed system based on myths that everyone once knew to be cultural attempts
to explain reality rather than actual history, but which later were interpreted
as theological facts and then canonized as virtual dogmas, there is little hope
for transformative power. The existence of the religion as it has come to be
defined and organized is at stake. Such a religion has become what the great
psychologist Gordon Allport called a "security-centered religion" rather than
a "growth-centered religion."[15] It also becomes an addictive (and often abusive) system rather than a healthy, life-giving organization.[16] Only an open
way of being—as identified with spirituality—can possibly make the transition from a closed to an open organization, a security-centered rather than a
growth-centered religion, an addictive system rather than a life-giving way of
life. This now invites us to revisit the chart above but with the response to its
early dynamics made by Wilson:

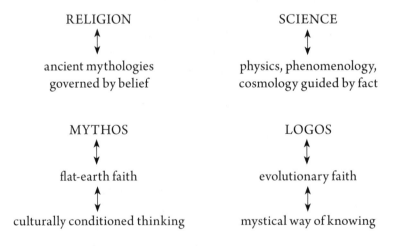

REVISITING E. O. WILSON'S RESPONSE
The way the world really works: realm of science
The way God works in the world: realm of religion

RELIGION   SCIENCE
↕   ↕
ancient mythologies   physics, phenomenology,
governed by belief   cosmology guided by fact

MYTHOS   LOGOS
↕   ↕
flat-earth faith   evolutionary faith
↕   ↕
culturally conditioned thinking   mystical way of knowing

MEANING MAKING
SPIRITUALITY

Based on the assumptions about religion being controlled by ancient mythologies that govern subsequent belief, Wilson noted that religion would be rendered irrelevant by what we have come to know from key areas of science such as physics, neuroscience, and cosmology. The only way one could lead an authentic life, given such "facts," would be to employ a new meaning-making model that would reflect the best of what we mean by "spirituality."

This insight invites a return to Chapter 1, to a key insight of one of the "four horsemen" representing the "new atheists," Sam Harris. While rejecting "man-made" and "fear-based" forms of religion (and their accompanying mythologies) he actually promotes religious experience and mysticism (which he virtually identifies with spirituality) as something that can be explained and defended scientifically. In this he reflects the thinking of Charles Taylor, who finds spirituality to be the antidote to secularism.[17]

While rejecting "religion" as "reason in exile" whose "myths seem to have granted us perfect immunity to outbreaks of reasonableness in our public discourse,"[18] Harris makes it equally clear that he finds to be very *reasonable* the observable patterned phenomenon of religious experience as this phenomenon has been articulated by mystics and others relating such experiences. He argues that it can be demonstrated "that spirituality can be—indeed, *must be*—deeply rational, even as it elucidates the limits of reason. . . ." Such reasoning actually echoes Karl Rahner's famous saying: "The Christian of the future will be a mystic or he will not exist at all."[19] Harris argues,

> Science will not remain mute on spiritual and ethical questions for long. Even now, we can see the first stirrings among psychologists and neuroscientists of what may one day become a genuinely rational approach to these matters—one that will bring even the most rarified mystical experience within the purview of open, scientific inquiry. It is time we realized that we need not be unreasonable to suffuse our lives with love, compassion, ecstasy, and awe; nor must we renounce all forms of spirituality or mysticism to be on good terms with reason.[20]

There is a root connection between mystery (*mystērion*), as well as mysteries (including mysteries as in magic), mysticism, and meaning (*muein*).[21] Thus, while the etymology of the words are themselves a mystery, in the Synoptics, Jesus explains the *meaning of the mystery* of the "Kingdom of God" in the form of parables (Mark 4:11; Matt. 13:11; Luke 8:10). The challenge of spirituality is to *understand* the *meaning of the* mystery of the "Kingdom" one has experienced mystically and to manifest one's initiation and participation in that mystery through one's individual, communal, and collective behavior. All such "mysteries promise their devotees salvation (σωτηρία) by the dispensing of cosmic life."[22] This brings us to the levels of meaning that have an impact on Catholicism today.

Even though I know my following remarks may not resonate exactly with James W. Fowler's celebrated taxonomy of the *Stages of Faith*,[23] I have concluded, from my own experience of the way the Catholic faith has been (and still is being) practiced by a large number of its adherents, that a good number of practicing Catholics do so from a mechanistic model. There is a sense that "*the* church" has little to do with themselves (except insofar as they belong to an organization to which they pay dues with the parallel expectation that "it" will provide goods and services, whether these are tied to demands around the sacraments or the doors of the schools that must be open to their children). The consequence of such an approach to membership in the Catholic Church has resulted in effective disengagement from a lived experience of faith. Pierre Hegy's analysis of the data from the U.S. Congregational Life Survey shows that "out of 10 basic variables or church strengths, Catholics rank lowest on 7."[24]

Along with this first, mechanistic model, there are three other levels of *muein* that seem to reflect the attitudes of many, especially in ethnic enclaves where "belonging" is still identified with obligation (and fear of hell for non-Mass attendance) and in the suburban parishes defined by good preaching, good music, good welcoming, and good schools. Church is treated like any other business transactions: because I pay I can play. Not only that, because I pay I am *entitled* to the goods and services such payment expects.

As I noted before, however, the vast majority of Catholics who are still practicing their faith in parish settings that are dominantly white (found mainly in the suburbs), African American, Hispanic, as well as those serving the "newer" ethnic groups such as the Vietnamese and Pacific Islanders, *will not be concerned about the kinds of matters discussed in this book*. This very large percentage of Catholics are not Culture I and would be hard-pressed to describe what it means to be Culture II (which they probably are). This is because of their positive Sunday experience at their local parish or non-territorial worship site. In this they are a kind of ecclesiastical equivalent to Tip O'Neill's famous saying that "all politics is local." Because they benefit from their local church they are not that impacted or concerned about issues in the wider church. Simply stated, church "works" for them. Issues such as those raised in this book regarding the *institutional* model of the church at levels beyond the parish just don't impact or interest them.

The second level of *muein* involves the "magical" or "miraculous." This involves deep and unquestioned belief in the traditional Catholic myths in which they have been formed. At this level the *mythos* becomes, de facto, *logos*, especially around interventionist notions of God's actions in history.

When one examines the scriptures at certain times of the year, especially the infancy narratives and the texts from Resurrection to Pentecost, it becomes quite clear that, with angels appearing and dreams revealing God's plans, such miracles are simply taken for granted as part of the heritage of faith. Instead of understanding (and appreciating) their historical basis more as literary devices reflecting notions of *mythos* that the people knew to be much more than provable historical facts, we define these literary genres to be factual, then make such "facts" theological or dogmatic and, finally, create systems without realizing their origin was based in the *mythos* rather than the *logos*.

Many Culture I Catholics, I believe, fall into this category wherein religion is highly identified with the miraculous, usually interpreted literally. Angels appear to people giving them a message from God; the angel becomes a form of *logos* instead of *mythos,* and we call the "fact" of such a literary device faith. I have often said that if I had angels appearing to me to tell me something as clearly as I have been taught (such as the annunciations of angels to Mary and Joseph in Luke's and Matthew's infancy narratives), "I would believe as well." However, I have never had the visitations of such angels and still believe.

Probably nowhere is this *mythos*-become-*logos* approach to faith more evident than in the doctrine of transubstantiation. While I believe in it as any Catholic must, I also must ask myself what this doctrine "means" (as I must do with all faith pronouncements). I must be willing to examine its meaning with good scriptural exegesis[25] and, above all, as a pastor, be concerned about the data that show substantial numbers of Catholics do not believe in it (probably because its deeper scriptural meaning has not been balanced with its more "miraculous" interpretation).[26]

When this second level of faith prevails, there often follows an unquestioned acceptance of the religion and its rituals and rules—at least until some kind of personal crisis arises, such as having a son "come out" as gay or a daughter define herself as lesbian. Or one has a bad experience of an official of the church. Or one reads about abuses of authority by church leaders. With such "jarring experiences," a deeper questioning that is more systemic begins, thus reflecting dynamics in the "hermeneutic circle" discussed on the next page.

Loss of meaning results from such questioning. This leads to the third level of faith. People find meaning at a deeper level and proceed with their lives or enter a stage where the religion and its beliefs become less and less meaningful. People who have found meaning in science or some other fact-based approach to life now experience their often-unquestioned religion and its beliefs as increasingly meaningless. Another term for this, we have shown, is the "crisis of faith." Here the honest questions about the myths and the miracles get no credible answer from religious leaders who themselves have never allowed themselves to do such questioning. When this happens long enough or when these questions about the teachings might be accompanied by abusive dynamics on the part of those who have defined themselves as the official teachers, the "falling away" begins. First it comes in the mind, then the heart, and, finally, if there is not enough guilt or fear to keep them from leaving the religion, they "fall away" completely.

When I give workshops, one of the most helpful models I share addresses the issue of "meaning" as it involves theological understanding at times of questioning. I show how the "hermeneutical" question (i.e., the question of meaning, after Hermes, the messenger of the gods) involves a fourfold process. (1) Some experience jars the accepted (theological) worldview of someone committed to faith. This leads to (2) a deeper questioning of one's worldview, including the faith that sustained this worldview. This involves a faith "crisis" of some kind. This elicits different reactions ranging from denial and delusion to rejection of "the faith" or a re-examination of it. (3) When people begin to re-examine their faith and its claims they need to return to the scriptural underpinnings as well as an enlightened view of their tradition. Hopefully this process will lead to (4) a new understanding that enables one to bring a revival of meaning to life and the dynamics that once led to a crisis of faith.[27]

The fourth stage gets to the heart of the matter. This involves the Greek notion of *muein* as a deeper entrance or experience of the mystery. Oftentimes this *muein* or mystery is translated as "the secret," but it really means "the heart of the matter." Here the myth at the heart of the mystery is *understood* in the sense of being *experienced*. An example of this was Jesus' parables shared with the insiders to whom the secrets were explained (see Mark 4:11; Matt. 13:11; and Luke 8:10).

At this fourth stage of faith-meaning there often arises a uniting metaphor (based on Aristotle's notion of a metaphor being the name of something that is applied to something different), such as I will suggest in Part II with the metaphor of "house"). This helps sculpt and redefine the core myth(s) with contemporary relevance. Grounded in this kind of worldview, mysticism (informative and performative) is not only honored and encouraged; it is taught and mentored. The *mystagogia* also comes alive with revitalized symbols and rituals. The aesthetics of meaning come to the fore in new cultural forms of music, painting, poetry, and the other key arts.

This fourth level of faith, involving the unveiling of meaning, represents the way of spirituality more than the way of religion, at least as it is practiced in mainline Catholicism today. Here one finds faith renewed and full of purpose. Here one enters the heart of the mystery to find the meaning to one's life and life's deepest questions.

The notions of "mystery" and "spirituality" have been described well by the mystics of Catholicism, and we will discuss this further in Part III when we speak about contemplation. However, here, I think it very important that we discuss its dynamics from the lens of one of the "four horsemen," the avowed atheist Sam Harris. He writes,

> A kernel of truth lurks at the heart of religion, because spiritual experience, ethical behavior, and strong communities are essential for human happiness. And yet our religious traditions are intellectually defunct and politically ruinous. While spiritual experience is clearly a natural propensity of the human mind, we need not believe anything on insufficient evidence to actualize it. Clearly, it must be possible to bring reason, spirituality, and ethics together in our thinking about the world. This would be the beginning of a rational approach to our deepest personal concerns.
>
> Mysticism is a rational enterprise. . . . The mystic has recognized something about the nature of consciousness prior to thought, and this recognition is susceptible to rational discussion. The mystic has reasons for what he believes, and these reasons are empirical. The roiling mystery of the world can be analyzed with concepts (this is science), or it can be experienced free of concepts (this is mysticism).[28]

In other words, given the data that show that a crisis of faith in Catholicism arises from its institutional dynamics more than its actual dogmas, any reclaiming of an authentic faith that represents the best of what it means to be Catholic must find its adherents grounded in the mystery of the Trinity. At the core of this mystery that must become the ground of a truly "Catholic" spirituality will be the reappropriation of a viable metaphor to give it life in the sense of what Joseph Campbell has written about his "impulse to place metaphor at the center of our exploration of Western Spirituality."[29]

In Part II we will show that this mystery, in which we have been baptized, will find us embracing the "mystery" of the "Kingdom of God" with renewed meaning, vision, and purpose. This will be done by a deeper insight into the dynamics of the evangelical metaphor of the "house."

5 _____

The Apocalypse Facing Catholicism

An Invitation to Convert

In 1964, two years before I was ordained a priest, the Quaker economist Kenneth Boulding published *The Great Transition: The Meaning of the 20th Century*. He referred to the twentieth century as part of the third great transition in human history, after agriculturally based civilization and the industrial world. He described major environmental, biological, and technical challenges that demanded a new consciousness on the part of humans. He concluded by envisioning a future wherein we might "find ways of organizing a self-conscious society of those committed to the transition."[1]

Unfortunately we have paid little heed to his all-too-prescient narration describing the vast scope of the germinating crisis whose full bloom he only envisioned and which we have seen come about more fully. Consequently we are witnessing the results of humanity's agency of another transition of critical proportions. This crisis has impacted our world's climate, its bio-geochemical cycles, the chemistry of its oceans, the color of its sky, and even the flow of its rivers. According to a May 2011 cover feature in *The Economist*, we have reshaped the natural processes of "the planet itself on a geological scale—but at a far-faster-than-geological speed." As a result, because "the extinction rate is running far higher than during normal geological periods," scientists "are increasingly using a new name for this new period. Rather than placing us still in the Holocene, a peculiarly stable era that began only around 10,000 years ago, the geologists say we are already living in the Anthropocene era: the age of man."[2] Whereas we humans once interacted more sustainably in cooperation with creation in a kind of holarchy defined by mutual interdependence, now the output of human activity is emitting nitrogen and carbon dioxide into the atmosphere at such levels that nature can no longer sustain itself.

While such a conclusion might serve as a kind of apocalyptic warning,[3] the editorial concludes with an approach which this chapter will identify as truly capturing the best of what "apocalyptic" means: the end of one era that contains the seeds within it of something even better—as long as all people do their own part in addressing the problem. It concludes,

> For humans to be intimately involved in many interconnected processes at a planetary scale carries huge risks. But it is possible to add to the planet's resilience, often through simple and piecemeal actions, if they are well thought through. And one of the messages of the Anthropocene is that piecemeal actions can quickly add up to planetary change.[4]

As we develop this chapter, we would be well-advised to consider two Greek words found in the book of Revelation (popularly known as the Apocalypse): *krisis* and *kairos*. *Krisis* refers to God's divine judgment on a situation or system of injustice (Rev. 14:7; 16:7; 18:10; 19:2). *Kairos* is a word referring to time. Unlike *chronos*, the root of chronology (which means time that is repetitive and expected), *kairos* is unexpected and sudden; unannounced inbreaking. It refers to an occasion of deep grace in the face of a reality of overpowering violence and sin (Rev. 1:3; 11:18; 12:12, 14). In this sense, a biblical *krisis* does not reflect what the Chinese characters for "crisis"—challenge and opportunity— are said to entail. Rather this *krisis* makes it clear that what is being described cannot be identified with God and, indeed, stands opposed to God's vision or plan for God's people. It is human made and, therefore, stands opposed to the vision of God. Consequently, for people of faith, it must be challenged.

True and False Apocalypse

The day I began writing this chapter, I happened to see a huge sign in the outlying suburbs of Milwaukee that caught my eye: "Judgment Day," it proclaimed. The billboard declared that May 21, 2011, would usher in the end of the world. The alarm came from a Christian radio broadcaster, Harold Camping.

I have known about Harold Camping for many years. Often, returning from my evening workout, I would listen to his unique interpretation of the scriptures. This included his conviction that churches of any kind represent infidelity to Christ. Earlier, he had predicted that the Rapture would occur in September 1994. When it failed to materialize, he said he had used the wrong data to calculate the "exact date and hour." Now he was absolutely clear that all the scriptures pointed to one indisputable truth: the Rapture would come May 21, 2011. On this day Jesus would return to gather up the "saved" and bring them to heaven. Five months later, God would completely destroy the whole universe, including the earth. Again, the scriptures were clear: that day would be October 21, 2011.[5]

The evening I saw Pastor Camping's billboard, I went for my usual workout.

When I returned to my car I saw that a van parked next to me had a bumper sticker announcing the end to take place on May 21. So I left a note on the windshield asking for more information. A couple hours later I got a call from the owner. Without telling him my background I asked how Pastor Camping knew so clearly this time how all this was going to happen, especially when Jesus in the Gospels of Mark and Matthew said "of that day and hour no one knows, not even the angels of heaven, nor the Son, but the Father only" (Mark 13:32; Matt. 24:36).

The man patiently explained to me that the End would begin in Australia at the exact time calculated by the count-down clock on the website. This would be accompanied by huge earthquakes that would open all the graves of those to be caught up into the Rapture. This would be followed by more convulsions of the earth. This great tribulation, ending on October 21, 2011, would end the world and send to the fire of hell all those who remained.

He also said he had gone with a group of three other men to pass out tracts about May 21 at the University of Wisconsin in Madison. "But we were ridiculed, just like they did to Noah before the Flood." When I noted that since Pastor Camping had been wrong in 1994, he might be wrong now, he said, "Nobody in my family believes me, but I'll continue to listen to him because he knows the scriptures so well and I've already learned so much from him." From his own certainty regarding the scriptural interpretation of Pastor Camping, he just *knew* Pastor Camping was right. But Pastor Camping admitted error. He died soon after.

While most Culture I and Culture II Catholics don't subscribe to such fundamentalist and literal (and subjective) interpretations of Bible texts, I do detect a kind of apocalyptic messianism in the absoluteness with which many Culture I Catholics identify themselves as the only true believers. In this sense they appear to me to have defined themselves as the remnant among the many backsliders, the 144,000 who have washed their ritual robes in the blood of the Lamb. They are the Catholics who have been chosen by God; they alone will be saved. Their teachings are spotless; their cause is God's.

This sense gets carried over in the rhetoric of many of those individuals, including priests and bishops, who call themselves "John Paul II Catholics." This apocalyptic notion of the remnant being saved is featured on the websites of various groups—from the Eternal Word Television Network (EWTN) to the *National Catholic Register* to those insisting on a formal consecration of Russia to the Immaculate Heart of Mary. Many feature the apocalyptic words attributed to Karol Wojtyla on a 1976 visit to the United States. However, rather than speaking about the final battle between *Christ* and the Antichrist, the quote speaks about the ending conflict between "the *church*" and the "antichurch." It alleges the future pope as warning, "We are now standing in the face of the greatest historical confrontation humanity has gone through. I do not think that wide circles of the American Society or wide circles of the Christian Community realize this fully. *We are now facing the final confrontation between the Church and the anti-Church, of the Gospel versus the anti-Gospel. It is a trial which the Church must take up.*"[6]

Apocalyptic warnings like this and those of Harold Camping are not limited to the religious sphere (although they have a tendency to get much traction when they can find their justification in divine revelation). We need only think of the "doomsday" predictions around Y2K with the advent of the third millennium. Other doomsday scenarios involve impending catastrophes to be expected if we vote for certain political candidates, raise the debt ceiling, cut taxes, or drink fluoridated water. On the other hand, we find naysayers who refuse to believe in the possibility of some scientifically established *real* global problems, such as possible water and food shortages, increasing deforestation and the consequences of climate change. These denials often come with appeals to individual, fringe scientists rather than bodies of scientists who agree with the naysayers.

Apocalypse as Death of One Reality and the Vision of Birth for Another

At the heart of many apocalyptic warnings is the sense that the promised doomsday is nigh. However, this is only half true. A truly apocalyptic pronouncement does not just predict the end of something; it promises the beginning of something new, like a phoenix rising from the ashes or even the process of natural selection wherein a new reality emerges from something resistant to adapt. This fuller notion is well summarized in the words of John Galt, the hero of Ayn Rand's controversial novel *Atlas Shrugged*, which has become a kind of "Bible" for free-market individualists and Tea Party activists. In the book's final, apocalyptic scene, the heroine, Dagny Taggart, turns to Galt and declares, "It's the end." At that he corrects her, saying, "It's the beginning."

The hemorrhaging of participation in the institutional form of the Catholic Church in the West is best understood if we consider it in apocalyptic terms. I came to realize the scriptural significance of this image as I prepared to give a talk in Dublin, Ireland, on May 18, 2010. I had been invited to the 50th Anniversary of the founding of CORI, the Conference of Religious of Ireland. This is the organization of the leaders of the women's and men's religious congregations in Ireland.

The request came months before the public onslaught related to the abuse scandals in Ireland that involved priests, brothers, and sisters. Indeed, for the whole week I was there, not a day went by without the Irish papers narrating stories of bishops being accused of misuse of their power over many decades regarding the allegations of abuse by priests and religious. Such accounts elicited rage on the part of most everyone, including priests, brothers, and sisters. They now found themselves being scapegoated because of the past sins of their peers.

My Capuchin brother, Dan Crosby, suggested I frame the resulting crisis of the organized church in Ireland from the perspective of "apocalypse." This led me to a deeper examination of its meaning in the scriptures. I discovered that apocalypse involves an "unveiling" or "uncovering" of a reality beyond something that appears to be cataclysmic. According to Robert Corin Morris, such an apocalypse exposes not just the failure and "inadequacy of present structures to deal constructively with human life" but God's persistent effort, evidenced by such upheaval, "to bring forth the kingdom 'on earth as it is in heaven,' as Jesus puts it."[7]

Most scripture scholars agree that the actual last book of the Christian scriptures, popularly called the Apocalypse, but more aptly called the book of Revelation, was written to a church under persecution. Imperial and religious enemies—outsiders—were besieging the true believers. A superficial interpretation of the texts limits their meaning to encouragement of those being persecuted to persevere, to be strong, and to remain faithful because the End was near. However, the more I read commentaries on the book of Revelation, a deeper interpretation came forth (especially from passages like Rev. 2:1-3:22). These warnings served as a challenge to the churches who naïvely accepted "the teachings of false prophets ... from laxity in their commitment to the faith."[8] More than a jeremiad about the future, they served as a call to recognize the death-dealing dynamics of the existing ecclesiastical situation, the Christian's complicity in the system, the judgment of God on their complicity, and a vision or promise for an alternative reality, a new community. In other words, it spoke of God's judgment revealing the death of one way of being church and the beginning of another. In much the same way, at the opening Mass of the Synod of Bishops on the Eucharist, Pope Benedict XVI captured this notion when he talked about how "the threat of judgment affects us also, the Church in Europe, the Church of the West in general."[9]

Naming the Death of the Destructive Dynamics in the Institution

The more I prepared my CORI talk, the more this notion of "the death of one era and the beginning of another" came to haunt me. What exactly was dead, I wondered? On Tuesday, April 6, less than two weeks before my CORI presentation, it became clear. I was on my way to present a program in Berkeley, California, on "the church." As I drove I felt a deep probing pain in the pit of my stomach. I had only experienced such pain twice before. I knew exactly what it meant. This led me to call my Capuchin brother, Dan.

"Dan," I said, "I want to check out something with you." "Okay," he responded. "I never talked to you about this before, but the more I have been thinking of that expression of the "church" that will be part of my remarks in Dublin next week, the more I am having the same kind of feeling in the pit of my stomach as when Mother and [our brother] Pat died. When I think of this 'church' my gut feeling tells me what I can no longer deny: it is dead. The realization of its death gives me the same sense of pain I had when they died. Do you know what I mean?" He assured me he understood; it was consoling to know I was not alone in my pain at its "passing."

Naming this feeling put into words the unwelcome sense of unease that had been building in me for years. I first articulated this sense of loss a decade before while teaching at an institute at the University of Notre Dame. It was becoming increasingly clear that key leaders in the church were keen on reverting to a Culture I form of Catholicism, even though they talked about a "theology of continuity." Protestations to the contrary, many of the official practices being promoted and/or promulgated indicated that a restorationist effort was well underway.

Teaching on the campus at the same time was my confrere, Kenan Osborne, an expert in historical theology and ecclesiology at the Franciscan School of Theology in Berkeley. He was lecturing at a summer course. We had decided that we would meet for lunch. As I had been watching some of the restorationist dynamics on the Notre Dame campus, I had begun to feel a deep unease. As I waited for him my unease moved toward a deeper sense of loss when I thought of the "church" that was now "taking over." After we greeted each other, I said, "Kenan, I've just had this powerful feeling when I think of what is happening in the church." "What's that, Mike," he said? "We've lost," was my simple response. "I know what you mean," was his equally simple response.

Years later, on that Easter Tuesday in Berkeley, my sense of loss became articulated ever clearer: the overly patriarchal, clerical, institutionalized model of church, while alive and well for some, is dead for many more. It may still be alive through the denial and delusion of those who believe its institutional form reflects God's will or Jesus' plan, but, to ever-increasing numbers of Catholics, it no longer is giving life; in fact, as an organization of human beings that has become closed to new life, it has died. This led me to recall the passage from Revelation: "When the Lamb opened the fourth seal, I heard the voice of the fourth living creature say, 'Come!' And I saw, and behold, a pale horse, and its rider's name was Death, and Hades followed; and they were given power over a fourth of the earth, to kill [i.e., take life]." Next it described the fourfold means by which that death would come about: the sword, famine, pestilence, and "by wild beasts of the earth" (Rev. 6:7-8).

Interpreting the Death of the Established Patriarchal, Clerical Church in Light of the Exile

I can think of no better referent to interpret the emotional reaction I experienced at realizing this church I have loved was dead than Israel's experience of exile. A once-persecuted community had overcome outside domination, entered a new land, and become established. Over the years it became a powerful political force in the world. Its religious leaders had achieved great dominance. However, such power, possessionsm and prestige led to its downfall based on a presumption related to the promise of God's abiding presence. Having conflated its covenant with God with its external expressions of religion, Israel gradually lost its soul and spirituality. The resulting exile spelled the death of that experience, including Israel's belief that God would always assure the survival of its land and temple.

For years I have given talks on the ecclesiology of exile, stressing the reality of being alienated from the national gods of materialism and militarism and the religious gods of patriarchal clericalism.[10] However, until now, my ideas were just that: intellectual ruminations. Now I experienced, for the first time, the *feeling* of being estranged and separated from something familial that had nurtured me, given me so much life, and with which I had fully identified. The sense of loss was quite overwhelming.

While someone like Edward Hays has written about the need to consider the Exodus as a metaphor for Catholics "who have trouble going to church,"[11] I prefer Walter Brueggemann's insight "that the Old Testament experience of and reflection upon exile is [both] a helpful *metaphor* for understanding our current faith situation in the U.S. church, and a *model* for pondering new forms of ecclesiology."[12] His image of "exile" as a "helpful metaphor for understanding our current faith situation in the U.S. church" fits well with the primary metaphor of the house that I will be stressing in the next chapters. These two metaphors of exile and house combine in a meaningful way in the writing of Sharon Parks: "At this pivotal, dangerous, and promising moment in history, the formation of adequate forms of meaning and faith—and perhaps the future of our small planet home—is dependent, in part, upon the liberation, reappropriation, and renewed companionship of the metaphors of detachment *and* connection, pilgrims *and* homemakers, journeying *and* homesteading."[13] While I believe these metaphors offer critical constructs to help us understand our reality, we must be aware that they are only metaphors. Indeed Sharon Parks herself cautions, "Every image and form is finite—even those we hold most sacred. Because every metaphor conveys both truth and untruth, image must contend with image in mutual correction and enhancement if we are to compose meanings worthy enough to ground both personal and social reality."[14]

The unrecognized and unacknowledged problem with Israel was that it had evolved in its history to the point that it became a religion without God. In its institutional model it had come to identify *itself* less as a people and more from its political, economic, and religious institutional expressions as the divinely ordained "chosen race, a royal priesthood, a people set apart." The exile was God's way of making it clear that such thinking was idolatrous. The God revealed by such dynamics was a god of human making.

As we further reflect theologically on the situation of the Catholic Church in the West, I find the pattern being replicated. This fact was made clear in Gary Macy's keynote address at the 2009 annual convention of the Catholic Theological Society. Acknowledging the data already discussed at the 2008 convention, Macy recalled the history of similar forms of religious leaders' amnesia regarding the equation of God's will with their human enterprises. He said, "When we clothe our frail and ephemeral human structure in eternal trappings, we cannot admit that we even have a history"[15] because everything is basically in place; nothing needs to change. When we fail to acknowledge that part of the institutional model of the church is of human creation, even though its mystical dimension may be divine, we will be caught in the trap of our own historical processes. He declares that we cannot

> begin to deal with the present church structure as a relic of the past until we first admit that that structure is part of human history and not intrinsically and eternally part of the divine plan itself. If the present church structure is understood as part of God's eternal plan, then the church cannot change, and has never changed. We have no future because we have no past. We are eternally trapped, frozen motionless and helpless in the eternal moment. Women cannot be ordained, for example, because Jesus did not ordain them, and therefore God did not intend them to be ordained from all eternity and for all eternity. And other examples could be given.[16]

Following the wisdom of addiction theory, Macy notes that, in order to "break out of this trap, we first must realize we created the trap in the first place," showing how the thinking that effectively divinized the human institution can be traced to the eleventh- and twelfth-century reforms. The consequence, he declared, is that "we inherited their story of the clerical church structure as eternally inevitable." Consequently, if we are going "to tell ourselves a different story, in order to appropriate other memories, we first have to admit that the vision of an eternally clerical church is itself a story, a set of memories, and only one of many to which we are heirs."[17]

By identifying the trinitarian God of mutuality and connectedness with its historically derived, hierarchical and patriarchal expression, the official church has led itself into an exile wherein increasing numbers of its members feel dislocated and disenfranchised. They no longer feel "at home"; instead they feel they been forced to become strangers. However, unlike the exile of the Israelites of old into Babylon, this Babylonian loss is experienced much more ideologically and theologically than physically and politically. As Brueggemann writes, "Exile is not primally geographical, but it is social, moral, and cultural."[18]

Brueggemann also shows that history reveals that for those who identify with such forms of "establishment" religion, the metaphor of exile will be more difficult to accept, since their perception of *their* church, though smaller and smaller, is "alive and well."[19] Brueggemann's insight is especially apropos when we consider the resistance of church officials in facing the abundant data regarding decline. Other data show how our perceptions involve an active process of meaning making that shapes and biases our particular stances in life. These perceptual biases distort our individual and group thinking in four critical ways: (1) we accept data that confirm our prejudices more vividly than data that contradict them; (2) we overvalue recent events when anticipating future possibilities; (3) we spin a host of differing data into a single causal narrative; and, finally, (4) we "applaud our own supposed skill in circumstances when we've actually benefitted from dumb luck."[20] The latter might be evidenced in the rapid rise of the Catholic Church in Africa, which keeps its declining numbers in the West more balanced.

As a young adult, Francis of Assisi lived in the "world" of the Holy Roman Empire and the papacy—heir to the eleventh- and twelfth-century ideology that equated the human church with divine mandate. One day he heard the call from the Crucified One: "Repair my house; you can see it is falling into ruin." This led him to live in relation to both his culture and his church as an exile, or, as he called it, "a pilgrim and stranger in this world." Today, when his followers are called to "repair" the house, fidelity to that charism demands that they too find themselves as pilgrims and strangers in "this world." Consequently, if his followers are faithful to the gospel, they too will find themselves in exile; they will have no *place* to rest their heads.

The meaning that the metaphor of exile gives us Catholics at this time, especially when we have found ourselves, against our will, actually *being made* exiles by the ideology of so many of our religious leaders, can offer us a particular lens by which we can view our predicament. As with all people experiencing death in its various forms, we need to find ways to admit the loss of one thing that gave life as we realize our responsibility to convert from our own ways that may have contributed to that death, admit the exact nature of *our wrong*, grieve over our loss, and commit ourselves to find ways to engage life with new meaning.

Apocalyptic Speech to Those Who Mourn

At my CORI presentation in Dublin I used allegorical images to outline the four forms of death announced in the book of Revelation. I showed how they might be experienced by Irish Religious in a way that put them in solidarity with the primitive church. The sword was the instrument used by those clergy and religious who had destroyed the innocence of certain young members of the church. There sins were being visited upon these members of CORI who never had anything to do with such abuse. Now this sword was stabbing their hearts. For them it would be the first of the fourfold forms of death (Rev. 6:7-8).

When I discussed the "famine" as the second death upon us, I recalled the words of the song *Galway Bay*, which I learned to sing both at St. Patrick's School in Fond du Lac, Wisconsin, and at home with my family. I recalled the Irish famine and its economic causes—those outside forces of control and domination—as well as the inside forms of collusion on the part of Irish Catholics elites who had "sold out" to the British. This led me to find contemporary parallels in the way the Irish became estranged from their roots, first by their docile submission to the many Jansenistic clerics who came to rule their lives, and then by their eager rush into the arms of the "Celtic Tiger," the rapid capitalist expansion of recent decades that ended up consuming them. Now they realized that such forms of clericalism and capitalism had given them a bitter pottage. Just as we in the United States had "bought the story" of upward economic mobility as Catholics, they too had embraced the Celtic Tiger only to see its lures leading them to bankruptcy and devastation—and now leading to a famine of the soul as well as of the land.

Just as Brueggemann talks about the way that "establishment Christianity and establishment culture have been in a close and no longer sustainable alliance,"[21] I showed that our own assimilation as Catholics into both clericalism and capitalism have led to us have little or nothing to offer those candidates coming to us who are seeking meaning in their lives. The consequence is evident in our own famine of new members and the unacknowledged dying of our own institutions taking place in front of us (evidenced by the white hair that dominated the participants).

Third, I reflected on the swarming of the pestilence in, among, and around us. I recalled the image used by Thomas of Celano, the first biographer of Francis of Assisi, as he described the culture of his time. A fatal disease surrounded it; a deadly disease threatened even religion (i.e., Catholicism); it was in dire need of a physician to come to its aid, to heal it of its malaise.[22] This made me think of the Spirit's challenge to the church in Sardis from the one "who has the seven spirits of God and the seven stars." "I know your works; you have the name of being alive, and you are dead. Awake, and strengthen what remains and is on the point of death, for I have not found your works perfect in the sight of my God" (Rev. 3:1-2).

Finally, I moved to the fourth form of death: the "wild beasts." This was code for the underlying structures of sin in the empire and the church that threatened the future of its members. Other words for the "wild beasts" that threaten the survival of its victims have traditionally been called the "powers and principalities." However, the image I used comes from another New Testament word, *stoicheia*. Paul showed that this represents the unseen forces controlling the interpretation of the law that suffocates the Spirit of Love (Gal. 4:3, 9). This religious system, combined with the devouring power of the unfettered, imperialistic market economy, I said, no longer gives us life. Unless, like Francis, we ourselves commit ourselves to turn from its ways, the disease threatens our very lives.

Engaging the Dynamics of Death
through Healing Forms of Grief

Addiction theory following a family systems model offers some insight here.[23] While we might salve our souls by blaming the death of the institution on the "identified" male members of the Catholic Church who are the leaders of this overly clericalized, patriarchal "family," we cannot deny how this death has impacted the whole family. Only when we acknowledge the debilitating consequences of the thinking that came to equate the human elements of the church with God's eternal plan can we begin. "Then," according to Gary Macy, "we can mourn what we have lost and that mourning can open up the possibility for a new and creative future."[24] Given his insight, I invited the members of CORI to re-appropriate the pattern of the traditional notion of the Irish lament. However, here I added a nuance that had been given me from Deidre Mullan, an Irish Mercy Sister who has spent the last ten years working at the United Nations.

Traditionally, she noted, when a death takes place that has been expected, the traditional Irish form of mourning follows time-honored cultural patterns of grieving associated with the *caoineadh*. However, because the death about which we speak here has come unexpectedly, we are faced with a much deeper loss. This, she suggested, might be faced if we look at the ancient Irish Brehon law (which defined the legal ways of Ireland before the arrival of Christianity). It involved a kind of Celtic-based *sharia* that guided the laws and customs of the relationships among the people that were interpreted for the kings and queens by the Brehons. These laws were created to reinforce the Celtic sense of their interconnectedness with one another and everything in creation. The official "death" of the Brehon and its related ways came with Queen Elizabeth I in the seventeenth century, the corporate personality of "the strangers" (i.e., the occupying British) who came to try to teach us "their" ways.

Applied to the rapid death of the institutional model of the church in Ireland, the revelations of the abuse by some priests and religious, accompanied by the deeper realization of the accompanying structural abuse on the part of so many of the bishops, has elicited not just a *caoineadh*; it has evoked the realization of an even deeper rupture of the *Brehon*—something utterly alienating and devastating and culturally disruptive. Rather than the *caoineadh* that calls on family bonds to ensure the continuance of the family at the time of death, the passing of the once-powerful Irish church now reveals a death much deeper. Sister Deidre said, "Rather than bringing us together as the *caoineadh* form of grieving is meant to do, this death points to the loss of the original Celtic ways whose archetypes still are in our cultural bones and which are so needed to be reclaimed in our church today. Consequently, it represents something about an understanding of the rupture in our very soul that finds us more alone than ever, more divided at this critical time than united."[25]

Hearing Deidre, I thought of how this way of being church had once given life to me and so many others. I also realized that, to this day, I have benefitted personally from its institutional dysfunction.[26] However, I also began to think of my work on Matthew's Gospel and the death of the innocents. Recalling the liturgy's words about "Mother Church inviting her children" to the Easter Vigil, I thought of Rachel's weeping for her children. With millions of Catholics abandoning "Mother Church" in my country, Ireland, and so many other places, it has become quite clear that, in all likelihood, "they will be no more." The once-powerful and dominant Irish church is dead. The institutional form that reached its apogee in the West has no life. This realization makes one ask: How are we to grieve the loss of that which had given us so much life and meaning?

Grief unacknowledged (much less denied) can immobilize those who suffer it. When loss is denied, those in denial will live in the past. Loss unacknowledged can paralyze the survivors from creatively picking up their lives and proceeding with new business. Those who suffer it can act as though "what was" can "be again"; but, deep down, even they know such nostalgic thinking only forestalls the inevitable. Life can begin again only when one faces the dynamic of death and finds a way to become free to find a new life filled with purpose.

This approach to loss and grieving is further complicated when one is hit with loss after loss. There is no time to grieve one loss before another has already occurred. The continued revelations of more child abuse in the past by some of the clergy and more incidents of protection of such accused molesters by some of the bishops without clear action on the issue by the Vatican erode the possibility of trust that things might be different.[27]

When we think of the wrenching realization of Rachel in the face of Herod's murder of Israel's innocents—that they will "be no more"—we will face all sorts of response ranging from delusion and denial that it really isn't so to rage and resentment that it has taken place. The fact or realization that the institution to which many of us gave our very lives will "be no more" can be the source of great loss. However, it can also serve as an invitation to make sure we use the exile to which it has brought us as an occasion of transformation into something ever more meaningful. In the meanwhile we must grieve our loss in the way noted by Brueggemann:

> The first task among exiles is to represent the catastrophe, to state what is happening by way of loss in vivid images so that the loss can be named by its right name and so that it can be publicly faced in the depth of its negativity. Such naming and facing permit the pain to be addressed to God, who is implicated in the loss as less than faithful in a context seen to be one of fickleness and failure. Such speech requires enough candor to dare to utter the torrent of sensitivities that cluster, such as pain, loss, grief, shame, and rage. For this naming and facing, of course, this ancient Jewish community found its best speech by appeal to the liturgical tradition of *lamentation* (which expresses sadness) and *complaint* (which expresses indignation).[28]

Not only sadness but indignation represents the normal kind of reaction of grief to something violent that has happened to us. An expert in grief counseling, Therese Rando, explains that such grief involves "the process of experiencing the psychological, behavioral, social, and physical reactions to the perception of loss."[29] Such grief gets expressed more concretely in a powerful pining for whatever has been lost or bitterness and anger about the loss, difficulty in moving on, and, above all (again), a sense that living has lost its purpose or meaning.

When I think of what has happened in my lifetime to Catholicism in its basic institutional expression—which has shifted from Culture I to Culture II to a mixture of both and, now, to an intentional effort by the clerical leaders to ensure the dominant patterns of Culture I Catholicism, I have spoken in terms of a "death." However, I think Rando's definition describes it better as a perception of deep loss. Having stopped the denial (or even delusion) about the death of the institutional model associated with an overly patriarchal and clericalized form of Catholicism, we must prepare to let go of the past, respectfully honor the remains, and move toward a new way of making Catholicism truly alive. And, as I suggested to the CORI members, while this belongs to everyone, those women and men who belong to official religious congregations and institutes in the church must accept this as their unique *kairos* moment, as they have throughout history, to show the *evangelical way* that new life can come from the dead bones around us. But before new life, we must lament the old.

We have found that the destructive (and deadly) impasse in which we find ourselves involves situations and dynamics of antithetical and polarizing ideologies as well as conflicting moral stances toward life itself. Their forms are political (right and left), economic (the 1 percent and the 99 percent), cultural (Fox News and MSNBC), and, unfortunately and too often, ecclesiastical (Culture I and Culture II Catholics). How, given such a deadening impasse, will we respond in a way that will bring those dead bones to life?

In discussing "ecclesial impasse," theologian Bradford E. Hinze writes, "ecclesial laments can serve as a catalyst for a prophetic critique of the church and society, for church reform and renewal, and inspire the formation of new communities, practices, and forms of life."[30] More concretely, how does one lament this kind of human-made loss of something that once represented such dreams and efforts? In my mind a new, rebuilt church can arise only when we admit its dysfunctional, debilitating, and death-dealing dynamics and allow this historically derived Vatican-form of the church to die in order to bring about a new kind of connected, organic life in our church. It must become an open system that is holarchically ordered instead of a closed system that could only be doomed to die as a result of its own self-inflicted, death-dealing ways. For those who have not given up, these apocalyptic times invite a form of mourning that must be actually ritualized in order to bring about a freedom from its paralyzing ways. In so doing, a new way—or as we shall call it, a *dao*—can be developed and embraced, giving greater meaning and life than before.

That new model will be revealed when we return to Jesus' original proclamation of the reign of God. This model will be reclaimed when we understand its trinitarian implications for our quantum age as well as for our personal, communal, and institutional lives. It is to this plan of God for our personal, communal, and institutional salvation that we now turn in Part II.

Part II

JESUS' *DAO* OF THE KINGDOM

Reclaiming the Metaphor

The thesis of Part II revolves around a threefold contention that has contributed to the crisis and challenge (which I addressed in Part I) facing the Roman Catholic Church, at least in the West. This challenge must be addressed if we are to have true evangelization in the church: (1) We have moved from the gospel proclaimed by Jesus in the Synoptic Gospels (2) to the gospel articulated by Paul in the Acts of the Apostles and his writings (3) to the gospel defined by the teachings of the whole apparatus of the Vatican, overseen by popes, curia, and local bishops.[1] The consequence of this is that many, if not most, Catholics define themselves more by the third gospel than the others. They identify their faith with membership in an organization called Catholicism rather than their baptism into a living body that makes them disciples of Jesus Christ.

This realization came to me years ago when I was asked to give input to students taking a scripture course at St. Scholastica's University in Duluth, MN. I had been asked to lead a Saturday session on some theme related to social justice. When a professor in the religious studies department heard that I was coming, he contacted me. He asked that I come a day early to teach his class on the New Testament, which was studying Matthew's Gospel.

When I entered the classroom that cold winter day I discovered three kinds of students. The first were the second-career people, all older women. They had their coats off, their notebooks open, and their pens ready (this was before notebook computers). The second were the young women. They had their coats off, but their notebooks were closed. The third were the young men. And, among these, the only ones I remember were those who looked like they just got off the football field, complete with their baseball caps on backwards.

Before I delved into Matthew's Beatitudes I thought I had better determine the students' degree of scriptural knowledge. I figured it would be good to go to data outside the scriptures that showed that Jesus did exist in a certain outpost in the Roman Empire. No interest. Then I tried to show how his disciples' experience of him being crucified was changed into their experience of him risen and alive in them and how this changed their lives.

Their boredom was evident, but I kept trying. I talked about how the "church in Jerusalem" met in house churches and how one of these seems to have been run by a woman named Mary, who was kin to Barnabas. But, not even the women seemed to be interested in this great insight of mine. Undaunted, I talked about how the new convert Paul and Barnabas were sent by the house churches in Jerusalem to Antioch where the widespread conversions there demanded more help. This led me to move, section by section, toward the famous text from the Acts of the Apostles. When I shared the words with them ("and in Antioch the disciples were for the first time called Christians" [Acts 11:26]) their total boredom was writ large.

Trying to salvage the class by making a connection between the text and their lives, I asked: "How many of *you* are 'disciples of Jesus Christ'?" Not a hand was raised. So I repeated my question again. Again no response. Then I asked: "How many of you are Catholics?" Almost all the hands in the room went up.

Then and there, in that classroom in Duluth, Minnesota, I concluded that if it was "at Antioch that the disciples were first called Christians," it would be from that time on in Duluth that I wanted to make sure that Catholics would be called disciples!

Jesus' "Way" invited people to move from one way of defining themselves—members of one family, business, or household—to his model of discipleship. This "way" (which we will call the *dao* in Part III) involved a definite model of life based on Jesus' teachings. He said that this new way of ordering their lives must be embraced by engagement; his teachings must be put into practice. By converting to his understanding of the "Kingdom of God," house-by-house, the underpinnings of the imperial kingdom or empire would be undermined, making way for a new way of bringing about God's vision on earth as it is in heaven.

The three chapters here in Part II concern Jesus' core message (at least as it is articulated in the Synoptic Gospels) as demanding a conversion to Jesus' "gospel of the kingdom of God." I will show that, in contemporary theological language this "kingdom of God" can be translated as the "rule or governance of trinitarian relatedness." Furthermore, I will argue why this trinitarian reign or authority must be replicated at every level of our world so its way of relating may come on earth as it is in heaven. Jesus' disciples of every age are to "put into practice" this way by following his *dao* of evangelical asceticism if they are to bring about the new order he envisioned.

6

THE "GOSPEL" OF THE HISTORICAL JESUS

The Reign of Trinity on Earth as in Heaven

In the aftermath of Vatican II, religious congregations were instructed to pursue reform and renewal by (1) reading the signs of the times; (2) returning to the gospel; (3) following the charism of their founders. Most religious congregations tried hard to follow these mandates. We did a pretty good job of reading "the signs of the times" and probed the historical context that gave rise to the "charism of our founders." However, we never really made any real "return to the gospel." Why? I believe that is because we always told ourselves, "We are already living the gospel."

The irrelevancy of such rhetoric about "gospel living" became clear to me decades ago. In our effort to adapt our own "appropriate renewal of religious life," my Midwest Province of Capuchin Franciscans embarked on an effort to discover what united us. If we discovered our commonalities, we surmised, we could develop the kind of necessary cultural symbols and behaviors that would enable us to be recognized and emulated by others and, hopefully, draw vocations. This task had become the project of the province's Research and Planning Committee (RAP), of which I was a member.

With the benefit of people involved in the dynamics of organizational development, we concluded that any or all of four key elements could display the unity among the disparate members of our far-flung group (which covered three time zones in the United States with many members in Latin America and the Middle East). These four possible unifiers were that we shared a common ecclesiology, a common lifestyle, a common apostolate, and a core value. With this belief, we proceeded to get expert advice on a sociological tool that would reveal whether any one or more of the four possibilities were manifested among our members. The resulting effort got organized into a very extensive questionnaire sent to all the friars.

The overall response exceeded our expectations. However, when it came to analyze the friars' response to data covering the four areas, we became increasingly frustrated. Based on what then was Avery Dulles's five "models of the church,"[1] we discovered we had no clear ecclesiology uniting us (although most fell into the "community" and "servant" models of church). Neither did we have a clearly agreed-upon lifestyle (although most of us would be considered "sympathetic innovators"). As to the third point, it was clear that we tolerated every kind of ministry, probably because we didn't want any outsider challenging our own. So we were left with the possibility that some core value or "story" about ourselves might be the glue that united us.

The glue seemed strong at first. Ninety-three percent of us agreed with the statement that our life was to "live the gospel." The glue no longer stuck when someone (knowing that all ecclesiologies come from some understanding of one's Christology or "story" about the core of Jesus' life and message) asked, "Which gospel—the servant, the community, the sacrament, the institution, or the herald model?" Since this experience, I have had a healthy cynicism when I hear someone or some group say, "We live by gospel values." Apart from love, it is hard to find any other "gospel value" that serves to bind us together and offers a sign of hope to ourselves and our candidates.

Why is there so much confusion about images related to the gospel? I think much of our confusion reflects the fact that we have never critiqued what these images really mean. As a result they represent untested assumptions. Another reason reveals our differences related to expectations regarding what "living the gospel" itself involves in our complex world. Another key reason relates to the fact that we are conflicted and, very often, compromised by "other gospels." As we will see, some very popular applications of the word "gospel" have little or nothing to do with the real gospel proclaimed by Jesus Christ.

The core of this chapter revolves around what Jesus meant by the word "gospel" (*euaggelion*). It is my contention that his gospel did not last very long; in fact, it virtually died with his death. Instead, the gospel Jesus proclaimed was quickly overshadowed and ultimately forgotten by what became known as the "gospel" of the early church: the death, resurrection, and embodiment of the historical Jesus, through his Spirit, in the lives and members of his disciples. In effect, the gospel of Paul eclipsed the gospel of Jesus. This becomes clear when we recall that Jesus' gospel was about the inbreaking of what he called "the Kingdom of God" and that Paul's gospel dealt with Jesus as the Christ. We find examples of this new understanding of "gospel" in sections of the New Testament identified with Paul.

Acts of the Apostles	*1 Corinthians*
Though they could charge him with nothing deserving death, yet they asked Pilate to have him killed. And when they had fulfilled all that was written of him they took him down from the tree, and laid him in a tomb. But God raised him from the dead, and for many days he appeared to those who came up with him from Galilee to Jerusalem, who are now his witnesses to the people. And we bring you the gospel that what God promised to our ancestors, this he had fulfilled to us their children by raising Jesus; as also it is written in the second psalm (Acts 13:26-33).	I am reminding you, brothers and sisters, of the gospel I preached to you, which you indeed received and in which you also stand. Through it you are also being saved, if you hold fast to the word I preached to you, unless you believed in vain. For I handed on to you as of first importance what I also received: that Christ died for our sins in accordance with the Scriptures; that he was buried; that he was raised on the third day in accordance with the Scriptures; that he appeared to Cephas, then to the twelve. After that he appeared to more than five hundred . . . at once, most of whom are still living, though some have fallen asleep (1 Cor. 15:1-6).

Paul and the evangelizers in the early church did not intend to preach the gospel of Jesus Christ in such a way that the radicalism of Jesus' own "gospel of the Kingdom of God" would be quickly forgotten. However, their experience of his passion, death, and resurrection (and, in the early years, their conviction that he would return very soon), combined with their understanding of themselves as the mystical embodiment of his presence in space and time, so overwhelmed their imagination that this experience became known as *the* gospel. In the process, the original subversive origin of Jesus' gospel gradually dissipated. It finally disappeared when it was virtually eclipsed with the establishment of the church in the time of Constantine. Consequently, we can say that the original gospel of the Kingdom of God proclaimed by Jesus was eclipsed by the gospel of the death/resurrection/embodiment of Jesus Christ in the church only to have both overshadowed by the gospel that too often has become proclaimed in deed if not in word that identifies the Kingdom of God with the institutional model of the church itself. The result is the type of Culture I and Culture II Catholics who, Cardinal Francis George of Chicago has stated, define "themselves vis-à-vis the bishops rather than vis-à-vis Christ, who uses the bishops to govern the church. It is not a Christ-centered church, as it is supposed to be; it is a bishop-centered church." This unfortunate reality, he adds, has been created in part by the bishops themselves.[2] When these dynamics occur, it is no longer the church of Jesus Christ but the church of the bishops; it is not the "my church" of Jesus that Matthew's Gospel talks about but "my church" of those bishops who see themselves as "*the* church" in their dioceses.

That Paul's notion of the "gospel" eclipsed that of the Gospels becomes evident from a simple word-count. In all, the Synoptics use the word *euaggelion* twenty-three times while John's Gospel never mentions the word at all. The Acts of the early church (i.e., the Acts of the Apostles) speaks about the "gospel" twelve times. In contrast to these usages, the writings attributed to Paul refer to "gospel" in seventy-seven places. This "gospel" of Paul appears more than three times than the "gospel" of Jesus is found in all the Gospels.

Given this background, since we must be faithful to the entire scriptural corpus, any "appropriate renewal," not only of religious life but of the life of religion itself in the Catholic Church, must reclaim the former gospel of Jesus in the Synoptics and balance it with that proclaimed by Paul. How do we go about doing this because both "gospels" must be fulfilled in our hearing? This demands a new kind of "evangelical obedience."

First, we must be re-evangelized by becoming ever more grounded in the gospel proclaimed by the early church, namely, the "good news" of the death, resurrection, and embodiment of Jesus Christ in us (individually, communally, and institutionally). Rooted and grounded in this presence, we must be evangelized to proclaim with power the dynamics of the gospel of the historical Jesus, within the tradition of the Catholic Church, in the midst of our imperial and ecclesiastical realities. This call involves our awareness that, as Jesus indicated in Matthew's Apostolic Discourse, these two powers also might crucify us for such preaching and witnessing in ways that challenge their institutional ways (see Matt. 10:16-20; Luke 12:11-12). This understanding must sculpt our contemporary way of being disciples of Christ Jesus crucified. The consequence of this way of being disciples involves the resulting "cross" that these entities will impose on us. This cross, however, is one that we must choose to take up and embrace if we are going to be faithful to our baptism.

What Did "Gospel" Mean at the Time of Jesus?

It is difficult for Christians today to appreciate the meaning of *euaggelion* when the media proclaims so many other messages as "gospel." I recall when the word "gospel" appeared quite innocently in Robert L. Short's highly acclaimed *The Gospel according to Peanuts*.[3] Its usage was sanctioned with a foreword by the eminent theologian Martin E. Marty. After that publication, during my seminary years, I began increasingly to encounter other culturally important gospels besides those of Matthew, Mark, Luke, and John.

In the parish to which I was assigned by my provincial in 1968 to "reconcile the whites and blacks," I studied the gospel according to Saul Alinsky regarding community organizing. Five years later, realizing I had failed in reconciling the parish because I was not equipped to deal with the social sins of racism and economism, I moved to the ministry of socially responsible investing and corporate responsibility. However, I then was confronted with the prevailing "gospel" according to Milton Friedman. I heard this gospel proclaimed continually (from Catholics and other Christians) when I'd go to stockholders' meetings on some social issue that might challenge their perception of "the bottom line." Indeed, it was only after the second economic crisis in 2008, which found the United States in its worst financial situation since the Great Depression, that I was able to share with such an audience the hard data about the divide between the rich and the poor, much less interpret it in light of the gospel message of Jesus. Before that, every time that I tried, I invariably would be labeled in demonic terms. During the Cold War, if I mentioned anything about the disparity of wealth or income in the United States, I'd be called a communist. After the fall of the Berlin Wall and the "triumph of capitalism," if I critiqued capitalism's monopolistic ways, the financial manipulations of Wall Street where investors were not investing for long-term growth but chasing money for immediate returns, or refer to the fall-out of Friedman's "free market" gospel, I'd be accused of fomenting class warfare (or, possibly worse, of being a Democrat).

Consequently, the first time I found myself free to preach the gospel of Jesus Christ about the "reign of God" to an audience formed by the gospel of Milton Friedman was at a suburban parish in poverty-stricken Youngstown, Ohio. Youngstown was once a booming steel town. Union workers and managers both found upward mobility there on an unprecedented scale. But then came the collapse of the U.S. steel industry as its production moved abroad. Now the congregants found that the life-long savings and pensions of both managers and workers faced a meltdown with the financial crisis. It was November 2008, during the three-month period that household wealth fell by $5.1 trillion (9 percent), the most ever in a single quarter in the fifty-seven-year history of recordkeeping by the Federal Reserve Bank.[4] This represented part of the biggest transfer of wealth[5]—not so much from those actually defined as poor (who had little or nothing to transfer) but from the middle-class—since the Depression. We only learned later from the *Wall Street Journal* that, during this same period, the median net worth of white households became twenty times greater than that of black households and eighteen times greater than that of Hispanic households.[6]

I was giving a retreat at St. Michael's parish in Canfield, Ohio. Relatively speaking, Canfield had been saved from some of the devastation experienced by Youngstown. Spiritually, the parish had been formed quite well; its people were formed in the mode of Culture II Catholicism. The theme for the parish mission was the notion of church in the New Testament. My message was being received well.

On the morning of my last conference, the Director of Religious Education told me she had been talking with the pastor. They had decided that instead of what we had agreed to be my final talk, I should talk on the topic "A Gospel Response to the Financial Crisis." I was quite surprised; even taken aback. "Do you really want me to speak on this topic? Do you know how the people might react?" I asked. "We think they are ready," she responded. "We want you to do this."

For the first time in my life, that night, in the context of what the economy was doing to further divide the rich and the poor (and bring more and more lower middle-class people into the ranks of "the poor") I was able to proclaim the gospel in a way that would represent "good news" for the poor. And my audience would not be liberal bishops, priests, or religious open to such a message. Instead it would represent middle- and upper-middle-class white Catholics in suburbia. As I set the context in our time for the gospel of Jesus in his time, I received no hostility. I was asked hard questions, but there was no defense of a political economy that they all knew had become indefensible.

Returning to my earlier comments about various secular meanings of the "gospel," I find another one that can be found in every bookstore's "personal development" section. Many of these are the equivalent of today's "Gospel of Oprah"! Such a "gospel" offers us answers to our deepest questions, as was intimated in a recent cover feature: "What's Your True Calling? An Easy-Does-It Guide to Finding (and Fulfilling) Your Life's Purpose."[7] Some of this invites us to become free of the guilt-producing, enshackling gospel of religion to embrace the enlightened message of great writers like Eckhart Tolle (whom I deeply appreciate). Indeed his 2008 book, *A New Earth*, a book-club selection by Oprah ranked #1 among all the others for the first decade of 2000. Then, as I created my own DVD series, *Choosing Compassion*,[8] I realized my need to become familiar with the recognized experts in organizational development. Top among these—at least at that time—was Marcus Buckingham. An article in the management section of *Business Week* about his message proclaimed, "Ladies and Gents . . . Marcus Buckingham! The Business Sage Is Spreading His Gospel via a Bus Tour—and Eyeing Wider Audiences."[9]

In a marketing environment such as ours, is it any wonder that a Christian, much less a Catholic (who is even less informed about religious terminology than agnostics and atheists[10]), would be confused about Jesus' original gospel message? Given this confusion, it is important to be clear about the historical context for Jesus proclaiming the gospel of the Kingdom of God. Since the historical Jesus seemed to know that his fidelity to the proclamation of that gospel would result in violence and death on a cross, the imperial instrument for subversives to its own imperial "gospel," it is essential that his followers today reclaim its real meaning for our time as well. This task is especially important in light of a challenge that comes to us from Theodore Jennings, a professor at Chicago Theological Seminary. He has written: "If the gospel is about transformation, how is it that two thousand years of proclamation have had so little effect? How is it that the gospel of Jesus Christ, so far from producing radical change, has instead become a cloak for avarice and arrogance, for a willful deafness to the cry of the poor and of the earth itself?" He concludes with the following challenge:

> It is only possible to speak of the gospel as a source for a remedy of the planetary crisis that we face if we are talking about a gospel that makes possible, indeed requires and in fact produces, a radical and visible transformation in all dimensions of life. Only a gospel that produces holiness, scriptural holiness, can transform the economy of death—or rather, abolish it and give in its place something that can really be "good news to the poor."[11]

Jesus' Alternative Gospel of the Kingdom of God

At the time of Jesus, the word *euaggelion* involved a broader as well as a more culturally relevant meaning. The broader notion of gospel referred to the proclamation of some kind of "good news," usually connected with the notion of salvation (being saved/liberated) from some kind of negative power/force. Often the salvation that prompted the good news referred to liberation of a military nature. This "gospel of salvation" came to possess a second meaning. It dominated the psyches of people in that part of the first-century Roman Empire where Jesus lived.

In this Judean outpost of Rome, such a culturally specific meaning of gospel involved an announcement of a special kind—the news of the expansion in space and time of imperial Rome's power (accompanied by the cult of its gods) that would save/liberate its citizens from the negative power/force identified with Rome's enemy. This was good news for the whole inhabited world or humankind (the *oikoumenē*) that was under the rule of the Roman emperors (see Matt. 24:14; Luke 4:5; Heb. 2:5; Acts 11:28; 24:5; Rev. 3:10; 16:14; 17:31) because, quite myopically, Rome's dominant rule was considered to be coextensive with the "whole" world. The umbrella for this notion of good news was another notion: *Pax Romana*. As long as people anywhere would not rebel against Rome, they would be assured its peace and salvation.

Whether related to space or time, this gospel's proclamation was identified with the extension of imperial rule and governance. In "space" it was proclaimed when Caesar's armies had conquered new territories. In "time" it was identified with the announcement that Caesar's wife (or daughters-in-law) had produced a male heir, ensuring the extension in time of imperial governance. The response of those hearing this gospel proclamation was to rejoice because this assured them of even greater security—as long as they did not challenge the *Pax Romana*. It was clear, therefore, there could be no other challenge to this gospel and the ultimate imperial authority it represented. All of these notions are summarized in part of a decree of that first-century era which proclaimed in its "whereas" statements that Caesar Augustus "has made war to cease and . . . put everything in peaceful order; and . . . the birthday of our god signaled the beginning of Good News for the world because of him. . . ."[12] Of course, this "god" was Augustus.

It was into this imperial world, based in Rome, that Jesus of Nazareth begins his public ministry. He had once been a disciple of John the Baptist. However, because John the Baptist challenged the marriage arrangement of Herod, the emperor's Judean representative, he had been imprisoned and executed. The mantle of the proclamation of the "Kingdom of God" turned to Jesus. Realizing that the justice he identified with John's proclamation (Matt. 3:15) must now be fulfilled in him (see Matt. 3:12-16), we read, "From that time Jesus began to preach, saying, 'Repent, for the kingdom of heaven is at hand'" (Matt. 4:17). A few verses later, Matthew equates this message that Jesus preached directly with "the *gospel* of the Kingdom" (Matt. 4:23). In other words, for those familiar with Rome's gospel, Jesus' gospel of the Kingdom of heaven stood diametrically opposed to the empire of Caesar and all that it encompassed, including the Jewish leaders' assimilation into it and its *Pax Romana*. His "gospel" was subversive to Caesar's.

Now that we have reflected on the meaning of the "gospel" of Jesus as it would have been understood at his time, we can turn to two other key words that were involved in its proclamation. Because it was the "gospel of the kingdom of God or heaven," we need to examine the meaning for our time of both "kingdom" and "God" as we have come to know God as "triune."

The Greek word for "kingdom" (*basileia*) actually involves a feminine notion, like "queendom." This is all the more evident when we go to its Hebrew derivation, *malkuth*. However, in the context of Jesus' day, given the overpowering and omnipresent reality of the *basileia tou Kaisaros*, it really meant the male (and, therefore, dominant) "empire" or imperial rule and governance (of the Caesars). While Matthew's original source in Mark invariably referred to the *basileia tou theou* (Kingdom of God), when the more-Jewish-oriented Matthean author wrote, being sensitive not to use God's "name," the notion of the *basileia tou theou* was changed to read *basileia tōn ouranōn* (Kingdom of

Heaven). In effect, the two images of "God" and "heaven" are quite synony-mous.

Given this contextual setting, what, then, can we understand by the under-lying meaning of Jesus' proclamation of the "gospel of the kingdom of God"? When we apply the meaning to our milieu (with the benefit of faith and sci-ence), we can conclude that the meaning of the "gospel of the kingdom of God" can be translated today to mean "the rule or governance of trinitarian dynam-ics" and that these dynamics or ways of relating must "come on earth as it is in heaven" at every level of life: personally, communally, and organizationally, especially in that institutional form of religion that is known as the Roman Catholic Church with its headquarters in the Vatican.

For years I tried to use the word "kindom" of God instead of "kingdom" of God, mainly to avoid sexist language. However, the more I probed the real meaning of *basileia* in its context then and what its parallel meaning would be today, with the aid of physics, I have moved from thinking of "kingdom" as a noun defined by place and time associated with the extension of Caesar's *basileia*, to thinking of it as a verb, a way of being. I got this insight while read-ing an article about Gibraltar. It remains in space and time part of the "reign" of what is left of the British Empire. The piece in *The New York Times* discuss-ing the phenomenon of the little monkeys that inhabit that colony was entitled "Where the British May Reign but the Monkeys Rule."[13] Since, in our quantum empire, all space- and time-experienced entities are various forms of massed energy, it became clear to me, as a believer, that "the reign" of God is the divine energy ruling at the heart of all reality. Furthermore, if this God is trinitarian relatedness and if relatedness or connectedness defines everything that is, all reality has been made by God to image trinitarian energy and power, triune attraction, connectedness, and self-giving.

When I give workshops and talk on this theme, the most-sought-after chart of my Power Point presentation on the topic is the one below wherein I offer different words for *basileia* and other trinitarian images for *theou*. Jesus' gospel of the presence of the *basileia tōn theōn* in his day can mean today (with the help of Nicaea and Chalcedon) the "kinship of trinitarian relatedness," which we must find and construct throughout our world. When we do so, far from supporting any kind of reinforcement of existing monarchical and/or patriar-chal dynamics in the church, especially when one considers the "Q" source, we see that "the standard of ethical behavior" connected to the notion of *basileia* cannot be found to "come any more from a patriarchal and kyriarchal figure";[14] rather, we will see, it will be now concretized in the new community of dis-ciples who are brothers and sisters under the one Father in heaven rather than under the *pater patriae*, the emperor, in Rome.

JESUS' GOSPEL OF THE *BASILEIA* OF GOD
TO COME ON EARTH AS IT IS IN HEAVEN

Other words for "kingdom"	*Other words for "God"*
commonwealth sovereignty reign rule	traditional trinitarian Nicea/Chalcedon formulae
realm project dream vision plan model	God as lover, beloved, loving
reality essence existence being life	God as knower, known, knowing
dominion dynamic force energy power	"I am"◄─►"you are" ↘"we are"↗
authority governance relatedness	the "I am" of male and female made as God images
Jesus' *basileia* as empire or kingdom	female and male made to be trinitarian
"kingdom" of yesterday = "kindom" of today	male and female made for kindom connecting

When we consider the implications of the chart above in a way that reveals the subversive character of Jesus' gospel in contrast to that of Caesar's gospel, it is little wonder that Jesus would die as a subversive for refusing to stop proclaiming it. When we realize that this gospel articulates God's plan that the dynamics and structures of trinitarian connectedness must be proclaimed to "all *ethnoi*" (Matt. 28:19) beginning with the church itself, should it come as any surprise that those who translate this gospel as applying equally for women and men in the church will be persecuted for trying to make it happen (see Matt. 5:10) but will find themselves part of that *basileia* for doing so? In the same vein, we can ask how anyone could be surprised by the historical fact that the further the early community moved away from its original experience of Jesus as "the Christ" who ushered in a new creation no longer defined by any "isms" based on economics (slave/free), ethnicity (Jew/Gentile), or sex (male/female), the male-controlled community would become more interested in promoting the gospel of Paul's notion of personal and individual salvation than the cosmic salvation intimated by the Synoptics' articulation of Jesus' message.

The fact that Jesus' theological proclamation of the gospel of the Kingdom of God was not to be limited to mere words but was intended to become performative theology is evidenced in the whole structure of Matthew's Gospel. We find it, above all, in the very way the Gospel is structured. Building on the accepted interpretation that Matthew sculpted the Gospel to have a beginning and an end, with five "books," each having a narrative and a discourse, we see that the core of the gospel reveals Jesus' vision for a new kind of social ordering in the empire. At the very center, in the third book, between the narrative and discourse, the traditional patriarchal family is contrasted with Jesus' vision of the new household under the one he called "the heavenly Father": "While he was still speaking to the people, behold, his mother and his brethren stood outside [the house], asking to speak to him. But he replied to the man who told him, 'Who is my mother, and who are my brethren?' And stretching out his hand toward his disciples, he said, 'Here are my mother and my brethren! For whoever does the will of my Father in heaven is my brother, and sister, and mother'" (Matt. 12:46-50).

Returning to the launching of Jesus' own ministry in Matthew 4, we find again Jesus' proclamation of the reign of God (which, we now know, can also be called the Rule or Governance of the Economic Trinity) that must come on earth as it is in heaven. Upon hearing of the arrest of John the Baptist, Jesus withdraws in a way that finds the scriptures fulfilled in him (Matt. 4:12-16). This empowers him to begin preaching: "Repent, for the kingdom of heaven is at hand" (Matt. 4:17). Immediately after this, he puts into practice at the micro-level this macro-message about the kingdom by calling Peter and Andrew and then James and John to inaugurate a new economic model or a new way of "doing business," not according to the principle of patriarchy but of equality (Matt. 4:18-22). To demonstrate the radicalness involved in this conversion, Jesus' call of Peter and Andrew, James and John (Matt. 4:18-22) is written to show that the new "family" Jesus was creating was not only a new household of equals or a new kind of *oikonomia*; it was a totally new way of doing business that would ultimately be recognized as a challenge to the religious leaders and to the imperial order and its way of doing business. No longer will the family business be modeled on "father" and "boats"; now it will be discovered in an alternative family of brothers and sisters under the one called the "heavenly Father."[15] This form of discipleship represents a totally new way of life, which we will discuss later under the title of the *dao* of "domestic asceticism."[16]

As Matthew's Gospel develops, it shows the members of Jesus' new household exhibiting the same conflicts found in every human household in one form or another, including the kind of traditional power and rank dynamics that Mrs. Zebedee advocated for her sons in Jesus' "kingdom" (Matt. 20:20-21). Yet Jesus' response to her and his arguing disciples also makes it clear that these ways of relating are no longer to be the norm among the members of his household in such a kingdom: "It shall no longer be so among you" (Matt. 20:26). Jesus' kingdom on earth is grounded in a political economy that begins in his new family. It is to be structured with a different *telos* or goal in mind: it is to reflect the perfection of the Economic Trinity (see Matt. 5:48) wherein

(1) all persons will be equal, and (2) their relationships will be ordered in a way of full participation, and (3) wherein all will have full access to all resources.

This new way of relating has already been outlined in the Sermon on the Mount with its fivefold stress on justice or rightly ordered relationships. By "doing good" in this way, his disciples will be those who not only bring light into the house but do so in a way that has cosmic implications in the way that makes them *salt of the earth* and *light of the world.* Thus, after saying that this light must enlighten "all in the *house,*" he immediately states, "Let your light so shine before men, that they may see your *good works* and give glory to your Father who is in heaven" (Matt. 5:16). Doing good is the original house-work; enlightened disciples are those who "do good" in a way that brings about the common good so that the world will mirror its original constitution. Matthew ends the Sermon on the Mount with Jesus' affirmation of those who build their house in a way that puts his words into practice (Matt. 7:24-27).

From everything that we have said, it should be clear that, in Matthew's world of the "house," not only the building but more importantly the relationships among the persons and resources that revolved around the "house" should reflect the same dynamics. The context for this vision is defined by the patterns of relationships in the towns and cities that created the infrastructure for the imperial household and Rome's political economy as well as ecclesial households at all levels. Consequently, the house (*oikia*) was the basic unit of the *polis* (city) and the *polis* was the basic unit of the empire (*basileia*). When Jesus, in Matthew 10, sends his disciples to every *oikia* in the *polis* their message is the gospel of another *basileia*: the rule or governance of what we now call a God of trinitarian relatedness that brings about a new social order (see Matt. 10:7-13). Furthermore, they were to move from house to house and from town and village with a message of salvation. This salvation promised from God rather than from the emperor would be defined by *shalom* rather than the *Pax Romana.* This gospel of peace and its modeling in his new family of ever-burgeoning disciples soon became such a threat to the religious leaders of Judaism, who had been co-opted by Rome, that they conspired with Rome to have him killed under the guise of saving the empire.

Before that killing, in the last use of the word *oikia* in Matthew, "when Jesus was at Bethany in the house of Simon the leper, a woman came up to him with an alabaster flask of very expensive ointment, and she poured it on his head, as he sat at table" (Matt. 26:6-7). In this one sentence we discover all the core dynamics of an economic transaction: a woman with an expensive resource and a man who would be in need of it. Their encounter led her to reorder her resource on his behalf. This economic transfer of wealth from the woman to the man was challenged by his disciples, who argued it should have been sold and given to the poor (Matt. 26:8-9). In response, Jesus "said to them, 'Why do you trouble the woman? For she has done a good deed to me. For you always have the poor with you, but you will not always have me'" (Matt. 26:10-11).

In these two lines we have two sentences: the first has been one of the most important but forgotten declarations of Jesus, while the other has been one of the most misunderstood but remembered sayings. That the second is one of the best remembered of Jesus' sayings involves the fact that "the poor you will always have with you" is part of the cultural lexicon. However, how Jesus interpreted the economic transaction of the woman on his projected need as a religious activity and linked to the divine and cosmic action of God's "good deed" at the beginning of the world has not been remembered.

The fact that we should remember what she did and not that the poor will always be with us is clear from Jesus' closing command (i.e., "Amen") in this section of Matthew's Gospel: "Truly, I say to you, wherever this gospel (*euaggelion*) is preached in the whole world, what she has done will be told in memory of her" (Matt. 26:13).

The anonymous woman is representative of all disciples. Her "doing good" represented both an economic activity (a redistribution of wealth) and a religious ritual: an example of the gospel economy of "doing good" that extends God's "good-doing" further into the world, bringing about a new kind of salvation. This notion, as noted immediately above, becomes even clearer when Matthew's Jesus declares, "Wherever *this gospel* is preached in the *whole* world, what *she did* will be told in memory of her" (Matt. 26:13).

Building on the assumed primary metaphor of the house, which will be discussed at greater length in the next chapter, it is important here to realize that it was in that house that such economic and religious activities were joined together in a way that put into practice the gospel Jesus had been proclaiming. Her "doing good" by sharing her resources with the one who would be in need represented the kind of evangelization that Jesus insisted should be replicated throughout the "whole world" for all time.

When the woman relates to Jesus *in the house* as a person generously sharing her resources with him in light of his anticipated need, she becomes the model disciple as well as an exemplar of evangelical living. In effect, she not only proclaims the gospel of the Economic Trinity; she witnesses to it. In this she furthers the purposes of the economy of salvation itself. Given Jesus' words about her economic/religious activity, the dynamics between her and Jesus must define the whole "world" of our (1) individual lives, (2) our group life, (3) our organizational or institutional life, and (4) of creation itself.

When we apply the metaphor of house at the level of our individual lives, it often appears in our dreams and in the revelations of many mystics as an embodiment of the self. In this sense, each of us is an *oikos/oikia*. Thus we find ourselves using the metaphor in terms of our self when we say such things as "I need to get my house in order." In this sense everyone is a "house-repairer."

We also see the metaphor dominating the relational life of Jesus in his world, beginning with the family. The management or ordering (= *nomos*) of the *oikia/oikos* involved family and associational groupings in a structure called *oikonomia*. How such houses were ordered when Jesus "entered the house" becomes important when we see how he preached the gospel of peace in them.

The third level, representing the whole inhabited world (especially its political and economic organizations and institutions with religion and its gods embedded within them, especially under the rule of the Caesars), was the *oikoumenē*. This is the origin of the word "ecumenical." By creating a *Pax Romana*, Caesar intended to bring the whole inhabited world under his reign.

Finally, building on the root words *oikos* and *oikia* we can call the whole cosmos the universe of the underlying connectedness of everyone and everything, the *oikologia*. When we humans relate to creation and one another with integrity in our relationships within our individual *oikos/oikia*, when we have integrity within our families and groups in their *oikonomia*, and when we also work to bring about collaboration and participative dynamics within the *oikoumenē*, we ensure the integrity of what we can call the *oikologia* itself. Integrity within the first three levels of the "house" ensures environmental integrity, a holarchy of peace throughout the whole cosmos.

The Diminution of Jesus' Subversive Gospel
Meant to Change Society

When one considers the *evangelical* radicality of this message of Jesus (which led him to be crucified as subversive to the imperial household), it is little wonder why the gospel of Paul came to eclipse this message of Jesus which he wanted to be proclaimed throughout the whole world for all time. The result of this stress on Paul's gospel rather than Jesus' gospel has taken its toll, especially in the West. A key proof of this is the church's failure to put into practice the profession of faith it makes in the trinitarian reality. No place is this therapeutic model of the gospel more evident than in the richest of the largest countries on the planet. No place but in the United States do we find the gospel that was once meant to bring good news to the poor who are always with us prostituted to such a degree that so many of its avowed followers actually believe fidelity to it will bring them wealth in the way wealth is created in the United States. How has this occurred? A September 2010 op-ed piece by the conservative Jewish columnist David Brooks made it very clear.

In a *New York Times* piece, "The Gospel of Wealth," he wrote about the days when the "United States once had a Gospel of Wealth: a code of restraint shaped by everybody from Jonathan Edwards to Benjamin Franklin to Andrew

Carnegie. The code was designed to help the nation cope with its own afflu-ence." While he showed that it gradually became eroded by selfishness and individualistic interpretations of the Gospels, he quoted those who have been challenging such assumptions. One of those he highlighted was a Southern Baptist minister by the name of David Platt. He referred to Platt's new book, *Radical: Taking Back Your Faith from the American Dream*. In it Platt made clear the essence of the gospel of the kindom of God: "The American dream radi-cally differs from the call of Jesus and the essence of the Gospel." He noted that Platt argues that the American dream emphasizes upward mobility, but that "success in the kingdom of God involves moving down, not up."[17]

It is not easy to proclaim a gospel that is good news to the poor when we live in a society wherein, as occurred in September 2011, newspapers reported on their front pages that poverty in the United States had reached a "52-year peak."[18] Why, when this was Jesus' core purpose in proclaiming the gospel, is it so foreign to so many of us citizens? One of the key problems that keeps us priests (along with bishops and popes) from truly proclaiming the gospel of God's vision that will bring good news to the poor resides in the fact that we have been immunized to recognize how our body-politic has been diseased by the consequences of an ever-increasing disparity of both wealth and income. Despite the data from conservative journals like the *Wall Street Journal* show-ing the ever-increasing gap in both areas,[19] one rarely hears the gospel pro-claimed in a way that will challenge the structural dynamics that have made this so. Because personal income has increased over the past hundred years, when average people read about wealth or income inequality, they do not feel the moral outrage that can be found in the more passionate egalitarian quar-ters of society;[20] in fact they don't really believe it. I must admit that I was "one of them."

The *Milwaukee Journal-Sentinel,* the paper where I live, features a "Truth-O-Meter" that investigates statements made by politicians and others as to their basis in fact. One that caught my eye was "Inequality Claim Checks Out." It sought to probe the veracity of the claim by filmmaker Michael Moore that, as the subheading of the article declared, "Moore Says Top 400 Own More than Bottom 50%; Figures Agree." It stated, "Moore correctly quoted *Forbes* [maga-zine], which said in a September 2009 article that the net worth of the nation's 400 wealthiest Americans was $1.27 trillion." Then, going to 2010 Federal Reserve Board data, the *Journal* concluded: "our assessment indicates that as of 2009, the net worth of the nation's 400 wealthiest individuals exceeds the net worth of half of all American households." It then concluded, "We rate Moore's statement True."[21] This made me a believer.

A key reason why people do not believe such data rests in the perceived gradualism by which more and more of the rewards of growth have gone to the rich and super-rich.[22] The result is that the four hundred richest people in the United States control more wealth than half of its citizens. This has taken place in a way that has found the rest of the nation falling behind. This fall has not taken place as much among the poor, but in the middle and lower-middle class.

In their well-received analysis of the current U.S. economy, *Winner-Take-All Politics*, Jacob Hacker and Paul Pierson outline the process of the past forty years in which corporations (defined as "persons"), with their bevy of lobbyists, have been able to bring about a massive change in the distribution of wealth and income in the nation. They show how their effective control of the legislative process through their selective placement of money has isolated the poor in a way that reinforces their own interests at the expense of the poor and middle-class. They conclude, "As money has become more and more prominent, our politics has become more and more like the parable in Matthew 13: 'For whosoever hath, to him shall be given, and he shall have more abundance.'"[23] Affirming their findings, David Brooks shows that the result of these dynamics is a new "leadership group" in Washington that has become "home [think of our metaphor of 'house'] to a vertiginous tangle of industry associations, activist groups, think tanks and communications shops" that not only has "overwhelmed the government"; but faced with less and less government regulation, they also do not "police themselves."[24]

Despite such overwhelming data revealing a growing chasm between the super-rich and everyone else in the nation, a key reason why U.S. citizens (unlike those in places like Israel) do not show more concern about the disparity and the resulting influence of the richest on our politicians rests in their belief that the nation is much more egalitarian than it is. A 2010 survey showed U.S. citizens think that the wealthiest 20 percent of Americans own 59 percent of the nation's wealth; in reality, the top fifth owns around 84 percent. The respondents further estimated that the poorest 20 percent own 3.7 percent, when in reality they own 0.1 percent.

This process has evolved slowly. In 1980 the richest 1 percent of the population got 10 percent of the total income; by 2011 this figure grew to 20 percent. Against such contrasts, data also show that U.S. citizens fail to act on their own best values. When they were asked to envision their ideal economy, they envisioned a breakdown wherein "the wealthiest fifth would control just 32 percent of the wealth, the poorest just over 10 percent." Such a distribution would not only put the ideal economic system for the average U.S. citizen closer to that of the gospel; it would be to the left of Sweden.[25]

Because of long-held myths about America being "the greatest" in everything, including equal opportunity (without considering the parallel need to consider equality of outcomes), notions about the basic fairness of the nation will not be easily challenged. The result will likely be even greater disparity between the rich and the poor reinforced by people's "buy in" to the "American Dream," which tells them that they too might be there some day, as long as they do the right thing. When so many people believe they will "make it" someday, whether the "it" happens to be the lottery or Las Vegas, the NBA or the NFL, the movies or the top one percent, it is not surprising that there would be little concern about those "others" who, for whatever reason, will not "make it." Again it is image over substance; the ever-more unrealizable gospel of the American Dream over the still unpracticed gospel of the Kingdom/Kindom. The result is increased household wealth and income for the very few instead of a new household of faith that reflects the "economy" of the trinitarian household that is open to all.

This leads us to our next chapter. There we will see how a deeper understanding of the metaphor of "house" in light of the trinitarian household of God, along with the implications of Jesus' proclamation of the gospel of that "economy" for humanity throughout the world, could upend much of what we have been taught by the official church.

Economics, the Economic Trinity, and the Economy of Salvation

Linking Science and Religion

In our last chapter we explained how a contemporary unpacking of the inner meaning of Jesus' message of the "gospel of the kingdom of God" can be understood today as his vision of bringing about on earth the "kindom of trinitarian connectedness" at all levels of life. The Jesus of history was not versed in the technical language of trinitarian theology, which was only defined in the course of protracted, and sometimes violent, debates in the third and fourth centuries. Thus, he would be intrigued with the "over-audacious claim" of the scientist-theologian John Polkinghorne that "a deeply intellectually satisfying candidate for the title of a true 'Theory of Everything' is in fact provided by trinitarian theology." Polkinghorne argues that "there are aspects of our scientific understanding of the universe that become more deeply intelligible to us if they are viewed in a trinitarian perspective."[1]

Ever since Augustine talked about creation containing the *vestigia* or footprints of the Trinity, people have been searching for scientific verification of their theological beliefs. This effort to link science and God recently received reinforcement from Francis Collins, director of the Human Genome Project and now of the National Institutes of Health. He called DNA the "language of God."[2] More recently, the notion of these *vestigia* in creation not only being like the DNA of God but, more specifically, of this trinitarian God has received more theological reflection in the writings of Elizabeth Johnson.[3] Perhaps its clearest expression thus far can be found in the 2010 statement of Robert D. Hughes III "that DNA may indeed be a *vestigium*, a vestige or footprint, of the Trinity." Even though he affirmed, with all theology, that he was speaking analogically, Hughes explained that "DNA as the very structure of life as we know it is a kind of resonance of the divine life, one of the myriad ways in which the self-expressive self-transcendence of the triune God evokes all drives towards self-transcendence in the creation."[4]

In this same analogical vein I gave a paper on the Trinity at the 2010 gathering of the Catholic Theological Society of America. I argued that an understanding of church that was faithful to what we know from science should support my thesis that trinitarian relationships should underlie reality at every level. Rather than resort to the hard sciences (about which I know very little), I decided to reflect on this theme from the perspective of the *social* sciences—particularly economics—in which I have been educated.

I realize that any effort to apply the "science" of economics to our understanding of the theology of the Economic Trinity[5] and the economy of salvation must be tentative and cautious. I am also aware that it could be questioned whether economics can even be considered a science. On this I was glad to come across an op-ed piece in the *Wall Street Journal* by an economics professor, Russ Roberts, that spoke to my question: "Is the Dismal Science Really a Science?" He cautioned, "If economics is a science, it is more like biology than physics. Biologists try to understand the relationships in a complex system. . . . We have the same problems in economics. The economy is a complex system, our data are imperfect, and our models inevitably fail to account for all the interactions." While addressing my question about the scientific status of economics, Roberts's remarks also find an echo in the mystery of the Trinity: it too represents "a complex system" about which we have imperfect data!

We have no objective data about God's triadic ways save what has been revealed in the one we call Jesus Christ and subsequent definitions of church councils. Therefore we need a good dose of humility as we try to make connections that further our understanding of how God is working in our world. Roberts writes of economics what we should be telling ourselves about the theological endeavor when we try to understand the Trinity:

> The bottom line is that we should expect less of economists. Economics is a powerful tool, a lens for organizing one's thinking about the complexity of the world around us. That should be enough. We should be honest about what we know, what we don't know and what we may never know. Admitting that publicly is the first step toward respectability.[6]

Much the same can be said of the economist we call God. God's basic mode of operating involves relationships within Godself—what we call the Economic Trinity. Once we recognize that God's essential nature is *relational* we find those relationships replicated throughout creation and its all processes (including economics). In this sense Denis Edwards writes, "Once the nature of God is understood as relational, then this suggests that the fundamental nature of all reality is relational." He adds, "The God of trinitarian theology is a God of mutual and equal relations. When such a God creates a universe it is not surprising that it turns out to be a radically relational and interdependent one. When life unfolds through the process of evolution, it emerges in patterns of interconnectedness and interdependence that 'fits' with the way God is."[7]

As we saw in the last chapter, God's way of relating, through the person and gospel of Jesus Christ, has extended God's family business or trinitarian household into creation and, finally, to humans within the economy of salvation. We come to a much deeper understanding of the radicality of this gospel when we consider the Economic Trinity and the economy of salvation from the perspective of economics and the social ordering it implies. But, to move toward a greater understanding of this connection, we need a primer in Economics 101.

Economics 101

"Economics" has its origin in the Greek words for house (*oikos* and *oikia*) and law or ordering (*nomos*). Together they create the word "economy" (*oikonomia*).[8] As we saw earlier, unlike the notion of "house" today, in the first-century Mediterranean world of Jesus, the house was not so much the building itself but the *ordering of relationships taking place within it among persons and their resources*. In the household, persons related to one another and their available resources according to established cultural patterns. Except for the more collegial, voluntary associations, these were almost always hierarchical and patriarchal. An *oikonomos* was "one who managed a household," while *oikonomia* involved "household management."

Whether we study micro-economics or macro-economics, analytically or descriptively, philosophically or historically, almost all agree that, at its core, the science of economics involves the study of a threefold reality: (1) persons, (2) resources, and (3) their relationships. These are ordered, managed, and structured in varying ways (usually under a "command" or "market" model). The underlying issue in economics is not so much defined by the persons or their available resources but the *way* those persons produce, distribute, and consume those resources. Thus, the basic definition of economics is the *ordering* of (scarce) resources among (competing) persons. In a socialistic model this ordering is done to meet basic needs of the members of the community. In capitalism, the ordering arises from the freedom that is ensured as individuals maximize their utility to respond to their unlimited wants.

The fact that economics is not as much concerned about the persons involved (i.e., "the market share") or the available resources (which are to be exploited) as much as the way these resources *are ordered* among persons holds significant trinitarian implications. Where theologians once approached discussions of the Trinity from the perspective of *persons* involving the Many (as in the East) or the *substance* of the One (as in the West), theologians today increasingly stress the relationships or the communion among the persons sharing the one substance.

Whether politically grounded around the poles of capitalism or socialism, each economic model has its own *telos* (goal or purpose) that undergirds its political choices as to what is the "best" way of ordering for the most people. That is why classical "modern" economic theorists such as Adam Smith, David Ricardo, and Jeremy Bentham more honestly called their theories "political economy."

Given the economic upheaval that has impacted countries like the United States, and the ideological mindset about the basic equality that sustains it, it is more important than ever that we point to the Economic Trinity as the ultimate *telos* of all personal and social ordering whether it is revealed in our economics, our politics, or our church. In light of the current crisis facing all these institutional realms, it is critical for us that we arrive at a true understanding of God as trinitarian relatedness, as the *telos* that should undergird not only these but all individual, group, and social relationships if they are to contribute to creating the common good. This brings us to basics on the Economic Trinity and the economy of salvation.

Trinity: One and Three

In 1988 Orbis Books published my doctoral dissertation *House of Disciples: Church, Economics, and Justice,* in which I argued that the dynamics associated with "house" (*oikos/oikia*) reveal the word to be the "assumed primary metaphor" in Matthew's Gospel.[9] In that same year, M. Douglas Meeks published *God as Economist.* Two years later, Catherine Mowry LaCugna wrote her groundbreaking *God for Us: The Trinity and Christian Life.* Both of them also suggested that the word "house" should be considered a key theological metaphor.[10]

Meeks argued, "My claim is that, according to the faith shaped by the biblical traditions, the metaphor Economist is a decisive and appropriate way of describing the character and work of God."[11] Reclaiming *theologia* and *oikonomia* (*oikos* + *nomos* = *oikonomia* or house ordering) as compatible rather than opposed,[12] LaCugna wrote, "Household is an appropriate metaphor to describe the *communion of persons* where God and creature meet and unite and now exist together as one. The reign of God is the rule of love and communion; God's economy is the history of this communion." She concludes, "The salvation of the earth and of human beings is the restoration of the praise of the true living God, and the restoration of communion among persons and all creatures living together in a common household. The articulation of this vision is the triumph of the doctrine of the Trinity."[13]

LaCugna's insights bring us to a more nuanced understanding of the "Gospel of the Economic Trinity" that Jesus preached. To help in this process, I will highlight some insights from the writings of the Franciscan theologian St. Bonaventure. Whether or not we will ever find clear scientific evidences of the footprints of trinitarian *vestigian* connectedness in creation or creatures, it is clear that Bonaventure's trinitarian theology can help us in this task even now.

Expanding Bonaventure's Scriptural Reflection Regarding God's Goodness to Find Its Trinitarian Traces Reflected in the Human Desire to Do Good

In Bonaventure's *The Soul's Journey into God* stress is laid on God's self-reality and consequent self-communication to us[14] as revealing God's Being as supreme goodness.[15] Since the essence of goodness involves giving, God's goodness is diffused in everything created as being "very good." In a chapter entitled "Speculation on the Most Blessed Trinity in Its Name, Which Is the Good," he supports this argument by reference to the story of Jesus and the rich young man who asked about what "good" he needed to do to be part of God's reign or reality. Grounding his reflections on the revelation of God's "I am" to Moses (Exod. 3:14), Bonaventure notes that Jesus first answers with reference to the Being of God: "No one is good but God alone." Bonaventure continues, "So Damascene, following Moses, says that, *The One Who Is*, is the first name of God. And Dionysius, following Christ, says that *Good* is the first name of God."[16]

In another place, Bonaventure showed how the "good" involves self-diffusiveness. He wrote, "For 'the good is said to be self-diffusive.' The supreme good, therefore, is supremely self-diffusive." He then argues that only when the dynamics reflect the supreme good will there be "a production that is actual and consubstantial" in a way that brings forth "both a beloved and a co-beloved, one generated and one spirated; that is, Father, and Son, and Holy Spirit. If this were not the case, it would not be the supreme good since it would not be supremely self-diffusive."[17] The self-diffusing good identified with the "I am" of the Father brings forth the "I am" of the Son and the Spirit. In much the same way, years later, faithful to the Damascene's stress on God's "I am" and Bonaventure's notion of God's self-diffusing goodness, Heribert Mühlen showed how God's "I am" necessarily involves relatedness to an Other "I am" in mutual self-giving. However, in the totality of their I-being-for-the-Other, a We is revealed.[18]

Despite Bonaventure's insight about God's self-diffusing goodness, it cannot be forgotten that the one who questioned Jesus about eternal life did so from another dimension of the "good," that is, *doing* good (*agathon poiēsō*). The text makes it clear that his desire to *do* good ultimately represents a desire to *become* godly. Such a desire for God involves, according to Bonaventure, a longing to be connected with "the highest good [which] must be self-diffusive" and also, according to Bonaventure, trinitarian. Thus, the rich young man's question about *doing good* and Jesus' response about God alone being good shows the connection between our activity of "doing good" and God's own divine goodness. This notion of our "doing good" being our way of revealing our longing to share in the Trinity's diffusive goodness is wonderfully summarized by Ilia Delio:

> It is goodness itself that provides the metaphysical basis for participating in the dynamic life of the Trinity. The human person must be diffusive in goodness as his or her creation is diffusive, for this is what it is to be and no real *telos* is achieved in its absence. To be God-like is to join in the intense generosity of goodness itself, a generosity that paradoxically grounds intimacy in diversity.[19]

The rich young man's desire to *do* good revealed something within him that was calling him to image God's own goodness. Furthermore, given the representational character of the rich young man, because we ourselves are made in the image of God who is good, the question about *doing* good vis-à-vis God who made us for that goal or purpose is at the heart of God's economy of salvation. How we work this out in community will determine whether the common good is becoming more perfected via patterns that approximate the dynamics of the Economic Trinity.

When the man says that he has "done" the commandments but seeks to "go further," Jesus links the notion of going further to God's own perfection. Thus the *telos* of humankind, according to God's project or economy, is not just to do good, but to be perfect (*teleios*) in the way the *teleios* of the goodness-of-God-communicated-as-trinitarian-relatedness has been revealed (Matt. 5:48).

Given the peasant economy of Jesus' day and the fact that any young man who was rich would have that wealth because of inherited family connections, when Jesus invited him to be part of his new family of disciples he made it clear that such a following demanded that he reorder not only his resources but his personal, familial ties toward those persons without resources, that is, "the poor." If he could do this, he would be perfecting his life on the pattern of what we call the Economic Trinity (Matt. 19:21).

The Perfection of God Revealed in Human Deeds of Goodness toward the Poor

The desire for God that was revealed in the rich young man's question about "doing good" (*agathon poiēsō*) evidences the fact that this ultimately represents a desire to become godly: to share in everlasting life. Jesus' response about doing good in a way that is evidenced in a reordered life on behalf of the poor, which serves as the entrance to the way of perfection, makes the connection even clearer.

The significance of this way of perfection, which represents what Bonaventure calls "the highest good," is evident from the conclusion of the six antithesis statements in Matthew (Matt. 5:20-48). This is especially clear when we consider the fact that Jesus' call for his disciples to "be perfect in the way your heavenly Father is perfect" (Matt. 5:48) envisions a total transformation of the existing culturally binding model of reciprocity that would be manifested among Jesus' new family of disciples.

As I have noted elsewhere,[20] there were essentially three types of reciprocity that defined the "limited-good world" in which Jesus and the authors of the New Testament lived. General reciprocity involved a house-ordering wherein some gave to others without expecting any return (i.e., parent/child dynamics). Balanced reciprocity defined relationships to the "neighbor" insofar as quid-pro-quo patterns defined the giving and receiving among kinfolk. The third form of reciprocity (negative reciprocity) was the exact opposite of the Golden Rule: you did to others what you would not want them to do to you, that is, hostility and warfare toward non-kin—the "enemy."

The context of the famous passage of Matthew 5:48 about being perfect in the way God is perfect is predicated on widening the circle of family to make home for the enemy: "Love your enemies and pray for those who persecute you, *so that you may be sons of your Father who is in heaven; for he makes his sun rise on the evil and on the good, and sends rain on the just and on the unjust.* . . . You, therefore, must be perfect [familial], as your heavenly Father is perfect" (Matt. 5:44-45, 48). Since the first part of the final antithesis statement accepted the assumptions behind the existing familial forms of reciprocity—which undergird the whole imperial social order—it becomes clear from this passage that a new kind of perfect social order was envisioned by Jesus.

The fact that the word *teleios* ("perfect") is used only one other time—in Matthew's Jesus' invitation to the rich young man to extend his resources to the "other" who was poor (Matt. 19:21)—reinforces the radicality of the new human, familial household dynamics that are not only to be reflective of a general reciprocity for a few; now the very ones defined as outsiders—the poor and even one's enemies—must be considered and treated as kin. They are to be one's equals. Consequently, if he truly wanted the perfection of eternal life as a disciple of Jesus and Jesus' gospel, his life must be modeled on the perfect self-giving that is revealed in the Economic Trinity. While Matthew's Jesus later will say that all who do good toward the poor will inherit eternal life (Matt. 25:31-46), here reordering one's resources on behalf of the poor is defined as the sine-qua-non of authentic discipleship.

While Matthew's anonymous youth in Matthew 19 failed to reflect the *teleios* of God's trinitarian ways, in Matthew 26, as we have seen, someone else does. This is the anonymous woman who anointed Jesus' head (Matt. 26:6-13). She not only *did* something that Jesus defined as good (*kalon*); he declared that "what she did" was "performance theology"; it witnessed to the heart of the gospel of the "kingdom of heaven." She engaged the other in his anticipated lack of resources by sharing her resources on his behalf "while he was at table" in the house. Matthew's Jesus canonizes her economic/religious activity as an embodiment of the gospel of the Economic Trinity, which will bring about the economy of salvation (Matt. 26:13).

It is critical that the context of this passage be highlighted here: in Matthew's version, the "good deed" of the woman who engages Jesus in a clearly economic transaction (as indicated by his own followers) takes place "in the house"; furthermore it takes place while he is at table. However, as we can see from the whole structure of Matthew's Gospel, this kind of relating within the house represents the essence of gospel living and the way of discipleship.

Ensuring the Replication of Trinitarian Dynamics

In November 2009, Pope Benedict XVI discussed the trinitarian theologies of Hugh and Richard of St. Victor. Richard had argued for more than one person in the Godhead because of the nature of love, which is the giving of self to the other. This communication of love creates a communion of love. Thus the pope concluded his reflection with an insight apropos the opening of this final section: "The Trinity is truly perfect communion! How the world would change if in families, in parishes and in all other communities relationships were lived following always the example of the three Divine Persons, where each one lives not only with the other, for the other and in the other."[21]

From this papal teleology, it is clear that we need to do a better job of de-linking discourses about the Trinity from categories defined by East and West, substances and essences, and even traditional philosophical and metaphysical treatises about the "one and the many" to stress the need for God's trinitarian economy for the world to find its expression in everyday *relationships* at all levels: personal, communal, and collective, including our institutions of economics, politics, and religion, starting with the church.

If the church is to be a sacrament of God the trinitarian economist, it must reflect the Economic Trinity at all its levels, especially organizationally to be salt of the earth and light of the world. This involves words and deeds that promote the dignity of every person as an equal, that make the resources of its commonwealth (from its administration to the sacramental) available to all, with relationships of power ensuring that there will be no more abuse of that power to protect any interests, structures, and dynamics that are untrinitarian and, to that degree, ungodly, and, to that degree, sinful. This conclusion arises from my understanding of what Pope Benedict XVI envisioned in *Caritas in veritate*. He said:

> The reciprocal transparency among the divine Persons is total and the bond between each of them complete, since they constitute a unique and absolute unity. God desires to incorporate us into this reality of communion as well: "that they may be one even as we are one" (Jn 17:22). The Church is a sign and instrument of this unity. Relationships between human beings throughout history cannot but be enriched by reference to this divine model. In particular, *in the light of the revealed mystery of the Trinity*, we understand that true openness does not mean loss of individual identity but profound interpenetration.[22]

Returning to Russ Roberts's insights about "some things that have stood the test of time," we find that a study of economics as well as the Trinity continually reveals the same three key components as core to their way of operating:

Economic Studies Show How	*Trinitarian Studies Show How*
Different PERSONS	The THREE PERSONS
are in RELATIONSHIP with one another	are in RELATIONSHIP with one another
vis-à-vis the available RESOURCES	vis-à-vis the RESOURCES they share

In my talk at the CTSA I said that the theologian's task is to be faithful to the evangelical vision more than to any institution. The task of what I called the "trinilogian" (in contrast to the "theologian") is to ensure orthodoxy and orthopraxy around the notion of the Economic Trinity and how its pattern must be worked out in the economy of salvation. This demand should lead us, as theologians, to critique our own lives, our communities, and our institutions in its light and let our light shine before all in the house so that God's trinitarian goodness might be diffused more clearly to the ends of the world. This is especially incumbent on us whenever we find ourselves part of a church that may be constitutively trinitarian but evidences in its institutional structures and dynamics untrinitarian relationships. We must apply to the church the same principles of Catholic social teaching we apply to other structures.

Building on the economic base for my interpretation of the Economic Trinity and the economy of salvation, I said:

> When we find patterns and structures manifesting untrinitarian dynamics, especially if they occur in our own church, we should not

be afraid to practice the truth in love in order to make those communities (including the institutional church) more trinitarian (see Eph. 4:15). Furthermore, when we become convinced that the economy of salvation is being co-opted by another "gospel" that is untrinitarian and of the flesh rather than of the Spirit, we must be faithful to the legacy of Paul with the Galatians and expose it as ungodly and, therefore, sinful. Finally, if any organizations are structured in an untrinitarian form, especially religious ones, and are buttressed by an appeal to "God" and "God's will" that justifies this injustice, our task as theologians is to unmask that idolatry and replace its gods with a God that is credible. Faith seeking understanding demands nothing less.

I concluded that talk as I will this chapter: "The integrity of the theological process is at stake; so is the integrity of the Economic Trinity we call God."

8 _____

Jesus' Call to Asceticism

Contemporary Discipleship as a New Catholic Dao

One of the perks in teaching at the School of Applied Theology in Berkeley, California, is the gift of free passes to the YMCA. One evening, in the Spring Session of 2011, I was relaxing in the sauna after my workout. Only one other person was there. I watched in wonder as this young man went through some ritual gestures. These involved his whole body and controlled his whole concentration; he seemed oblivious to my presence. When he seemed to break his concentration, I asked him what he was doing.

He explained that he was disciplining his body as a way of practicing aikido. When I asked him to explain how such gestures helped him, he said that aikido, like many related words having a *dō* at the end (such as tae kwon do or hapkido) stresses the *practice* of a teaching more than the teaching itself. While he knew it was important to know the teachings of "the masters" who had taught him and whom he had read, he found it to be much more important to put these teachings into practice. Indeed, he was not as concerned about getting the teachings right; he was concentrating on the bodily practice to help him get the teachings translated in his life.

His brief and simple explanation turned the lights on for me. From my knowledge of the way Jesus is portrayed in all four Gospels, he clearly evidenced more concern for his disciples putting his teachings into practice than being correct about their articulation. Orthopraxy trumped orthodoxy every time. Thus, in Matthew's Gospel, all those who hear his words and *do* them (puts them into practice) reflect authentic discipleship; they have built their house on rock (Matt. 7:24). Indeed, all those disciples who *do* the will of his "Father in heaven" reveal themselves to constitute the mothers, brothers, and sisters in this household or family (Matt. 12:48-50). In Luke's Gospel too, this notion is echoed in Mary's words about having God's word "be done" in her (Luke 1:38). In other words, what the young man talked about regarding the *dō* in some practice like aikido is what Matthew's Jesus talks about in the "doing." Even of himself he declared that his actions would determine whether or not he reflected the promises related to the Messiah (see Matt. 11:6).

Jesus' theology, to use the adjective used so many times by Pope Benedict XVI, was much more "performative" than "informative." It seems the first Christians understood this much better than we do. They first described themselves simply as those who belonged to and practiced "the Way" (Acts 9:2; 19:9, 23; 22:4, 14, 22).[1] Their practice of love defined them as Christians, and even today Pope Benedict XVI points to the ethos that defined them: "The Gospel is the greatest power for transformation in the world, but it is neither a utopia nor an ideology. The first Christian generations called it rather the 'way,' that is, the way of living that Christ practiced first and invites us to follow" as contemporary disciples.[2]

Right after the young man explained to me what he meant by *dō*, an older man (i.e., my age!) entered the sauna. He was very thin, with white hair and a white beard. He looked like some kind of guru, an impression reinforced when he also began another kind of ritual gesture with his body. As I had done with the young man, I asked him to explain what he had been doing. Again, the word *dao* was the term he used to describe the discipline he had been practicing. Unlike the young man, however, he defined himself not just as a practitioner of his particular *dao* but as one of its teachers. He explained that he was a Sufi.

Building on the comments of the young man, I asked the Sufi all sorts of questions about his notion and discipline of *dao*. He seemed more than eager to teach me. So, for the next half hour or so, inside and outside the sauna, sitting in our white towels provided by the YMCA, it became clear to me that while both men had been highly formed in their different traditions, the unifying element for both practices revolved around clear *dao*s that would evidence fidelity to certain teachings.

As noted earlier, this realization made it ever clearer to me that we need to take more seriously the insight of Pope Benedict XVI about the rightness of our theologies being performed or practiced in our lives. It also made me wonder if this may be the reason why, because he has awareness regarding other religions and their *dao*s, Pope Benedict XVI is now stressing the need for the church to witness to a performative theology to evidence the real personal effectiveness of any informative theology.

The *Archē* for a "Way" or *Dao* of Be[com]ing a Disciple

The last two chapters showed how, as a way of making his evangelical proclamation a performance (or his informative theology, performative theology), Jesus embodied its translation in his words and deeds. Immediately after *informing* people of the gospel or good news that the reign of God had broken into the universe in a new and powerful way, Jesus enacted this message in the way he called his disciples. Thus, Jesus' Synoptic proclamation of the new reign of the divine family's trinitarian connectedness (Matt. 4:17) was immediately put into practice in the way Jesus called Peter and Andrew, James and John, to move from the old way of familial relatedness defined by patriarchal ways to a new one (Matt. 18-22) that would be evidenced in a family of equal brothers and sisters no longer under patriarchal forms of domination leading all the way to the emperor in Rome but all the way to his "Father in heaven" (Matt. 12:46-50).

In reading the Synoptic accounts, we find that all three show clearly that Jesus called for a new way of doing business. Thus, in the way he called the first disciples, they *left* the one business model based on patriarchal patterns and turf dynamics vis-à-vis fishing; they *embarked* on another model wherein they became defined in a pattern of equal brothers and sisters under a "heavenly Father" rather than the *pater patriae* in Rome.

Clearly, in his human form, Jesus himself may not have interpreted the dynamics involved as I have tried to unpack them here. The underlying pattern, however, shows clearly that he was issuing a call to replicate at every level of human relationships the divine household and its pattern of belonging. In this fashion, the pattern of the divine, trinitarian architect would be replicated in all patterns of human relationship.

Archē (the root for words like "architect," "archetype," and "overarching") means "originating or original source." Other meanings include "beginning," "first cause," "prime mover," "ultimate ruler or authority." *Archē* also is the root for many words dealing with *power*: monarchy,[3] patriarchy, hierarchy, kyriarchy, and even anarchy. *Archē* can also involve a kind of originating "type" or model able to be replicated. If God is the *archē* of everything, we can only come to one conclusion. Given this quite-brief development of images connected to *archē*, it does not take much to conclude that the Trinity, as ultimate *archē*, made male and female to image itself. How? By constituting all creaturely architecture in a way that would be patterned on the divine archetype. The architecture of this divine archetype has been imprinted in everything that has been created not only as its source but its goal.

Building on this notion, we can conclude that Jesus' proclamation of the gospel of what we now call "the kindom" reveals a plan (an "economy") that evidences a certain modeling. Every house follows a certain architectural plan, a blueprint; this involves a plan meant to be followed at every stage of development. Likewise, the "ordering" of the house (*oikia*) that has been revealed in the Economic Trinity is the *archē* to be built at every level of life: the personal, the communal, and the collective. Following our metaphor of the "house," the *archē* of the Trinity is the archetype as well as the underlying architecture that must be patterned in our personal *oikia*, at the level of the *oikonomia* (communal) as well as the whole *oikoumenē* (global) for the integrity of the *oikologia* (creation) itself.

Since the Trinity has made/makes us as male and female to image the divine way of being and connectedness, we have been constitutively formed "from the beginning" to be connected to one another and everything in a way that reveals our identity as images of God's trinitarian connectedness. Like each person in the Godhead, none of us can say "I am" except in equal relatedness to another "I am." Thus, we have been called or elected from the beginning to be the very architectural embodiment of the divine *archē*. The primal power or *archē* of trinitarian connectedness, informed and performed in and through love, constitutes the basis of our identity (our "I am"). Everything and everyone, as we shall later explore, has been made in and because of that love to reveal and perform that love in our lives for the integrity of the whole created universe. Using contemporary language, we can say that, since all the information that defines the Trinity was made flesh in the Word, we who have been formed by that Word are called to put into practice the reign of that trinitarian God in our world that is the ultimate source and energy at the heart of each and every one of its constitutive parts .

Pope Benedict XVI made this connection abundantly clear about the Trinity's relationships in heaven as constituting the font, source, or *archetype* on earth that is revealed throughout creation when he said (on the Feast of the Holy Trinity in 2009):

> The Trinity does not live in a splendid solitude, but is rather an inexhaustible font of life that unceasingly gives itself and communicates itself.
>
> In some way we can intuit this, whether we observe the macrouniverse: our earth, the planets, the stars, the galaxies; or the microuniverse: cells, atoms, elementary particles. The "name" [i.e., reality] of the Most Holy Trinity is, in a certain way, impressed upon everything that exists, because everything that exists, down to the last particle, is a being in relation, and thus God-relatedness shines forth, ultimately creative Love shines forth.

Going further in applying the "divine model" to human relationships that have been made to reveal the trinitarian architect, he said: "Using an analogy suggested by biology, we could say the human 'genome' is profoundly imprinted with the Trinity, of God-Love."[4]

Making Sense of the Trinity in and for a Quantum World

Having outlined the vision of how the plan of God for all creation is to have its architecture modeled on the trinitarian archetype, while being faithful to our traditional understandings of its dynamics (as highlighted in both the Eastern and Western churches), we would do well to find a way to frame what we can explain about the Trinity that reinforces what we know from science about the way the world (made by this Trinity) really works. This leads us to stress a little-discussed dimension of the members of the Trinity that has always been at the heart of the trinitarian theology of the Eastern Fathers: their relationships. Faithful to this approach, the Orthodox theologian John Zizioulas says that the originating *archē*, or primordial and ontological reality, is what grounds all persons within the one divine substance. He insists that "the being of God is a relational being: without the concept of communion it would not be possible to speak of the being of God."[5]

In this quantum age, such an approach is necessary not only for the sake of providing more helpful approaches to the trinitarian mystery but to preclude aberrations arising from existing stresses. Indeed, for some time, theologians from the Protestant Jürgen Moltmann to the Catholic Catherine Mowry LaCugna have clearly shown how any "theologizing" that stresses "the *One* in Three" rather than "the *Three* in One" and, even more, their relationships, can undermine not just the theological project but subtly sustain and justify untrinitarian ecclesiastical structures. (Later we will see that both forms fail to stress the "in"). Thus Moltmann writes:

> As long as the unity of the triune God is understood monadically or subjectivistically, and not in Trinitarian terms, the whole cohesion of a religious legitimation of political sovereignty continues to exist. It is only when the doctrine of the trinity vanquishes the monotheistic notion of the great universal monarch in heaven, and his divine patriarchs in the world, that earthly rulers, dictators and tyrants cease to find any justifying religious archetypes any more.[6]

Having said this, I am aware that LaCugna cautions against "projecting" trinitarian relationships onto human ones as a way to support either "a hierarchical *or* egalitarian vision." When either *monē archē* or *triadikē archē* becomes the sole lens, theology and theologians become "blind to their own ideological construction of reality, likewise supposedly rooted in the nature of God's inner life."[7] Arguing for a "Christian trinitarian monotheism," LaCugna concludes that, had we adapted this balanced model, "a different political and social order likewise would have prevailed."[8]

With LaCugna's conclusion in mind, we need to recall why Jesus' vision of the reign of what we have called the Economic Trinity brought him into conflict with the religious leaders of his day. It envisioned a different social and religious order than the prevailing ones. The fact that he actually created a basic community to serve as an alternative to the dominant imperial and religious models by calling his disciples to form a new "business" model of organization in contrast to the prevailing underlying metaphor of hierarchy and patriarchy as the model for house-ordering cannot be discounted either. Even further, by subtly linking such discipleship with a way of economic modeling that would help his disciples be "perfect in the way" of the Economic Trinity (see Matt. 5:48), he demands that we model all relationships at all levels on earth as they are in heaven.

Signs of the "Kindom" of Heaven Meant to Be Manifest on Earth

As we consider the relationships "in heaven" that must be replicated in human relationships, we would be well advised to disabuse ourselves of any notion of heaven as a *place* we enter or go to ("up there") when we die. This is especially important when we read in the Gospel stories about Jesus looking up to heaven in conversation with his "Father," or the one in Luke that says that, after his death and resurrection appearances to his disciples, Jesus "was carried up into heaven" (Luke 24:51) or, as Acts articulates regarding the Ascension, how "he was taken up" (Acts 1:2). The traditional notion of heaven as a place gets even more challenging when space/time images are used of Mary's Assumption "into heaven" when the official teaching states of "the Immaculate Virgin" that, "when the course of her earthly life was finished, [she] was taken up body and soul into heavenly glory."[9]

In my mind, one of the most important and far-reaching teachings of Pope John Paul II involves his locutions about the last things: heaven, hell, and purgatory. In these Wednesday discourses, Pope John Paul said that heaven and hell were not places one "went to"; rather they were *states* of being. In other words, they reflect the actual experience of (not) being in relationship with the trinitarian God. Heaven and hell are not places but eternal ways of being.

When I was a novice, we were taught a passage that remains with me to this day: "Heaven begins on earth or it never begins at all." What I have come to learn about the power of these words is that, when Jesus in the Synoptics spoke about the "kingdom of heaven," he was, above all, talking about a way we were to be in relationship with one another that imaged that of the trinitarian relationship. We were to put into practice his teachings about this reign that would be expressed in such dynamics of love-in-action as mercy, forgiveness, justice, peace, and compassion. Such virtues define the force-field of God's reign.

In his teachings, especially his parables, he revealed quite clearly the *dao* of what we must do to be part of God's reign. Since Jesus revealed God to be a lover whose love spilled over into creation and the incarnation, it is evident that those who remain in that love and evidence that love in their relationships abide or remain in God. But our understanding of his teachings about heaven goes further too. This involves the notion of the signs of the kingdom of God revealed by Jesus to represent divine *energies* or *powers* that are in us; these are meant to be extended to others in the ways we *energize* and *empower* them, especially in their needs for such things as mercy, forgiveness, justice, peace, and compassion, thus our grasp of them as force-fields of energy.

Various writers have distinguished between God's "I" (God's nature or *ousia*) and God's activities or action (*energeiai*), saying that, until Jesus Christ and his announcement of the reign or action of God in the world, God was known only in God's *energeiai*. These energies revealed God to be merciful and forgiving, faithful and truthful, just and peaceful, caring and compassionate. When God's people revealed these energies in their lives, they would be giving evidence that their lives were revealing God's holiness (Lev. 19:2).

With the advent of Jesus and his proclamation of the reign of God or "energies of trinitarian connectedness," which he revealed in his person and practice, Jesus showed how these energies were signs of the *basileia*. From the loving practice of mercy and forgiveness, fidelity and truth, justice and peace, and care and compassion, it follows that when we reveal these dynamics to others who need them they also reveal the ultimate energy source within us. To the degree we reveal them to others in need, this will be the measure of our ultimate share in the divine energy itself. In our *dao* of them we actually extend the reign or power of God into those relationships in our life and world that still remain in need of them. The image that comes to me when I think of this yin and yang way of remaining in and revealing the *basileia* in and beyond us revolves around a certain kind of energy. From within we are impelled to witness to this reality; however, the parallel to this impelling within us is propelled by the need for these signs of the *basileia* to be revealed in the face of any need for them throughout creation.

This understanding of the way we are called to experience and express the signs of the kingdom is very evident, for instance, when we look at one example taught by Jesus regarding the way we are called to extend to others the mercy and forgiveness of debts we have experienced ourselves. These become concrete ways we hear and put into practice the impelling/propelling challenge: "You, therefore, *must be* perfect, as your heavenly Father, is perfect" (which means that we are to be trinitarian in the way God is trinitarian [5:48]).

Within the bookends of what it means to be part of the *basileia tōn ouranōn*, we hear the promise that those who show (evidence) mercy will receive (experience) mercy (Matt. 5:7). Later in the Sermon on the Mount, we find that authentic prayer involves that kind of jubilee justice that demands that we have the courage ask God to "forgive us our debts *as* we have forgiven our debtors" (Matt. 6:12). This Matthean text means we must seek realistic ways not only to forgive personal transgressions as God forgives us, but especially social debts (including those contemporary debts that find people fearing foreclosures or those held by the Christian West regarding their brothers and sisters in less economically developed nations). Such an interpretation of the text becomes even clearer when we recall that kingdom story told by Jesus in Matthew 18 as part of that Gospel's vision of a new order for the house churches regarding their *dao* with one another.

Responding to Peter's frustrated question about the limits of forgiveness that might be extended to recalcitrant members of the community, Jesus tells the story of the man who was in debt—to the tune of ten million days' wages. Since he had no way to pay, he was treated as any other common debtor. However, because he made his need known to the authority holding the debt and asked for patience (a sign of the Spirit [Gal 5:22]), the heart of the debt holder was propelled to do something. The ruler was "moved with compassion" in a way that led to the debtor's release and the forgiveness of his debts. Now that he has experienced this energy of God's *basileia* it can be expected that he will be impelled to extend the same power of that forgiveness which he has received to those, who, like him, may be in need of it *from* him.

But this does not happen. Instead, when he sees another in need, he refuses to forgive him his debt. As Jesus tells the story, this is not just a matter of a refusal to cancel a small payment of 100 days' wages; it represents an affront to God insofar as this person has refused to extend the reign of God's forgiveness which he has received by sharing it with another in need. Thus the condemnatory words: "You wicked servant! I forgave you all your debt because you besought me; and should not you have had mercy on your fellow servant, as I had mercy on you?" (Matt. 18:32-33).

Being part of and practicing the *dao* of the "kindom of trinitarian connectedness" is like a circle: the more we practice its dynamics of forgiveness and mercy, along with justice and peace, fidelity and truth, the more we become transformed or energized by these dynamics themselves. Because this energy (to forgive and show mercy, plus all the other signs) is within us, empowering us, we are able to do such things. If we do not reveal such forms of God's loving perfection, we put ourselves outside the reign of that perfection. The yin and yang of this dynamic move us ever more into the perfection or Trinity of God. If we choose to be part of these dynamics we will be part of the heavenly reign; if we choose not to participate in them, we are free to do so. But that freedom not to be part of the reign of God's dynamics will find us in what we have known to be hell. We put ourselves outside God's energy.

Discipleship as the Christian *Dao*:
The *Dao* as Asceticism

When Jesus began his public ministry by saying "Follow me" (Matt. 4:19; see Matt. 4:22; 9:9), he made it clear that his notion of following involved a way of moving away from one culturally received model related to how business was to be conducted to another one: from a patriarchal way to a familial model defined by the equality of brothers and sisters living in the *basileia* of the one he called *our* "heavenly Father." The form of "following" which this entailed involved a definite counter-cultural way of being and doing. This defined a transformative model for the whole imperial and religious reality of Jesus' day, beginning with the constitution of a new kind of household-, family- and economic-order. Using a contemporary phrase, this involved a whole new "business model." Discipleship in such a way demanded discipline; this discipline would have to outline a clear *askēsis* (literally, practice of worship, filial piety, or way of engaging in business). In Jesus' call, it involved the way his received teaching would be translated in one's life. The way this form of discipleship would be lived out can be defined as domestic asceticism.

I came to this insight and significance as I was preparing to give a keynote address in 2010 at the Washington Theological Union. The theme chosen for the annual Franciscan Symposium there was "Greed, Lust, and Power: Models of Fraternal Economics." I don't think I have ever been given such an intriguing topic.

Given the financial crisis facing the nation at that time, it was quite clear that greed, lust, and power represented key underlying (capital) sins that had contributed to the crisis being experience in the nation. In fact, a pair of authors had only recently referred to the dynamics of "outsized ambition, greed, and corruption" that led to the "Economic Armageddon" experienced by the United States and the whole global financial system. Echoing our metaphor of house, the authors pointed to the breakdown of the U.S. economy as being linked to the market manipulators or "housers," as they have been called.[10] Given the market mindset that is reinforced by the ideology of the market and the greed it masks that has claimed the hearts of so many who claim to be disciples of Jesus, it became evident to me that these capital sins could be countered effectively only by a viable alternative. This would have to encompass a life-giving, counter-cultural "way." This demanded a new kind of evangelical asceticism.

While preparing my remarks, I discovered the work on New Testament asceticism by Leif E. Vaage. In 1995 he wrote a chapter in a volume on asceticism edited by Vincent Wimbush and Richard Valantasis. In it he described asceticism as:

a certain disciplinary techne of the body as the specific means deemed most likely to permit the achievement of a stipulated end. All share, in other words, the same form of cultural "engineering," a discernible and distinct style of "crafting" the social self. Thus the pragmatic and theoretical wager that, through "asceticism," one can enjoy a still unrealized, but progressively anticipated, greater sense of personal well-being.[11]

While I liked Vaage's description of asceticism, another definition of and dynamics associated with asceticism (especially its counter-cultural ones) by an editor of the above book captured my attention and imagination. Richard Valantasis wrote that authentic asceticism involves "performances within a dominant social environment intended to inaugurate a new subjectivity, different social relations, and an alternative symbolic universe."[12] Continuing his thoughts reflecting a counter-cultural power lens, he argued, "Asceticism does not simply reject other ways of living. . . ." Any resulting rejection occurs "precisely in order to embrace another existence, another way of living embodied in a new subjectivity, alternative social relations, and a new imaging of the universe."[13] The consequent threat to prevailing power dynamics and relationships becomes evident in his conclusion: "This intentionality has power—power to create a new person, power to restructure society, power to revise the understanding of the universe."[14]

If the house was the basic unit of the whole imperial household as the apex of the pyramid of households organized into towns and the towns into cities and the cities, with their trade routes creating and maintaining the empire, to call for a new kind of household, like Jesus did, also involved a call for a converted social order. To achieve this demanded a whole new discipline; this entailed the creation of a new kind of "architecture," a new power dynamic that would be expressed in domestic asceticism.

When I consider the dynamics involved in Jesus' proclamation of the "kingdom of God" and the execution of the new order implicit in that proclamation through his performance of it in the calling of the disciples then and in the future (Matt. 28:19-20), I can no longer interpret them apart from *power* dynamics. Using Valantasis's definition, Matthew's way of communicating the "call" to discipleship in that outpost of imperial Rome clearly reveals the fact that Jesus meant to create "a new subjectivity, alternative social relations, and a new imaging of the universe." History has shown that, while this might look like a small beginning on the shores of a small "sea" called Galilee in an outpost of imperial Rome, it would have cosmic reverberations. The invitation to Peter and Andrew, James and John "to leave" their home and its way of doing business was a call to change the underlying power dynamics throughout the then-known world. It had economic, political, and, above all (given Jesus' confrontation with his own religious leaders), religious and spiritual consequences that would be universal, impacting generations to come. That this power sharing is to continue, aided by the abiding presence of the *exousia* of Jesus Christ, is evident from the wording of the Great Commission (Matt. 28:16-20).

In 1999 Vaage, along with Vincent L. Wimbush, edited *Asceticism in the New Testament*.[15] However, it was his article in the *Catholic Biblical Quarterly* ten years later that captured my immediate attention. As I have mentioned, because I wrote my doctoral dissertation on the metaphor of "house" (*oikia/oikos*) in Matthew's Gospel and how this metaphor imaged an entirely new social order, I was intrigued by the title of Vaage's piece in the *CBQ*: "An Other Home: Discipleship in Mark as Domestic Asceticism." In this article on Mark's Gospel (which I applied to Matthew's), Vaage made a connection between Jesus' house of disciples and the *dao* of the religions of the Indian Subcontinent.

> I reflect the fact that the household is here [in the Gospel of Mark] the site where the otherwise "anti-(conventional) family" and "familiar" habits of discipleship are supposed to be practiced. I also mean to suggest something else. I take the phrase "domestic asceticism" from Patrick Olivelle's discussion of the history of Brahmanism, in which Olivelle has demonstrated how older Vedic forms of religion came to incorporate (and thereby to co-opt) the challenge to the traditional social order(s) of the Indian Subcontinent, which the more radically world-denying asceticism of early Buddhism and Jainism embodied. Something similar, I think, is true for Mark vis-à-vis other more radical or utopian early Christianities such as those represented by "Q" [as found in Matthew and Luke].[16]

With such insights he concludes, "the proper and most effective way to enter the kingdom of God is by redoing life at home. This may be the evangelist's most enduring challenge to us."[17]

If Jesus created a new business model that involved joining his newly ordered family of disciples, this meant he was calling for a new way of religious belonging that would have cosmic implications (insofar as the empire was viewed to be the center of the world with all households together creating its base). Fidelity to his way or practice of ordering life demanded what we thus can call the *dao* of discipleship. Building on our metaphor of "house" and realizing what Jesus came to bring about, through a change in the basic domestic household, we see the inbreaking of the household of trinitarian relatedness, the practice of the *dao* of discipleship, as becoming evident when we work to bring about trinitarian patterns at every level of the world into which we are sent (see Matt. 28:16-20). The fact that Matthew has reworked the asceticism of Mark and made it more clearly identified with Jesus' disciples for all time is evident in a comment by Mary Ann Tolbert. She writes, "The Gospel of Matthew, with its concern for the perfection of the Christian and the learning that fits one for the kingdom of God, is much more amenable to the picture of later ascetic spiritual formation than anything that can be found in Mark."[18]

When I was writing this chapter, the bishops of England and Wales had just called on Catholics in those nations to abstain from meat on Fridays throughout the year, not only Lent. Their reason involved the effort to realize "a clear and a distinctive mark of their own Catholic identity." They argued that a communal expression of this fasting would evidence the belief that the "best habits are those which are acquired as part of a common resolve and common witness."[19] When I read the actual statement and purpose of it, it became clear that imposing such an obligation (albeit one that they said could be rejected in favor of some other unnamed obligatory penance) might reinforce the kind of sacrifice that appeals to Culture I Catholics; however, it would be rejected as a throw-back by Culture II Catholics and become as meaningless as other fasts that are called without a clear purpose save the practice of asceticism itself.

This led me to realize that Culture II Catholics cannot just reject such sincere attempts to preserve a Catholic identity. *They must develop their own ascetical practices* that offer to a new culture of meaning. And, as I have argued thus far in this book, the key ascetical program as outlined by Jesus himself, was the evangelical embrace of "the cross" that would come from practicing that form of discipleship that would insist on the performance of trinitarian relatedness at every level of life. When communities of equality, beginning with the Roman Church itself, would witness to such structures, and, in the words of the bishops, become "visible in the public arena, then it is also an important act of witness." Abstaining from meat will not get anyone crucified; however, when we develop new forms of asceticism that create "a new subjectivity, alternative social relations, and a new imaging of the universe" in our church and nation, contemporary forms of crucifixion will not be far behind. Such ascetical practices that challenge the existing economic, political, and ecclesiastical order will incur the same response for the disciples that the teacher promised (Matt. 5:10-11; 10:16-23). This may not reflect some of the asceticism found in our tradition, but it is at the core of how the scriptures define any true disciple.

When we probe more deeply the "*dao* of discipleship," we find it involving a key ascetical discipline associated with the notion of "withdrawal." Indeed, the notion of withdrawal (*anachōrein* [verb form]) has always been associated with the dynamics of the ascetical life. Asceticism demands a withdrawal from one way of living to embrace an alternative form of life. Thus we find in four places in Matthew's Gospel (Matt. 2:13-15, 19-23; 4:12-16; 12:14-21) a Matthean triadic structure centered on the dynamics of "withdrawal." It describes (1) some kind of destructive pattern expressed in the form of a conflict or violence of some sort; (2) the consequent action of "withdrawal" (*anachōrein*); and, finally, (3) the realization that through this withdrawal (and only through it), will the scriptures be fulfilled in that person as well as that situation.

The assumption guiding this triad is the insight that God's work and God's will, as revealed in the scriptures (which are informed in order to be performed), cannot be fulfilled in conflicted situations and violence. In order for the scriptures to be fulfilled in people, they must find a way to withdraw from the way of violence, at least in their minds, to become free from "the sin of the world"; the *dao* continues the process with commitment to "put into practice" the core vision of the gospel and becoming discipled to that.

While tradition has it that the "Matthew" (*Matthaios*) of Matthew's Gospel was the one who sat "at the tax booth" and followed Jesus (Matt. 9:9), few contemporary scholars following the historical-critical method agree. The question thus arises as to who was the "Matthew" identified with authorship of the First Gospel. It has been my contention that, since the disciples of every age (according to Matthew) are those who put into practice "everything" Jesus has taught (Matt. 28:20), the Matthew of the First Gospel appears likely to have been a collective personality represented by any disciple (*mathētēs*) who has been taught (*mathēteutheis*) and who understands (*synienai*) the personal, communal, and institutional implications of that teaching, that is, the need to put these teachings into practice—to make performative the words of which one has been informed.

The Matthean notion of understanding (*synienai*) differs from its Markan source precisely here: while Mark's notion involves a lack of cerebral understanding of what is taught, the Matthean redaction invariably points to the need to act on what has been taught and understood. Thus Jesus asks at the end of the third sermon that constitutes many of the Matthean parables: "Have you understood (*synienai*) all this?" and they answer, "yes" (Matt. 13:51). At this Matthew's Jesus immediately links two of the metaphors we have used throughout this book (*basileia* and *oikos/oikia*) in declaring: "Therefore every scribe who has been trained (*mathēteutheis*) for the kingdom of heaven is like the master of a household (*oikodespótēs*) who brings out of his treasure what is new and what is old" (Matt. 13:52).

Of all the Gospels, only Matthew uses the word *mathēteutheis*. It means "one who is learned" in the teacher's ways, "one discipled" to a teacher who puts into practice the master's teachings. Here the word is used of *any* "householder." Later it will identify Joseph of Arimathea (27:57). The final time it is used is in the Great Commission, or final words of Jesus on the day of resurrection. Having earlier said he had been "sent only to the lost sheep of the *house* of Israel"

(15:24) and having himself sent his own apostles only "to the lost sheep of the *house* of Israel" (10:6), the resurrected Jesus now breaks all boundaries. This demands that those now united to him evidence his teachings throughout the *whole world*: "Go therefore and make disciples (*mathēteutheis*) of all nations, baptizing them in the name of the Father and of the Son and of the Holy Spirit, and teaching them to obey everything I have commanded you. And remember, I am with you always, to the end of the age" (28:19-20). Ultimately then, all persons who fulfill the words and works of the Gospel of *Matthaîos* are to be its *mathēteutheis*. As such they are to be its final redaction in the world; they are to become its living embodiment—personally, communally, and organizationally.

Years after this proclamation I was in a part of the "whole world" that found me meeting two men in the sauna in Berkeley. Their conversations about their particular *daos* invited me on a journey that has shown the need for a new kind of Catholic asceticism, as envisioned in Vaage's insights. The more generic *dao* of domestic asceticism as envisioned in Jesus' call to discipleship in Matthew's Gospel needs to be enfleshed in clearer signs or *energies* of that *basileia* (as in mercy and forgiveness, etc.). Along with these, they will demand seven new ways of living for contemporary Catholics, which will be outlined in Part III.

PART III_____

THE *DAO* OF BEING A "KINDOM" CATHOLIC

The Practice of Seven Contemporary Sacramentals

In Part I, I discussed the crisis that faces the culturally and historically conditioned institutionalized model of Roman Catholicism. I highlighted the resulting lack of meaning that it represents for ever-increasing numbers of people in
the West. In Part II, I showed how this overly institutionalized model of church
reflects some of the same dynamics that Jesus faced as he came proclaiming his
gospel. Increasingly, as the meaning of his message became clearer and people "left" the "received" interpretations of their religion for his proclamation
of the "kingdom/kindom of God/Trinity," he found himself opposed by the
religious leaders with their interpretation of the Law. He declared that their
ways put them outside the fulfillment of justice (the original purpose of the
Law and the demand of the prophets before him). These leaders had "eyes to
see but would not see" and "ears to hear but would not listen." They were not
open to real dialogue because they believed they possessed the truth. Their
only response to his message would fit the culture of the day: challenge and
counter-challenge, retort and riposte. The result was his rejection of their ways
with the words: "For the sake of your tradition, you have made void the word
of God. You hypocrites! Well did Isaiah prophesy of you, when he said: 'This
people honors me with their lips, but their heart is far from me; in vain do they
worship me, teaching as doctrines the precepts of men'" (Matt. 15:6-9; Mark
7:6-8).

From there I showed that his notion of discipleship invited people to follow him and join together in bringing about another way of living within that
religion and the wider empire that encompassed it. I suggested that this "way"
must ground all asceticism in future Roman Catholicism in the West.

How this way can be outlined and followed is the challenge of this third
and last part of my book. I call this the *dao* of contemporary Catholicism. I
see it involving an additional seven "sacramentals" that envision, through their
practice, a new and hopeful way of practicing Catholicism in a way that might

123

enhance and enrich our church. However, at this point in this book I must explain here why I think such a *dao* is needed.[1]

My conclusion about the need for a Catholic *dao* was germinated at a colloquium at which I spoke at Loyola Marymount University, April 24, 2004. Probably because I had written a couple books on celibacy[2] I was asked to represent the "Catholic" approach to celibacy at the Catholic-Hindu Dialog that was to take place that day. The theme was "Sacred Celibacy: A Hindu-Catholic Dialogue." I had decided that my approach to the "way" one could be a healthy Catholic celibate would revolve around the triad of "fasting" from, for, and with, as I had discussed in my books.

When I finished my sharing I thought I had done a pretty good job. However, upon listening to the Hindu representative, Adrian Piper, speak, I was embarrassed at my inability to articulate a real "way" to be celibate that came from official Catholicism. She had come from Wellesley College to share her insights on the Hindi notion of *brahmacharya*. She had developed this approach in an article she wrote for the book *How We Live Our Yoga*.[3]

Her *dao* of *brahmacharya* revealed a highly developed discipline. It is meant to help those practicing celibacy embrace it with the help of a step-by-step practice that enabled its adherents to bring meaning to their lives and commitment. The more I heard her, the more it became clear to me how lacking we are in our own tradition to help all those we say are "called" or expected to be celibate or chaste "for the kingdom." This call (in its official interpretation) involves five groups: those who are not yet married; those who are widowed or divorced; diocesan priests in the Latin Rite and vowed religious and members of secular institutes; and homosexuals. While stressing the biblical basis for this celibacy (which I have critiqued elsewhere[4]), the *Catechism of the Catholic Church* offers little or no guidelines or way this can be lived out. Indeed, I have found no real practice, or *dao*, to guide celibates in a *Catholic way to be celibate* anywhere, whether in the writings of the Fathers or the teachings of those considered to be the founders of religious congregations. Any discipline related to the practice of celibacy seems to echo a Nancy Reagan equivalent of her suggestion for those tempted to use illicit drugs: "Just say 'no.'"

Subsequent to this experience I heard from others, especially younger people desiring a Catholic identity, that they could find no help in their effort to remain celibate. As one young man told me, "We are told to do many things by Jesus and have been given many commands, like the great command or others associated with mercy and forgiveness, compassion and even prayer, but we have never been given the tools for practicing celibacy. We're told what we must do but not how we can do it."

The *dao* had its origins in China.[5] Believing that the same energy empowering the universe lay deep within one's own physical body, the Chinese developed practices whereby one could move toward greater harmonization of these macro- and micro-energies that were taught by their masters. These teachings and practices involved a *dao*.

Interpreting the beliefs of one religion (i.e., Catholicism) from the centuries-old and highly developed practices of another religion (such as Buddhism, which does not believe in a personal God) can do a disservice to both or be accused of a new kind of religious colonialism.[6] Aware of this danger, I think we need new rituals to help the upcoming generations become "practicing Catholics" in ways that include but go beyond their participation in Mass and the sacraments and their acceptance of our basic creeds.

The subtitle of this book is *Becoming a "Kindom" Catholic*. While I have spent quite a bit of time thus far explaining that "kindom" involves the new kind of family of equals, imaging the trinitarian God, at all levels of life and the seven new sacramentals to clothe it, I will not be spending any significant time developing the notion of what it means to be "Catholic" in light of such insights. I do this for one main reason: it has already been done, and better than I could ever do, by Ilia Delio, OSF, in her wonderful 2011 book (also from Orbis) *The Emergent Christ: Exploring the Meaning of Catholic in an Evolutionary Universe*.

Grounded in the convictions discussed in Part II, this final part of the book outlines a contemporary Catholic *dao*. It builds on the traditional notion of communal sacramentality (external signs or practices) to help its disciples or practitioners be more consciously connected, in Christ, to everyone and everything in the universe in a way that will be both contemplatively and compassionately grounded. This kind of *dao* for Catholics of the twenty-first century might not offer specific ways to live more celibately or chastely or provide other religious practices that already are part of the tradition of being Catholic, such as private devotions like the rosary and adoration of the Blessed Sacrament. Rather, these practices can evidence a *Catholic dao* that fulfills the great command of Jesus under the umbrella of relevance or meaningfulness. This includes a sevenfold approach to God, self, and others that involves the practice of cosmic awareness, Christic centeredness, increasing consciousness, greater connectedness, deepening contemplation, and expanding compassion, all of which find their best realization in what is truly Catholic: life-giving community.

Welcome to the *dao!*

9

THE COSMIC WAY

Building on the material outlined in Part II, this chapter begins Part III by grounding our approach to the *dao* of being a contemporary Catholic in the cosmos or creation itself. Given Edward O. Wilson's comments about developing spirituality from an understanding of how "the world really works," this seems appropriate. Given the crisis of the Catholic Church in the West, the need to begin with the story of the universe echoes the oft-quoted sentiment of St. Thomas Aquinas that ignorance about creation will lead to a mistake about God.[1] Building on this insight we can also conclude that without a solid grounding in the cosmic story, any "Catholic Story" will be suspect and, quite possibly, susceptible to continued myths that make less and less sense. Even though we will never have the degree of certitude regarding our religious faith that we find in science, this faith, at the least, must be reasonable if it is to provide meaning.

The word "catholic" involves the notion of being "universal"; universal reminds us of the word "universe." The universe has been made to be a self-creating, living system that reveals a way wherein life comes from non-life and consciousness evolves from non-consciousness. Thus, it is fitting that we offer a contemporary *dao* for Catholicism (along with its received creeds and seven sacraments) that begins with the universe, or the cosmos, itself. In other words, the "universality" that should somehow be found in what it truly means to be a contemporary "Catholic" must now start from what we know about the universe itself. This approach gets reinforced when we realize that, in its broadest meaning, *dao* involves the "way" the universe itself functions and the path that natural events evidence as being part of this functioning. Individuals who practice the *dao* do so to bring better balance to their lives.

At this time in the Catholic Church, especially in places like the United States which evidence a lack of harmony among Catholics who define themselves as Culture I or Culture II, such a *dao* is sorely needed. This need becomes especially critical when the data have shown that our imbalance and lack of harmony in our ecclesial body ultimately does not involve matters of creed or sacraments (i.e., dogma) as much as ecclesiastical or institutional issues around governance and who will be doing the governing. The need to honestly address this issue takes on special importance when, as we saw in Chapter 2, some truth-claims which are called "divine givens," in effect, have been more human in their origin than attributable to the Jesus of history. This invites us to a truly "Catholic" way of integrity that reflects a balance between scripture and tradition wherein neither reinforce unenforceable mythologies. This demands a more scientifically grounded faith that leads one to the "facts" that are found in what science tells us about the world in which we do our believing.[2]

The stress on beginning with solid grounding in cosmology as we seek for meaning in our faith rests on an important assumption about truth itself, especially how we understand and interpret the whole created order. If something is shown to be objectively true in one area of life, such as science, it cannot be contradicted by another, especially if that other source is not grounded in fact as much as faith. When one's faith is contradicted by science, the results do not demean science as much as one's religious beliefs. When religious institutions continue to promote such ungrounded faith as facts they only reinforce the conviction of others about their irrelevance.

Another way believers refuse to ground their faith in what we know from science in ways that continue myths that no longer offer meaning is compartmentalization. This involves the process of thinking that enables one to separate the "truth" of one field from the "truth" of another when they are no longer shown to be compatible with objective facts. Such cognitive dissonance is most often associated with issues around the science available to us about creation and a literal interpretation of the Bible as to how creation came to be.

This dichotomization gets expressed when such an unfounded truth becomes ideological and absolutized into an "ism," in this case, the "ism" of fundamentalism. When this happens, as we saw in Chapter 2, the adherents of such an ideology stubbornly cling to that absolutized truth in a way that colors the rest of their worldview. This absolutizing truth becomes all-embracing in a way that results in this viewpoint becoming the monolithic embodiment of truth: "the only way to interpret."

A good example is the front-page story in *The New York Times* entitled "Believing in Scripture but Playing by Science's Rules." The piece discussed the 197-page doctoral dissertation in geosciences written by Marcus R. Ross, which he submitted in 2006 at the Kingston campus of the University of Rhode Island. It discussed the abundance and spread of mosasaurs. He wrote that these marine reptiles vanished at the end of the Cretaceous era about 65 million years ago. His findings were interpreted as "impeccable." However, the article noted, these findings clashed with his faith-life. The author noted, "Dr. Ross is hardly a conventional paleontologist. He is a 'young earth creationist'—he believes that the Bible is a literally true account of the creation of the universe, and that the earth is at most 10,000 years old."[3] The *Times* piece elaborated on how Ross subscribes to "creation science": the "fact" that, because the Bible says so, God created the world exactly as the Bible says.

Ross is not alone. Gallup data in 2010 showed that, in the United States, his stance of "creationism" is supported by at least 60 percent of people who attend church at least weekly. At the opposite side of the debate about science and creation we find those who support "naturalistic evolution." This promotes a kind of "scientism" which does not allow for a god having anything to do with the origin of creation. In between we find people like me. We believe in the theory of evolution (beginning with the Big Bang 13.4 billion years ago, the coalescence of stardust developing earth about 4.5 billion years ago, the beginning of life a billion years ago, and the evolving of that life through natural selection that has led to the creation of human beings), but also believe that its origins are attributable to the one we call "God." This balance we articulate in the creedal phrase, "I believe in God . . . the creator of heaven and earth."

God's way of creation involves everything we know about God as the energy that energizes the heart of all matter. Thus God *is at the heart of creation.* God's trinitarian "I am" is the archetype of everything and everyone that is because the "is-ness" of everything and everyone is coinherently connected to everything and everyone else. How this happens is secondary; that it is has not been contradicted by any truth connected to the evolutionary process. As a consequence, when we consider animate creation and see that its evolutionary processes have been shown to be evolving for millions of years through natural selection, we who believe should only rejoice that this natural selection is an evolutionary manifestation of the kenotic principle that is at the core of all spirituality. This reveals a dynamic in us and all around us that keeps pressing us forward. In the process, we are energized to move toward ever-greater forms of life (i.e., consciousness for us humans). Furthermore, for us humans, this involves not only a "letting go" of whatever might be an obstacle to the survival of our species and the planet itself but also the realization that the survival and growth of the one is intrinsically interconnected to the other.

Grounding Every Story in the Cosmic Story

Our observable universe contains at least a million galaxies, with more stars than there are grains of sand on all our earth's beaches. Even more, today cosmologists are openly asking if there might not actually be parallel universes to ours. They call this the "multiverse."[4] In this vast quantum world of interconnectedness, the cosmic story is the lens through which we are called to interpret all of our other key stories. Because an understanding of its reality impacts everything in creation, its narration will impact how we understand

and interpret anew the key stories dealing with our nations and our church, our scriptures and our spiritual lives.

According to Terrence J. Moran, C.Ss.R., when we realize that "our generation of humanity is the first to have access to a scientifically accurate story of the origins of the universe," we realize the tremendous responsibility contained in this fact to make sure our other stories do not lie outside that basic story. He explains:

> The new story of cosmic origins comes not from inspired sacred texts or from religious authority figures but from empirical observation. This new story, therefore, has enormous unifying possibilities. No longer can the central religious concern of our day be the competing and often contradictory claims of faith traditions [such, I would add, as are found in ideological adherence to the "stories" of Culture I and Culture II Catholicism]. Rather, the central question of the age is how every religious tradition might integrate the awe-inspiring and truly sacred story of the universe's origin that comes from science. We are the first humans to be graced by this blessed opportunity. We are also the first humans to struggle with the immensity of this question.[5]

As we find our common grounding in the cosmic story, we become more attuned to the possible contradictions that may undermine the integrity of the narratives of our other stories. This demands that we find a way to "completely revise our approach to nature," as Pope Benedict XVI said in 2011.[6] This should invite us to free ourselves from the "isms" and ideologies of the religious, national, and scriptural stories (including our own personal stories) that will find us grounded in the cosmic story in a way that honors what is authentic in the stories of everyone and everything. Their "truth" will be objective to the degree they reflect, in their narration, the dynamics revealed in the patterns of that cosmic story from which all these stories ultimately derive. What I have articulated here also represents the conviction that drives the evolutionary evangelists Michael Dowd and his wife, Connie Barlow. They have summarized this endeavor in their wonderful book *Thank God for Evolution: How the Marriage of Science and Religion Will Transform Your Life and Our World.*[7]

The chart and discussion on page 134 illustrate how four stories (the country's story, the church's story, the scriptural story, and our personal story) are grounded in the cosmic story—how they interact with it and one another and how we must discover any ideological biases or absolutizing in any of them in order to become free to celebrate their authentic narratives in our collective spiritualities. This demands that all our stories be grounded in the cosmic story that is faithful to what we know from science about the way the world really works. In this *logos* we bring our *mythos* of belief that the trinitarian God is the archetype that must be at the heart of *every story*, not only creation's. This is beautifully summarized in the words of Denis Edwards: "I suggest that the foundation for a theology that takes evolution seriously can be found in the trinitarian vision of God as a God of mutual relations, a God who is communion in love, a God who is friendship beyond all comprehension."[8]

Since everything in creation is in relationship in a way that mirrors trinitarian connectedness, we can say, with Thomas Berry, that "the universe as such is the primary religious reality, the primary sacred community, the primary revelation of the divine, the primary subject of incarnation, the primary unit of redemption, the primary referent in any discussion of reality or of value. For the first time the entire human community has, in this story, a single creation or origin myth."[9] If this be the case, then, especially as we have seen the devastation to creation that humans have done to such a degree that we have now entered the Anthropocene Age (see Chapter 4), the "cosmic story," or what Berry calls the "universe story," is that key story that "is now needed as our sacred story."[10] In this Berry reflects what we have already discussed about the insight of St. Bonaventure that all creation is an emanation[11] of the triune goodness and love. It is a book or story in which creation's maker, the Trinity, is revealed as vestige, image, or likeness. Thus, Ilia Delio, writes, "The created universe, therefore, possesses in its inner constitution . . . the imprint of the Trinity as well."[12]

The cosmic story must undergird all other major stories in a way that creates and sustains the story that defines each of our own personal stories. Combined, these four key stories are true to the degree they are grounded in creation's story, including the story articulated in our scriptures as well as any story told by our country or our church. This includes our story about God because only in light of creation do we apprehend a creator. Without each breath we take that makes us depend totally on creation's breath we can never even imagine a God whom we believe to be the Breath that fuels all breathing in the universe. Consequently, I find it very important to ritualize this realization in my breathing itself, especially when I try to make conscious contact with this creator-trinitarian God. So, breathing in everything in the universe, my diaphragm inflates like a balloon; breathing out it deflates, giving back to the universe only my desire for its good.

Breathing in this way helps me become more conscious of my connectedness with the God of this universe. It makes me more aware of what Thomas Berry meant when he wrote that existentially "there is no God without creation and there is no creation without God."[13] Truly the original meeting place of God and humans is creation, the original incarnation. Creation is the foundation for everything else in the universe, including our understanding of evolution itself and everything else.

Addressing a full session of the Pontifical Academy of Science, Pope Benedict XVI highlighted the "story" notion of creation when he reminded its members, "To 'evolve' literally means 'to unroll a scroll,' that is, to read a book. The imagery of nature as a book has its roots in Christianity and has been held dear by many scientists."[14] An understanding of this evolutionary groundedness and interconnectedness moved Thomas Berry to declare: "For the first time we can tell the universe story, the earth story, the human story, the religion story, the Christian story, and the church story as a single comprehensive narrative."[15]

In a wonderful way Jennifer ("Jinks") Hoffman has shown how all these stories, combined together, create a cairn. A "cairn" is a pile of stones that is built for various reasons. However, the primary reason for a cairn is to serve as a pointer or marker on one's journey. While Jinks Hoffmann finds us working together to make a cairn of our personal stories, I also think that the stones found throughout creation itself can create a "creation cairn," which, in turn, can serve as the solid foundation for all the other stories to make an even more impressive cairn. Serving as the source and goal of each and all we find pointers to God:

OUR STORIES

Jennifer (Jinks) Hoffmann   September 26, 2008
It is our stories
our sacred, chaotic, blessed stories,
our lonely, peaceful, frightened stories,
our awe-drenched, doubting, joyous stories;
it is our stories
that are the stones
of God's language
on the rocky, jagged, radiant
path of life.
It is the holy listener
who helps arrange these stones
into cairns
which point the way to
God's desire for our lives
and
God's desire for our every moment.
The cairns, if patiently balanced,
uneven though they be,
if patiently balanced,
by the two who gather in God's presence,

> if patiently balanced,
> can point the way to heaven.
> Heaven, after all,
> is making God-serving meaning
> of our stories
> on this rocky, jagged, radiant
> path of life.[16]

Building on this book's previous chapters, it follows that the primary or root metaphor for all our personal and collective stories, including our God Story of the Economic Trinity, can be interpreted from the metaphor of house (*oikia/oikos*). The primary metaphor of the cosmic story has replaced the earlier metaphor of the machine composed of various parts with that of a living organism wherein the whole is in each and every part and each and every part creates the whole. This organism thus houses its own ecology (*oikologia*) or way of ordering relationships that reflects that of a house at every level, like Russian nesting dolls. When we read our nations' stories, the image of "homeland" immediately comes to mind. The same applies to the "Church's Story." Thus it is not surprising that the words to St. Francis of Assisi from the crucifix at San Damiano involved the mandate to "repair my house which, you can see, is falling into ruin." Repeating what we have already discussed regarding "Scripture's Story," we have already shown how the spirituality of the Synoptic Jesus involved the proclamation to every "house" of a certain gospel. This involved the inbreaking of the governance or rule of the Economic Trinity in the economy of salvation. It was behavioralized in Jesus' creation of a new household, or family of equals, under the one he called his Father in heaven. Finally, in dealing with our own personal story, whether in our unconscious expressed in dreams around the image of the house or in our mystical experience, we find that the metaphor of "house" describes God's way of "remaining with" us and we with God and God's people. We must be about God's business.

We have said thus far that the four stories are grounded in the cosmic story and that all five stories are more understandable from perspectives connected to the metaphor of "the house." These insights reveal a meaning that just may offer a new model of faith that will speak to the longings of people everywhere. Without going into further details about the five stories, it should be apparent from the "isms" at the extremes of all three sides of the four stories and the two sides of the cosmic story (see the figure below) that the integrity and relevance of each story vis-à-vis the other stories will be compromised to the degree that they are equated with their particular "isms." Such "isms" become weapons in the war of ideas that keep us from getting to the heart of the real story. These reflect ideological and self-serving or group-interested ways of telling the core stories that reflect bias and absolutizing tendencies with polarization the result.

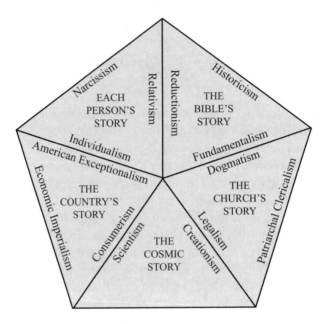

Unpacking the First Words of Our Creedal Statements

When we consider our Church's Story in light of the cosmic story, the supposed differences between Culture I and Culture II Catholics seem quite petty. This becomes all the more evident when we realize that the adherents of both (if they are not going to be ideologically driven) declare regularly their common faith in the Nicene Creed at Mass and in the Apostles' Creed when we pray the rosary. Whether it is the Nicene Creed or the Apostles' Creed, with our individual credos of what we hold in common, we profess in each phrase some aspect of our personal faith in God as the originating and ultimate source of everything in the universe. This personal faith in this God is expressed in a consciousness that everything has emanated from this source and that, as source, everything is still emanating from this source. This is the ground for all other beliefs about which we agree or disagree.

Furthermore, as people of faith, we believe that from "the beginning" of creation, God's creative power has functioned in the one we call the Word. However, because science has shown us that everything in creation is what it is because of the way information has been structured to make everything be what it is, taking these notions about information being at the heart of every structured part of reality, we can give the name "Information" to that One we call Word. Thus, in the beginning, there was not only "the Word"; this Word was/is Information. In the image of this Information everything lives, moves, and has its being. "In the beginning there was Information and that Information revealed God." This Information of God has been wired into everything that has ever existed because, as Margaret Wheatley reminds us, "Information organizes matter into form, resulting in physical structures." She shows that every system is merely an information system that is manifest in matter.[17]

Because of our belief that God is the Information that informs all reality, we constellate such beliefs in our creedal statements. Consequently, we can never forget that they are *faith* statements, not demonstrable facts. Such belief automatically puts us in the realm of *mythos* more than *logos*, as much as we might want it to be clearer. Consequently, our approach to every phrase in our creeds (at least ideally) should be accompanied by a desire to get to the core meaning behind these words and the myths they reveal. Furthermore, if we seek to unpack the meaning of these words and the myths they embody, we should be the first to realize that "fidelity to our faith" statements demand that we be as concerned (or even more concerned) about clearly embodying them in our lives as in insisting on our interpretation of what they mean. When the latter approach dominates discussions about such creedal statements they can easily be used ideologically. Further polarization will be the result.

As noted earlier, the more I think about God from the perspective of my faith in that God who has been revealed as unconditional and unconditioned love, the more I realize that the freedom not to believe in such a God must be at the heart of all theoretical discussions about God. A need-based God, much less a fear-based God, is not worthy of being called God. Like any healthy father or mother, the God that is the parent God must be worshiped as the One who brings his/her children into the world risking the fact that those children may never reciprocate in love. But if they do not, God allows them the freedom to remain outside the reign of that God. While this may be hell, a loving God allows us to "go there" and remain outside that One's love. Any God believed to be the "maker of heaven and earth" will encourage rather than demand our loving response; as such, our relationship with a God worthy of being God will never be grounded in any form of control—only unconditioned care that includes our freedom to remain outside the reign of that God, even if forever.

Probing more deeply regarding our belief in God, we find that the opening image of our core creedal statements themselves are grounded in the cosmic story. We begin by saying we believe in God who is "almighty" and "creator of heaven and earth." Unfortunately, this God all-too-often looks like the God we see on the ceiling of the Sistine Chapel. And, no matter how much our theologizing about this God reveals a non-anthropocentric being, the image remains. Consequently, it colors our ability to have a personal faith in such a creator whose power gets translated more as control in a way that compromises our freedom. Furthermore, when the language about this God continues to be male centered, it is very hard to truly believe that this creedal God we call "Father" is equally "Mother." This dilemma has been compounded in the Catholic Church, and any effort to bring a better balance between the divine masculine and feminine gets undermined for ideological purposes. This was evident when the official paper of the Holy See, *L'Osservatore Romano*, failed to include the section of a speech before 900,000 people in which Pope John Paul I said that while God is a Father, God also could be considered "even more Mother."[18]

The dissonance between a theory of God that is beyond sex and the male-centered terminology related to this God is no better evidenced than in the *Catechism of the Catholic Church*. It talks about God creating male and female to be images of the divine reality rather than the other way around. It states, "In no way is God [made] in *man's* image. *He* is neither man nor woman" (emphasis my own).[19] Another example is found in the 2011 "Statement" on questions related to the "theology of God" found in the writings of Elizabeth Johnson by the Committee on Doctrine of the United States Conference of Catholic Bishops. They agreed with her that "the Catholic theological tradition affirms that no human language is adequate to express the reality of God. Catholic teaching maintains that human concepts apply to God only in an analogous fashion."[20] This is followed by a quote from the *Catechism of the Catholic Church*: "We can name God only by taking creatures as our starting point, and in accordance with our limited human ways of knowing and thinking" (no. 40). However, in the sentence immediately preceding this quote as well as in the next section (no. 41), discussion of God is limited to male pronouns. Theologically the point is clear: God is beyond sexual categories; however, linguistically it is compromised by a continued reference to God that uses exclusively male pronouns. The result is a persistent sexist notion of God. The subtlety of this male bias related to God is evident when the "Statement" challenging the writings of Elizabeth Johnson includes mention of her reference to the Spirit of God as "she."[21] The whole approach mirrors the reality that has been wonderfully described in the dialogue between Shug and Celie in Alice Walker's *The Color Purple*: "When I found out that I thought that God was white, and a man, I lost interest,"[22] Shug says to Celie.

When such a sexist approach to God gets reinforced in official Vatican texts, intentionally or unintentionally, especially after appeals for greater inclusivity in terms related both to God and humans, it becomes clear that the Vatican's insistence on exclusive language, dictated unilaterally by males, reflects the use of language in the form of ideology to reinforce the continued domination model that can belie an absolutist approach to Culture I Catholicism rather than the partnership model that is at the heart of a Culture II church.

Just as I noted in Chapter 1 that we have two different understandings about church that help define our place between the poles of Culture I and Culture II Catholicism, so I believe we have two basic constructs of God from which we build our consequent theologies and, I would add, our spiritualities. And, as I offered the previous chart on church without comment, I do the same here:

TWO POLES IMPACTING OUR UNDERSTANDING OF GOD

I	II
• Reflects a flat-earth worldview	• Reflects fidelity to evolutionary worldview
• God as "other there"; the divine "other"	• God as "everywhere"; at heart of all
• God as transcendent and interventionist in creation	• God as immanent and participative in creation
• Hierarchical dynamics dominate organizations	• Holarchical dynamics dominate organizations
• Mediators needed to make God present	• God's presence in world as sacramental
• The Fall necessitating God's "coming to earth" to save people from their sins	• No necessary reason for God to come to earth except love that is unconditional
• Anthropocentric (human centered); everything existing for human beings	• Ecozoic (cosmic centered); everything has its unique part in the cosmic story
• Ensoulment and death as determined by God's direct decision for each person	• Ensoulment and death as determined by God's power in the evolutionary process
• Humans ruling over creation without that much concern for negative impacts	• Humans as part of creation's processes to bring about ever-greater sustainability

Given this background related to the powerful God of creation which begins our creedal statements, we can return to the response of E. O. Wilson to the question raised by the writer from the *Wall Street Journal* regarding the survivability of religion in light of "what science is telling us." Wilson concluded, "The more we understand from science about *the way the world really works*, all the way from subatomic particles up to the mind and on to the cosmos, the more difficult it is to base spirituality on our ancient mythologies."[23]

When we try to unpack Wilson's words about "the way the world really works," we recognize the fact that the notion of *world* differs in four main ways. First and foremost, Wilson's "world" refers to that part of creation called the "cosmos." This is the domain of scientific study. In Chapter 3, we have shown the cosmos to represent the domain of *logos*; it involves the area of reason that arises from what scientific facts reveal. This world is defined by what is observable "all the way from subatomic particles [physics] up to the mind [neuroscience] and on to the cosmos [cosmology]." Second, there is the world that seeks to explain what *logos* cannot. This is the world of *mythos*: that which is not observable but believed. It is that part of what one believes to constitute a reality that exists beyond the senses and pure reason. Third, we find the worldview that undergirds both how we live *logos* (reason) and *mythos* (faith). Sometimes this worldview is grounded in truth. Other times it reflects ideology. Finally, for people of faith, we have "the world" of human beings that is the domain of grace as well as sin that represents our lives.

These four levels are brought together eloquently in a passage from the "Second Life" of St. Francis of Assisi, the founder of my community of Capuchin Franciscans. It was written by Brother Thomas of Celano, within a couple decades of the death of the saint he admired so much. They offer us a wonderful insight into the fact that whatever "world" we may be thinking about, they all exist because of that world called the Cosmos: "This happy traveler, hurrying to leave the world as the exile of pilgrimage, was helped, and not just a little, by what *is in the world*. Toward *the princes of darkness*, he certainly used it as a field of battle. Toward God, however, he used it as the clearest *mirror of goodness*."[24]

Creation: The Mirror of God's Diffusive Goodness

In my lifetime, a host of books have been written on a faith-based approach to the "new cosmology" and "the universe story." I have benefitted immensely from such groundbreaking insights, starting with Pierre Teilhard de Chardin and continued in the writings of the "geologian" Thomas Berry[25] and Brian Swimme.[26] These have been brought to a deeper christological perspective by theologians like Ilia Delio[27] and John Haught as well as Nancey Murphy and Philip Clayton (to say nothing of the wonderful way all this was popularized by the late Judy Cannato[28]). Because they have articulated much better than I a faith response to creation and its causation, I will "not go there" here. Neither will I probe theories such as morphogenic fields, the Higgs boson (more popularly called "the God particle"), or the work of Francis X. Collins, the director of the human genome project, who almost evangelically argues for the existence of God. Rather, in this book, I want to approach God as Divine Goodness and to understand our experience of the good and doing good as manifestations of the reign of that God. In so doing, I want to stress how I understand creation or the world to be connected to the God of religious experience or, in the words of Thomas of Celano, to be "the clearest *mirror of* [that kind of divine] *goodness*."

Previously we approached creation as the mirror of divine goodness. This mirroring of the divine reality reveals itself in the vestige of every creature and in our imaging of this divine goodness in our identity as females and males. And, since (as Pope Benedict XVI has stated), each of us as males and females carries an imprint of the Trinity in our genetic material,[29] we become likenesses of this Trinity when we become conscious of this and replicate this goodness in our effort to bring about the same mirroring in our own lives, relationships, and institutions by "doing good." Such a notion undergirds Franciscan cosmology and ecological theology. As such, it is not only informative but performative insofar as it empowers us to reveal the goodness of God's trinitarian connectedness in our lives and relationships. This awareness makes us all the more committed to Jesus' core message of the reign of this divine goodness. It challenges us to evidence our participation in it in the way we do good to everyone and everything. In this way the smallest act of goodness impacts the whole cosmic reality.

Goodness and doing good define the core of Jewish spirituality.[30] Indeed, according to David Gelernter, the very purpose of the earth as well as of humankind involves the extension throughout the cosmos of that goodness: "to create what might be (if we succeed) the only tiny pinprick of goodness in the universe—which is otherwise (so far as we know) morally null and void. If no other such project exists anywhere in the cosmos, our victory would change the nature of the universe." If one would ask, "Why seek goodness?" Gelernter's answer is simple. It is in our genes: "Because most humans desire goodness. For most (not all!) humans, this urge is easily ignored in the short term, but nearly impossible to uproot over the long haul."[31]

Since all matter in the universe is "energy-massed," those who believe in God as the Ultimate Power or Energy, believe that, at the heart of all energy-massed, is some ultimate energy or *archē* we call God. For us Christians, this "God" is the triune architect of everything and everyone who has ever existed. As such, the Trinity is understood to be the all-embracing and all-encompassing form of relationship and identity that undergirds everything in creation. Furthermore, males and females, precisely because they have been constituted by God to image God, have been created to relate to each other in such "blessed" ways of solidarity, participation, and *perichoresis* (or mutual indwelling or coinherence) that the reality of the reign or power of that trinitarian God might be revealed in and through them, drawing all things to their maker and ultimate cause.

Saying all this in another way, the first sign of God the Almighty or All-Powerful Energy—before any humans ever became Energy-Massed-in-Self-Consciousness—is creation. Because it is in the nature (the "being") of goodness to be diffused (to "do good"), God, being personified goodness, can only be and act out of goodness. Because God made *everything* "very good," everything is constituted to image trinitarian goodness and love. Everything in the cosmos made by God somehow has been made to uniquely image God's diffusion of goodness. This involves self-communication that is realized only in the mutual giving of self to and in the *other*.

In this sense everything connected to the beginning and continuance of creation in time and space is, in its "self" (insofar as its "self" is "in" the other) a self-expression of trinitarian dynamics. Given that the archetype of everything is the Trinity, its way of relatedness is to be reflected in the architecture of everyone and everything in creation. As we noted in Chapter 5, this modeling is revealed when we "do good" in a way that does to the other the good that we would want the other to do to us.

As we conclude this chapter, it is important to recall that it was not just male and female that were defined as "very good" but that *everything* made by (the trinitarian) God is not only "very good" but can only be "very good" in relationships of mutuality that reflect trinitarian goodness. As we come to share our stories, we need to be aware of the way the different ideologies connected to them can undermine the divine goodness that should be narrated in each of them. Especially as we ground ourselves in the cosmic story in an age of ecological destruction, we need to move from a human-centered (anthropocentric) worldview to an ecocentric or creation-centered stance toward all of life. Rather than view creation as existing to serve humans, we must reclaim the wisdom of a mystic like Francis of Assisi in a way that finds us becoming "subject and submissive to everyone in the world, not only to people but to every beast and wild animal as well."[32] This stance will lead us with another mystic, Ignatius of Loyola, not only to find God in everything but to love and serve God's divine majesty in everything.[33] When we are faithful to this kind of interconnectedness with everyone and everything in the cosmos, we will witness to a credible spirituality that finds God throughout the cosmos "all the way from subatomic particles, up to the mind and on to the cosmos."

10 —————————————————————————

THE CHRISTIC WAY

Until I left for college, I lived on Bank Street in Fond du Lac, Wisconsin. In between our street and Melrose Boulevard (where the rich people lived) there was a large vacant lot. It covered the whole inside of the four sides of the block. We had basements in Fond du Lac; and when someone built a new home they would just put their dirt in ever-larger piles on the vacant lot. When I was a child, these provided the hills and mountains we needed when we would play "war" between Bank Street and Melrose Boulevard.

One day during a truce than enabled us to eat our peanut butter and honey sandwiches, Carol Fishelson, the granddaughter of one of the wealthiest Jews in town, told me that her older brother Bobby "was not a good Jew." When I asked her why (not quite knowing what a Jew was), she said, "Every night I pray that I will be the mother of the *messhiach*, but Bobby doesn't pray that he'll be the father of the *messhiach*."

I did not know what Carol was talking about then, but it was important enough for me to remember it to this day. In the process I have become fascinated by the notion of the *messhiach* (which the Greek translated as *christos*): the one in whom God's purposes and the peoples' dreams would converge. Whether the *messhiach* would be an individual, a remnant community, or the nation itself, the notion of the *christos* captures the Jewish notion of a corporate personality in such a way that the stress on anyone being called "the christ" has more to do with the community recognizing the person as "the christ" for the community and nation rather than on who that one may be as an individual.

The Christian Story of How the Historical Jesus
Became the Christ in Whom We Believe

To this day, in the Jewish community, there remain varied understandings regarding the identity of the *messhiach,* and many debates regarding whether the anointed one has come (as in the creation of the State of Israel) or is still to come (or will ever come). The competing claims range from those of Menachem Mendel Schneerson (1902-1994), whom many believed to be the Messiah during his lifetime, and, even after his death, continue to await his return as the Messiah, to the "Jews for Jesus," who try to use the scriptures to convince fellow Jews that the historical Jesus fulfilled the scriptures, especially interpreting the "Suffering Servant" text found in Isa. 54:13-53:12 in a way that makes him the messiah.

The Christ-search of the Hebrew Scriptures undergirds the whole New Testament understanding of the historical Jesus. There it becomes very evident that the lens through which its various writers interpreted the Jesus of history was the belief that, because of his death and their conviction of his resulting resurrection, he was/is "the Christ." However, lest we make too great a dichotomy between the Jesus of History and the Christ of Faith, it is very important to realize that this Jesus was embodied in his human body, the very stuff of creation itself. Ilia Delio elaborates on this connection in a beautiful passage:

> The body of Jesus, like every human body, is made from cosmic dust birthed in the interior of ancient stars that long predated our planet and solar system. The iron that ran through his being, the phosphorus and calcium that fortified his bones, the sodium and potassium that facilitated the transmission of signals through his nerves—all make the incarnation a truly cosmic event. Jesus participated in the unfolding of life and the emergence of consciousness, just like any other human being; his humanity is our humanity; and his cosmic earthly life is ours as well.
>
> However, in Jesus something new emerges, a new consciousness, a new relatedness, and a new immediacy of God's presence—in short—a new Big Bang. Jesus Christ symbolizes a new unity in creation: non-duality; reconciling love, healing mercy, and compassion. Jesus brings a "new heart" to humanity, both on the individual and the collective planes. Humanity becomes a new "creative center" within the evolutionary process in such a way that the path of this evolution now becomes explicitly directed; evolution has a goal.... "The suffering and death of Jesus were a radical manifestation that faith in God liberates the individual to accept the full implication of his freedom and responsibility" (quoting John Cobb). The awareness of God's immediacy and a sense of ethical responsibility (for example, feed the hungry, clothe the naked, compassion for the poor) marked the new Christian consciousness.[1]

While Jesus might not have been the political messiah anticipated by many Jews (see Luke 24:21), his fidelity to God's plan brought about their realization that his suffering and death resulted in his resurrection, which they had come to experience and/or believe in (Isa. 42:1-9; 49:1-13; 50:4-9; 52:13-53:12).

Furthermore, it became the conviction of those who believed this and were baptized that they too became participants in the life of this Christ as the *christoi*, through their baptism and anointing in the Spirit. Partaking in this divine life as the *christoi*, they were empowered and commissioned to witness to and bring about a new order in creation. Being part of Christ in this way makes clear the cosmic implications. In the words of Ilia Delio, "Jesus Christ is *the* human . . . who symbolizes the capacity for all human persons to be united and transformed in God."[2]

This chapter is my attempt to expand on the ideas outlined in the previous chapter of the cosmic story. It will also build on notions contained in Part II with the goal of presenting the Christ of our Faith as the Cosmic Christ in whom, through whom, and for whom everything and everyone has been made. This Christ is the one through whom the Economic Trinity has been revealed in a way that its "economy," or plan, for the world has been ushered in to bring about the fullness of its salvation, its *shalom*, its fulfillment. This is to be accomplished by our participation in the very body of this Christ, the church.

The purpose of this economy of salvation is to bring about the reign of trinitarian connectedness on earth as it is in heaven through the abiding presence of the Cosmic Christ in the church. Indeed, the only way we can understand the *God of Jesus Christ* is as Trinity. As Catherine Mowry LaCugna wrote years ago, "trinitarian theology arises out of Christology and is unthinkable apart from it."[3] The chart below (see p. 145) shows how the Economic Trinity's economy of salvation fulfilled in Jesus Christ has taken place in history (each line leads into the dynamics in the line below) and is now to be worked out in the church in each and every member of this body of Christ.

As we have come to know God from "the beginning," we understand this God to be a "kindom" of trinitarian love wherein each person is perichoretically united in and to the others. *Perichōrēsis* (being in one another) is the theological term used to describe the mutual indwelling, or interpenetration, of the three persons *in one another*. A more understandable word may be *coinherence*. Everything done by the one is done by the others since the only thing that differs among them is each one's unique "I am"; everything else about them, including how they function, is communal. A good symbol of this interconnectedness in the Trinity is the Celtic knot.

While we know all action of God is trinitarian, we attribute the creation of the universe to that member of the Trinity we call the Word. In the energy or Spirit of the trinitarian God, our world stands as the first sacrament of God's loving presence in the whole cosmic reality. Everything in creation, then, in its unique "is-ness," is made to image God as a vestige, an image, or a likeness of God's trinitarian relatedness and loving.

Because of (and only because of) God's unconditional love, the second great incarnation of God's self-giving love was revealed in the Spirit-attributed (Matt. 1:20; Luke 1:35) enfleshment, embodiment, or "creation-ment" of the historical Jesus. As we have seen, he came with a gospel of the rule and governance of trinitarian relationships. This gospel inspired others to follow him as disciples. When their numbers grew, the religious leaders became threatened; his authority challenged their hegemonic control (Matt. 7:28-29). This led them to call for his death. To achieve this goal they sculpted their real rationale (their loss of power and control) in terms of his threat to imperial power. This resulted in his crucifixion, the form of death reserved to enemies and threats to the power of the state. Given our previous discussions about atheism, it serves our considerations well here to recall a trenchant insight of Barbara Brown Taylor of why this crucifixion occurred: "Jesus was not brought down by atheism or anarchy. He was brought down by law and order allied with religion, which is always a deadly mix. Beware of those who claim to know the mind of God, and who are prepared to use force, if necessary, to make others conform. Beware of those who cannot tell God's will from their own."[4]

Within three days of his death on the cross, one disciple after another began experiencing him as alive in their lives. This became known as the resurrection—the experience and resulting conviction that the Spirit of the Christ was in each of them and among them whenever they would gather. Hearing the "good news" of the death of Jesus and his resurrection in and among them drew even more disciples. This created a whole new threat to officialdom in Judaism.

This whole phenomenon came to constitute the core religious experience of Saul of Tarsus, who had been trying mightily to stop the spread of this message. This experience occurred to him on the way to Damascus and made it clear to him that the individual members of the house churches he had persecuted in Jerusalem and now was trying to stop in the Damascus synagogues were not just part of some organized groupings called "church" or "synagogue"; they were the embodied members of a living, organic enfleshment of the Christ.

The chart below summarizes the ideas I shared in the above four paragraphs. For believers, it outlines the economy of salvation that began and continues because of God's trinitarian love. This love has now been entrusted to us to be extended into creation by our evangelical witness as members of the Body of Christ. As we see how the trinitarian love of God, revealed first in creation, then in the incarnation, and reaching its apogee in the crucifixion, has been enfleshed by the Spirit in the living members of the Body of Christ, we find in seminal form the two poles between which the members of the church must be grounded. On the one hand, it will be a "what": an observable institution that will be structured according to historical and cultural conditioning that will differ, depending on time and place. On the other hand it will be a "who" composed of the living members of the organic body of Christ wherein, individually and communally, the abiding presence of the Christ remains in the whole and in each and every part.

Because the organic and organizational dynamics represent poles on the continuum of what it means to be church, the human "what" will always reflect humanness, and therefore, some forms of sin. The mystical grounding that defines the organic grounding of the church will serve as a continual call to all the members, individually and as a whole, to reflect in its institutional expression the trinitarian dynamics in which its baptized members have been called. With this background we see how one reality flows into the next.

REAL PRESENCE of TRINITARIAN GOD/LOVE

WORLD (sacrament)   COSMIC WORD (indwelling)

The BREATH/SPIRIT/ENERGY/LIFE FORCE

INCARNATED SELF-GIVING   GOD-WITH-US/JESUS

THE EMPIRE'S GOSPEL   JESUS' GOSPEL

THREAT TO SYSTEM   GROWTH of DISCIPLES

ULTIMATE SELF-GIVING   JESUS' CRUCIFIXION

DISCIPLES' EXPERIENCE OF JESUS: RISEN, COSMIC CHRIST

ASSEMBLY/QAHAL

VISIBLE ORGANIZATION   MYSTICAL ORGANISM

Synagogue   House/Church   Corporal Body of Risen Christ
ש ‬ש ‬ש ‬ש   ✝✝✝ ✝✝✝✝ ✝✝✝   "Why do you persecute me?"

A Meditation on the Trinity and Creation
and Their Connection through Christ

I experienced an insight into the connectedness between the Economic Trinity and the economy of salvation and its relevance for our lives in January 2010 when I made the *Spiritual Exercises of Saint Ignatius*. In the First Prelude for the First Day and First Contemplation of the Second Week, Ignatius invites the exercitant to reflect on "how the Three Divine Persons look down upon the whole expanse or circuit of all the earth, filled with human beings" and decreed "that the Second Person should become man to save the human race."[5]

Having prayed for the necessary openness and indicated my desire to experience as fully as possible the meaning of the mystery involved (in this case the two great mysteries of the Trinity and the Incarnation), I began by meditating on the dynamics that brought about the inbreaking of God's trinitarian life in creation through the person of Jesus who became the Christ.

On the first round of meditations nothing unique happened. However, when I went through the meditations on the second round, a rush of insight came to me. Somehow my economics degree became the lens through which my second effort to meditate on the Trinity and the next meditation unfolded. The following is my meditation as I recorded it:

> When I started thinking of the Trinity, maybe because of my own Master's in Economics, I started thinking of its members as constituting a "family business," an *oikonomia*. The family members were quite happy going about the business of their business, of being the loving persons they were, giving themselves totally to each other in mutual love. At one point, however, just because their love was so expansive they decided to expand their family business. This resulted in creation. And creation evolved to the point that some creatures became conscious of themselves. However, despite the different ways the owners tried to communicate, they did not really know what it meant to be images of God and to create their relationships modeled on the original family business. As a result they were kind of without much direction.
>
> Consequently, again only because of love (which alone can motivate One Who is Love), the members of the family had a business meeting to discuss what they should do. It was decided the humans needed something much more concrete to reveal to them how they should conduct their business. Before either of the other two could say anything, the middle member said, "I'll go."
>
> Now that it was decided who would go, the question became: how can we take our business "public"? Thus it was decided that an IPO, an initial public offering, would be made. In considering the conduit for this, it was decided that a young maiden from Nazareth would be chosen; through her the private business would go public. When they sent an emissary to ask about her willingness to be such a conduit, Miriam said, "I'm all in."
>
> So her child revealed in his humanity, especially in his words

and deeds, what it meant to be part of the family business and what it would take to become a stakeholder in it. However, in the process it became clear that the Economic Trinity had even more wondrous expansion plans. Not only would those who patterned their lives on its economic model be stakeholders, but by sharing in their very life-force or Spirit, they would be made joint heirs as children.

We are the children whom they have planned, in their *oikonomia*, to have inherited the family business. Jesus entered a human family, and then created an alternative human family, *oikonomia*. In sharing his own life-force, he empowered all of us as disciples, his followers, to enter the family business which he came to establish on earth as it is in heaven. Because of the Incarnation, we, including Mary, are all equal members of the family business as long as we "do the will of the heavenly Father." Now we are not just heirs; we have become adopted children.

At that I began wondering about this "economy" planned by God and thought of its articulation in Ephesians 1:3-23 and Colossians 1:15-20. Somehow this led me to ask a further question: "Well, what exactly *is* the 'family business?' What does it make?" At that, my meditation moved to the concluding words of the Colossian Hymn: the family business is all about "making peace by the blood of his cross" (Col. 1:23), the ultimate act of trinitarian self-giving love.

The resulting *Our* Father took on new meaning.[6]

What I experienced in this meditation is what Ilia Delio finds in Bonaventure's identification of creation with the incarnation in a way that becomes the key to a true cosmic Christology in an evolutionary universe.[7] It also led me into a deeper experience of Bonaventure's doctrine of exemplarity. As discussed in the previous chapter, this means that God's goodness is diffused in creation and humans through what Bonaventure calls the vestiges, the images, and the likeness of God found everywhere. Building on the notion of the book (or what we have called "story") as a form of communication, Bonaventure writes:

From all we have said, we may gather that the created world is a kind of book reflecting, representing, and describing its maker, the Trinity, at three different levels of expression [i.e., communication]: as a vestige, as an image, and as a likeness. The aspect of vestige is found in every creature; the aspect of image, only in intelligent creatures or rational spirits; the aspect of likeness, only in those spirits that are God-conformed. Through these successive levels, comparable to steps, the human intellect is designed to ascend gradually to the supreme Principle, which is God.[8]

The basic difference among each of these three "icons" (*eikōn*) is their degree of consciousness regarding their identification with God's trinitarian being. John Duns Scotus found God's being, or "I am-ness," iconically linked for everyone and everything in their own unique *haecceitas*—their special "thisness." The thisness or *haecceitas* of everything in the universe is, in some manner, an *eikōn* of God's "I am." Since the "I am" of God is expressed in a Trinity of "I am-ness" and connectedness, this same way of connecting defines each and everything and everyone in creation as a unique *eikōn* of God's trinitarian connectedness. This has been revealed to us in the Incarnation of God's Trinity in the person of Jesus Christ.

The theology of Bonaventure and Scotus found contemporary expression[9] in the following free verse I composed shortly after my meditation on the Trinity and the Incarnation. Its inspiration came from different kinds of squirrels that were scurrying around the retreat house grounds on a day when the blue sky was dotted with large cumulus clouds:

BE-ING ABOUT THE BUSINESS OF BEING

The business of squirrels is squirreling;
the business of flowers is flowering;
the business of rain is raining;
the business of clouds is clouding;
the business of everything in creation
is to be about its unique business of being
that each and every "thing"
may do its thing
as trinitarian sacrament of the Word
that makes its own be-ness
to be about its family's business.[10]

The business of each member of the Economic Trinity is to be about its business of ensuring the effectiveness on earth of the family business. Given the expansion of their business in creation and the Incarnation that leads to a new model of "doing business" revealed by Jesus Christ, the business of each creature in the universe, especially those who belong to the business called church, is to be about its business of being its unique is-ness of witnessing to the Economic Trinity in its words and deeds. In a nation ideologically captured by the gospel of Milton Friedman, who preached that the "business of business is business," our business is to "mind our own business" in a way that *perichoretically* or mutually contributes to the integrity or coinherence of the "is-ness" of everyone and everything else. This will find us working together to bring about God's trinitarian relatedness at all levels of life. When we do this, the common good will be achieved; even more, the Commonwealth of the Economic Trinity will have come on earth as it is in heaven, and the economy of salvation will have come ever that much closer to its fuller realization.

The Son of Man as the Cosmic Christ

As noted in the first section of this chapter, after the Easter event the disciples of Christ interpreted the Old Testament passages as evidence that the historical Jesus was the Christ of their faith. They did this by an appeal to the "Suffering Servant" passages from Isaiah noted above. Another image that does the same thing has never received sufficient theological treatment. It revolves around the Son of Man passages.

I believe a deeper examination of Jesus' reference to himself as the Son of Man can mean, in contemporary language, that he is the "Cosmic One," the Cosmic Christ. I have come to this conclusion from a study of two of the main constellations of the Son of Man texts used by Jesus: (1) references to himself as the one who must suffer/be rejected/and crucified "by men" but who will rise on the third day; and (2) references to his cosmic power that is linked to his final coming in "the clouds" in a way that will have him triumph over the supposed cosmic powers of this world. Indeed, the first reference almost relies on a link between the Son of Man passages and those identifying Jesus as the Suffering Servant.

Among the Old Testament's 107 usages of the term "Son of Man" (in Hebrew, *barnasha/enas* or *bar/ben adam;* and in Greek, *ho huios tou anthrōpou*), the main themes involve God's name for Ezekiel (89 times). It also is used of a Davidic, divine-like eschatological redeemer who will overthrow God's enemies and establish God's reign among the people (Dan. 7:13-27; 8:17). Finally, to a lesser degree, the image can also refer to humanity itself in its lowly status before God and the heavenly powers (Num. 23:19; Job 25:6; Pss. 8:4; 80:17; 146:3; Isa. 51:12; 56:2).

In the New Testament we find among the fourteen uses of the term in Mark a special connection with the image of power (*exousia*), so much that Australian theologian Anne Dawson writes:

> Jesus is not only asserting his freedom to act on man's behalf, but is also challenging the controlling power that the scribes hold within the social system. The . . . allusion to the Son of Man (Mk 2:10) is to be found in Daniel 7, where the Son of Man confronts the dominions of oppressive power. Thus it is obvious that the author is further emphasizing Jesus' understanding of his mission as that of exposing oppressive practices that were endemic within the society.[11]

In addition, Dawson points to the subversive way Mark and other authors use the term "Son of Man" in order to identify Jesus with the cosmic powers heretofore attributed to Caesar. She concludes:

> Mark's gospel emphasizes how the challenge to the prevailing ideology of power extended not only to the structures of government and those exercising power through these structures, but also to those who claimed allegiance to Jesus as his disciples. For the followers of Jesus, claiming discipleship meant being called to a radical understanding of the meaning of *exousia* and also a radical way of living out of this new understanding.[12]

Moving to the rest of the Gospels, we find eight references to the Son of Man in Matthew and Luke together (i.e., the "Q" Source), seven uniquely Lukan passages, and ten found only in Matthew. The thrust of most of these, faithful to Mark, identifies Jesus with a divine, cosmic power (*exousia*) over everyone and everything in creation. This threatens the ruling powers. Knowing this, Jesus warns his followers that his gospel way of life, of necessity (*dei*), will lead to the cross. He declares that all those who will be faithful to this gospel (in contrast to the gospel of empire) must follow him by "taking up" their cross until the Son of Man, the Cosmic One, returns. The three predictions by Jesus in the Synoptics regarding his suffering, rejection, and killing as the Son of Man have their parallel in John's theology of Jesus' being lifted up. In the Synoptics, his passion and crucifixion bring about Jesus' resurrection; in John, the resulting salvation brings about eternal life for those who believe.

More than any other title used by John of Jesus except "the Christ" and "Son of God," "Son of Man" is used by Jesus of himself. The heart of John's usage of "Son of Man" follows Synoptic usages, except for the notion of the "Son of Man being lifted up." This includes the famous passage in John 3:14-15 about the necessity of the "Son of Man" to be "lifted up" in such a way that "whoever believes in him may have eternal life." Rather than being the source of shame, this lifting up not only will bring about glory for Jesus; it will be the source of life for all those who believe in him.

In the three other New Testament passages referring to the Son of Man we find them all linking the appearance of this one with cosmic power (Acts 7:56; Rev. 1:13; 14:14). Thus we can conclude that the imagery of the "Son of Man" involves a redemptive, salvific collective notion that binds those who believe in this one into a *body of believers*, the church. This brings them together in sister/brother connectedness, in this One, to everyone and everything in the universe. This takes place in, through, and for the Cosmic Christ. This Cosmic Christ (1) is our entry into the triune Godhead; (2) empowers us to bring about the rule of trinitarian relationships; and in the process (3) restores creation to its original purposes.

The Economic Trinity as the Pattern for the Economy of Salvation in Ephesians and Colossians

A deeper examination of the passages related to the Cosmic Christ also reveals a deep connection to those passages that refer to the primacy of Christ. These passages, found in what Benedict XVI has called the "twins"[13]—Ephesians 1:3-22 and Colossians 1:15-20—reveal a new cosmic order of the Trinity-Communicated-in-Christ that has been envisioned "from the beginning" to bring about God's plan ("economy") for the salvation/peace of the world.

Pope Benedict XVI also has said, in effect, that the economy of salvation is patterned on the "architecture" of the Economic Trinity. Quoting Ephesians, he outlines its dynamics. This involves "a plan for the fullness of time, to unite all things in him, things in heaven and things on earth" (Eph. 1:10). He added that, "prominent in this 'plan,' in Greek 'oikonomia,' that is, in this harmonious plan of the architecture of being and existence, is Christ, head of the body of the church, but also the axis that recapitulates in himself 'all things, things in heaven and things on earth.'"[14] In yet another talk, the pope made a further link between God's plan for the world in the economy of salvation and the [Economic] Trinity. He declared: "The 'Program' of God's Plan which is valid for every follower of Christ . . . is centered on Christ himself, who must be known, loved and imitated to live in Him the trinitarian life, and, with Him, to transform history to its fulfillment in the heavenly Jerusalem."[15]

The purpose of "the Christ" in Ephesians and Colossians is to wrap the historical Jesus in the cosmic mantle of the Christ and to endow that mantle with cosmic power and primacy over all creation. Below is a summary of this plan:

- This one is the image of the invisible God in whom the fullness of the Godhead (Trinity) is pleased to dwell.
- This one is before all (i.e., pre-existent) and the firstborn of all creation in whom all visible and invisible things in heaven and earth (thrones or powers) were/are created; in Him all these exist.
- This one is the beginning and firstborn of the dead.
- This one is head of his body (the church), whose members we are. We complete in our flesh what is wanting in the sufferings of Christ for his body which is the church (Col. 1:24).
- This one achieved redemption/reconciliation and peace/*shalom* for all in the cosmos in himself.
- This one accomplished all this (for us/creation) through the blood of "his cross."

From our understanding of God as trinitarian and God's vision for human creatures to image God (i.e., Trinity), it follows that an authentic theological anthropology that reflects the Economic Trinity in the economy of salvation will be better understood, as we have seen, using the metaphor of house. This will have as its goal (1) the dignity of the person realized in freedom; (2) the commonwealth shared by all in a way wherein needs are fulfilled, so that (3) the relationships among the persons vis-à-vis the resources are ordered for the purpose of communion. From this it follows that to ensure no. 1 there can be no discrimination among persons at any level of life; to realize no. 2 there can be no deprivation of the goods of the commonwealth; and, finally, to enable nos. 1 and 2 to be realized relationships there must be communion rather than domination. If any form of discrimination, domination, or deprivation would be structured into the relationships, they would be "untrinitarian." They would not only undermine the commonwealth or common good; they would denigrate the personal perfection in which all human beings are called to share. Pope John XXIII said that the common good is "the sum total of those conditions of social living, whereby men are enabled more fully and more readily to achieve their own perfection."[16] And this "universal call to perfection" will be an icon of God's perfection to the degree the community reflects trinitarian relatedness.

Becoming the New Cosmic, Christified Order

Connecting to the section above on the Son of Man of Jesus' understanding being the Cosmic Christ of our understanding, I believe this image echoes almost everything found in the passages from Ephesians and Colossians regarding the cosmic nature of the Christ. Even though we do not find the previous image applied to Jesus Christ, God's "economy" for creation finds definite parallels between those passages discussing the Son of Man as the Cosmic One with the passages discussing the primacy of Christ. Among these parallels we find that:

- Both have a pre-existent identity that has become enfleshed/incarnated.
- Everything in creation finds its own identity and purpose in this one.
- This one stands over the dominance of the principalities and powers, visible and invisible.
- A new cosmic order of reconciliation is realized through the suffering, rejection, and crucifixion ("blood"/life-force) of this one at the hands of global forces of economic, political, and/or religious domination.
- In this one all of humanity, human history, and the future of the cosmos find their grounding.

- Consequently, the Son of Man, the Cosmic One, holds primacy over everyone and everything in the cosmos.

This is the one in whom all creation (insofar as it has been made through this Cosmic One) finds its own unique "I am" and in whom all believers find their identity (common cause) in the way we become members of Christ. As the *Christoi,* we take up our cross. In so doing we become partners in God's economy of salvation. Given our awareness of being members of the Body of the Cosmic Christ sharing in this one's cosmic destiny and purposes, I would like to conclude this chapter with a personal story.

I was canoeing with a good priest friend of the Archdiocese of Milwaukee, Joe Juknialis. At that time I was about sixty-five and he three years younger. He was recalling a recent dinner party he had attended with old-time friends from his first assignment. These were four couples who attended the parish where he began his ministry as a young priest. The women at the dinner party were recalling a recent luncheon which they attended, along with four or five other women—all Catholic.

As they shared their conversation, they found they all were being challenged by the reality of their husbands retiring and wanting to help around the house. They interpreted this willingness to help as interfering with their decades-old patterns of being housewives. Furthermore, their children had moved far from Milwaukee, so they could not babysit for their grandchildren. This new phenomenon led these Catholic women to discover they no longer knew what their "purpose" in life entailed. They knew what it meant to be "wife" and "mother"; now they questioned what their future purpose might be.

At that Joe said to me something like, "So, Mike, you're sixty-five; in the business world you could retire too. You've accomplished almost everything anybody in your shoes would want: leadership, travel, and success. So now that you have accomplished everything you could imagine, what is *your purpose* in life?" His direct question came as a surprise. I had never been asked it quite that way. So, to deflect it, I responded by giving the traditional *Baltimore Catechism* definition: "The purpose of my life is to know, love, and serve God in this life," I said, "and be happy with *Him* (stressing the "Him") in the next."

"That's not good enough," Joe said. "It's got to come from yourself. So, seriously, what do you see as the purpose of your life now?"

Coming from some place, I spontaneously found myself saying, "I want to become the Christ." The words astounded me. At the same time, however, I knew I would not take them back.

At first the phrasing sounded quite presumptuous. But upon further reflection they began to make sense, especially if we understand the Christ to be the one(s) in whom the scriptures are to be fulfilled. This means that all of us are called to become the Christ. But the image of "becoming the Christ" means even more. It involves something deeper than informative theology. Rather, it becomes that kind of performance theology that leads to our gradual transformation into the Christ. This Christification follows a definite pattern: inspiration leading to imitation; imitation moving toward integration; integration leading to illumination;[17] and, finally, through ever-intensification of embodying the gospel, to identification. The reality of this identification is summarized in such words as "I want to become the Christ."

Not long after my conversation with Joe, I found exact scriptural verification for my claim that I wanted to "become the Christ." Paul wrote to the members of the Church of Galatia: "My little children, with whom I am again in travail until Christ be formed (*morphein*) in you" (Gal. 4:19). This morphing into the Christ represents a kind of natural selection in which we evolve to a higher level, leaving what is unsustainable and sinful behind. Such a "morphing" into the Christ in each and every part of Christ's cosmic Body demands the realization of a new social order in each and every part of this Body. Thus, "for as many of you as were baptized into Christ have put on Christ. There is neither Jew nor Greek, there is neither slave nor free, there is neither male nor female; for you are all one in Christ Jesus" (Gal. 3:27-28). In us the new order begins.

Given the whole notion of what it means to be "in Christ" and to have Christ be "in" each member of the Body, the church, as an organism and organization, must mirror this new cosmic order. Pope Benedict XVI reiterated this idea in 2009 when he said, "Christ brought down the wall of separation and unites all of us into one body. In the body of Christ, we become one people, the people of God." He added, "He brought down the wall of distinctions among peoples, races and cultures; we are all united in Christ."[18]

The image of the church as the embodiment of the new cosmic order becomes even more clear if we look at the wider Pauline corpus. Thus we see from 2 Corinthians that the empowering dynamic of this reality takes place in our bodies. "We hold this treasure in earthen vessels" (2 Cor. 4:7). This means we are to be transformed in such a way that it is the treasure, not the vessel, the inner contents rather than the outer envelope, that defines our individual and corporate participation in trinitarian life through this Christ. Thus "if *anyone is in Christ* that one is empowered to be a new creation; the old [order of structuring life] has passed away" (2 Cor. 5:17).

The power and mystery of these passages cannot be underestimated. Maybe it is precisely because they have not been tried and found wanting but never even understood that the old order of clerical, patriarchal, and Western European colonizing ways still define the institutional structures of the church. But the dream—indeed, the demand—remains: if anyone is in Christ that one, combined with all the "ones" who are believers, must have as their purpose "to become the Christ" in such a way that a new order based on an absolutely trini-tarian way of structuring reality will be realized "on earth as it is in heaven." Until that day comes, our purpose in life must be ordered to help bring it about in our personal lives, our communities, and congregations as well as in the whole male, clericalized organization of the church itself. And, to the degree its leaders resist the realization of this goal as their pattern of governance, to that degree they will find themselves outside the reign or governance of the trinitarian God.

The old order of patriarchy and control has been put to death; now, who-ever is in Christ constitutes a trinitarian family of equals under God the Economist. This insight led Francis of Assisi to call everyone and everything "brother" and "sister." Furthermore, imitating the Trinity's self-giving love, he felt called to "be subject to them" in a way that would create a new *Haustafel,* or familial way of doing business. Consequently, Ilia Delio writes, "one who lives in Christ no longer calls Christ by the name of Jesus but by the name of 'brother' and 'sister.' To live in the experience of Christ is to live in the experi-ence of relatedness, to be a member of the cosmic family, because Christ is the Word of God through whom all things are related."[19] The effective realization of this economy of salvation involves the dismantling of any divisions based on inequality of any male and female made in God's image, whether this be based on sex, gender, orientation, nationality, tribe, ethnicity, age, race, or clerical status. If, in Christ, the new order has begun on earth in a way that reflects the trinitarian reign of God in heaven, the *Christoi* must be those in whom no dis-crimination, domination, or deprivation will be found or allowed anywhere.

What greater purpose could one have than to be committed to bringing about in one's life its divinely ordained purpose? In his book *Drive: The Sur-prising Truth about What Motivates Us,* Daniel Pink builds on the work of Edward Deci, Richard Ryan, and Mihaly Csikszentmihalyi. All of them show that we do our best work when we are self-directed regarding the use of our time and decision making and when we function from a sense of purpose.[20] To be in Christ and to proclaim the gospel of the "kindom of trinitarian connect-edness" is the ultimate purpose of a Christian, especially a Catholic Christian. To fulfill such a purpose should be the goal of our lives.

11 _____

The Way of Consciousness

Following the saying of Edward O. Wilson regarding the need for spirituality to be free of "ancient mythologies" and, instead, to reflect the "way the world really works, all the way from subatomic particles, up to the mind and on to the cosmos," we have touched upon subatomic particles as representing those forms of matter that are the building blocks of our universe. We have also spent more time in Chapter 9 considering the cosmic story and, in Chapter 10, how the Cosmic Christ is the story behind its story. Now we turn to the third element of what we know about the way the world "really works," which involves the "mind," or our consciousness.

Traditionally consciousness has been defined as the ability to be aware of one's self. In this sense humankind is creation conscious of itself. However, from another perspective, consciousness can be consider in a broader sense as well. From the world's beginning more than 13 billion years ago, communicative information has been at the center of how all matter is organized; everything has within itself those dynamic processes or information codes that enable it to be structured into its unique "is-ness." As Margaret Wheatley explains, "In a constantly evolving, dynamic universe, information is the fundamental ingredient, the key source of structuration—the process of creating structure."[1] And, in thoughts that will frame this chapter, she adds, "If the capacity to deal with information, to communicate, defines a system as conscious, the world is rich in consciousness, extending to include even those things we have classified as inanimate. Consciousness occurs in systems that do not even have an identifiable brain."[2]

From the world's beginning during a span of billions of years, we also have seen an evolution of consciousness within creation. As it emerged into life forms and that life developed in greater complexity, a parallel increase in consciousness has taken place. And where we once were dazzled at the discovery by psychologists of such things as the conscious and the unconscious, the collective unconscious and the unconscious archetypes, we now are discovering from neuroscience basic attributes of the unconscious and patterns of thinking that we once believed resulted only from personal decisions grounded in freedom and choice.

While not accepting the approach of some neuroscientists who might find themselves labeled as scientific reductionists,[3] people of faith should have some elementary understanding of what neuroscience, especially cognitive neuroscience, is telling us about how our consciousness has evolved to this point. When we examine neuroscience, even tentatively, we quickly discover that its data make some of our traditional thinking about consciousness tentative at best. This involves such questions regarding where the unconscious ends its influence and where our consciousness takes charge of our thought processes.

Cognitive neuroscientists are discovering that "the way the brain really works" involves a greater interplay between the unconscious and conscious workings of our brain than previously imagined. One of these neuroscientists is David Eagleman. In his book *Incognito: The Secret Life of the Brain*,[4] Eagleman has demonstrated that the dynamics involved in the unconscious are so powerful and pervasive that they almost overpower our consciousness and mode of thinking. Such data invite us to ask whether we are as conscious about being self-directed as we would think. His findings (as well as those of others in this field) also challenge some of our heretofore unquestioned assumptions regarding traditional notions of self-control and free will.

David Brooks has highlighted the possible disconnect between what we know from science and what we know from our religious mythology in a May 2008 column in the *New York Times* aptly titled "The Neural Buddhists: When Brain Research Meets the Bible."

Referring to the arguments against religion made by the "new atheists," Brooks begins by presenting their key challenges and theories. These involve the materialist argument that the existence of God has arisen from evolutionary processes that reveal that point in humanity's conscious development wherein "people perceive God's existence because their brains have evolved to confabulate belief systems."[5] What he does not discuss from the new atheists is the conviction of Sam Harris that spirituality does have a rational basis in human consciousness and evolution, as we will see below.

In his column, Brooks notes that the past several years have seen a large amount of data from neuroscience that reinforces some of the key ideas that I have been developing in this book. He notes that "the momentum has shifted away from hard-core materialism. The brain seems less like a cold machine. It does not operate like a computer. Instead, meaning, belief and consciousness seem to emerge mysteriously from idiosyncratic networks of neural firings. Those squishy things called emotions play a gigantic role in all forms of thinking. Love is vital to brain development." The consequence, he reports from his studies of the neuroscientists, is that an understanding of the way the world really works vis-à-vis our "minds" does not support the arguments of the atheists. "Instead, he says, it leads to a kind of spirituality that he calls "neural Buddhism."[6]

I believe human beings are creation that has evolved to consciousness of itself. I also believe that part of being human is to understand one's limitations and, in this understanding, come to believe in a power higher than oneself. While I would like to agree with the conclusion of the psychologist and philosopher Nick Humphrey that the purpose of consciousness is to awaken our awe, he offers no data to support his statement.[7] Consequently I find Brooks's summary of the findings of neuroscience instructive for our purposes here. In his column Brooks summarizes the main findings on what neuroscience is telling us about the way our consciousness influences how we "see" the world. As I read his précis, my belief became all the stronger in how the Trinity is the archetype for all human consciousness and interrelatedness.

> First, the self is not a fixed entity but a dynamic process of relationships. Second, underneath the patina of different religions, people around the world have common moral intuitions. Third, people are equipped to experience the sacred, to have moments of elevated experience when they transcend boundaries and overflow with love. Fourth, God can best be conceived as the nature one experiences at those moments, the unknowable total of all there is.[8]

Moving beyond the traditional arguments that have characterized the materialistic mindset that has influenced the approach that has been used to discuss the relationship between religion and science (and without mentioning Sam Harris's positive understanding of religious experience as spirituality), Brooks concludes that the materialist approach "was the easy debate. The real challenge is going to come from people who feel the existence of the sacred, but who think that particular religions are just cultural artifacts built on top of universal human traits. It's going to come from scientists whose beliefs overlap a bit with Buddhism."[9]

Unwilling to abdicate the future of religious meaning to the *dao* of Buddhism, my reading of Brooks invites us Catholics to return to the core insights of our great mystics (who remained faithful to being both Catholic and mystics in their generations). In the process we will discover our own Catholic *dao* that will evidence "in unexpected ways" how "science and mysticism are joining hands and reinforcing each other."

Awakening Leading to an Understanding Heart

In various places in this book I have referred to my 2011 experience of talking about notions of the *dao* that were shared with me by the younger man and the older self-described Sufi whom I met in the sauna at the Berkeley YMCA. In the midst of our conversations, both told me that a key reason for their practice of their respective *daos* involved bodily movements. Both also said that they went through such bodily exercises to enable them to "be awake." They subscribed to the conviction that the intentionality with which they brought to their various bodily movements would help them remain more conscious of their connectedness to everyone and everything in the universe. As the young man explained it to me: "It's my way of remaining awake." Later the Sufi told me that his practice was meant to help him "stay awake." The acknowledged need of this younger and that older man to remain "awake" recalls the famous story of the Brahmin priest and the Buddha.

One day the priest happened to encounter the Buddha sitting very still, the result of some unknown discipline. Sensing a powerful presence at work in what he was witnessing, the priest asked the Buddha: "Are you a god, sir?" When the Buddha said, "no," the priest asked if the Buddha was some kind of angel or spirit. To whatever the priest could imagine to be the source of the strength getting expressed in the quiet demeanor of the Buddha, the Buddha said "no."

This led the Buddha to explain how he could discipline himself in such a way that he would be able to free himself of his ego and self-centeredness and experience himself consciously connected to everyone and everything. This would enable him to be enlightened. He concluded his "teaching" to the priest by returning to his earlier questions about who he might be. "Remember me," the Buddha said, "as one who is awake." Indeed the title of "Buddha" actually means "one who is awake." Consequently, what Buddhists call "mindfulness"[10] is their practice of staying awake or being consciously connected in the here and now.

As the Sufi in the sauna patiently explained to me the process he uses to "be[come] awake" and "remain awake," lights began to be turned on in me. For him it was clear that this awakeness or awareness meant being alive to the world around himself, transcending his own ego, emotions, and even some of his beliefs in order to better comprehend reality in a way that led him to sense his connectedness to everyone and everything. His insight echoes what Antonio Damasio writes in *Self Comes to Mind: Constructing the Conscious Brain.* Damasio notes that consciousness involves wakefulness, self-awareness, reflection, mindfulness, and the kind of "knowledge of one's own existence and of the existence of surroundings." These impact a person's whole stance toward life.[11]

Listening to the Sufi, I recalled a key passage from Isaiah's mystical/prophetic call (Isa. 6:9-10). It talks about the hardness of heart of the people in words that indicate their eyes and ears were "not awake": "Go, and say to this people: 'Hear and hear, but do not understand; see and see, but do not perceive.' Make the heart of this people fat and their ears heavy and shut their eyes; lest they see with their eyes and hear with their ears, *and understand with their hearts*, and turn and be healed."

Without telling him my background or even my scriptural sourcing from Isaiah, I said to the Sufi, "Is the purpose of disciplining your eyes, your ears, and all your senses so you can 'be awake' in a way that moves your center from your head to your heart another way of saying you want to develop an 'understanding heart'?" The Sufi's face lit up from ear to ear. "That's exactly what it means," he said with a twinkle in his eyes.

I had never before equated "staying awake" with "an understanding heart." However, the deeper I probed the meaning of both images, the more I see that the ground of any Catholic *dao* involves the discipline of bodily practices to help us see and hear with a greater sense of our common connectedness that will reveal an "understanding heart." That this kind of meaning connected to this text should be put into practice by the church of every age takes on greater meaning when we realize it is the only Old Testament passage that is found in all four Gospels in one form or another.

The radicality of this Isaian passage becomes even more evident when put it in its context. Isaiah was a priest. As such he was perceived to be "holy." However, his experience of God's "holiness" was so diametrically opposed to his own "holy priesthood" that, when his eyes and ears were opened to recognize God's holiness, he saw the unholiness or sinfulness of his own life and state, as well as that of the people.

While the whole Isaiah 6 will be developed at much greater length in Chapter 14, I think it is incumbent on us to realize the different kinds of consciousness that lay beneath the words of the text. As a priest, cultic holiness set Isaiah apart from everyone else. In the process he developed a consciousness that now stood opposed to the religious experience of God's holiness. This experience of God—which invaded his total consciousness—gave him a new consciousness. In the process of experiencing *God's* holiness, his eyes and ears were opened to recognize the "sinfulness" of his own brand of holiness and that of his co-religionists, especially the priests. This new "understanding with the heart" gave him a totally new perspective on the world—as well as his mission to call it to conversion.

The Isaian passage demonstrates that an "understanding heart" is one that is moved to convert one's self and to call one's world from ways that do not match the new consciousness of the God of one's religious experience. When this happens in the church, as the 1971 Synod on the Ministerial Priesthood stated, the church "not only preaches conversion to God to individuals, but also, almost as society's conscience, she speaks as best she can to society itself and performs a prophetic function in this regard, always taking pains to effect her own renewal."[12]

Applying the Isaian passage to today's world, when we understand with our "heart" rather than our head, we begin moving from forms of seeing and acting that represent ways of domination and control to ways of greater connection and care. We move from a clericalized way of seeing that reinforces the isolationist forms of a Culture I Catholicism to see how it can blind us to become a small exclusive group that sets itself and its believers apart from others. Authentic biblical "understanding with the heart" involves a turning.

Increasingly a key lesson of adulthood as well as of conversion involves a process of unlearning those things that are no longer important but to which we can cling mightily. Abraham Lincoln addressed this tendency when he spoke about the need to disenthrall ourselves from "the dogmas of the quiet past" in order to "think anew." Applying his notion of "the dogmas of the past" to Catholicism in its institutional dynamics that reflect an ever-increasing clericalized tradition, we can ask, What blocks us priests from "seeing" with our eyes in a way that keeps us from being converted in a manner that will lead us to proclaim the political, economic, and religious consequences of patterning our personal, communal, and collective lives on the reign of God's holiness? The Isaian passage makes it clear that the reason why an individual or a people will not turn and be converted is personal and collective hardness of heart (*sklērokardia* [Mark 10; 16:14; Matt. 19:8]). It also reveals the depth of heretofore unconscious and unacknowledged sinfulness.

Probing the Isaian text more deeply, we find that its later use in the Synoptics refers to the "them" represented in the clerical group opposed to Jesus' message. At the same time it invites us today (especially us priests) to ask: Is it possible that these same dynamics are found among us who tell ourselves we belong to the "holy" priesthood? Why do we continue to separate ourselves in the name of our "holy" priesthood from that of the people and the *universal* call to holiness? What is the *mythos* behind the belief that we are somehow *more* holy or in a state more holy than theirs? Why are so many of us in this clerical group of Catholics so resistant to change?

A key reason anyone resists changing involves the fact that we don't think we need to change. This is compounded when we equate our ordination with a divine sanction for what we say or intimate is God's will. Such psychological shortcomings easily get projected into serious institutional problems. Because we believe we are impervious to bias and ideology (sometimes going so far as to believe we somehow are divinely ordained to actually *possess the truth*), we fail to have the eyes to see how we have become blinded. This becomes more serious when we have ears to hear but do not communicate in a way that evidences we are listening. Such closed mindedness results in closed institutions that tell themselves they are open to truth. Consequently, some researchers on this phenomenon in other institutions have stated that "the only way to get objective data is to have institutions that assume objectivity doesn't exist."[13] Using the scriptures to justify now-unjustifiable traditions demands that we be aware of such "pre-understandings," to use the image of the Pontifical Biblical Commission in its document on the proper interpretation of the Bible in the church.

Oftentimes, such warped understanding and reasoning mask what scientists call "confirmation bias"; in everyday language it is called "pigheadedness." This happens in a group or organization when people focus on data that support their views and ignore data that count against it. Science has shown how we humans can easily develop an irrational loyalty to our beliefs and work hard to find evidence to support those opinions and to discredit, discount, or simply pay no attention to information that rejects them.[14] Such faulty reasoning can be particularly susceptible when one's rationale in seeking the truth is more for apologetic purposes (to prove one's position to be right) than for the sake of truth itself.

Dan Sperber and Hugo Mercier have demonstrated a critical consequence of apologetical argumentation in an insightful piece "Why Do Humans Reason? Arguments for an Argumentative Theory." They show that reasoning involves that part of our evolution that serves the purpose of argumentation and persuasion. They share evidence that, when people argue in order to prove themselves "right" rather than to seek the truth (even when seeking "the truth" may be given as reason for the argument), the truth itself can be compromised. They say, "Reasoning is generally seen as a means to improve knowledge and make better decisions. However, much evidence shows that reasoning often leads to distortions in our thinking as well as poor decisions." A failure to recognize the resulting bias involved in such "reasoning" can undermine legitimate truth-claims. Knowing the truth requires not just true belief but also a right approach in knowing how and why that truth is communicated. The realization of the fact that it is not only "truth" that is important but how it is communicated as well is also critical to know. Sperber and Mercier continue:

> Poor performance in standard reasoning tasks is explained by the lack of [acknowledging its] argumentative context. When the same problems are placed in a proper argumentative setting, people turn out to be skilled arguers. Skilled arguers, however, are not after the truth but after arguments supporting their views. This explains the notorious confirmation bias. This bias is apparent not only when people are actually arguing, but also when they are reasoning proactively from the perspective of having to defend their opinions. Reasoning so motivated can distort evaluations and attitudes and allow erroneous beliefs to persist.[15]

Besides some of the factors noted above, another key obstacle that keeps change from happening involves fear. This has been shown by Margaret Heffernan in her *Willful Blindness: Why We Ignore the Obvious to Our Peril.* The core of the author's argument is that we all succumb, in different degrees, to ways of thinking that can actually undermine our effectiveness. Given the huge amount of information that can inundate us, we sometimes filter it in ways that counter some of the professed beliefs that we insist constitute our individual and corporate identities. These filtering mechanisms that blind us as individuals, groups, and institutions can actually undermine our moral grounding and emotional integrity. Heffernan demonstrates that love, ideology, fear, and the impulse to obey and conform all represent significant forces that blind us to dynamics that actually can be devastating to our personal and organizational lives. This blindness can lead us to keep quiet in the face of dynamics that actually undermine our core beliefs because of our various fears, especially rejection coming from officials of the group to which we belong.[16] Again, the result can be a kind of false consciousness that is blinded by the need we have to "belong."

While I was writing this book I read a *New York Times* summary of still more data that show how false consciousness can take over individuals and groups especially around notions of moral self- or group image. I found this piece to be particularly important for church leaders like myself to realize. The *Times* writer outlined "the many ways that people subconsciously maintain and massage their moral self-image. They rate themselves as morally superior to the next person; overestimate the likelihood that they will act virtuously in the future; see their own good intentions as praiseworthy while dismissing others' as inconsequential." In addition, the author stated, "scientists are beginning to learn how memory assists and even amplifies this righteous self-massaging. In piecing together a life story, the mind nudges moral lapses back in time and shunts good deeds forward . . . creating, in effect, a doctored autobiography."[17]

Even though such patterns exist throughout the wider population, they can be compounded when religious leaders see themselves as being divinely ordained with a teaching authority that is not to be questioned. This gets further compounded when their teachings get questioned in a way that those who see themselves as being in "possession of the truth" secretly are not sure of the facts to support their "truth." Again, research shows that the more people doubt their beliefs, the more likely they will actually proselytize in favor of them. Similarly, the data also show that those forced to confront evidence counter to their beliefs advocated for them more forcefully.[18] The consequence of such behavior, especially among high-achieving leaders, other data show, finds their very leadership actually compromised by a fear of showing their limitations.[19] When this occurs, such leaders can become *their own* worst enemies.

The *Dao* of an "Understanding Heart":
An Evangelical Invitation to a New Consciousness

Given the pervasiveness of the kinds of cultural obstacles that create false consciousness, even among true believers and religious leaders, it becomes all the more imperative that we examine where our eyes may be blind and our ears deaf to such data in a way that keeps us from conversion. This demands an even-greater awareness of the need for the kind of "understanding with the heart" noted by Isaiah and the Gospels' portrayal of Jesus. As Catholics, individually, communally, and within the leadership of the church itself, we need to develop the discipline or *dao* of consciousness which is a sign of the "awakeness" of the one (or ones) who practice it.

The Isaian text above makes it clear that the key obstacle to the kind of conversion that accompanies an understanding heart involves two main aspects: the closed ways of perception that keep us from a whole-hearted vision and how we hear in ways that do not reflect authentic listening. This realization takes on critical importance when we consider the kind of consciousness that is demanded of us as we work to overcome the crisis in the church of the West which this book is trying to address. This demands clear vision and dialogue.

Albert Einstein is supposed to have said two things that are apropos here: "We cannot solve problems by using the same kind of thinking that created them"; and "No problem can be resolved from the consciousness that created it. We must see the world anew." This demands a new way of seeing and listening. We must break with the old ways that have led to the problems we now face, especially around the issue of meaning. Simply put, whether as individuals, groups, or institutions, we cannot develop an evolutionary consciousness if we remain imprisoned by a flat-earth mindset.

The necessary change involved will be further compromised by dynamics that reflect wider institutional patterns of fear and control that go unrecognized and unacknowledged because of the desire to be seen as loyal to the group. Study after study shows that the behavior of individuals is highly influenced and shaped by what they consciously consider to fit the appropriate and acceptable norms of the group to which they belong or desire to belong. Even more, these norms not only influence the behavior of the members; they actually come to define their attitudes. In a fascinating summary of these dynamics reported in the *Wall Street Journal* ("Under the Influence: How the Group Changes What We Think"), the author demonstrates how "Norms serve a basic human social function, helping us distinguish who is in the group and who is an outsider. Behaving in ways the group considers appropriate is a way of demonstrating to others, and to oneself, that one belongs to the group."[20] The infamous Stanford prison experiment is another example.

Given all these obstacles that serve as barriers to a new kind of consciousness, how might we take the tentative steps that are necessary for a change to take place? In my mind, if science has told us clearly about the obstacles to such consciousness we might also find in science some sense of the possible ways we can bring about a commitment to this new consciousness.

Neuroscience has demonstrated that our brains are divided into a left and right hemisphere or sphere of influence. The left hemisphere is logical and analytical, seeking ways to dominate. The right is intuitive and inclusive, always seeking ways to move to greater wholeness. These two ways of thinking are organized into power dynamics defined by dominating patterns that evidence "left brain thinking or consciousness" or collaborative ways or relating and solving problems that reflect "right brain thinking or consciousness."

My generation was raised to think "with the head" in a way that highlighted the left brain: this was the male way. However, increasingly, especially among those working to bring about change in organizations, right-brain thinking is being stressed, not as a substitute but as a balance to our heretofore over-reliance on left-brain thinking. Returning to Isaiah and Jesus and noting the ways we can become blinded and deaf (which are identified with thinking with our "head" (left-brain consciousness), we see even more reasons to balance such head-thinking to "understanding with our heart" (right-brain consciousness). Daniel Pink has written the following in his best-seller, *A Whole New Mind*:

> Today, the defining skills of the previous era—the "left brain" capabilities that powered the Information Age—are necessary but no longer sufficient. And the capabilities we once disdained or thought frivolous—the "right-brain" qualities of inventiveness, empathy, joyfulness, and meaning—increasingly will determine who flourishes and who flounders. For individuals, families, and organizations, professional success and personal fulfillment now require a whole new mind.[21]

In the previous chapter we saw that if anyone was truly "in Christ," that one would be a new creation. The old order would be gone. Just to have the humility of heart to recognize the need for such a new creation demands a new consciousness that recognizes the futility of clinging to old ways that have proven to have failed in meeting the needs that challenge us. "A whole new mind" is a matter of individual and organizational success and fulfillment. Even more, it represents fidelity to the core message of Jesus Christ regarding an attitude that reflects openness to his "gospel of the 'kindom' of trinitarian relatedness": a change of mind, a change of heart. This change will determine the degree to which we expand our consciousness into a greater awareness of our connectedness to everyone and everything. In Hebrew, such a consciousness is called *mochin d'gadlut,* or open mindedness. This stands opposite ways of constricted consciousness that reflect what is meant by the Hebrew image of *mochin d'katnut,* or small mindedness.

The ability to change our way of thinking or consciousness reveals dynamics that will show whether a person, group, and institution is open or closed. When our bodily systems start shutting down, death is not far behind. The same can be said of the organizational body. I have learned, from my struggle with adapting to ever-new forms of communication in this information-formed world, that when we no longer have anything to learn, we become increasingly irrelevant to that world to the point that we might not even be aware of its language. When this happens to human organizations it is a sure sign it is becoming brain-dead and quite possibility on the way to extinction. The data about the decline of living members in the church of the West give some evidence of this dynamic taking place.

We know from science that all matter is ultimately energy and that all the forms of connectedness enable everything to be its particular *it.* Knowing this makes it abundantly clear that the connecting that enables every "it" to be its unique "it" involves some kind of consciousness. Each "it" contains its own kind of consciousness or information which is communicated at each level to create the next level in ever-more-complex forms. The ability to process and communicate information defines every person and all systems as conscious. Information-based consciousness thus involves the energy that grounds all materiality, be it the smallest neutron, proton, or the basic quark itself. In humans all are organized holarchically up to the system we call "brain." Applying this reality to our personal lives and systems, we must be aware of the consequences of what physicists, biologists, and neuroscientists are telling us: because closed systems involve a shut-down of consciousness and entropy, we humans must be open to ever-new forms of information and consciousness all around us if we and our systems will survive. Thus Margaret Wheatley writes:

> If we understand consciousness from the viewpoint of machine imagery, this makes no sense. If there is no identifiable part that handles thinking and communication, then there can be no such activity. In the past, we measured an organism's capacity for intelligence by counting the part of it brain (or noting the lack of one). . . . Instead, consciousness is a property that emerges when a certain level of organization is reached. Anything capable of self-organizing, therefore, possesses a level of consciousness. A well-ordered system is defined not by how many brain parts it has, but by how much information it can process. The greater the ability to process information, the greater the level of consciousness.[22]

In every living system, such as our bodies, there is a form of conscious-ness in each and every part. Connected together, these contribute to a deeper consciousness. Science shows that this is not only evidenced in the brain but throughout the whole body—thus the saying that we should "listen to our bodies." Science shows that our skin, our heart, and other organs have their unique "minds" and ways of knowing and remembering. These may not be identical to what we identify with our brains, but they do seem to have a mem-ory of their own. Together, these contribute to our bodies being living sys-tems. When shut-down occurs in our kidneys and other organs, death will not be far behind.

Applying this data to larger systems that organize people, we find that in a closed system there is no new consciousness nor anything new to learn. In an ideologically closed system everything needed to be known has already been received. If Wheatley is right about well-functioning organizations being dependent on being open to new information, then we can see an even-deeper reason for the crisis facing the Catholic Church, especially the role of its lead-ers, regarding which model will guide their decision making. According to Wheatley, "In the traditional model, we leave the interpretation of informa-tion to senior or expert people." However, when the interpretation is limited to such a small group, even when its members may be aware of the tendency to be selective in their interpretation, it also means they will be able to observe "only very few of the potentialities contained within the data."[23] Despite what science is telling us about such a situation, when the traditional model revolves around the *mythos* that ordination itself metaphysically endows the bishop with teaching authority, there is no need for further intellectual or intelligent discussion and/or development, only insistence on a certain kind of ortho-doxy. When this happens in any organization, the free flow of information is restricted, if not denied altogether. Following quantum theory, living systems (be they individuals, groups or institutions) have built-in dynamics for gener-ating and absorbing information, for feedback, and for self-regulation. When the freedom of such flows is restricted or denied, there can be no nourishment in the system. Because such flows enable everything to exist and survive, with-out such flow, a vacuum will arise.[24]

The experience of the present vacuum of meaninglessness, I believe, is but one explanation why the institutional church is "dead" to so many.

Growing into a New Consciousness

The notion of consciousness came into academic discourse less than five hun-dred years ago. Despite this, what consciousness itself means (or involves) has always elicited deep debate. What might seem self-evident, upon further investigation, leads to the need for ever-more-nuanced insights to determine consciousness itself as well as the various levels of consciousness.

The psychotherapist Philip Chard is the first I have read who has outlined the process of moving into ever-deeper forms of being "awake" in our consciousness. His writings outline the gradual way human awareness involves "levels of inner experience."[25] To achieve the deepest type of consciousness (which is mysticism) involves five stages, which will be developed below.

The first and outermost realm involves those dynamics that include our thoughts and primary, unreflective forms of sensations such as sight and sound (as noted by the Isaian text above), pain, and basic emotions. Closing our eyes and just being awake to these characteristics of our "self" represent the first level of being "conscious" of our consciousness.

Second, when we slow down or quiet our senses we become aware of a connectedness that lies beyond what we ordinarily see or hear. This moves us to the next level of consciousness. This is called visualization or, in some spiritualities, meditation. "Once there," he writes, we "just allow mental images to bubble up without trying to censor or control them. You may experience a cavalcade of scenes, memories and seemingly random imagery." He notes that this level is where "many artists and creative thinkers hang out."

The third level goes beyond the other two stages to arrive at what some call "the sixth sense." Here people discipline themselves in order to enter a realm beyond normal ways of thinking and feeling. It is the area of illuminating insights, aha moments, and intuitive leaps. Here a deeper sense of our connectedness to everyone and everything is experienced. Sometimes its dynamics are discussed in paranormal phenomenon and near-death experiences.

The fourth level is very important for our purposes in this book. It is "a transitional zone where one's sense of self (the ego) starts to evaporate." Chard cautions that this "can be a scary state for many (it feels a bit like dying mentally), although mystics pursue it in hopes of growing close to God." I would add to Chard's explanation that this is where one's whole goal in life is to "become the Christ" or to be dissolved in the Godhead of the Trinity.

This critical fourth form of consciousness deserves deeper analysis. It is here that the notion of consciousness emerging through natural selection in order to be more consciously connected to others in their consciousness makes more sense. However, at an even-deeper level, again building on what we know about natural selection, we find that it involves the kind of *kenosis* or "letting go" of our selves at one level to let emerge or give birth to a higher form of consciousness. This is described eloquently by the author of the letter to the Philippians:

> Have this mind among yourselves, which was in Christ Jesus, who,
> though he was in the form of God, did not count equality with God a
> thing to be grasped, but emptied (*kenoō*) himself, taking the form of a

servant, being born in the likeness of men. And being found in human form he humbled himself and became obedient unto death, even death on a cross. Therefore God has highly exalted him and bestowed on him the name which is above every name, that at the name of Jesus every knee should bow, in heaven and on earth and under the earth and every tongue confess that Jesus Christ is Lord. (Phil. 2:5-11)

The "mind" or consciousness that was "in" Jesus Christ that evidenced his evolution to the point of such love that he would be willing to lay down his life only to have it emerge into an awesome form of cosmic consciousness has been called the "epistemology of the cross." It involves the level of a human's consciousness that realizes only in dying can new life evolve, even if this means death on a cross. It involves the awareness and consciousness that the "cross" imposed on such a person by closed-minded people for having such a consciousness come because of the undeveloped level of consciousness that is represented in those who impose that cross. Since the story of Jesus involves him freely embracing the cross as the consequence of his fidelity to the gospel of trinitarian connectedness, the author of the letter to the members of the Body of Christ at Philippi reminds them that they too must have that same mind" or consciousness if they are ever to be transformed into the love that is represented in such self-giving. The *dao* of the disciples called to "take up their cross" demands no less.

Epistemology studies the nature of knowledge, its scope and limits and how we humans come "to know." However, for those whose "knowing" is colored by their faith in the power of the cross and resurrection, there is a kind of epistemology of the cross that offers a faith perspective on knowing that can deeply transform our personal, communal, and collective lives. In her writing on this epistemology of the cross, in which she addresses the psychology of knowing, Eleanor Godway suggests that the "traditional model of knowing involves something of domination, which in the end we will need to give up." She shows that as such a dominating way of knowing "set the subject 'above' the object known, it came about that the subject assumed a position of privilege. One of the features of privilege apparent in many situations of oppression is that it tends to become invisible to the holders of that privilege, especially if they form a group."[26]

Being a white, male cleric in the Roman Catholic Church in the United States represents a clear position of privilege. If I am going to embrace the "emptying" way of knowing that was revealed in the *kenosis* of the Word in becoming human, Godway's conclusion makes all the sense in the world. She writes, "We have to 'unlearn' what we have been colluding with as we have been co-opted by privilege, and the outcome of this unlearning will allow us to handle the violence [of the dominating way of knowing and acting] differ-ently—that is why I make so bold as to refer to an 'epistemology of the Cross.'"[27]

The discipline of *kenosis* invites us to the fifth level of becoming conscious at the deepest level of our "I am," the awareness of being connected at our core with the source and ground of all being. This cannot be described, only experienced. "You just have to be there," Chard writes. This, he explains, is the level of religious experience or mysticism. Sam Harris also calls it "spirituality." Chard explains, "mystics call it a timeless state of pure being in which the feeling of separation ('me' as distinct from everything else) dissolves, replaced by an experience of complete oneness with . . . creation, God, one's higher power, etc." This is what Chapter 14 on contemplation will describe as the "Shug Experience."

It should be evident from what has been said in this chapter that a critical component in our human development involves ever-deepening forms of awakening to ever-greater consciousness. While the actual experience of contemplation is not the work of human hands, humans can develop their consciousness in such ways that evidence its dynamics. However, while this highly evolved form of consciousness may not be reflected in those who consider themselves religious, it certainly is within the realm of those who know about spirituality. As such, it has been well articulated by Andrew Cohen, editor of *EnlightNext* magazine in an interview with Ken Wilber:

> I'm beginning to see that so much of spiritual development is really about finding ways to creatively compel ourselves, through our own inspired will and intention, to actually evolve. Ideally, I believe, we will get to the point where the experience of enlightenment, which is the direct awakening to consciousness, becomes automatically fused with the experience of a higher level of cognition.[28]

How does one move through these stages? For our purposes here, the whole process of moving from our head to our heart, from left-brain thinking to a more balanced life involving right-brain consciousness, begins with a process of slowing down. A very helpful way to achieve this is to consciously direct our senses and sensations toward a kind of centering wherein our eyes cannot only see but perceive relatedness and connectedness and our ears might not only hear but listen in a way that makes us be at the loving service of everyone and everything with whom we feel a deeper relatedness and connectedness. This process of developing an understanding heart moves us from head-thinking to heart affectivity. The way to the heart involves the discipline of silence.

A time-honored way to move into a way of silencing our senses involves the discipline or *dao* related to inhaling and exhaling, of taking deeper and deeper, longer and longer breaths. When I work with people trying to practice deep breathing, I suggest they get into a comfortable but intentional body posture with the back straight and feet on the floor. Then, after a quick breathing out, I suggest they breathe in as deeply and as long as they can without straining. This involves inhaling by ballooning their stomach and exhaling by letting the diaphragm relax. By concentrating on bodily breathing one can move more easily toward non-mental ways of knowing, or deeper and deeper consciousness of the type outlined above by Philip Chard.

Chard himself is convinced that virtually every emotional state is enhanced or undermined in ways that are associated with our breathing. Since most of our breathing is unconscious, he, like many psychotherapists, is convinced of the need to bring greater consciousness to our breathing. He notes that when people are stressed out they breathe in a tight, restrained way; when they are deeply conscious of their breathing, they inhale deeply from the diaphragm. He also believes that what is becoming increasingly clear to people in his field of therapy has been known for centuries by people involved in the spiritual life: "This is why so many spiritual disciplines, such as meditation and yoga, employ specific kinds of respiration to center and ground the spirit. Meditative breathing can clear the mind, calm the heart, and anchor the soul."[29]

Some directors suggest the use of mantras (usually not more than seven syllables). One half of the mantra is used as one breathes in, and the other half is silently uttered as the person breathes out. These mantras can come from a host of sources, ranging from a passage in scripture to a word summary of where one wants to be in one's relationship to God, self, and others, including everyone and everything in creation. Others suggest using images on which one might center one's gaze. Still others stress the breathing pattern itself, free of any thoughts, mantras, or images, as the essential pattern that brings about a sense of greater quiet and connectedness. Whatever the approach used, the goal is to help the person move from the head to the heart, from sensate thinking to an ever-greater consciousness of our connectedness—a sense of belonging to something much bigger than one has experienced. In the process of this breathing we enter more deeply into the kind of "understanding with the heart" or consciousness that makes one feel a greater clarity about what is important in life and a deeper sense of belonging. Using our metaphor of house, John Donohue describes the power involved in such breathing in his *Anam Ċara*: "Through breath meditation, you begin to experience a place within you that is absolutely intimate with the divine ground. Your breathing and the rhythm of your breathing can return you to your ancient belonging, to the house, as Eckhart says, that you have never left, where you always live: the house of spiritual belonging."[30]

This notion of breathing-leading-to-greater-consciousness that brings about a deeper sense of spiritual belonging leads us to our next chapter. It outlines how we can "belong" in ways that bring about ever-greater forms of our conscious connectedness to everyone and everything in the cosmos.

THE WAY OF CONNECTEDNESS

Richard Feynman, considered by many to be the greatest physicist of the last half of the twentieth century, received a Nobel Prize in Physics in 1983. The award was given to him for the way he explained the interaction between electrons and protons in terms of quantum mechanics. In the world of quantum reality (unlike the machine world of Newton), everything is what it is because of its relationality. Everything that exists involves relationships continually seeking connectedness. In a query that reflects our desire to create a spirituality faithful to what science is telling us about the atom, Feynman once asked, "If, in some cataclysm, all of scientific knowledge were to be destroyed, and only one sentence passed on to the next generations of creatures, what statement would contain the most information in the fewest words?" He responded to his own question with his own one-sentence summary: "I believe it is the atomic hypothesis (or the atomic fact, or whatever you wish to call it) that all things are made of atoms—little particles that move around in perpetual motion, attracting each other when they are a little distance apart, but repelling upon being squeezed into one another."[1]

Whether it involves the law of attraction or the law of repulsion, nothing exists apart from relatedness or connectedness. When we apply this quantum fact to human relationships, we know they will be most effective and productive when people are conscious that they are a part of one another rather than apart from one another. Consequently, when we speak of becoming conscious of the connectedness that is at the core of all reality and apply this scientific fact to humans we better understand humanity's deep need for connectedness in our individual, communal, and institutional lives. Such connectedness represents the core of our "I am." Not only is this God's view for humans (that it is not good to "be alone"); it is an established scientific fact. "To be is to be with," or, as Martin Buber said so eloquently, "All life is meeting."

My deepest experience of this came on the infamous day of September 11, 2001. The weekend before I had been a guest speaker at a Catholic Charities convention in Newark. My hotel room had a clear view of the World Trade

Center and the Statue of Liberty. From there I had taken a train to Manhattan to stay with the Capuchins at St. John's Friary on 31st Street.

September 11, 2001 was a beautifully bright blue day. And then came the devastation. In order to see it, one needed to go to the "Avenues" and look downtown. All that appeared there in that beautiful blue sky was the dark cloud rising to reveal the degree of destruction.

Two days later I walked outside (not able to get transportation out of New York) to be met with an equally blue sky as on "9/11." However, it was only a few seconds before something strange happened in my body. My eyes started to itch, my nose felt clogged, and my tongue got dry. It did not take me long to figure out what had happened: the wind had shifted. What was in that observable acrid cloud downtown had moved invisibly to Midtown. Now it had entered my body; it had become part of me. I now held within my own body the remains of the guilty and the innocent, the perpetrators and the victims, those who died full of revenge and those who died full of love.

That day made me aware of a key dictum of quantum reality in a way I never imagined. I learned through this tragedy that we are all connected not just in some nebulous way, but truly, in the very air we cannot see but breathe into our bodies. My next breaths led me to a mindfulness I never experienced before. It involved a consciousness of the fact that every breath I take in life takes in the good and the not-good. As I consciously breathe these realities into the core of myself, I must stop the violence. I must absorb the negative energy and give back only what is positive. My heart must act like a purifying force that breathes back into the universe only that which repairs and builds up. Such an understanding is much like the Buddhist meditation of *tonglen,* wherein a person breathes in other peoples' suffering and the negativity of our world (*dukha*) in a way that transforms that negative energy and exhales into our world only goodness and kindness, care and empathy.

To build on the previous chapter, as our level of consciousness increases in ways that free us from our ego and false self, an ever-greater awareness of our connectedness to everyone and everything increases exponentially. This sense of my interconnection with everyone and everything finds me moving from dynamics of control to seeking the right kind of order that enables the best functioning in my relationships at every level. The more I relate in ways that free others from my control and the more I can experience relationships wherein I am free from others' control, the more I move (consciously or unconsciously) to a higher level of integrative being. As the systems scientists Erich Jantsch writes, "In life, the issue is not control, but dynamic connectedness."[2]

As my consciousness of my connectedness moves to greater integration and wholeness, I grow in my desire to experience and seek ever-more inclusive ways of being *with*. Why? Because I have become conscious that this is more integrative of who I am and who I am meant to be. Meaning happens when I come to realize that, at the highest level (or is it the deepest level) of consciousness, I cannot say "I am" apart from being consciously awake to my connectedness to everyone and everything.

We experience our need for connectedness at our birth when we are confronted with the fear of separation anxiety. This need continues to be expressed (in positive and negative ways) until we are faced with death, where our only desire, as my dying brother Pat taught me, is that our loved ones just "be with us." In between it gets expressed at the beginning of the day when we read "Dear Abby," when it becomes abundantly clear that all life involves our conscious or unconscious striving for connectedness. At the same time, given the conflicts described in each of those letters, we also must admit that, despite all the advice, we human beings have not quite learned the recipe of how to connect in a way that will bring about greater meaning in our lives.

Unfortunately, especially in non-communally oriented cultures like our own , we often feel more apart than connected. This separation results in patterns of relating that truly are "unnatural," if quantum laws rather than those of Newtonian mechanics represent what we know about our world. This has led to the development of an egocentric "I" mentality rather than an interconnected "we" way of thinking that impacts our stance toward life. When such an ideology is sanctioned politically ("get government off my back"), economically (resistance to taxes in any form), and culturally (which we will discuss later), it can take a very long time, if not a lifetime, of ascetical practice to disassociate ourselves from thinking that we are the center of the universe (or, at least, our world). This applies to us as individuals as much as it does to us in our organizations, be they political or religious. When any one individual or group interprets their understanding of reality as the best or only way, one or one's group becomes the center of the world. The result of such thinking is that, when we are the center, everyone else is at the margins and, thus, marginalized—if not totally outside the center of our lives. The result: we become disconnected to many more than the few in our small sphere with whom we see ourselves connected.

While a culture of individualism exaggerates this human tendency to be the center of the world, the fact that the world, being round, has no center makes it easier for each of us to be self-centered rather than other-oriented. The result is a disconnect from creation and its processes. Because of this self- and group-centeredness, it now takes a lot of discipline to de-center ourselves in ways that will make us, as Francis of Assisi urged us, to be "subject to every human creature for God's sake" or how Ignatius of Loyola asked us to recognize how we could find the reign or reality of God and lovingly serve that reality in *everything*. Why? Because God is everywhere.

The invitation to make this way of thinking ever-more conscious in our psyches has been evolving in me over the years. In the winter of 2011, just before writing this book, the awareness of this need became more immediate to me while at a meeting in Bangkok. Years before I had visited Bangkok simply as a tourist. What happened there in 1986 became a prelude to my later, 2010 experience of how this evolution in my consciousness was taking place.

In 1986, I was given a tour of Bangkok by Fr. Eugene Pocernich, a priest of the Archdiocese of Milwaukee. He was ministering in Bangkok as a Maryknoll volunteer. We walked around the city a long time, took rides on its canals, got a Thai massage, and visited its many temples. We were in our shorts, which was taboo for Thai males. But why did we need to care about this? We were "Americans." After quite a few hours of walking, I needed to use the men's room. Luckily this need arose while we were in that area of Bangkok where the large hotel chains were located. So we walked up the steps of one of the famous intercontinental hotels. Immediately the doorman greeted us with a smile and opened the door without a question as to why we were there. As I was passing him, I realized that, had I been a Thai male (even one in long pants), I would have been stopped at the door. I would have been asked what business I had coming to such a place. While the whole reality assumed I belonged (in *his* country), a Thai male would have been challenged about his connection. At that I realized how privileged I was as a white male, and, in addition (from the assumption of the doorman looking at my shorts), an American.

This time in 2011, however, my thoughts went in another direction. Now I began from the realization that I was in "their" country. Now I knew I was an outsider; not a member of their body, not a part of their world. Aware of this sense of being not a part of their reality, I found myself wanting to find a way to be better connected to the hundreds of people who passed me by, who waited on me in stores, or looked at me in a way that let me know I did not "belong."

One day as I stood on a busy five-way corner in one of the key market areas of Bangkok, fascinated by the way the motor scooters made their way to the head of the line while the cars waited for the light to change, the realization came to me that every single person who existed within my vision was the "center of the world." This insight led me to realize that, only when I would begin being conscious of them as such and treating them as such would I truly be connected to them in a trinitarian way.

This experience at that place of five corners was not exactly the same as what Thomas Merton called his "Fourth and Walnut" experience of contemplation. However, it did help me move more deeply into a contemplative attitude toward the people who had opened my eyes to perceive in a way that gave me a more understanding heart. Indeed, that day, I turned a little bit—away from myself to make each of them, rather than myself, the center of *my world.*

The weekend after I returned to the States, I drove from Milwaukee to Clinton, Iowa, to give talks to the Clinton Franciscan Sisters and their Associates. As I drove the interstate highway, my Bangkok experience came alive again. I began looking at the people in the cars passing me and going in the other direction. I somehow tried to get inside each of the houses in the towns and villages, the farms and the shops I passed by. I did so with the realization that every one of these human beings (at least as far as their consciousness was concerned) was the center of the world. Only when I would grow in my consciousness of their consciousness would I begin seeing them as such and treating them as such. Only then would I truly be connected to them so that I could be "in" them and they would be "in" me.

Everything about the way I understand my connectedness depends on my consciousness. When I make myself the center of the world, this represents a "false consciousness"; I deny what is true in science. This is reinforced from passages attributed to two of the greatest scientists of our modern world: Albert Einstein and David Bohm. When we place them next to each other, we see how their thinking coincides regarding the false consciousness that too often results in our acting more separated than united:

Albert Einstein	*David Bohm*
A human being is part of the whole called by us universe, a part limited in time and space. We experience ourselves, our thoughts and feelings as something separate from the rest. A kind of optical delusion of consciousness. This delusion is a kind of prison for us, restricting us to our personal desires and to affection for a few persons nearest to us. Our task must be to free ourselves from the prison by widening our circle of compassion to embrace all living creatures and the whole of nature in its beauty. We shall require a substantially new manner of thinking if humankind is to survive.	Fragmentation is now very widespread, not only throughout society, but also in each individual; and this is leading to a kind of general confusion of the mind, which creates an endless series of problems and interferes with our clarity of perception so seriously as to prevent us from being able to solve most of them. . . . The notion that all these fragments are separately existent is evidently an illusion, and this illusion cannot do other than lead to endless conflict and confusion.

When we see ourselves not just separate from others but actually separated from them, the likelihood exists that we will think, feel, and act toward others as though we are *apart from* them rather than *a part of* them and they of us. Such thinking, we will see, not only stands against the core theology of discipleship in John's Gospel (which revolves around us *remaining in* Christ in the relatedness of love *as* Christ remains in the Godhead); it actually is shown to be unnatural, if we look at the way "the world really works all the way from subatomic particles, up to the mind and on to the cosmos." From these we learn four great rules about our connectedness to everyone and everything:

1. The universe is a web of interconnected relationships that evidence the "natural" fact that everything is connected. Each whole is its whole because of the wholeness of its individual parts. Every whole is itself a part of another whole, structuring everything by holons. This makes everything in our universe defined by holons wherein, at each level, every part is in the whole and the whole is in each and every part.

2. Because holons emerge holarchically, any isolating individualism, with all its consequent social expressions that are expressed in unequal power dynamics (as in institutional "isms") are, to that degree, not "normal" but purely human constructs. Since all hierarchy in the universe is the result of holarchy, authentic hierarchy must be holarchical.

3. The conclusion of this, especially for human beings and human organizations, is that our "I am" cannot be realized apart from connectedness to the other—indeed, all others. We are wired for connectedness; to the degree we disconnect or disengage from others, we move into entropy and lose a key source beyond ourselves that ensures our survivability.

4. The universe, despite its periodic upheavals, is intrinsically ordered toward ever-greater forms of evolution, including increasing consciousness about the core connectedness of the universe. Personhood involves the sum total of these relationships in their evolving consciousness. The apogee of such personhood involves a community of persons interconnected.

Margaret Wheatley brings together these notions in a wonderful passage that shows how nature is telling us that connectedness is the essence of what science is telling us about our whole world and, by extension, how we must relate connectedly or die disconnectedly:

> To live in a quantum world, to weave here and there with ease and grace, we will need to change what we do. We will need to stop describing tasks and instead facilitate *process*. We will need to become savvy about how to build relationships, how to nurture growing, evolving things. All of us will need better skills in listening, communicating, and facilitating groups, because these are the talents that build strong relationships. It is well known that the era of the rugged individual has been replaced by the era of the team player. But this is only the beginning. The quantum world has demolished the concept of the unconnected individual. More and more relationships are in store for us, out there in the vast web of universal connections.[3]

The basic difference between a cultural consciousness of individualism and separation that makes us "apart from" vs. a "quantum consciousness" that makes us feel "a part of" can be outlined in the following grid:

Viewing Ourselves as Being Apart from the Other	Viewing Ourselves as Being a Part of the Other
A personal sense of being disconnected	A sense that our "I am" is connected to all in the universe
Desire to be apart within our groupings	Desire to work with others; collaborate for better outcomes
Partisanship of groups with regard to others	Participative model regarding problems and problem solving
Institutionalized apartheid in the "isms"	Institutionalized structures of holarchy mutually interdependent
Morally stresses sin; works of the flesh	Morally stresses fruits of Holy Spirit

Being born and raised in the United States acculturates us to the notion of apartness because of its characteristic individualism that seems not only excessive but is increasing. This is evidenced culturally in everything from our advertising to our music. This was noted in an April 2011 New York Times article. It featured research that made it clear that today's songs "are more likely about one special person: the singer."[4] While self-centeredness has been the sign and consequence of humanity's original sin since the beginning, such data prove the fact that "American self-involvement is actually reaching an apogee in the age of Facebook and Twitter."

Pointing to this research, Ross Douthat opined in one of his columns in the New York Times: "Younger Americans are more self-absorbed, less empathetic and hungrier for approbation than earlier generations—and these trends seem to have accelerated as Internet culture has ripened. The rituals of social media, it seems, make status-seekers and exhibitionists of us all."[5] In terms of the topic of this chapter, the social media (which was created to help us connect) actually has often resulted in a sense of greater disconnectedness and isolation. Sherry Turkle summarizes what many are saying in this regard in her book Alone Together: Why We Expect More from Technology and Less from Each Other.[6]

The blame for such an individualistic approach to life cannot be laid at the doorstep of U.S. culture alone. Its twin is alive and well in a theological form of individualism that finds home in an individualistic approach to salvation. Those who are saved are "apart" from the unsaved; even their communities are based on an individual member's personal salvation. It is not so much that "Jesus saved us" but "Jesus is my personal savior." This "parts" mentality in Christianity has been well described by Ilia Delio:

Christianity has focused so intently on sin and salvation that it has lost sight of Christ as the new creation emerging from within. The dominant Hellenic influence on the shape of Christian thought has imparted an unhealthy otherworldly focus, reinforced by dualistic thinking of matter and spirit, soul and body, as if separate parts come together by the power of God for the construction of the human person. A "parts" mentality has led to an understanding of the whole creation as parts distinctly separated from one another: humans from trees, Catholics from Jews, men from women, cleric from lay, and the litany goes on. A Christology of parts mirrors a cosmology of parts.... Instead of becoming whole-makers, following the example of Jesus, we have become parts people, fragmenting the cosmos into little pieces and setting parts over and against one another. Christianity must move beyond fragmentation if it is to remain true to its identity in the person of Jesus Christ.[7]

As the chart above indicates, when we look at the fragmentation noted by Ilia Delio and link it to the "apartness" we have been discussing, it is not difficult to see how an exaggerated individualism works out its dynamics structurally in the ever-increasing partisan divide we see manifest in all new forms of organizational and institutional apartheid, be this political (as between ideological Republicans and Democrats in the United States), economic (as in the ever-increasing divide between rich, poor, and middle-class), and religion, be it Islamic between Sunnis and Shias or Catholicism (between Culture I and Culture II expressions). And just as it was an ecumenical group of religious leaders in South Africa who recognized the ungodliness and sinfulness of its apartheid system, so, in our own religion, we must call the structured inequality between men and women "ecclesiastical apartheid." This demands that we no longer consider such apartheid a matter of God's will but name it the sin that it is. Furthermore, when church leaders continue to insist that such ecclesiastical apartheid is a matter of God's will, that definition of this structural sexism needs also to be exposed as idolatrous because such leaders are asking their followers to worship a God that is false and made by men. Rather than imaging male and female as equal "I am's" in the church they are promoting a form of idolatry wherein men image God more fully than women. This is not only untrinitarian; it is ungodly and, as such, must be exposed and resisted.

Recalling our reference to the two ways of thinking (along with their parallel moral stances) discussed in Chapter 3, we find that the insights about the United States being "a nation divided over right and wrong" of the economist Paul Krugman in January 2011 also have resonance when we deal with what we have called Culture I and Culture II Catholicism.

Even though Krugman describes the opposing moral grounding for each position and concludes "there's no middle ground between these views," I am not prepared to say the same of Culture I and II Catholicism. This is especially true when, as we have said many times, such positions are based not in dogma but in other issues that are treated as dogmatic. However, I do agree with Krugman that "the real challenge we face is not how to resolve our differences—something that won't happen any time soon—but how to keep the expressions of those differences within bounds." He notes of the divide regarding government what others have said of the divisions in the Roman Catholic Church: "But what we're talking about here is a fundamental disagreement about the proper role of government."[8] If we can agree on our core dogmas, and if Pope Benedict XVI has said we need a change of mentality that does not see the laity as under the bishops and priests but co-responsible with these clerics, can we not see that this should be the basis for a new form of governance in our church? If we can agree with the pope on this, which involves a matter of governance (even though he never said so), can we not set aside the other issues dealing with non-dogmatic differences and, together, be "a part of" a common effort to address the deeper crisis facing the church in the West, especially in our own nation?

It seems to me this challenge is critical for our future when we move from what we know from science about the way our world works to the Scriptures, especially John's Gospel, to discover Jesus' vision of what it means to be a "church" whose governance is grounded in the form of organization found in the trinitarian Godhead. When we consider the prayer for unity offered by Jesus in John's Gospel, we find that it constitutes as many chapters (though not as many verses) as the whole passion, death, and resurrection narrative, including the added ending of the Gospel (John 21:1-25). From the beginning of the Gospel narrative after the Prologue, one common theme is woven through its trial-like tapestry: *remain* with me *as* I *remain* with the one he called "Father."

In no other place in the New Testament do we find the word "remain" (*menein*) and its parallel "to be in" (*einai en*) developed as thoroughly as in the writings attributed to John, be they the Fourth Gospel or the three letters. Mark uses these words only twice; Matthew uses them three times, while in Luke they are used seven times. However in the Johannine corpus they appear almost five times more (sixty-seven times) than the three Synoptic Gospels combined. This includes the forty times they appear in the Fourth Gospel and the twenty-seven times we find them in the letters.[9] It goes without saying that John's theology revolves around notions primarily associated with the words *menein* and *einai en*.

We get a better grasp of the breadth of their meaning related to our chapter's concern about *connectedness* when we consider the various words the Latin uses to translate the Greek: *manere, permanere, remanere, sustinere, habitare*.

Whatever the translation, it becomes clear that these words describe and outline a radical new way of being connected to one another and God in the way
the members of the Godhead are connected to each other. This way of relating is meant to define those who will be disciples of Jesus and belong to his
newly constituted family. Along with *einai en*, these notions bookend John's
Gospel from the beginning when John the Baptist sees the Spirit remaining
with Jesus (John 1:32) and does not try to stop two of his disciples who follow
Jesus only to remain with him (John 1:39) to the last five verses of the Gospel
wherein the Beloved Disciple (in contrast to Peter)[10] is to remain with Jesus
until he returns (John 21:20-25). All these passages are brought together in
the high theology of John regarding the Eucharist (John 6:56) and, in a more
developed way, through the metaphor of the vine and the branches wherein
Jesus describes the connectedness he has with his followers (John 15:1-6) as
patterned on his connection to the Godhead.

In speaking about this kind of connectedness or belonging, Pope Benedict
XVI has said: "This belonging to each other and to him is not some ideal,
imaginary, symbolic relationship, but—I would almost want to say—a biological, life-transmitting state of belonging to Jesus Christ."[11] In relation to
the metaphor used throughout this book, that of the "house," we find the consoling promise Jesus made to his disciples whose hearts were troubled regarding his physical departure from their midst: "In my Father's house (*oikia*)
there are many places to remain (*monai*); if it were not so, would I have told
you that I go to prepare a place for you" (John 14:2).

Maybe it was because I was writing this book in the spring of 2011 or just
plain grace, but, during the Easter season when we read John's Gospel, another
word besides *menein* and *einai en* kept making a demand on my theological
imagination. It is the word "as" or "just as" (*kathōs*) that we read in the Gospel's most mystical section: John 17. This demand became very clear to me in
the context of a Provincial Chapter that we celebrated as Capuchin Franciscan
brothers June 7-10, 2010. There, blessed with fifteen to twenty young men in
initial formation, more than one hundred of us perpetually professed brothers
gathered with still more brothers from three other continents. At the Mass on
Thursday, we heard in the Gospel Jesus pray to the one he called "Father" not
only for those who surrounded him that evening of his death, but also this evening of June 9 for us with whom he has promised to *remain* and who believe in
him on the word of such writers as the Synoptics, Paul, and John:

> I do not pray for these only, but also for those who believe in me
> through their word, that they may all be one; even as (*kathōs*) you,
> Father, art in me, and I in thee, that they also may be in us, so that the
> world may believe that thou has sent me. The glory which thou hast
> given me I have given to them, that they may be one even as (*kathōs*)

we are one. I in them and thou in me, that they may become perfectly one, so that the world may know that thou has sent me and hast loved them even as (*kathōs*) thou hast loved me. Father, I desire that they also, whom thou hast given me, may be with me where I am, to behold my glory which thou hast given me in thy love for me before the foundation of the world. O righteous Father, the world has not known thee, but I have known thee, and these know that thou has sent me. I made known to them thy name, and I will make it known, that the love with which thou has loved me may be in them, and I in them. (John 17:20-26)

Simply put, the dream of the trinitarian reality and its dynamics, incarnated in Jesus Christ, who has come to remain with us, revolves around the "gospel" of having the trinitarian dynamics of love constitute the members of Jesus' community so that they are organized just as (*kathōs*) the Trinity is organized. This is the structuring envisioned "before the foundation of the world." This trinitarian way of relating within the Godhead is not only continued in us in the same way (*kathōs*); it is to be manifested to the world in the same way: through our way of relating that is trinitarian. And if any part of the world rejects this way of relating, it is a sign that it knows neither Jesus nor the one who sent him. All-inclusive, self-giving love is the hallmark of the Trinity; all those who *remain* in that Trinity/Love must also be all-inclusive and self-giving without any distinction.

We are to remain in God and *in one another* personally, communally, and institutionally in a way that mirrors the Holy Trinity. Theologians have told us that, just as the love of God has been revealed communally, so the way the members of this community remain with one another is through such dynamics as have been described as *condelictus, perichōrēsis*, indwelling, and coinherence. Whereas, in the past, great debates would revolve around which dimension of the Trinity would be stressed—its oneness (the members sharing one substance or *ousia*) or three-ness (wherein the one God is revealed as three persons or *prosopoi*)—so, now, in this quantum age, the stress should be put on the relationship that exists between the one and the three. No member of the Trinity can say "I am" apart from that one's relationality with each of the others and without them able to say equally "I am." Indeed, without community or being "a part of," there can be neither one nor three. God cannot be trinitarian apart from being communitarian. John Zizioulas says that it is "unthinkable to speak of the 'one God' before speaking of the God who is 'communion,'" that is, the Holy Trinity.[12] Communion is the "I am" or being of God. This communion is what males and females have been blessed by God to image. Not only that, this is what Jesus meant by praying that *all* of us may be one *as* he celebrated his oneness with the Father through their relatedness to the Spirit.

The chart below shows that whether we stress the "three" or the "one" (as in "one in three" or "three in one") in describing the Trinity, we can never forget that the "in" is the link that is at the heart of the connectedness between the one and the three. Increasingly we are realizing that it is not so much the one or the three but the relationality or communion (i.e., their "in-ness") that makes the one three and the three one.

TRINITY: MUTUAL INDWELLING

ONE ⟶ THREE
GOD ⟵ - - **IN** - - ⟶ PERSONS
(*ousia*) ⟵ (*prosōpa*)

Aware of what would divide his followers the night before he died, Jesus was "troubled in spirit" (John 13:21). This led to his prayer for those actually with him physically that night and for us who would "remain" with him in the future. The prayer was that they and we might be one "just as" (*kathōs*) the trinitarian members remained with each other. This prayer asked that we might relate to each other perichoretically in the way Jesus experienced in the Godhead. It also reflected the way all relationships are expressed in nature as well as humanly: holarchically, that is, each part creates the whole and the whole is in each part; no one is apart from; all are a part of. This way of relating, based on the indwelling of the Trinity throughout creation, which reaches its apogee in humans and its full expression in the church, demands that everyone exist together perichoretically and holarchically. Any hierarchy (such as how we lamely try to describe the generations in the Trinity) only can be imagined (much less structured) to be at the service of holarchy, of the wider communal reality. What science tells us about the way nature is ordered and what theology tells us about ordering in the Trinity must define the way we remain ordered in our human relationships at all levels of life, especially the church. Just as the members of the Trinity experience their own unique "I am" by co-inhering in one another and being perichoretically identified in one another, so must we, if we are to proclaim in our bodies the "gospel of the kindom of trinitarian relatedness."

Noting Francis of Assisi's intuition of this trinitarian mystery at the heart of all creation (and not just of humans), creating a new kind of trinitarian family on earth as it is in heaven, Robert Barron offers an eloquent insight into the meaning of co-inherence and *perichōrēsis* when he writes:

A further implication of the doctrine of creation from nothing is that all of God's creatures are intimately connected to one another in an echo of the primordial co-inherence of the Trinitarian persons. Since all creation is centered in God, all finite things, despite their enormous differences in size, position, quality, or metaphysical status, are linked together as ontological siblings. When Francis of Assisi spoke of "brother sun and sister moon," he was using language not only poetically evocative but also metaphysically precise. All creatures are like islands in an archipelago, separate on the surface, but connected at the depths.[13]

13 _____

The Contemplative Way

I begin this chapter narrating my first awareness of a contemplative or mystical experience. It was the late 1980s. I was almost fifty years old. I had been saying prayers since I was a child and trying to pray since I entered the Capuchin Franciscans when I was nineteen. It occurred while I was pursuing a degree in New Testament Spirituality at the Graduate Theological Union in Berkeley.

At that time (1985-1990) the United States was still testing nuclear weapons underground, in Nevada. The exact place was a good hour from a town called Mercury, Nevada. For years anti-war activists concerned about the proliferation of nuclear weapons would come to Mercury to stand outside the perimeter of the Nevada test site. The land was claimed by the Western Shoshone Indians, but the United States government also claimed it. The dispute over the land resulted in the Shoshones' putting in escrow the monies the U.S. government paid them for the disruption caused by the testing.

One weekend I joined other Franciscans from around the world to protest outside the test site. This began early in the morning. We would stand by the side of the road and wave to the workers on the buses going into the test site. Our wave usually took the form of the two-fingered peace sign. The response from the workers on the buses did not always include both of those fingers, but, when they saw the Franciscans year after year, many of the workers themselves would return the peace sign.

After this ritual, the leader of the protest invited us to find a place in the desert where we could spend some quality time reflecting. I found a rock on which I could sit. As I began my breathing to get centered, my senses started to get in greater synch with my surroundings. Since that part of Nevada is a living desert, part of this awakening led me to begin seeing little green plants in various places around me. Then my eyes began to move from seeing to perceiving when I realized there was a diminutive pink flower at the tip of some of these little green plants. Wanting to examine further one of these little flowers, I bent over to pick it. Just then a clear command came from within me: "Don't you dare; let it be."

At that moment I experienced a sense of oneness with the flower, with the plant, with everyone and everything in that desert and with everyone and everything in the whole universe, including God. This was accompanied by a sense of deep love that pervaded every inch of my being. The feeling of this loving connectedness gave me a sense of overwhelming peace and deep joy. I *knew* that I had just experienced God. I just had a mystical experience.

My experience of contemplation initiated by the reality of the little pink flower is much better described in Alice Walker's *The Color Purple*. Earlier I quoted the dialogue between Shug and Celie regarding their insufficient images of God (Shug: When "I found out that I thought that God was white, and a man, I lost interest"). Now, however, the dialogue about God continues in a way that has Shug calling God "It," much to the consternation of Celie.

> But what do it look like? I ast.
> Don't look like nothing, she say. It ain't a picture show. It ain't some-thing you can look at apart from anything else, including yourself....
> She say, My first step from the old white man was trees. Then air. Then birds. Then other people. But one day when I was sitting quiet and feeling like a motherless child, which I was, it come to me; that feeling of being part of everything, not separate at all. I knew that if I cut a tree, my arm would bleed. And I laughed and I cried and I run all around the house. I knew just what it was. In fact, when it happen, you can't miss it.[1]

Shug's experience of her connectedness to everything in the universe, expressed in her awareness that if she would take the life of a branch she would be doing violence to *herself*, was the same experience I had outside the test site in Nevada. If I were to pick that flower, I would take its life; and this would do violence to me. The flower and I were one; we were no longer separate at all. This sense of communion pervading every part of one's being, of being connected to everyone and everything, is the mystical experience of God's "remaining" with us. But not only us; everyone and we too are "in them and they are in us." This is contemplation; the mystical experience of oneness. It's what Jesus prayed for his followers: the experience of loving, trinitarian con-nectedness *just as* the members of the Trinity experience and express this love in and among themselves.

While I have put a Christian or trinitarian lens on mysticism, there is a deeper core that grounds all authentic religious experience. Communion with the Ultimate we Christians call God was also discovered by the therapist Abraham Maslow as he listened to such experiences recounted by his patients. He described their "sense of the sacred glimpsed in and through the particu-lar instance" as a "peak experience." He noted that the degree of our psycho-logical health depends on the degree we express such peak experiences in our daily living. Thus, those who indicated to him some kind of peak experience evidenced greater creativity, inner strength, and resilience in their day-to-day living.

The rest of this chapter will highlight the dynamics of the mystical, or contemplative, experience. It will then outline an approach to contemplative prayer. Finally, building on the notions of contemplation itself and contemplative prayer, it will take the ideas we have already developed about the *dao* of being a kindom Catholic and discuss how we might enhance a contemplative stance toward life.

The Pattern Uncovered in the Mystical Experience Called Contemplation

Some time after my experience in Nevada, I spoke at the Los Angeles Religious Education Congress. There some of my friends who also were speakers invited me to a party in one of their rooms. How our conversation turned to mystical experience, I can't recall. However, we somehow found ourselves talking about our various religious experiences. The whole tenor of our conversation changed the mood; it became very serious, deeply personal, and collectively uniting, a holy experience in itself.

When we finished it became abundantly clear that, while each of us had had our own "Nevada experience," a common thread became clearly apparent in all our separate stories. Each experience encapsulated five dynamics: (1) It came totally unannounced, unanticipated, and unsolicited; (2) this inbreaking was all-encompassing and experienced throughout our whole being; (3) it made us feel connected to everyone and everything around us; (4) we *knew* this experience was not "of" God but was God; and, finally, (5) the reality experienced became the basis for a new consciousness or construct that we now envisioned for our world, that is, harmony for all. This fifth element was well described by Thomas Merton in the experience that occurred to him on the corners of Fourth and Walnut Streets in Louisville, Kentucky, where he suddenly realized that "the whole illusion of a separate holy existence is a dream."[2]

This pattern of authentic religious experience has been highlighted in scientific terms by none other than Sam Harris, one of the "four horsemen" of avowed atheism. While the other atheists spend their time debunking the god of religion, Harris has studied the dynamics of belief, faith, and religion and found them wanting. What he deeply respects, however, is the experience that corresponds to the question "What do we need to be happy?" In his mind, the traditional human guarantors of happiness (health, wealth, and good company) all will fail. True happiness, such as that felt in religious experience, must be "of a sort that can survive the frustration of all conventional desires."

Traditionally, happiness has been identified with eating, drinking, being merry, and having a good sex life, or, more specifically, with having the best of health, lots of wealth, "fulfilling" relationships, and a perfect job. At the core of our longing for happiness is our desire for meaning and purpose. According to Harris, true happiness can only be fulfilled in soul-meaning, which he otherwise calls "spirituality," "religious experience," and "mysticism."[3] He sees these grounded in the kind of conscious desire that we described in the fifth dimension of religious experience above: the desire to construct a new reality for one's own life and world that reflects the reality that one has experienced. Or, as he writes, it is the desire "to change our relationship to the contents of consciousness, and thereby to transform our experience of the world."[4]

Building on these notions, we can elaborate on our five points:

First, the experience comes unannounced, beyond any human effort or discipline. We know this from two classic examples: the "Damascus experience" of Saul of Tarsus and the "leper experience" of Francis of Assisi. Contrary to some pious thinking, this experience is not limited to any one kind of person, whether an unbeliever like Saul or a searcher like Francis. The mystical experience can come to anyone.

Second, the inbreaking of the experience is all encompassing. It affects the mind, the emotions, and the sensations. Francis of Assisi said the embrace of the leper (in which he discovered the crucified Christ) changed him in mind and body. The all-pervasiveness of the experience is overwhelming. It is clear from Shug that "the feeling" that came upon her invaded her body as much as her mind. It is an experience of deep love and connectedness; its energy reaches to every part of a person's being like no other "normal" experience. In many ways it can be said to take one "outside" oneself, even though the experience is felt deeply within. As such it is ecstatic, like the famous depiction in Bernini's sculpture "St. Teresa in Ecstasy."

Third, the experience (of love) is understood as a sense of connection to everyone and everything without discrimination or domination. The sensation is one of absolute solidarity with complete strangers, a feeling of oneness from "the least" to "the greatest." One finds oneself, one's "I am," in the other's "I am" and vice versa. In such communion with the other, any hierarchical notion of least or greatest is non-existent. Even such thoughts seem to do violence to the experience because there are absolutely no categories except oneness and connectedness that define the experience.

The fourth dimension is critical. The person who has this experience comes to understand God from *this experience* in a way not understood from previous religious categories. These now cease to give meaning; indeed they often represent illusion if not idolatry. One gets to the "heart of the matter" or the "ground of all being" or the "absoluteness" that now undergirds all reality. The person realizes that this is "God," this is love, this is what is "really real." The

God of one's religious experience becomes the God that pervades not only one's self but all creation. Angela of Foligno, a Franciscan mystic, wonderfully describes this experience:

> I beheld the fullness of God in which I beheld and comprehended the whole of creation, that is, what is on this side and what is beyond the sea, the abyss, the sea itself, and everything else. And in everything that I saw, I could perceive nothing except the presence of the power of God, and in a manner totally indescribable. And my soul in an excess of wonder cried out: "This world is pregnant with God!" Wherefore I understood how small is the whole of creation—what is, what is on this side and what is beyond the sea, the abyss, the sea itself, and everything else—but the power of God fills it all to overflowing.[5]

Finally, because of the power of this experience, all previous forms of reality become relativized. As the fox said to the Little Prince, "What is real is invisible to the eye." The religious experience now takes a person "out of" commonly accepted forms and definitions of truth and goodness and becomes the lens through which one views all reality. Thus, Paul of Tarsus *now viewed* everyone and everything as somehow connected to the "me" that he heard in the words "Why do you persecute me?" For his part, Francis of Assisi *now discovered* the living, crucified Christ in the broken members of the Body of Christ that he had previously regarded with disdain and persecuted by his insensitivity.

This religious experience results in a demarcation between the "then" and the "now." What once defined one's worldview now no longer gives meaning. The consciousness of self and others that reflected a closed world now opens up a new perspective on everyone and everything. The way of thinking that defined one's past no longer provides meaning for one's future. The experience deconstructs the past worldview and now offers the lens through which reality is defined and relationships are ordered. The old order, the old memories, are gone; the new ones take over. When the old memories are "undone and absorbed by the fire of contemplative love," the Carmelite Constance Fitzgerald writes, we come to a new understanding of "the truth that has no borders."[6]

Because of the overpowering reality of this experience, all other reality will be judged as real or unreal, valid or untruthful, good or harmful, right and just or false and violent to the degree that its dynamics mirror the core reality known through this experience. And when it does not, the mystic feels compelled to challenge the falseness or sinfulness in one's "world," even if its representatives are part of the structures heretofore identified with holiness and God.

The desire to transform one's world to reflect the reality now experienced is the reason why so many (but not all) mystics have been agents of social change.

From their experience of God they were given a lens to recognize the sinfulness of their previous way of seeing as well as an accompanying grace that impelled them to call for a new way of living. In this line of mystics and prophets, just in our tradition, we begin with the historical Jesus, move to Francis and Clare of Assisi, go on to the likes of Catherine of Siena and Bridget of Sweden and, in our own lifetime, to Caryll Houselander and Thomas Merton. One can go so far as to say that the authenticity of their mysticism was realized in their efforts to bring about social transformation so that society would more closely mirror the reality they had experienced.

Nowhere is this pattern outlined as clearly as in the sixth chapter of Isaiah. There the priest Isaiah has a mystical, religious experience of God's holiness. This experience makes him realize his own sinfulness as well as that of his compatriots (which would include his fellow priests). It leads him to feel called to bring about a transformation of society that will reflect a new way of being holy.

We have noted earlier that the one passage from the Old Testament that is used in our four Gospels as a fulfillment text comes from Isaiah. It is in the first part of the Book of Isaiah, which is not as "pro-priest" as later parts arising from the exile. Matthew uses the text in chapter 13 to represent the hardness of heart on the part of religious leaders to Jesus' message of the rule of what we are calling trinitarian relatedness. Society's hardened reaction to the prophet's call for conversion (Isa. 6:9-13) is a consequence of Isaiah's faithful efforts to bring about in his world patterns of holiness that would reflect his earlier mystical experience (Isa. 6:1-8). Isaiah's mystical/prophetic theology corresponds, for Matthew, to Jesus' spirituality. In turn, Matthew's Christology corresponds to his ecclesiology. And Matthew's ecclesiology, finally, supplies the content of our spirituality.

As many of us find ourselves in a kind of internal exile within our own *oikonomia* as well as our *ekklēsia*, a reflection on the steps involved in Isaiah's call to prophecy (Isa. 6:1-8) might encourage us in fidelity to our own call to be mystics and prophets for our generation. To this reflection I now move.

Isaiah 6: The Archetype
of the Mystical/Prophetic Experience

No better biblical articulation of the key components of the mystical/prophetic calling can be found than in chapter 6 of First Isaiah (chapters 1-39). This occurred in 742 BCE, the year King Uzziah of Judah died. Using powerful, almost apocalyptic images, Isaiah describes what happened to him when the mystical/prophetic call invaded his life:

> In the year that King Uzziah died, I saw the Lord sitting on a throne, high and lofty; and the hem of his robe filled the temple. Seraphs were

in attendance above him; each had six wings: with two they covered their faces, and with two they covered their feet, and with two they flew. And one called to another and said: "Holy, holy, holy is the Lord of hosts; the whole earth is full of his glory."

The pivots on the thresholds shook at the voices of those who called, and the house filled with smoke. And I said: "Woe is me! I am lost, for I am a man of unclean lips, and I live among a people of unclean lips; yet my eyes have seen the King, the Lord of hosts!" Then one of the seraphs flew to me, holding a live coal that had been taken from the altar with a pair of tongs. The seraph touched my mouth with it and said: "Now that this has touched your lips, your guilt has departed and your sin is blotted out." Then I heard the voice of the Lord saying, "Whom shall I send, and who will go for us?" (Isa. 6:1-8a)

A summary of this passage shows the consequences of experiencing contemplatively a vision of God that puts a person at odds with the prevailing notions of holiness and righteousness. Given what we said in the previous chapter about *consciousness*, this passage narrates how Isaiah's religious experience overpowered him with an entirely new consciousness of God's holiness. This consciousness evoked in him a deep sense of his own priestly unholiness. It also made him conscious, seemingly for the first time, of the sinfulness in his society that profaned the holiness of God. Aware that this new consciousness of God's holiness was now at odds with the notion of holiness in his culture, he reassured himself: "Yet my eyes have seen the King, the Lord of hosts." This realization of God's word not only healed him of his own unholiness and sin; it empowered him to go to his own people to call them to convert from their unholiness and sin.

When he accepted the call, he was told that his message would not be received. Ideologically convinced of their own righteousness his people would reject the message. When Isaiah asked "How long, O Lord?," God answered that his prophetic vocation would not be concluded until cities would lie in waste without inhabitants and the land would be "utterly desolate" with everyone being sent "far away." Only one ray of hope would be allowed to break through: when the only thing left standing would be the stump of an oak, a holy seed would be the stump (Isa. 6:11-13). New life would come forth from the death of the old. A remnant would come forth; a refounding and rebuilding community would rise up and take the place of the unrepentant priests and their institution.

Evelyn Underhill notes that the elements contained in Isaiah's experience of God's holiness constitute the heart of every prophetic/mystical vocation.[7] Given the fact that there exists, by reason of everyone's baptism, a "universal call to holiness," we need to examine its dimensions and how they apply to all of us today. In the process we will find the dynamics paralleling the five dimensions of religious experience that we discussed earlier:

1. The unanticipated call occurs within concrete historical exigencies: In the year King Uzziah died (Isa. 6:1a).

Isaiah tells us his call came to him while he was in a house. The fact that his vocation came to him in a house is significant because, as we have seen throughout this book, the Greek word for house is *oikia* or *oikos*. In the Mediterranean world, house (*oikia*) did not mean just a building; it implied a whole world or network of interconnected relationships at every level of life, of what we have discussed as the *oikia, oikonomia, oikoumenē,* and *oikologia.*

Unlike those who want religion to be divorced from reality or a church removed from the culture, Isaiah's vision makes it clear that all authentic spirituality must be lived in the world as it is. This world, above all, is interconnected at every level and exists within everything holarchically. This is a world not of the past or future but of the now. Accordingly, our own mystical/prophetic vocation to be faithful to our call cannot be divorced from this reality. This demands an entirely new way of seeing how everything in the universe must be in relationship for the common good, how everything in the universe is meant to be at the service of the holy.[8]

For Roman Catholics in the United States, this places our call within the political dynamics of a growing imperial presidency, of an economy built on insidious greed, and of a church whose clerics—especially those at the highest levels—have abused their power and undermined the people's trust. This dominant culture constitutes the only milieu in which we can hear our call and respond to it spiritually. In this world the call breaks into our lives.

2. This all-pervading call imprints on our consciousness a new awareness of the reality of God's own holiness (Isa. 6:1b-4).

Isaiah writes that he "saw the Lord sitting on a throne, high and lofty" (6:1b). Such language reinforces for many the primitive anthropology of God being located in some geographic place called heaven, which exists beyond the dome of the heavens that cover the earth. However, his choice of words merely expresses in human language the ineffable and indescribable experience Isaiah had of being transported into the vision of God's ultimate transcendence; his "seeing" was his experiencing.

Once we experience the reign, the realm, the reality, and, indeed, the rush of God's presence and power breaking into our lives, this becomes the ground of our lives for the future. Everything else becomes relativized; indeed, we come to interpret our past understanding of God and God's holiness as illusory.

It is this contemplative experience of God that we prophetically express in our world at all its levels through our participation in community that I call spirituality. This spirituality represents the way we feel divinely called or impelled to proclaim the holiness of God in the context of the unholiness we now find around us. It defines a new way of being holy in the contemporary world. However, while such spirituality demands that we *express* this holiness in an unholy world, its foundation is in our *experience* of the holy that makes us look at the world in an entirely new way. "Holy, holy, holy is the Lord of hosts; the whole earth is full of his glory," the "holy" priest Isaiah heard one of the seraphs call to another (6:3).

In his reflections "The Threefold Testimony of the Most Holy Trinity," St. Bonaventure points to the threefold use of the word "holy." He finds it speaking to how "the God-Trinity manifests and gives testimony to this trinitarian reality throughout the whole of the created universe." He continues,

> And yet it is the eyes and ears of the faithful alone that are opened to hear and to see the testimony by which the divine mysteries are revealed, according to what is said in figurative language in Isaiah 6:1-3: "I saw the Lord seated on a high and lofty throne, and all the earth was filled with His majesty. . . . The Seraphim were standing above it, and they cried out to each other saying: Holy, Holy, Holy, Lord God of hosts, all the earth is full of his glory." In their words the mystery of the Trinity is expressly declared in as far as they say "Holy" three times. And with this, all the earth gives the most glorious testimony to the most blessed Trinity, so that it can be truly said with Psalm 92:5: Father, "your testimonies are very credible." For by means of the vestige of the Trinity, all heavenly and earthly things give witness to the highest heaven, that is, to God three and one. Or rather, it is through this that the triune God gives testimony of himself. Therefore, there are three who give testimony in the highest heaven.[9]

Considering Isaiah's experience of seeing the "whole earth" full of God's glory in the light of Bonaventure's reflections, one can only think of how everything in creation is revelatory of the trinitarian glory of God. Before such a vision, one can only stand in awe and reverence, recognizing the divine present in everything and everyone. This experience is another name for contemplation. Without contemplation, the experience of the holy, there can be little or no authentic prophetic utterance.

The contrast between Isaiah's "received" notion regarding the holy priesthood and God's notion of it can only be appreciated if we realize that the Hebrew Scriptures outline three related ways one could be holy. The *wisdom* writers highlighted the need for individual integrity in the sight of God; the *prophets* stressed the need to make a connection between worship, social justice, and conversion; and the *priestly school* of the exile insisted on the observable practice of the "holiness code" in order to fulfill the scriptural imperative, "You shall be holy, for I the Lord your God am holy" (Lev. 19:2).

Even though Isaiah 6 was supposedly written before the exile and the rise of the priestly school, it seems clear that this passage challenges the third form of "holiness" that came to be equated with the priestly school and which reinforced the status of its priestly class. Thus, one can imagine the surprise that came to Isaiah in his experience of true holiness. He had been culturally conditioned to believe in a notion of holiness that involved the separation of the priests from the people. Now, overcome with what true holiness entailed, Isaiah came to realize that his received notion of holiness was anything but holy; indeed, it was sinful. Thus, the next element in Isaiah's call.

3. Experiencing God's holiness gives us an enlightened consciousness of the reality of sin that was once part of our received notions of holiness defining our individual and social ways of relating (Isa. 6:5a-b).

In response to his experience and awareness of the true meaning of holiness, Isaiah, a member of the holy priestly class, could only respond: "Woe is me! I am lost, for I am a man of unclean lips." At the same time, his new consciousness of how he personally was falling short of God's glory made him deeply sensitive to sin in his surrounding religious world and its institutional expression. This led him to add, "and I live among a people of unclean lips." The experience of God's holiness gave Isaiah a new lens through which he came to perceive not only the meaning of true holiness but a sense of the unholiness and sinfulness in and around him.

4. This new way of looking at reality made Isaiah aware that he would be challenged by his fellow priests and that he needed to be sure of the basis for his new understanding (Isa. 6:5c).

Knowing the assumptions about holiness shared by his fellow clerics, Isaiah realized they would never be able to grasp what he now knew to be defined as holiness. Only one who had been "taken out" of the old way of thinking would understand. Not only that, but his vision would be rejected; quite possibly, he himself would be rejected. I can just imagine the wavering and second-guessing that would overtake his ruminations about what lay ahead. This made him return to his original experience to be assured he would be standing on solid ground. Thus he reassured and consoled himself that, indeed, he had experienced the vision: "Yet my eyes have seen the King, the Lord of hosts!"

I can also hear what his fellow priests would say when they heard his challenge: "And who do you think you are?" "What (or who) gives you the right to challenge what the scriptures have told us about holiness?" "Do you think you have some great new insight into holiness?" Aware that the authenticity of his contemplative experience would marginalize him from his peers, he had to reassure himself of the authenticity of that experience in face of his expected rejection by his fellow priests and peers: "Yet my eyes *have seen* the King, the Lord of hosts!" Another way of saying this would be: "I know it happened; it's really real; nobody can tell me I'm crazy!"

Until this experience of God's holiness, Isaiah seems to have been quite comfortable in the world of meaning that had been mediated to him through the dominant consciousness of his clerical culture. Herein the injustice of the political and religious economy was sanctioned as just by the religious leadership of his day. With his mystical experience of *God's* holiness, his world of "holiness" was turned on its head. His mystical experience generated in him a gut-wrenching stirring of conscience. His mystical insight became a moral imperative. What before his conscience had considered "moral" and even sanctified was now failed, profane, and sinful.

Conscious that his contemporaries would consider his vision bogus because it did not correspond to their "royal consciousness," he reminded himself that his experience really happened. The truth of his mystical experience revealed the lie that sustained the political, economic, and religious worldview that heretofore had mediated meaning for him. Never again could he look at these forces with the same eyes, hear their message with the same ears, or accept their ways with the same heart. He had had a conversion.

5. The recognition of sin in our lives opens us to be purified and empowered by a force beyond us: the word of God (Isa. 6:6-7).

If we cannot acknowledge that we are sinners, we will never convert. If we cannot admit that our human structures (divine in origin as they may be) just might reflect serious social sin, there is no possibility of conversion. Refusing to see the need for conversion, we remain the same. If we stay the same, we will remain in our sins. Righteous in our sins, we can easily convince ourselves that we are holy. The real "unholy" ones and "sinners" will be those apart from us. Unable to see how far we have moved from God's trinitarian holiness, we will never be empowered to live holy lives if what profanes our lives controls our thinking about them. This demands a purification of our memories themselves; a new way of thinking is demanded.

In her major address at the 2009 Catholic Theological Society of America's annual assembly, Constance Fitzgerald explained why John of the Cross wrote so much "on the purification of memory": "In the deeper reaches of a contemplative life, a kind of unraveling or loss of memory occurs which can be more or less conscious. Then one's usual way of harboring memories is incapacitated. A person's past becomes inaccessible as a basis for finding meaning."[10] Furthermore, she writes, this purification which involves "the annulling of the memories" that now have been deconstructed finds us "dispossessed of the autonomous self" that also makes us conscious of the "impotence" of past seductive ways of thinking.[11]

I know about such seductive power—what Walter Brueggemann calls the "royal" consciousness—from my own experience. The religious experience of God, leading to the consequent realization of my own sinfulness, gave me a fresh understanding of how Isaiah, only after he had recognized his own sin and could admit it publicly, could be purified of its influence and hold over his life. Once he had admitted the exact nature of his wrong, "one of the seraphs flew to me, holding a live coal that had been taken from the altar with a pair of tongs. The seraph touched my mouth with it and said: 'Now that this has touched your lips, your guilt has departed and your sin is blotted out'" (Isa. 6:6).

Not only did the coal—which most take to represent God's word—heal Isaiah of his own sinfulness; it empowered him to live from its healing energy. Now, in the power of this word grounding him in God's holiness, he realized he had been commissioned to proclaim authentic holiness to a sinful nation.

Applying this part of the passage to ourselves, anything falling short of God's trinitarian holiness is, to that degree, unholy or profane. The experience of God's healing word in us invites us to live reordered lives. It also serves as a mandate to spend our lives proclaiming the gospel of God's trinitarian reality that must come on earth (at all levels, above all, in the church) as it is in heaven. Anything falling short of this holiness must be invited to conversion—be it the culture itself or our religious system.

6. Empowered in this word, we accept the invitation to go into the world as God's ambassadors (Isa. 6:8).

Isaiah's experience of being healed by the burning coal made him realize that his life was not just freed of his past sins; this freedom from his sin involved an empowerment or commission to "take away the sin" of the world of which he was a part. The burning coal of God's word had fired in him the desire to proclaim its message in his world.

According to Abraham Heschel, traditional religious experience tends to be "a private affair in which a person becomes alive to what transpires between God and himself, not to what transpires between God and someone else; contact between God and man comes about, it is believed, for the benefit of the particular man. In contrast," he says, "prophetic inspiration is for the sake, for the benefit, of a third party. It is not a private affair between prophet and God; its purpose is the illumination of the people rather than the illumination of the prophet."[12] This understanding applies here to Isaiah's experience.

At the heart of every mystical/prophetic call is the concomitant demand that one's religious experience of God be accompanied by a commission to be present in the world in an entirely new way: as one who has been empowered to proclaim the rule of God's sovereign presence and power in the midst of contrary imperial pretensions and infallible proclamations.

"Whom shall I send, who will go for us?" God asks. This is a question everyone called to the prophetic vocation must be open to hear. Frightened at the consequences of saying "yes" or reluctant as they may be, such prophets must also be willing to act upon the invitation. In effect, the prophet is the ambassador of God, the one whose words are divinely authorized. Divinely inspired prophets speak with power because they have been empowered in the word to proclaim the imperative of God, whether that proclamation be one of words or works, gesture or symbol.

7. Preaching God's holiness to a sinful society that identifies its ways with "God's will" promises rejection by those whose hearts have been hardened by their own imperial/ infallible consciousness (Isa. 6:9-13a).

When individuals and their groupings have not been grounded in the true God, they will rely on a God who has been historically conditioned to give them understanding. Without being freed from such notions, they cannot but believe their understanding of God is true. Those whose religious worldview is defined by the archives of the past can never become the architects of another kind of religious future because their experience of God is defined by past memories that have not yet been purified.

That is why, upon accepting his divine mission, Isaiah was told that nobody would listen; he would be a failure. The force that had enfleshed God's word in him said, "Go and say to this people: 'Keep listening, but do not comprehend; keep looking, but do not understand.' Make the mind of this people dull, and stop their ears, and shut their eyes, so that they may not look with their eyes, and listen with their ears, and comprehend with the minds and turn and be healed" (Isa. 6:9-10).

This passage about the people seeing but not perceiving and hearing but not listening, lest they understand in their hearts and turn and be converted is the only text from the whole Hebrew Bible that is quoted in all four accounts of Jesus' life. All four Gospel writers refer to this passage to explain the resistance Jesus received from *his own* religious leaders, including those of the "holy" priesthood. This fact reminds us that the insensitivity and hardness of heart Jesus encountered might happen to us as well—if we faithfully translate his message of trinitarian connectedness into our world and clerical church.

As Isaiah's vocation prefigured that of Jesus, so his prophetic call must echo in our hearts, both individual and corporate. Such a vocation can be exercised only in the midst of the hardness of heart that is found in the dominant culture of our political economy of corporate capitalism and of the dominating dynamics of our church. The fact that we will be resisted by the "true believers" and that their resistance will be justified by their sense of righteousness does not mean they are evil people. It should not be surprising that they would call us unpatriotic and anti-capitalist or disloyal to the pope and "no longer Catholic" when we dissent from their interpretation of God and God's will. After all, it was promised that this would happen, that the time would come when we would be excommunicated from "their" synagogues and hailed into "their" courts. Such charges will come because they think that the ideologies that keep their systems going represent incontrovertible truths. While we see these as forms of idolatry that profane the holiness of God, they honestly believe them to be divinely blessed. They also believe they have the right to sanction anyone who deviates from their vision. And they are ready to do so.

8. Despite rejection, an alternative community will serve as the seed for implementing the new vision of God's holiness (Isa. 6:13b).

We will discuss this new community in the next chapter. Suffice it to say—whether we are dealing with the history or the sociology of religion, I have yet to be shown any place where an old and established religious institution of any significant size was able to truly be transformed. But more on this later.

Moving toward Prayer That Is Contemplative

Even though the experience of pure contemplation is something unattainable by human effort, contemplative prayer nurtures the dynamics described above, especially the sense of being connected to God and everyone and everything in the cosmos. The essence of such prayer involves moving from our head to our heart in a way that finds us praying with more understanding hearts, that is, more mindfully. Here our prayer becomes freer from distractions. We become more conscious of our loving union with God and all those loved by God (i.e., the whole cosmos). The purity of heart that is developed by the effort to "pray always" begins with the effort to move from bodily and sensate feelings to a deeper consciousness of our connectedness to everyone.

Despite having the images of "praying with a pure heart" and "having always the spirit of prayer and devotion to which all things should be subservient" in my Franciscan background, I never was offered a *dao* as to how these ways of prayer might be incorporated in my life. Indeed, it was only when I read J. D. Salinger's *Franny and Zooey,* while studying theology, that I learned about the ancient practice of praying with a mantra. Franny is talking to her boyfriend, Lane, about her fascination with Jesus' words about "praying without ceasing." She discovers that this could be facilitated by the recitation of the "Jesus Prayer," which says, "Lord Jesus Christ, have mercy on me." She says,

> If you keep saying that prayer over and over again—you only have to do it with your *lips* at first, then eventually what happens, the prayer becomes self-active. Something *happens* after a while. I don't know what but something happens, and the words get synchronized with the person's heartbeat, and then you're actually praying without ceasing. Which has a really tremendous, mystical effect on your whole outlook.[13]

The goal of contemplative prayer is to move beyond the sensing and feeling of reality outside one's self to a sense of centeredness in one's self where one also senses the presence of a power beyond one's self, the Other. While it may begin with vocal prayer, mental prayer, or meditation on some mystery of the Gospels, the goal of contemplative prayer is to experience more fully the love of God with one's whole heart (thus the notion of "praying with a pure heart") in a way that gets expressed outside of prayer in ever-greater love of neighbor. This notion of love, especially trinitarian love, as the goal of all other forms of prayer is well described in the words of Pope Benedict XVI: "Prayer is life and it develops gradually at the same pace with the growth of the Christian life: It begins with vocal prayer, passes to interiorization through meditation and recollection, until it attains union of love with Christ and with the Most Holy Trinity." Reflecting on the life and prayer of St. Teresa of Avila, Benedict XVI notes her "fullness" of contemplation as being realized in the "indwelling of the Trinity, in union with Christ through the mystery of his humanity,"[14] again showing that, to be "in Christ," is to be in the trinitarian God.

In praying with such "purity of heart," one rarely has a contemplative experience; however, the sense of the presence of the Other becomes the core of the prayer. In this it is best expressed in the passage "Be still and know I am (God)."[15]

While the outlines of such prayer of stillness and quiet take different forms, depending on the teacher (whether classical teachers such as Teresa of Avila,

John of the Cross, Bonaventure, and Ignatius of Loyola, or contemporary teachers such as Thomas Keating and John Main), I find the approach to contemplation outlined by Clare of Assisi particularly helpful. I find it especially helpful as a way to make performative in one's life the experience of contemplative prayer itself. In this sense such contemplative prayer becomes the experiential grounding that finds its authenticity to the degree its fruits become evident in the prayers' actions.

In her Third Letter to Agnes of Prague (who jilted the Holy Roman Emperor to become a "Bride of Christ"), Clare wrote, "Place your mind in the mirror of eternity; place your soul in the brilliance of glory, place your heart in the figure of the divine substance and transform your whole being into the image of the Godhead Itself [i.e., trinitarian Love] through contemplation."[16] From here she outlines a four-step process leading to spousal love: gazing on, considering, contemplating, and imitating the divine spouse.

Contemplative prayer begins with a simple gaze. Deeper prayer moves toward deeper gazing. Deeper gazing leads one to desire a deeper connectedness with the one upon whom one gazes. Clare used the word *intuere* to describe this kind of gazing: intuiting or "getting into" the heart or reality of the Other. She visualized this intuitive gazing with the image of the mirror. She envisioned being drawn into the object seen in a way that would make this object the sole or ultimate object of her desire.

From simple gazing, one is moved to a deeper consideration. This might be understood as the meditation on the mysteries of the life of Jesus in a way that would lead to contemplation of divine love itself, as promoted by Ignatius of Loyola in the *Spiritual Exercises*. In her own Franciscan way, Clare's approach, which she called *considere*, could not be done apart from contemplation of the Beloved One on the cross. Thus she wrote in her Fourth Letter to Agnes of Prague: "That Mirror, suspended on the wood of the Cross urged those who passed by to consider: '*All you who pass by the way, look and see if there is any suffering like My suffering.*'"[17]

The third stage in this prayer is actual contemplative union (*contemplare*) between Clare and her spouse. In this embrace, the soul, using bodily images, becomes absorbed in the Beloved. Clare captured this sense in her First Letter to Agnes of Prague. It is filled with familial images based on Jesus' vision of the new family of brothers, sisters, and mothers of Jesus Christ. Based on these images of intimacy, she urged Agnes to think of Christ as the Love of all Loves, inviting spousal love in return: "When you have love [for the Bridegroom] you shall be chaste; when you have touched [the Bridegroom] you shall become pure; when you have accepted [the Bridegroom], you shall be a virgin."[18]

Unlike other teachers in contemplative prayer, Clare shows that the authentic practice of the first three steps toward contemplation are evidenced in the fourth step of "imitation" (*imitare*). The authenticity of prayer must be evidenced in one's day-to-day living. This kind of prayer was inseparable from the proclamation of the gospel itself. Thus she wrote to Agnes in another letter, using the image of imitation that was used so often by Francis—to "walk in the footprints" of Jesus Christ: "You have become such a diligent imitator *of the Father of all* perfection [that] His eyes do not see any imperfection in you.... You have held fast *to the footprints* of Him to Whom you have merited to be joined as Spouse."[19]

The goal of this fourfold process is transformation into the object of our desires: to be one. Clare summarized this transformation in that most mystical image noted above wherein one coinheres one's "I am" in the very life of the trinitarian community: "Transform your whole being into the image of the Godhead Itself through contemplation so that you may feel what his friends feel."[20] When we experience our union with the Beloved *as* that One experiences it within the other members of the Trinity, we experience what it means to *feel* ourselves as friends of God. When we imitate this friendship by expanding the boundaries of our love to include those once considered enemy, we evidence a mystical way of life in the world.

Developing a Contemplative Stance toward Everyone and Everything in Life

After the experience of contemplation itself, supported by contemplative prayer, the *dao* of contemplation involves the discipline connected to the development of a contemplative stance toward life. This practice is enhanced when we keep trying to grow in that kind of consciousness that will find our hearts growing in a mystical stance in life that reflects our religious experience. We will approach life with an understanding heart. Such a stance makes us more aware of our cosmic connectedness, in Christ, to everyone and everything in creation. Since the Isaiah passage about an understanding heart is linked to changing our ways to match the experience of God that now has been understood, it invites us practitioners to ongoing conversion to the personal and social proclamation of the good news that this experience entails. This notion was well captured in a passage from the *Ministerial Priesthood* by the 1971 Synod of Bishops. It stated:

> Impelled by the need to keep in view both the personal and social aspects of the announcement of the Gospel, so that in it an answer may be given to men's most fundamental questions, the church not only preaches conversion to God to individuals, but also, almost as society's conscience, she speaks as best she can to society itself and

performs a prophetic function in this regard, always taking pains to effect her own renewal.[21]

Given this passage, one can say that the authenticity of the church's experience of God's reign is expressed in the church's ongoing renewal and reformation. When anyone or any group has had a truly mystical or contemplative experience, the likelihood exists—because that experience now becomes the transformed lens through which one interprets truth, goodness, and right relationships—that that one will develop ascetical practices that promote a contemplative spirituality. This demands a contemplative *dao* that tries to replicate, as closely as possible, the dynamics of the mystical experience. This involves the effort to integrate a conscious form of prayerful connectedness, in Christ, to everyone and everything in the cosmos. This invites its practitioners to a radical de-centering of one's self to find one's self with the other.

Though he never used the word "contemplation," Francis of Assisi associated this contemplative stance in life with the notion of "being subject" or at the service of everyone and everything. He developed this notion of being subject to others in different ways: to each other in the same "house"[22] and "to all humans."[23] And, if the "all" were not clear enough, this contemplative, nonviolent way of relating was to be extended throughout all creation insofar as his followers were to "be subject to every human creature for God's sake," including those considered by the Christians of his day to be the enemies of Christendom, that is, the Muslims.[24] This approach to ministry was not limited only to those brothers who were to go to unbelievers and Muslims. He urged all his followers, as his brothers and sisters: "We must never desire to be above others, but, instead, we must be servants and subject to every human creature for God's sake."[25]

Solidly grounded in Francis's spirituality,[26] Ignatius of Loyola begins his *Exercises* in a similar way. Although he too does not use the word "contemplation" in the sense we've discussed (but rather as a form of meditation), he invites the exercitant "to see and find God in all things and all things in God." However, as I discovered myself when I made the *Ignatian Exercises*, at the highest point of love, at the end of the *Exercises*, Ignatius invites the exercitant not only to see and find God in all things, and not only to "love God in all things," but to "love and serve" God "in all things."[27] This is Clare's notion of *imitare*. This is the apogee of the *dao* of discipleship and the fulfillment of Jesus' prayer about having the love of the Father that was in him being "in them" too, that they might also be one as (*kathōs*) the members of the Trinity are one. This is the goal of contemplation of the love of God.

Developing a contemplative stance toward life and all it contains, besides finding God in everything and being subject to everything for God's sake, necessarily involves the practice of "letting go" of as many forms of control as possible. This involves the active practice of nonviolence. Such nonviolence, expressed as a basic stance, colors every kind of relationship of which we are a part. And, once we realize, with Mahatma Gandhi, that nonviolence is a power or energy that is always available to us, we must make a decision as to how we will use power (as a force for building up the house or for contributing to its ruination) in our relationships at every level of life: toward ourselves when we do something wrong, in our families, communities, and workplaces, as well as in our politics, economics, and, above all, in our church. Using the U.S. bishops' definition of violence as any way one uses to control another through fear and intimidation,[28] we see that a nonviolent, contemplative stance invites active engagement to right the wrongs around us and to bring about a world that ever-increasingly reflects its trinitarian maker at every level. This demands the contemplative effort to bring about trinitarian relationships defined by equality rather than discrimination, mutuality rather than domination, and solidarity rather than deprivation. Furthermore, being grounded in contemplation and committed to address those situations where people are marginalized and violated at any level of life demand that one's heart be moved with compassion to bring about a change of that situation toward an ever-more trinitarian reality.

Toward this end we now move to our chapter on compassion itself.

14

The Compassionate Way

When I was a student in philosophy, before the Second Vatican Council, I was flummoxed by the fact that we said so many prayers to God each day but spent little, if any, time indicating our concern for what God was concerned about, namely, people who were poor. It seemed to me that if prayer involved a two-way communication with God, the "God" we were praying to seemed awfully quiet, if not indifferent, about the concern for the poor that the God-with-Us called Emmanuel, Jesus, defined as core to his identity as the Christ (Matt. 11:2-6). This concern has never left me.

Having spent the last chapter talking about contemplation, we can take our reflections on contemplation and apply them to the topic of this sixth way of developing a Catholic *dao*: compassion. For believers, compassion is the necessary consequence of having experienced the totality of God's loving embrace that gets expressed in the effort to include in that embrace those whom society or circumstances have left out.

This chapter begins by distinguishing between natural empathy and biblical compassion, showing that the former involves a feeling with the pain of an other, while the latter involves action to remove the pain. This will naturally lead us to probe the famous Lukan passage on "compassion" as found in the story of the Good Samaritan. From here we will show how we can remove the obstacles on our path in the way we develop "hearts moved with compassion" by examining Matthew's five uses of the word. In the process I hope to show how compassion is the compass we use to locate ourselves in conscious connection with everyone and everything in the world, especially those who are most marginalized and in need and who must be welcomed into the ever-expanding house of our hearts.

Compassion will be shown to be the power and force of non-violent love released, without exceptions or boundaries, into our own personal, institutional, and communal universe. It reflects an empowering care that extends into the whole universe once the realization comes that something or someone is in need. Such care identifies us as human; thus, not to care about someone in need (even if we cannot always do something directly to alleviate that need) makes us, to the degree of our lack of care, inhuman. Such care consists of efforts to address the wrongs around us in ever-widening circles and to embrace the world with such care that we not only work to alleviate its pains but we try to empower those who have been violated so that they can be healed and walk free of those forces that have kept them in need. In our work for compassion, as the 14th Dalai Lama has shown in a wonderful *New York Times* op-ed piece, we find ourselves linked to people of all the major religions of the world.[1]

Unfortunately, the word "compassion" suffers from "compassion fatigue," becoming too often a self-serving buzzword. Now we even have *The Self-Compassion Diet*. Such therapeutic (and even entitlement) approaches to compassion are compounded politically when we hear a president promote "compassionate conservatism" only to find it masking economic processes in which *more* people are left behind, battered, and robbed on the way to the Jerichos of our nations. Such prostitution of the word begs that it either be retired from our lexicon or explained more honestly in a way that will give it more meaning and urgency for our day.

Empathy: The Gateway to Compassion

Neurobiologists have discovered that a secretion from our pituitary glands called oxytocin is a key hormone in mother/infant bonding. It is also found in men, though in a lesser degree. A sign of its activity is found in the expression of care on people's faces when they are near a child. The production of oxytocin manifests itself in empathy. It seems to be produced more when people are at the service of others. Some have called it the "milk of human kindness."[2]

This chapter will not discuss further how oxytocin may or may not be the stimulant for empathy. Rather, I will show how empathy or care for those who are vulnerable or suffering is the hallmark of being human.[3] Empathy is also the glue of connectedness. It involves a way of understanding and imagining the feelings of others. This does not always mean that such an empathetic person really cares about another's feelings in a way that shows a willingness to do anything about those feelings.

The fact that empathy is a noble human characteristic does not mean that other creatures are incapable of empathy. Primatologist Frans de Waal has traced the actual origins of empathy beyond us humans by showing that chimpanzees and other primates console one another, share with others in need, and take care of their injured members.[4]

Acknowledging the source for empathy early in our evolutionary processes, current science offers other evidence to show quite clearly that human beings actually seem to be wired for empathy. Neuroscientists have shown how certain parts of our brain are triggered when we come face to face with the suffering of others, especially those close to us. While disagreeing on some of the nuances of this phenomenon, they point to three factors that consistently determine feelings of empathy. Empathy represents (1) an affective response to another person which often but not always involves some kind of sharing in that person's emotional state; (2) a cognitive ability to take on the perspective of that person; and (3) the ability to determine what kind of emotional response one will make to the situation experienced by the other person.[5]

Again, as noted above, such feelings do not always mean one can or will do anything about the situation. One response to this feeling of empathy can be to exploit it; another is evidenced in a "feeling with" that remains only at the level of feeling—that is, with some vague sense of solidarity that does not lead to involvement with the other or a commitment to change the situation.

Studies in neuroscience also show that much of what seems to be altruistic in our empathy might actually mask self-interest. Other studies show it can come from group interest, especially when the survival of the group is at stake. Regarding the latter motivation, Jonathan Haidt has shown that natural selection occurs not only when individuals compete with other individuals for survival but also when groups compete with other groups for survival. While both forms of competition exemplify patterns related to the "survival of the fittest," when groups compete, "it is the cohesive, cooperative, internally altruistic groups that win and pass on their genes."[6] This notion of group selection thus serves as a balance to natural selection.

With the evolution of our human consciousness into a kind of capitalist consciousness, it is not surprising that marketers have found a way to exploit people in need in ways that might not always meet their real needs but which always are assured of generating a profit. Such "capitalistic compassion" became clear to me while I was writing this book. I read in the opening paragraph of an article entitled "Save the Poor. Sell Them Stuff. Cheap!" the following words:

> The first slide comes up on the white-walled lecture room's double display screens. In capital letters, it declares: "EMPATHY."
> The 40-odd Stanford students gathered in a semicircle of plastic chairs on the cement floor blink at the screen, awaiting explanation. Almost all of them are pursuing graduate degrees in some form of engineering or business—disciplines known more for unemotional logic and bare-knuckle competitiveness than getting in touch with someone else's feelings.[7]

The article describes the brainchild of Jim Patell, a professor at the Stanford Graduate School of Business. He noted that for all the decades of aid to developing nations ($1.5 trillion over sixty years), one billion people still live on less than a dollar a day. Given this reality, Patell envisioned a way to market products that such people might consider useful or desirable in a way that would make them "actually want it and use it." And, even though the "world's poor don't have much money individually . . . there are billions of them," insuring "colossal profits to be made."[8]

Patell's understanding of empathy may have some semblance of genuine care for the other; yet the self-interest part of it compromises what most people mean by empathy. While its aim is to help the students put themselves in the place of the world's poor, its ultimate goal is not care of people as much as care for profits. Hence, genuine empathy is something much more than the market-manipulating approach of this Stanford course. Rather, real empathy involves a genuine feeling of not wanting to be in the situation of someone in need. This involves a feeling of solidarity that echoes dynamics that speak to what all religions call the Golden Rule.

In our friary in Milwaukee, where people of all colors and religions congregate and serve at our daily "Loaves and Fishes Meal Program," we have a very large picture featuring a symbol of the world's great religions with their equivalent of the Golden Rule. Ten are depicted. In one way or another they say treat all people as you would want to be treated. While our version in the West frames the rule from the perspective of doing unto others what we would want them to do to us, in other traditions the same meaning is cast negatively: do not do to others what you would not want them to do to you.

In her writings, talks, and website on compassion, Karen Armstrong shows that, with its empathic core, the Golden Rule serves as the ground of compassion in most of the world's great religions. In his tome on empathy, Jeremy Rifkin argues that the evolution of empathy reached a new stage with the advent of Christianity. With Armstrong he writes that "all of the great axial movements stressed the importance of the Golden Rule." However, he adds, "it was in Rome that the full impact of the new dictum came to the fore with the rise of a new urban religious sect that would be known as Christianity. The early Christian eschatology represented both the final flowering of the empathic surge of ancient theological times and the bridge to the modern era of humanism and the secularization of empathic consciousness."[9]

In highlighting "the secularization of empathic consciousness," Rifkin highlights the etymology of the word (*em-pathos*, "feeling in or with") as containing two of the previous key elements of the *dao* we have outlined earlier: consciousness and connectedness. For him, empathic feelings arise from a conscious awareness of the plight of another in such a way that one feels connected to the other in that one's plight or need.

A particularly instructive section of Rifkin's book shows how "shaming cultures" often lack compassion and, to that degree, are not equipped to manifest compassion. This occurs when their patterns of honor and shame involve dynamics meant to exclude the other when that one offends the dominant or dominating mores. When this happens, the leaders in the group, despite their protestations of care, are incapable of truly empathizing with those their own rules or rituals exclude. The resulting pain of institutionalized exclusion for such excluded ones comes especially in tradition-bound societies. He writes,

> Shaming cultures, throughout history, have been the most aggressive and violent because they lock up the empathic impulse and with it the ability to experience another's plight and respond with acts of compassion. When a child grows up in a shaming culture believing that he must conform to an ideal of perfection or purity or suffer the wrath of the community, he is likely to judge everyone else by the same rigid, uncompromising standards. Lacking empathy, he is unable to experience other people's suffering as if it were his own and therefore is likely to judge their plight as their own fault because they failed to live up to the standards of perfection expected of them by society.[10]

In reading Rifkin's words, I could only recall the many conversations with women[11] and gays that I have had for years. They feel excluded and "less than" because of the preaching they have heard from many church leaders as well as the documents that invoke God to justify their exclusion from full participation in the life of the institutional church. They find these patterns especially confusing when they deeply believe their own "I am" has been made "very good" by God. Within such structures, it is incumbent on the part of male, straight priests to truly empathize with those committed women and homosexuals who *feel shamed* when church leaders define them as unfit for ordination. The same empathy from such priests is needed when lay people experience the imposition of rules in which they had no say which exclude them from roles that have been needlessly reserved to the clerics in the church.

While stressing the affective component of empathy that finds us feeling with others in their pain and suffering, Rifkin acknowledges that it does not do enough to eliminate such hurt. Thus, he highlights compassion as "the action component" of empathy.[12] When we actually try to prevent or eliminate the suffering of another through our action on behalf of the one in need, we move from empathy to compassion.[13] With this understanding of the key differences between empathy and compassion, we can now articulate more clearly the *dao* of how we can grow in the Christian notion of compassion as it is found in the New Testament even if it has not yet been developed and promoted in the official teachings of our Catholic faith to the same degree that some of its other key components, like mercy and justice, have been articulated.[14]

Unpacking the Dynamics Involved in Luke's Story
of the Good Samaritan

The story of the Good Samaritan (found only in Luke's Gospel) follows Jesus' words about loving the neighbor as one's self (which are also found in the other Synoptic Gospels). In Luke's version we discover that such love of neighbor is much more inclusive than might be assumed in the Golden Rule. Having responded to the lawyer's question about the heart of the Law as loving God and the neighbor as oneself, the lawyer probed Jesus further: "And who is my neighbor?" (Luke 10:29) Jesus' response becomes more than the lawyer expected. Jesus' story of the Samaritan involves two dimensions: (1) a rejection of religious codes when they do not ensure compassion; and (2) his redefinition of the neighbor to include as objects of our compassion the very ones that religion can put at the margin. The next paragraphs further probe these two dimensions:

1. Jesus eclipses or rejects religious codes when they undermine compassion.

The setting for the story of the Good Samaritan involves the layman Jesus and a Torah scholar or scribe. It begins with the lawyer's not-so-subtle effort to undermine the teachings of Jesus (and, therefore, his power vis-à-vis the lawyer and his cohort). This becomes clear from the stated context: "A lawyer stood up *to put him to the test.*" The question he posed to Jesus about what was needed to inherit eternal life was not sincere; true to the honor/shame society of that day, it reflected a query. Equally true to the *mano-a-mano* interaction being played out, Jesus responded to the lawyer's challenge with a riposte of his own: "What is written in the law?" When the lawyer responds with the wording of what we now know as the great command of love that is to be extended to God "and your neighbor as yourself" (Luke 10:27), Jesus actually compliments him on his response.

Rather than accepting Jesus' compliment, the lawyer still pursued the culture's one-upmanship. He felt a need "to justify himself," to prevail in the religious debate in a way that would make Jesus look wrong. He failed in this tactic when he made the mistake of asking Jesus to define the meaning of "neighbor." Rather than give a theoretical definition Jesus told a story that made it abundantly clear what *he* meant by "neighbor." Today we call it the story of the Good Samaritan.

Jesus' narration of the story has provided the world one of the great examples of what it means to have a heart *moved with compassion.* But at a deeper, more subversive way realized by his audience, Jesus was also exposing the bankruptcy of those patterns in his own religion that religiously sanctioned mores that created a system based on exclusion through the perpetuation of false notions of holiness. In this, the limitation regarding the existing notion of holiness discussed in Isaiah 6 in the previous chapter receives further rein-forcement. More than a story about a Samaritan doing good as any good Jew was called to do, the system behind the text is shown to be bankrupt insofar as it is sustained by clerical codes of separation and superiority which elevated one's own class and dehumanized others. This dynamic is evident at the end of the story when Jesus asks the lawyer: "Which of these three, do you think, proved neighbor to the man who fell among the robbers?" (Luke 10:36). Still incapable of speaking the truth because of his cultural biases, the most he could do was to refer to the outcast Samaritan as "the one who showed mercy" (Luke 10:37).

Jesus' story (Luke 10:30-35) begins with an anonymous man on a journey. He "fell among robbers, who stripped him and beat him . . . leaving him half-dead." At this point, it is not other anonymous people but two representatives of the clerical class, a priest and a Levite, who enter the scene. They pass by the one in need.

This simple statement, again, reveals another, deeper and more subversive part of this famous story that often goes unrecognized. Why, among all the people Jesus could have used to show the lack of compassion, did he point to two exemplars of his religion's ruling class? Why does he specify that it was first a priest and then a Levite who saw the Samaritan in his plight and "passed by on the other side" (Luke 10:31, 32)? Clearly, Jesus was not accepting the holiness codes that dictated that they walk by. At the same time, he made clear his own understanding of what true holiness entailed.

The story retains its subversive challenge for our own day. With an ever-increasing effort in Culture I Catholicism to return to its own clerically defined, culturally conditioned codes of exclusion, it is important that we examine the dynamics behind the lack of compassion by religious leaders of any day. Sim-ply stated, their notion of holiness, insofar as they demand separation, exclude the possibility of compassion. Why is this so? Again we are told by the Lukan Jesus about the unfortunate results of a clericalized, dualistic way of thinking about the practice of holiness that actually undermines the core passage of the Priestly Holiness Code of Leviticus 19:1-2: "Say to *all the congregation* of the people of Israel, You shall be holy (*kaddish*); for I the Lord your God am holy (*kaddish*)."

The meaning of what it meant for God in heaven to be holy (*kaddish*), given the worldview of people of that day, involved separation from humans. When applied to humans, it resulted in a hierarchical order that reflected structural separation and exclusivity of one group regarding outgroups because, as Mar-cus Borg writes, "purity was political."[15] Bruce Malina and Richard Rohrbaugh write: "To 'hallow' or 'make holy' means to endow something pure with exclusivity. What is holy or sacred is always exclusive to some person—something or someone set apart for that person. To hallow is to draw a boundary separating what is designated [holy] from what is not and so define its status and meaning."[16] Because holiness was identified with purity and purity was equated with cleanness and cleanness with non-bleeding, it followed that women would, "by nature," be at the bottom of the structural hierarchy of classification related to holiness. Among the men, there would be a hierarchy of holiness, with priests and, especially, the High Priest at the top. Such a construct around "holy" and "unholy" defined by notions of exclusion and separation can be shown in the following chart:

Holy	Unholy
sacred	profane
pure	impure
clean	unclean
non-bleeder	bleeder
male	female
inside	outside
priest	non-priest

Even allowing for some form of dualistic interpretation of holiness and the desire for some kind of separation from what would be defined as unholy, the model of holiness became the special domain of the priestly class with the virtual equation of "clean" with those who did not bleed, that is, males, and "unclean" with those who did bleed, that is, females. Females who by nature were made to bleed and to be found by God as "very good" by so doing thus found themselves among those classified (by the males who did not bleed) as unclean. Such polarizing and dichotomizing thinking serves an ideology of patriarchal clericalism defined as willed by God, the Holy One.

Returning to the original Levitical call to holiness from God that was meant for the whole "congregation of the people of Israel" (as Max Weber shows of every religious organization's original ethos), we find that this universal call to holiness gradually becomes identified with and virtually limited to a special clerical class of "holy" people, namely, the priestly/Levitical group. Weber calls it the "clerical propendum."[17] This group was at the top of the pecking order of those considered holy. Consequently, by the time of Jesus, according to Luke, priests and Levites were in the top tier of the list of those who were pure. Given the faulty premise that defined holiness in a way that demanded separation rather than involvement, a whole litany of practices had come to define ways the holy ones had to remain unpolluted and unspoiled. Furthermore, because Samaritans constituted Israel's "enemies," they would be lucky even to be on the list. They were what religions have traditionally called heretics or unbelievers.

Given this "world before the text," it should not be surprising why the priest and Levite would "pass by" the Samaritan. They were only following orders. They were just being faithful to the rules.

2. Jesus redefines the neighbor to include as the objects of our compassion the very ones that religion puts at the margins.

In our earlier discussion of reciprocity, we showed that Jesus' gospel of radical inclusion went beyond the cultural patterns of kinship that created a "balanced" way of relating that fit the Golden Rule. In his culture "doing unto others as you would have them do to you" was limited to one's kin; it excluded the "other," who was beyond one's immediate family and kin. The other was enemy. For Jesus, immediate family and kin included every child of the household of the heavenly Father. Therefore, love of the enemy had to be concretized by hospitality rather than exclusion. This ideal is now exemplified in the story of the enemy who refused to follow the religious norms that named him an outsider. The boundaries of hospitality are expanded to make the other a virtual member of one's own family. In this story, the Samaritan is shown as exemplifying the true code of holiness as compassion toward the other, the marginalized one.

In Luke's Gospel, besides the story of the Good Samaritan, the two other times the Greek word for compassion (*splagchnizesthai*) is used also involve a veiled challenge to culturally honored household dynamics. The first comes with his restoration of a dead son to his widowed mother who would have been quite totally marginalized without him (Luke 7:13). The other involves the heart of the father of the household "being moved with compassion" at the return of the Prodigal Son. Here Jesus promotes a familial dynamic that goes beyond issues of inheritance to the deeper "kindom" bond of relatedness, connectedness, and belonging. Not only because of his own alleged impurity for consorting with prostitutes and pigs, but from another legal perspective, the son had disinherited himself. Nonetheless, the heart of the father was "moved with compassion" at the sight of his son. Not only did he embrace him; he brought him back into the family (Luke 15:20).

Before the political situation in the United States moved so far away from real biblical compassion,[18] Maureen O'Connell wrote a little-heralded examination of Luke's understanding of compassion.[19] Concentrating on the story of the Good Samaritan, she took the world of that text and applied it to our own context. She points to our cultural blinders that keep us from seeing in a way that would enable our hearts to be moved with compassion. In particular, she points to the "isms" of Americanism and capitalism in our nation to show how subtly the cataracts on our eyes make us gradually blind.

Like the lawyer in the story of the Good Samaritan, our blindness is directly linked to our position of privilege. This results in the tendency to interpret some others negatively based on culturally received biases and to see ourselves in terms of our righteousness (i.e., holiness). Like the lawyer, in our effort to "justify ourselves," we often immunize ourselves from doing anything to alleviate the suffering around us, especially the causes of suffering that may result from our own position of privilege, including moral codes or practices that virtually exclude various groups (such as women and homosexuals) from sharing in the fullness of life. This is compounded by two other factors, O'Connell says. First, because we have an individualistic rather than a communal approach to salvation, "we tend to associate compassion with individual acts of charity rather than with collective commitments to social change." Second, despite it being a core characteristic of the followers of Jesus and his gospel message, "compassion has never been among the central principles of Catholic social teaching that guide the people of God in engaging social questions regarding the state, society, and the world."[20]

I find an example of the first obstacle to compassion noted by O'Connell in what I know now to have been the well-meaning but misguided use of the word in the first inaugural address of President George W. Bush, delivered on January 20, 2001. I had not voted for Mr. Bush, but, being a political junkie, I watched his address to the nation to discover how he would outline his vision for us as a people. As he moved into the heart of his speech, I was surprised to hear him "affirm a new commitment to live out our nation's promise" through four C's: "civility, courage, compassion, and character."

When he developed the notion of compassion, I began thinking that we might just be getting a statesman president. To my astonishment, I heard him solemnly and sincerely declare:

> Where there is suffering, there is duty. Americans in need are not strangers; they are citizens, not problems, but priorities. And all of us are diminished when any are hopeless.
>
> Government has great responsibilities for public safety and public health, for civil rights and common schools. Yet compassion is the work of a nation, not just a government. And some needs and hurts are so deep they will only respond to a mentor's touch or a pastor's prayer. Church and charity, synagogue and mosque lend our communities their humanity, and they will have an honored place in our plans and in our laws.
>
> Many in our country do not know the pain of poverty, but we can listen to those who do.

And then he said something that I remember to this day: "And I can pledge our nation to a goal: When we see that wounded traveler on the road to Jericho, we will not pass to the other side."[21]

As the British would say, the intuition of the president was "spot on." However, the ability to bring about the compassion of the Samaritan he invoked was perhaps too much to ask of this kind of president, or of any other politician. The national family he envisioned was composed of too many concerned about their own welfare. The consequence of President Bush's failure to put his words into practice by the end of his second term was revealed in a *Wall Street Journal* op-ed piece. There the conservative columnist Daniel Henninger described the exact opposite of compassion in writing about indifference to the suffering of others and the contributing violence that has hardened our hearts as a people. It was entitled "The Numbing Down of America."[22]

Truly, in Luke's use of the word, compassion becomes all-inclusive and all-encompassing, especially for the ones rejected by the existing religious codes of "belonging" that demand separation for those considered unholy or deviant. Compassion envisions a new kind of household where all can find their place at the table with a house-pitality or hospitality of inclusion rather than exclusion. Extending the boundaries of the house even beyond our own kin to include the enemy and even further than this to include the universe, we see the need for an approach to all ecology that shows compassion for everyone and everything insofar as all creatures, including the planet in its need, are recognized as inviting our response. This demands universal compassion, a compassion without walls.

The Steps to Developing a Compassionate Heart as Outlined in Matthew's Gospel

In the 1960s, when I was yet in seminary, I was impressed by a book that linked psychological health, or well-being, with spiritual health, or holiness. Its title was *Holiness Is Wholeness*.[23] Maybe that is a reason why I find the biblical pattern of developing a compassionate heart grounded in good psychological or therapeutic insights. This reveals the fact that the dynamics of what the scriptures call "a heart moved by compassion" follow a definite pattern of seeing (something/someone in need), having this trigger something related to deep care at one's core, followed by a desire and effort to do something to alleviate the need. This pattern of seeing, caring, and doing basically follows the observe, judge, act model of social involvement.

If we examine these steps from a therapeutic model, we find a good approach in the insights of Michael E. Cavanagh. The first element of compassion constitutes a way of seeing the plight of others around us. Dr. Cavanagh calls this the "cognitive" element. It involves a certain way of perceiving and comprehending another's situation of need. Recognizing the plight of those who are poor and marginalized makes us aware that something is wrong about this. We would not want it to happen to us. We try to find out the dynamics in the person's life and background, social setting and environment that are keeping this person in such a negative situation.

The second step in compassion is what Cavanagh calls the "affective" element. The realization of this need triggers feelings of deep concern in the depths of our hearts. The Christian scriptures call this form of care "a heart moved by compassion." This compassion moves beyond the kind of care that reveals an empathic concern insofar as it places a moral judgment on the reality that is reflected in the need, that is, it is wrong. This evokes in the compassionate person a desire to right the wrong being experienced in the pain of the other(s). The person feels compelled to do something about remedying the situation.

The third and final step of compassion involves the effort to act in such a way that the plight of the one(s) in need will be alleviated. In addition, this action is undertaken in a way that seeks to create the dynamics that will keep it from happening again. This third step of acting on behalf of the suffering one is what Cavanagh calls the "behavioral" component. It "means responding to another in a way that is helpful."[24]

When I consider the five uses of the word *splagchnizesthai* in Matthew's Gospel (9:36; 14:14; 15:32; 18:27; 20:34), I find these same dynamics of seeing, judging (with care), and acting. The first three involve compassion that is extended to "the crowd" that was harassed and helpless (9:36), suffering and sick (14:14), and in need of something to eat (15:32). The fourth use of the word identifies it with a key way of being part of the reign, or way, of God. Here compassion addresses the limitless debt owed others in a way that forgives the debt, thereby empowering the forgiven one to extend that same forgiveness to others in need of it (18:24-27). Recalling our link among God's holiness, perfection, and mercy, we are told that the mercy we have received must be returned to others as it has been shown to us. Finally, the fifth use of the word *splagchnizesthai* involves two *blind* men. When asked to enable them to see, Jesus was moved with compassion. The request moved him to touch "their eyes, and immediately they received their sight and followed him" (Matt. 20:33-34). Summarizing these five uses of the word *splagchnizesthai*, we find that in every case there is a need (involving relationships that are one on one, a twosome, or a "crowd") that becomes recognized in some way. This triggers the "heart moved with compassion" to action to take away the need.

What I find fascinating about these five uses of the word (which is the key word in a Matthean triad involving seeing, compassion, and acting) is the final story. It involves two *blind* people "sitting by the roadside." Their disability systemically puts them outside the mainstream of society. They are, by definition, unclean. They and their cries for help only bring rebuke from the crowd. Only in response to their repeated cries for help does Jesus stop. He asks them, "What do you want me to do for you?" These words indicate that he perceives himself to be one who desires to be there for them to free them from their need. When they ask to have their "eyes be opened," his response of compassion, accompanied by the action of touching "their eyes," enables them to *see*. The passage ends with the simple words that, upon receiving their sight, they "followed him."

This kind of "following" Jesus does not mean simply walking behind him but rather becoming committed to put into practice in their own lives the teachings and practice of the master. Such a form of discipleship demands that all of Jesus' followers, if they will be authentic in their discipleship, must (1) develop ways to see the needs of those around them (from one-on-one encounters to the smallest group and up to the level of the "crowd"); (2) allow their hearts to be moved with compassion in a way (3) that will bring about a resolution of the need. When they embrace this compassionate way of putting into practice the teachings of Jesus, the reign of God's compassion in them will be extended into ever-more parts of our world with its many needs.

In his book *The Compassionate Life*, the 14th Dalai Lama has written, "Genuine compassion is based not on our own projections and expectations, but rather on the needs of the other: irrespective of whether another person is a close friend or an enemy, as long as that person wishes for peace and happiness and wants to overcome suffering, then on that basis we develop genuine concern for their problem. This is genuine compassion."[25] Unless I misunderstand what seems to be a condition on whether or not compassion will be shown ("as long as that person wishes for peace and happiness and wants to overcome suffering"), my understanding of the evangelical form of compassion (*splagchnizesthai*) in Matthew's Gospel differs from the Dalai Lama's on two counts: while not denying compassion to an individual in need, its stress is on "the crowd"; and, while not denying that some people in need may not wish for peace and happiness," the main motivator of the one showing compassion is simply to help an individual, a group, or a whole mass of people "to overcome suffering." In this sense compassion has no conditions for its largesse. Recalling our chapters on consciousness and connectedness, we find it is only when we begin to see and hear in ways not defined by indifference but by care that we can nurture the kind of understanding in our heart that reveals that our hearts "have been moved by compassion."

Authentic compassion involves the kiss of mercy and justice in an embrace that links empathy with awareness of the structural obstacles that hinder the realization of that compassion. It involves making the connections between what seems to be a problem and what insures that the problem continues. An example of the structural blinders that benefit some at the expense of many has been raised by Pope Benedict XVI regarding global hunger and ever-rising food prices. Noting that the ethic "to feed the hungry" involves the kind of compassion that is "inscribed in the heart of every person,"[26] he pointed to the structural obstacles that prevent that kind of compassion from being realized when market dynamics go unchecked and unchallenged. He said,

> Poverty, underdevelopment and hence, hunger, are often the result of egoistic behavior that, coming from man's heart, is manifested in social behavior, in economic exchanges, in the market conditions, in the lack of access to food, and is translated in the negation of the primary right of all persons to nourish themselves and, therefore, to be free from hunger. How can we be silent about the fact that even food has become an object of speculation or is linked to changes in a financial market that, deprived of certain laws and poor in moral principles, seems anchored only in the goal of profit?[27]

In addressing underlying structural obstacles to compassion, Maureen O'Connell promotes her own understanding of the threefold approach I have used, especially in articulating the blinders that keep us from seeing the systemic obstacles to compassion that arise from a position of privilege. Without making such links, she insists, effective love of the neighbor in this globalized world can easily become a pious fiction. Consequently, the "seeing, caring, and acting" that I have articulated above needs to include a structural and systemic element as well. This involves "the *ability to perceive* our connections to the causes of others' suffering; the *willingness to interpret* contexts of injustice from the perspective of those who suffer; and an *active commitment* to create new relationships with the capacity to reform the neighbor, ourselves, and the social reality."[28]

Maureen O'Connell's insights are especially helpful for any of us who benefit from our position of privilege in countries like the United States, which is too often blinded by economic imperialism. Given the fact that ours is a globalized economy, unless we "see" the victims of our excess and exploitation in a way that moves our hearts to compassion in a way that energizes us to "change this world" and the mentality and structures to support it, we will not be following Jesus Christ in the kind of contemporary *dao* demanded of us today.

This leads us to our final chapter on the seventh *dao* involved in becoming a "kindom Catholic." Just as the disciples' "following of Jesus" was not in isolation but part of becoming involved in a community of disciples, so we now move to see how our following Jesus invites us to move from our cultural ways of individualism to join a community of like-minded disciples to support us in our discipleship.

15

The Way of Community

Over the years, learning from my mistakes, I have developed three sayings that have helped guide me in my relationships: (1) "correction without care is control"; (2) "where there is testing [in a relationship] there is little trusting"; and (3) "what adult have you ever changed?" This chapter builds on the insight of the third saying and applies it to our existing institutions.

Adults do not change unless they make a decision to do so. Nobody can force another person to change unless the former is using forms of control and the latter is not free. When it comes to effecting change in situations where people are free of dynamics of control, the most we can do is to *influence* others in such ways that *they decide* to change. When people decide to change, it comes from a realization that life will get worse without a change, or, conversely, life will get better with a change. This thinking represents the core of the Twelve-Step Program: when I admit my powerlessness over someone or something I become open to change my way of relating toward that person or thing.

When we apply this notion to groups it becomes even clearer: what group have you ever changed? I may have influenced many group members but to think I have actually changed any group (where I have not used forms of control and its members are free) gives me much more significance than I have. If we cannot really change a person, what in the world makes us think we can change a group? Change can take place in a group if it is forced to do so through negative power such as coercion, domination, or manipulation, or if its members are under some kind of control that denies them real freedom. In such a group, all it takes is the removal of such forms of control to discover how quickly any perceived change disappears.

Finally, when we apply this notion of "what adult have you ever changed?" to institutions, it becomes almost impossible—unless the leaders in such an institution realize it is in crisis, cease denying the situation, and admit that structural change is necessary to keep the institution from dying. An example would be a political party that lost an election in a landslide. Its leaders realize that changes will have to be made, at least in strategy, in order for the party to survive. A better example would be a business that loses market share to the point that its stock drops precipitously, its rating are downgraded, and its creditors are at the door. At this point, arguments that hope is around the corner fall on deaf ears. Short of filing for Chapter 11, the business admits the need to develop a hard-nosed rescue plan as the only way to save the company.

When I look at religious institutions, especially my own Roman Catholic Church in its current crisis in the West, I see some faint signs from its clerical leaders that there just may be some institutional issues that need to be addressed. However, at a deeper level, resistance to change overrides any real effort on their part to "make all things new." Instead, as I have argued elsewhere, because of the leaders' underlying obsession in preserving the male, celibate, clerical way of being "the church," no real change in such an addictive system itself can be expected.[1] It still is overly defined by a denial of the "exact nature of the problem" (to use Twelve-Step language to refer to the addictive and abusive nature of patriarchal clericalism). Whether it be the denial of the addictive dynamics by the church's leaders or their delusion regarding the deeper structural forms of abuse that are somehow equated with "God's will," it is clear both dynamics of control will continue in the family of Catholicism.

Besides applying the wisdom of addiction theory to the institutional dynamics of the Roman Church, I also find the same patterns in play from social science to support my supposition that the existing institutional and organizational way of the Roman Catholic Church will not change.[2] Besides the traditional reactions of denial, other forms of resistance are based on the conviction by the leaders that the present historically and culturally derived institutional model of the church is divinely sanctioned. This is reinforced by various factors: delusional thinking, ideological biases, and, sadly, a conflation of historically derived dynamics that have nothing to do with the church's mystical nature but are man-made patterns with a clerically controlled magisterial veneer that justifies such dynamics as God's will.

Whether it be addiction theory, the scientific study of religion (especially the sociology of religion), or a review of history, all have shown that when religious groups become institutionally dysfunctional to the point that a sense of meaninglessness (anomie) appears among a good proportion of the members, the only hope lies outside these institutions—in the evolution of alternative communities wherein an embodied form of an enlivened spiritual life creates new hope and meaning from the dead bones within which it arises. In such communities individuals are defined not by dynamics of control but by a trust that finds all members sharing in the governance of the group in ways that enhance its relevance rather than reinforce its dysfunctioning.

As Francis of Assisi outlined in his Rule, such a community will manifest a new way of obedience that is faithful to the vision found in the Gospels. It will find all members serving one another in a way that is not preoccupied with rights, rules, and rituals as much as with the members' organic connectedness as members of the Body of the Cosmic Christ. It will not be defined by appeals to overly controlling patterns that worked in past cultures but, even more, by the bond of love and commitment that the group's members have toward Jesus Christ and which they show one another. Such small communities, Pope Benedict XVI has said, help in meeting our desire to experience God's goodness, give voice to our inner longings, and become the source of enlivened and deepened friendships through prayerful adoration of God and shared commitment to finding "new paths to evangelization."[3]

Greg Esty and Mary Testin envision such dynamics as those that must characterize pastoral practice in a postmodern church. They declare:

> Until we are concerned first with our identity as people whose life is grounded in Christ, we will continue to be caught in a cultural consumer trap that teaches that our value comes from producing religious "products"—more outreach, better liturgies, friendlier parishes, and building more Catholic schools. These ministries are not enough. It is only when the community identity with Christ is deep that an authentic response to the gospel can happen. In the work of conversion, the Church must boldly challenge the effects of individualism. Christianity is more than being "nice" and we must face the fact that calling people to conversion won't always make everyone happy. How can this conversion happen in an age when a distrust of institutions is so endemic to our lives? Remember the postmodern principle: My experience—the Truth. A church of conversion to Christ is only possible when the experience of community is personalized. Individuals need to be invited into a deeper faith life.[4]

The Rise of the New Community within the Old

In Chapter 13 we showed how, given the anticipated resistance and rejection of Isaiah by his fellow priests and co-religionists, the only way the mystical/prophetic call could be realized was in the creation of an alternative community. Isaiah was asked to go to his own people and invite them, as an ambassador of God, to change their way of being holy in order to reflect the way God is holy. When he accepted the call, he was told his message would be resisted by those who have "eyes to see" and "ears to hear" lest they "understand with their hearts" and then, "turn" and be converted. Today, given the parallel assumption that those presiding over and canonizing the existing institutional arrangements in the Roman Church will resist the call to conversion, the only hope rests with the promise of new shoots that will rise up from the stump: *"Despite rejection, an alternative community will serve as the seed for implementing the new vision of God's holiness (Isa. 6:13b)."*

As noted above, the mindset that demands the creation of alternative communities living by the *dao* of a new kindom way of being Catholic can be found in the ideology (and theology) that virtually equates the present form of church governance with God's governance or God's will. Because this human system has come to be so identified with divine "holiness" in the eyes of the church's hierarchy, not even the application to its institutional patterns which we find in Isaiah and which were replicated in Jesus' effort to bring about a new way of being holy (see Matt. 5:20-48) will bring about any admission of the exact nature of the problem, much less conversion. Since this conversion will not take place because of the ideological justification of this clericalized, patriarchal model, the only thing that will be new will be the rise of an alternative form of Catholicism within its institutional patterns. There, within the existing structures and sacraments of Catholicism, it will offer a new way of life that gives meaning "to all in the house."

To question the present form of dominating governance in the church that is sustained by control and fear invites a "repair" of this household of faith in an unprecedented way. Furthermore, it demands a new model of governance, authority, and obedience within such alternative communities. Again, I believe these will reflect what we know from science about the way the world really works. In these communities and their gathering together, all hierarchy will be at the service of holarchy, in much the same way that was the case in the early church when charisms defined its social ordering.

In my experience of how power and authority is lived in my own Capuchin Franciscan Order (which has been approved by the official church), I find a kind of "evangelical" model that Francis used to govern his community. He called it "being received into obedience." It involves a way of being at the service of one another that honors the role of the *elected* leaders as well as the responsibility of those leaders to meet the needs of the brothers. When the leaders fail to do this in serious ways, the Rule proscribes the brothers to remove such offenders of evangelical obedience. Given Francis's insight that his way of life was divinely inspired within the existing church model (which he never critiqued directly, contrary to what I have done in this book), his "gospel way" of life outlines the best way we can respond to Jesus' words to him: "Repair my house which you can see is falling into ruin." In my mind, this evangelical form of governance, authority, and obedience best represents a trinitarian-based community wherein all the community's members are "obedient" in a way that empowers them to exist at one another's service in self-sacrificing love and submission.

In Chapter 1 I defined spirituality in its broadest sense as the integration of one's religious experience of what is ultimate with the lived witness of that transcendent experience within some kind of community. When we speak of "Christian spirituality" or, more specifically for our purposes, "Catholic spirituality," it always implies some kind of shared experience and expression of the divine (God, Christ, the Trinity) with *others*, that is, in some kind of community. This book has shown that, for the Catholic Christian, what is ultimate in one's life, that which gives meaning, is "to be in Christ," especially Christ being crucified in his living members, in a way that becomes the embodiment of trinitarian connectedness.

This notion has been wonderfully articulated by Ilia Delio as she unpacks the theology of St. Bonaventure, which we have discussed in Chapter 7:

> Bonaventure's doctrine of the Trinity which gives rise to a world view with Christ as center rectifies the malady of the Christian faith that has persisted through the centuries. In the created world there can be no other way to live in the heart of the Trinity than by living in Christ. Christ *is* the heart of the Trinity in the created world. Bonaventure underlines the fact that it is Christ's human and, in particular, his suffering humanity, that manifests the love of the triune God in the world. There is only one way, therefore, to live in the Trinity of love and that is to live in personal relationship to Christ Crucified in whom the Trinity is expressed. The relationship between the Trinity and Christ is the essential meaning of the *Itinerarium*. The journey into God is the journey into Christ in whom the triune God is expressed.[5]

Since God's life is ultimately communitarian, there can be no truly *Catholic* (much less Christian) spirituality that exists apart from community. Applying this and other insights we have learned from our quantum world, we find that the problem arises when the communal dimension of the religious expression of Catholicism gets identified with dynamics that are neither Christified nor trinitarian. Indeed they actually stand counter to Christ to the degree that they do not witness to a redeemed social order and new creation wherein there will be neither Jew nor Gentile, slave or free, woman or man, or any other such division. Such untrinitarian and, therefore ungodly, dynamics will exist to the degree the church's communal or institutional way of ordering testifies to discrimination rather than equality, domination rather than mutuality, and deprivation rather than abundance and insofar as the basic sacraments are denied for the many in order to limit one of them just to male celibates.

In this new remnant community, dedicated to personal, communal, and institutional forms consciously witnessing to trinitarian connectedness and wholeness, a new kind of perceiving and listening (and ongoing conversion) will define its structuring. The Latin word for hearing is *audire* and the Latin word for obedience is *ob-audire* (we listen together). Evangelical obedience will not be coercive or dominant in controlling ways that elicit fear, pain, and violence; rather it will provide trusting and cohesive models that bring about ever-greater trust and collaboration among church members. These will evidence an energizing kind of obedience that reveals an enlivened, continually renewing community wherein any hierarchy will be holarchical.

Reclaiming the Communal Character of a Renewed Catholicism

When I began my Ph.D. studies in 1985 one of the first courses I took was under Robert Bellah at the University of California-Berkeley. He had just published his exposé of the entitlement spirituality that has overly dominated our times. He summarized his research and that of his colleagues on the cultural psyche of the United States in *Habits of the Heart: Individualism and Commitment in American Life*. What he found has been updated in the moral relativism that Christian Smith and his colleagues described in their 2011 book *Lost in Transition: The Dark Side of Emerging Adulthood*.[6]

Bellah found an exaggerated form of individualism undermining community encapsulated in the "Sheilaism" that a young woman named Sheila used to describe her faith life. Bellah described her faith life as "a perfectly natural expression of current American religious life, and what that tells us about the role of religion in the United States today."[7] As a counter to such a mindset that undermined the possibility of commitment in American life, Bellah and his co-writers proffered the need to create alternative, mediating communities that would provide new meaning to counter the individualism that they found rampant in the nation. Again, their conclusion reflects what we know from science about the way the world really works regarding the way individualism trumps relationality.

Nowhere is the communal reality clearer than what we see in the universe itself. Any type of relationship that falls short of this relational way of being connected cannot be said to be of God (the Trinity) because it denies the way it has been constituted. Again, Thomas Berry has articulated this notion much better than I:

> Everything in the universe is genetically cousin to everything else. There is literally one family, one bonding, in the universe, because everything is descended from the same source. In this creative process, all things come into being. On the planet earth, all living things are clearly derived from a single origin. We are literally born as a community; the trees, the birds, and all living creatures are bonded together in a single community of life. This again gives us a sense that we belong. Community is not something that we dream up or think

would be nice. Literally, we are a single community. The planet earth
is a single community of existence, and we exist in this context.[8]

In an Internet world that proclaims individualism but really practices
ever-growing conformity, increasing signs are pointing to renewed efforts
to rediscover the communitarian character of life itself. Freudian and Dar-
winian notions characterizing the inherent selfishness of individuals (leading to individualism) are being challenged by data showing that children
are much more affected by the empathic attitudes and behaviors of adults
around them than by any inner drives that isolate them from others. The once-
sacrosanct theories of Freud and Darwin have been surpassed by those of the
pediatrician-psychologist Donald Winnicott. He has gone so far as to say of
babies that "it is not logical to think in terms of [them being] an individual
... because there is not yet an individual there."[9] In other words, otherness
actually creates the individual; relationships define our "I am." Just as we have
said of the Trinity in whose image we are our "I am," relationship defines the
essence and core of any "I am" that develops in a child's formative years.

Increasingly, an emerging understanding of what we have called spirituality
in the West is stressing its essentially communal character in a way that is moving it from the "self-help" section of our bookstores to its rightful place in communal dynamics. Indeed, as Thomas Moore has said, anything smacking of
narcissism should not even be called spirituality because it lacks a communal
dimension.[10] Such thinking challenges an overly rights-based and entitlement-
defined, highly personalistic and individualistic, mindset. So, while many in
the popular culture still celebrate individualism, entitlement, and narcissism
as inevitable consequences of evolution's natural selection, an increasing number of studies, starting significantly with Bellah's book, have been showing
that this notion is ill founded. In fact, we are "intensely social creatures deeply
interconnected with one another" to such a degree, David Brooks writes, that
"the idea of the lone individual rationally and willfully steering his own life
course is often an illusion." He reinforces his argument by pointing to the work
of cognitive scientists, neuroscientists, geneticists, behavior economists, psychologists, and sociologists and concludes: "What emerges is not a picture of
self-creating individuals gloriously free from one another, but of autonomous
creatures deeply interconnected with one another."[11]

I believe that, as we seek to enflesh in practice what such scientists have
revealed to be our true nature and reclaim the communal dimension of spirituality, we can be helped by those cultures that are less self-centered, personalistic, and individualistic and more communal, participative, and familial. As
Catholic Christians we can find no greater exemplar than the familial-based
culture of the historical Jesus himself. Thus, during his visit to the Cathedral of
the Holy Family in Barcelona in 2010, Pope Benedict XVI said that Jesus "has

taught us also that the entire Church, by hearing and putting his word into practice, becomes his family."[12] Here he was referring to the Matthean text about who constitutes the new family of equal disciples that followed Jesus (Matt. 12:46-50), an image we have been using throughout this book.

As we move from a more individual-based notion of salvation and spirituality to a more inclusive and familial-based model of church, I find much insight in the ecclesiology coming from Africa, which Pope John Paul II himself highlighted in his post-synodal Apostolic Exhortation, *The Church in Africa*. In his second such exhortation he wrote, "In African culture and tradition the role of the family is everywhere held to be fundamental." He then highlighted how its stress on the family separated it culturally from those groups that based their relationships on individualism:

> African cultures have an acute sense of solidarity and community life. In Africa it is unthinkable to celebrate a feast without the participation of the whole village. Indeed, community life in African societies expresses the extended family. It is my ardent hope and prayer that Africa will always preserve this priceless cultural heritage and never succumb to the temptation to individualism, which is so alien to its best traditions.[13]

Later in the post-synodal Apostolic Discourse, where he interpreted the church as God's family, Pope John Paul II stated:

> Not only did the Synod speak of enculturation, but it also made use of it, taking the *Church* as *God's Family* as its guiding idea for the evangelization of Africa. The Synod Fathers acknowledged it as an expression of the Church's nature particularly appropriate for Africa. For this image emphasizes care for others, solidarity, warmth in human relationships, acceptance, dialogue and trust. The new evangelization will thus aim at *building up the Church as Family,* avoiding all ethnocentrism and excessive particularism, trying instead to encourage reconciliation and true communion between different ethnic groups, favoring solidarity and the sharing of personnel and resources among the particular Churches, without undue ethnic considerations. "It is earnestly to be hoped that theologians in Africa will work out the theology of the Church as Family with all the riches contained in this concept, showing its complementarity with other images of the Church."[14]

Michael Battle is one of those theologians in Africa who have been working out the theology of the church as family in a way that also shows "its complementarity with other images of the Church." He offers a powerful witness to an alternative notion of salvation and spirituality to that of the born-again or more "evangelical" Christian who often will ask: Do you have a *personal* relationship with Jesus? He counters their question with one of his own: "How many times is the question asked: 'Do you have a *communal* relationship with Jesus?'"[15]

Whereas our Western theology, overly defined by Enlightenment theories, stresses the individual "I am," it forgets quantum theory that shows an individualistic approach is alien to the reality of the atom itself. No atom exists apart from its relatedness to others. Such scientific understanding has never been lost in those indigenous theologies that put the notion of "we are" before "I am." Where we have stressed the notion of the "I am" that, in relationship to others, enables us to say "We are," in these more communal societies, everything *begins* with a "We are" that defines each and every "I am." This notion is wonderfully summarized in the African word *Ubuntu.*

Ubuntu is a wide-embracing concept that means "because we are, I am" or, "because I belong, I am." The notion involves the realization that we are persons only through a community of other persons. This essentially trinitarian notion derives from the Bantu language, which serves as the root of the two-to-three-hundred tribal languages (and tribes) of most of Sub-Saharan Africa. I learned its meaning from Benson Kumbukani Makileni, a member of the Chewa tribe who immigrated here from Malawi. It was providential that I met him while I was writing this chapter. He explained to me that *Ubuntu* is "the stuff that makes all of us individuals, groups, and tribes one because of our common origin" (or what I have called in this book *archē*). He said, "I am a Chewa by tribe but a Bantu by origin." He added, "*Ubuntu* is the essence of being human and, since no human exists apart from humanity, *Ubuntu* is about our common origin and resulting interconnectedness; it is about how we belong to one another and everyone else." Mr. Makileni summarized this notion when he told me, "Because we are, I am."[16] In his own description of *Ubuntu,* Archbishop Desmond Tutu shows how it means "that we are made for togetherness, for friendship, for community, for family, that we are created to live in a delicate network of interdependence."[17]

The understanding of the "we" that defines the "I am" of every member of the community makes much clearer the trinitarian "we" which is the archetype of all creaturely relatedness and connectedness. This gospel was expressed in the new way of doing business that Jesus proclaimed and performed through the creation of a new family of disciples. This, we have seen, involved a turning away from one way of being family, which reinforced the empire of Caesar, to witness to an alternative community of equal brothers and sisters under the reign or governance of the one Father in heaven (Matt. 12:46-50).

We find significant parallels between the African synod's ecclesiology of the "church as family"[18] and Avery Dulles's model of the church as a "community of disciples."[19] As already stressed, when we examine the Synoptic Gospels through this lens (aided by the metaphor of house, which we have used throughout this book), we discover this is exactly what Jesus was announcing in word as well as deed: the creation of a new house, family, or community of disciples with an alternative way of doing business. Furthermore, his theology was not just informative through his preaching; it was performative through his actual creation of an alternative family model (Matt. 4:18-22) that he envisioned as an extension of the governance model of the Economic Trinity everywhere on earth as in heaven (see Matt. 28:16-20).

Just as Richard of St. Victor found in the perfection of human love a better understanding of that divine love that defines the Trinity, so it cannot be underestimated how this approach to the Trinity as community must guide our future theology of God and how we are called to image that God. Thus, Joseph Bracken has proposed, because "community" and "not individual substance" is the first category of being, "the Trinity should be conceived as a community of three divine persons who love one another in perfect freedom and through their continuous interaction with one another constitute that higher reality which is their unity as one God."[20] It is in the perfection of this community that humanity is to find its ultimate ground and goal.

Summarizing the *Dao* of Being a Kindom Catholic

At the heart of these new communities will be dynamics that ensure ways of relating that begin with trust rather than fear among their members. Returning to the thought of therapists like Donald Winnicott, we find that such trust is essential if people are to make commitments to one another in community. These dynamics involve what he calls "holding environments" or "envelopes of care."[21] Herein all members agree to affirm one another and be affirmed in what he calls *confirmation*. With such affirmation, the members can challenge one another to growth (which he calls *contradiction*). The result will reveal an ever-greater commitment (which he calls *continuity*).[22] In the kind of communities envisioned here, this will involve commitment in community to the core message of Jesus Christ and the "gospel of the rule of trinitarian connectedness." Such will create the environment of a new way of being Catholic.

Such communities will be continually developed and nurtured through the *dao* we have tried to outline in Part III. Grounded in deeper meanings for the core creeds that speak about God in trinitarian language, the person of Jesus Christ, and his teachings, and with the seven sacraments ensuring equal access for all the baptized, this *dao* will offer a new way to be Catholic that will not even be Western; it will be universal. It will be revealed in the ongoing, communal practice that makes its practitioners ever more consciously connected in cosmic and Christically grounded ways. It will be reinforced by deeply contemplative practices and evidenced in ever-increasing circles of compassion that embrace all of creation.

The rest of this chapter will show how these six contemporary "sacramentals" can find their full expression in the seventh core form of Catholicism: community.

1. The Cosmic Dimension of Community

Building on what has been shown to be the communal or relational dimension of nature itself as well as the "reign" or "kindom of trinitarian connectedness," we find that it becomes very clear that only a community defined by collaboration rather than domination will replicate what we know from science about the way the world really works and what we know from theology about the way the Trinity really works. Only when our own community building moves toward and reflects those dynamics will it be viable.

This notion is wonderfully summarized in an image of community articulated by Wendell Berry, one of the key naturalists of the late-twentieth and early-twenty-first century. He writes that such a "community . . . exists within a system of analogies or likenesses that clarify and amplify its meaning. A healthy community is like an ecosystem, and it includes—or it makes itself harmoniously a part of—its local ecosystem." He then invokes the metaphor of "house" to describe the nesting of one entity in another, from the individual level to the ecological depths of creation itself: "It is also like a household; it is the household of its place, and it includes the household of many families, human and nonhuman. And to extend Saint Paul's famous metaphor by only a little, a healthy community is like a body, for its members mutually support and serve one another."[23]

2. The Christic Dimension of Community

Paul's metaphor of what makes a healthy community arose from his mystical experience on the way to Damascus. Herein he came to an understanding never before imagined by any religion: that the individual members of a group, such as those worshippers whom he had persecuted in the house churches in Jerusalem and had been trying to drag out of the synagogues in Damascus, were not just participants in these organizations; they were living members of the Body of Christ extended in space and time. This Christ was the Cosmic One in whom, through whom, and for whom the whole universe was created. This communal extension of the Cosmic Christ in what he called the church could only be realized when all the members of the body interacted with one another in collaboration rather than competition, in community rather than division, in solidarity rather than isolation. Nowhere was this to be sacramentalized more fully than when members would gather together to celebrate themselves as the Body of Christ in the "breaking of the bread."

This notion of the Eucharist as the living Body of Christ invites its members to "build a house" where all will not only be welcome for the breaking of the bread but can safely dwell in such gatherings. This idea stands in contrast to ways that are based on separation rather than communion and laws and decrees that highlight and perpetuate apparent differences rather than quantum commonalities.

3. The Consciousness of Being a Community; Working to Deepen Our Familial Relationships

In all my reading and visits to the contemporary mega-churches, it is clearly apparent that their founders have worked to make their members consciously aware of their communal connectedness. With such strong familial ties come resulting responsibilities. These too will demand communal cultivation.

We also saw, from our discussion of the *dao* that defines many other religious traditions, the stress on the need to "be awake" or attentive to the ways the members individually are connected to everyone and everything, especially through various bodily disciplines. Furthermore, our probing of the mystical/prophetic call of Isaiah envisioned a community with an "understanding heart" that would enable its members to have eyes that could see and ears that would hear (and obey) and so bring about God's vision of transformation.

This kind of enlightened consciousness is critical today. Such a consciousness cannot be limited to individuals growing in personal awareness apart from their connectedness to others. Instead, we must promote new kinds of "communities of attentiveness" whose members learn and share a common perspective and discipline. This asceticism will find them working together to enliven the person and message of Jesus Christ and his challenge for us to be attentive to the signs of the "kindom of God" all around us.

In their 2010 book *All Things Shining: Reading the Western Classics to Find Meaning in a Secular Age*,[24] Hubert Dreyfus and Sean Dorrance Kelly bemoan the self-centeredness of Western society and envision a return to a more communal way of relating, such as we have noted above. They invoke the image of the Homeric hero whose life is one of public relatedness and responsibility. True to our discussion of the understanding heart in our chapter above on consciousness, they envision a new community of attentiveness. Herein the members will develop rituals that celebrate "a fully embodied, this-worldly kind of sacred."

If this is what such writers envision for the future of the West, how much more should these concepts appeal to Catholics who believe this "higher power" is the trinitarian God and that the awareness of the triune presence unites them in and among one another.

4. Developing Ever-Stronger Communities by a Sense of the Members' Conscious Connectedness

In the chapter discussing our *connectedness* to everyone and everything, I highlighted the Johannine notion of being "a part of" and "remaining with/in." I contrasted these mystical notions with the debilitating effects of the opposite way of remaining "apart from" others. This unnatural and untrinitarian dynamic reflects a lack of consciousness of our deeper connectedness, which goes beyond our categories of time and space to the energy that unites us all as members of one family, sharing kith and kin. In this sense, summarizing many things already discussed, Elizabeth Johnson writes:

> If separation is not the ideal but connection is; if dualism is not the ideal but the relational embrace of diversity is; if hierarchy is not the ideal but mutuality is; then the kinship model more closely approximates reality. It sees human beings and the earth with all its creatures intrinsically related as companions in a community of life. Because we are all mutually interconnected, the flourishing or damaging of one ultimately affects all. This kinship attitude does not measure differences on a scale of higher or lower ontological dignity but appreciates them as integral elements in the robust thing of the whole.
>
> Take, for example, trees. Their process of photosynthesis creates oxygen, the most essential, life-sustaining element in the air we breathe. Without trees there would be no animal or human life on this earth; we would all be asphyxiated. Now, biologically speaking, trees do not need human stewardship. Without human beings they existed very well for millennia. Human beings, however, positively need trees in order to breathe. Who, then, needs whom more? By what standard do human beings say that they are more important than trees? At this point in evolutionary history we form one mutually interdependent community of life. We are all kin.[25]

5. Creating Contemplative Communities of Ever-Deeper Ecologically Conscious Connectedness

Surprisingly, my first experience of being in a contemplative community did not come in my own group of Capuchin Franciscans but in London. More than twenty-five years ago I visited a friend who invited me to someone's flat for an evening of contemplative praying. I had never been part of something like this and really had no idea what it was about.

When we arrived, we were greeted by ten or fifteen others, who had come from all over the city. After making small talk we were invited to center ourselves through deep breathing. Then we sat in contemplative silence for forty-five minutes. It was a powerful experience. I sensed the presence of God in, among, and around each of us. The realization that we had come together to "seek the face of the living God" in itself was the source of deep peace. This sense of peace continued when, at the end of our contemplative sitting, the leader gently asked: "Did anything happen to you during your prayer that you would be able to share with the group?" This question led to more silence. It was not that kind of awkward silence where people feel challenged to say something. Rather it was a sacred kind of contemplative silence that seemed to be a communal sense of honor at the awe of each person's search and experience of God. As people gradually shared what they felt willing to communicate, another sense of silence came in the listening stance that took place between each person's sharing.

Whether it be this kind of contemplative prayer or body prayer or the kind modeled on the writings of spiritual leaders such as John Main or Thomas Keating, or even a type closer to the formal expressions of *lectio divina*, I believe that no Catholic community will be able to be truly communal without the cultivation of rituals that will find its members sharing their search for God in some kind of *dao* that involves a form of contemplative prayer.

6. Widening Our Communal Circles of Compassion

As we have mentioned, little exists in official Catholic theology or Catholic social doctrine regarding compassion, much less papal or episcopal teachings that invite a Catholic *dao* of compassion. Yet, when we consider the teaching of Jesus, especially related to how we are to be present to one another, notably to those whom society and religion itself consider outside and marginalized, it becomes clear why official Catholicism has not developed a theology of compassion. Too often, at least in the official church, some of the very ones who have been beaten up and left on the roadside are the victims of the teachings of the leaders in the official church itself.

If the future of our way of being community is to reflect the metaphor of house in its various familial and trinitarian dynamics, we must find ways to ensure that the very ones who feel rejected by official Catholicism find a home and hearth in these new communities. Such an approach can be found in the words of our Anglican Catholic brother Archbishop Desmond Tutu. Building on the African theology of *Ubuntu*, he stresses the communal dimension of compassion that originates in the "self-assurance that comes from knowing" that we belong in and to a greater whole. This consciousness of our connectedness to everyone makes it clear to us that we ourselves are "diminished when others are humiliated or diminished, when others are tortured or oppressed." This leads us to ever-greater solidarity with them in their effort to become free of whatever it may be that contributes to their diminishment.[26]

As we commune together to bring about a truly Catholic *dao* that learns to practice these seven contemporary sacramentals (and further refine them), we find ourselves ever-more conscious of our connectedness, in Christ, to everyone and everything in the cosmos. Contemplatively, we find in their images the face of the trinitarian God. With them we become ever-more transformed into the reign of that triune God in ways that are reflected in our loving passion to bring God's trinitarian reign into every part of the earth as it is in heaven. In this we will enflesh the insight attributed to Albert Einstein with which we end this book:

> A human being is part of the whole called by us universe, a part limited in time and space. We experience ourselves, our thoughts and feelings as something separate from the rest. A kind of optical delusion of consciousness. This delusion is a kind of prison for us, restricting us to our personal desires and to affection for a few persons nearest to us. Our task must be to free ourselves from the prison by widening our circle of compassion to embrace all living creatures and the whole of nature in its beauty. We shall require a substantially new manner of thinking if humankind is to survive.[27]

Introduction

1. Pope Benedict XVI, "In Our Affluent Western World, Much Is Lacking," September 24, 2011 (http://www.zenit.org/article-33516?I=english).

2. Some of these "isms" were articulated in the opening conclave homily of Cardinal Joseph Ratzinger that resulted in his election as Pope Benedict XVI. Included among these was the oft-reported "dictatorship of relativism," which he addressed.

3. The term "individualism" itself can have different meanings ranging from selfishness to self-expression to rational choice. In this book I interpret it from the perspective of Robert N. Bellah, Richard Madsen, William M. Sullivan, Ann Swidler, and Steven M. Tipton, *Habits of the Heart: Individualism and Commitment in American Life* (Berkeley, CA: University of California Press, 1985).

4. Like "individualism," the term "secularism" (in contrast to "secularity") can have different meanings ranging from being totally defined by secular values to being part of the *saeculum* or world. For a contemporary classic on the subject of secularism, see Charles Taylor, *A Secular Age* (Cambridge: Belknap Press of Harvard University, 2007). For an approach to the subject from the perspective of religion, see the special issue "Does Religious Pluralism Require Secularism?" *The Hedgehog Review: Critical Reflections on Contemporary Culture* 12, no. 3 (Fall 2010). For a Catholic slant, see Ronald Rohlheiser, ed., *Secularity and the Gospel: Being Missionaries to Our Children* (New York: Crossroad, 2006).

5. Another example supporting this statement came from Fordham University's Center on Religion and Culture while I was writing this book. Data released September 6, 2011 showed that just 16 percent of U.S. Catholics ever heard of the U.S. bishops' document "Forming Consciences for Faithful Citizenship," while only 3 percent said they read it. More to the point I am making, three-quarters of those who were aware of the document said it had "no influence at all" on the way they voted in 2008. Seventy-one percent said it would have made no difference even if they knew about it. Only 4 percent said the statement either was or would have been a major influence impacting their political choices had they known about it (Religious News Service in "Catholics Tuning Out Bishops' Voting Guidelines," *National Catholic Reporter*, September 16, 2011).

6. While this number seems extremely large, the fact that one in ten people in the United States were once Catholic makes this number over 30 million. Add to this the formerly "Catholic" countries of France, Spain, Ireland, and parts of Germany and you see that this number is not radical at all. As I wrote this, Archbishop Dairmuid Martin of Dublin noted that the designation of Ireland as a "bastion of Catholicism"

needed to be dropped, given the huge loss of numbers of practicing Catholics in his diocese, where Mass attendance in some parishes has sunk to less than 5 percent.

7. Pope John Paul II, *Sollicitudo rei socialis,* 36, December 30, 1987 (http://www.vatican.va/holy_father/john_paul_ii/encyclicals/documents/hf_jp-ii_enc_30121987_sollicitudo-rei-socialis_en.html).

8. These images will be explained more thoroughly in Chapter 3. Suffice it to say here that, since Western Catholicism has evolved historically, the approach of "Culture I" Catholicism involves a more institutional model of church that stresses hierarchy and obedience while "Culture II" Catholicism will not discount those elements of being Catholic but stresses greater collegiality and participative forms of "being church."

9. "The world" ("I left the world") and "sin" ("when I was in sin") were linked in Francis's view regarding the exclusive and persecuting ways that reinforced the religiously sanctioned violence of his day. This is attested by the opening lines of his Testament, wherein he speaks of his conversion as being divinely inspired. See St. Francis of Assisi, *The Testament,* in Regis J. Armstrong, OFMCap, J. A. Wayne Hellmann, OFMConv, and William J. Short, OFM, eds., *Francis of Assisi: Early Documents* I (New York: New City Press, 1999), 68.

10. "The community of the Trinity is the origin of and the model for the Fraternity" of Francis. See Julio Micó, "The Spirituality of St. Francis: Brothers to All," trans. Paul Barrett, OFMCap, *Greyfriars Review* 8, no. 2 (1994): 151. See also my *Finding Francis, Following Christ* (Maryknoll, NY: Orbis Books, 2007), esp. 128-41. For the trinitarian notion that informed Francis's whole spirituality, including his understanding of "the Spirit of the Lord and Its Holy Activity," see Optatus van Asseldonk, OFMCap, "The Spirit of the Lord and Its Holy Activity in the Writings of Francis," trans. Edward Hagman, OFMCap, *Greyfriars Review* 5, no. 1 (1991): 105-58.

11. St. Francis of Assisi, *The Earlier Rule* 7.2, in Regis J. Armstrong, OFMCap, J. A. Wayne Hellmann, OFMConv, and William J. Short, OFM, eds., *Francis of Assisi: Early Documents* I (New York: New City Press, 1999), 68.

12. St. Francis of Assisi, *The Earlier Rule* 19.1, in Armstrong et al., *Francis of Assisi: Early Documents* I, 77.

Part I. Catholicism and Apocalypse

1. The first occurred ten years earlier.

2. Avery Dulles, *Models of the Church,* expanded edition (New York: Image Books/Doubleday, 1987).

3. Donald Senior, *Invitation to Matthew* (Garden City, NY: Doubleday Image Books, 1977), 223.

4. Some of this harmful conflation of grace with nature is reinforced by the recent return to appellations such as "your grace" or "his grace" when referring to the hierarchy.

5. Daniel Kahneman, Dan Lovallo, and Olivier Sibony, "Before You Make That Big Decision . . . ," *Harvard Business Review,* June 2011, 51.

6. Pope Benedict XVI, "Lay People in the Church: From Collaboration to 'Co-

Responsibility,'" Address at the Opening of the Ecclesial Convention of the Diocese of Rome, 26 May, 2009, in *L'Osservatore Romano*, June 3, 2009.

7. Kahneman, et al., "Before You Make That Big Decision," 60.

1. Understanding the Various Forms of Atheism

1. This would not be too difficult. My first book in this genre was *Thy Will Be Done: Praying the Our Father as a Subversive Activity* (Maryknoll, NY: Orbis Books, 1977). Because I was rightly challenged for the approach I used for my scriptural sourcing as "proof-texting," I later updated this book using the historical-critical approach, which will be discussed in Chapter 2. This was published as *The Prayer That Jesus Taught Us* (Maryknoll, NY: Orbis Books, 2002).

2. My doubts about believing in a "need-based God" came at the same time that Stephen Hawking and Leonard Mlodinow published *The Grand Design* in which they said that, following the M-theory, which posits many universes created from nothing, "their creation does not require the intervention of some supernatural being or god." See Stephen Hawking and Leonard Mlodinow, *The Grand Design* (New York: Bantam, 2010), 8.

3. Vladimir Lossky, *Orthodox Theology: An Introduction*, trans. Ian and Ihita Kesarcodi-Watson (Crestwood, NY: St. Vladimir's Seminary Press, 1978), 73.

4. For more on this see the commentary on the "Pastoral Constitution on the Church in the Modern World," Part I, Chapter 1 by Joseph Ratzinger: "Over the pope as the expression of the binding claim of ecclesiastical authority there still stands one's own conscience, which must be obeyed before all else, if necessary even against the requirement of ecclesiastical authority. This emphasis on the individual, whose conscience confronts him with a supreme and ultimate tribunal, and one which in the last resort is beyond the claim of external social groups, even of the official Church, also establishes a principle in opposition to increasing totalitarianism. Genuine ecclesiastical obedience is distinguished from any totalitarian claim which cannot accept any ultimate obligation of this kind beyond the reach of its dominating will." In Herbert Vorgrimler, general editor, *Commentary on the Documents of Vatican II*, trans. W. J. O'Hara (New York: Herder and Herder, 1969), V.134.

5. Hawking and Mlodinow, *The Grand Design*, 5.

6. Richard Rohr, *The Naked Now: Learning to See as the Mystics See* (New York: Crossroad, 2009), 23.

7. For a CD/tape of his talk, contact CSD Digital Media: www.csctapes.com. #4-02 2011 Los Angeles Religious Education Congress.

8. An example would be his letter *De laude novae militiae*.

9. National Conference of Catholic Bishops, *When I Call for Help: Domestic Violence against Women*, 10th Anniversary Edition, November 12, 2002. http://www.nccbuscc.org/bishops/help.htm.

10. Ibid. While the bishops refer to forms of violence against women that represent *domestic violence*, I do not think they would be willing to say that violence against women in the church is justified. However, they seem unable to apply their own definition to the dynamics in the church against women and others and to name it sinful.

11. While I was writing this book, Pope Benedict XVI discussed with scientists how "the concrete nature of the nexus between faith and reason should and must always be plumbed anew" (June 30, 2011, http://www.zenit.org/article-32987?l=english).

12. Michael Dowd, *Thank God for Evolution: How the Marriage of Science and Religion Will Transform Your Life and Our World* (New York: Viking, 2008).

13. Fran Ferder and John Heagle, "The Inner Workings of a Hierarchy with a Sex Offender Mentality," *National Catholic Reporter*, August 2, 2010 (http://ncronline.org/print/19526).

14. Richard Dawkins, *The God Delusion* (Boston/New York: Houghton Mifflin Mariner Books, 2008), 73-74.

15. In later writings Dawkins seems to be moving toward the stance of a pure atheist, albeit with a form of reasoning that represents, to me, a straw dog God as Creator that he sets up and then tries to dismantle: "Making the universe is the one thing no intelligence, however, superhuman, could do, because an intelligence is complex—statistically improbable—and therefore had to emerge, by gradual degrees, from simpler beginnings: from a lifeless universe—the miracle-free zone that is physics." See Richard Dawkins, "Evolution Leaves God with Nothing to Do, Argues Richard Dawkins," *Wall Street Journal*, September 12-13, 2009, W2.

16. Dawkins, *The God Delusion*, 189.

17. Sam Harris, *The End of Faith: Religion, Terror, and the Future of Reason* (New York/London: W. W. Norton, 2004), 12.

18. Harris, *The End of Faith*, 65.

19. Ibid., 64.

20. Leisa Anslinger, *Turning Hearts to Christ: Engaging People in a Lifetime of Faith* (New London, CT: Twenty-Third Publications, 2010).

21. The National Survey of Youth and Religion had three "waves." The first was reported in Christian Smith, with Melinda Lundquist Denton, *Soul Searching: The Religious and Spiritual Lives of American Teenagers* (New York: Oxford University Press, 2005). This group was followed with another survey in 2005. Its participants served as the database in 2007-2008 for Christian Smith, with Patricia Snell, *Souls in Transition: The Religious and Spiritual Lives of Emerging Adults* (Oxford/New York: Oxford University Press, 2009).

22. Robert D. Putnam and David E. Campbell, *American Grace: How Religion Divides and Unites Us* (New York: Simon & Schuster, 2010).

23. James Allan David, Tom W. Smith, and Peter V. Marsden, *General Social Surveys, 1972-2006: Cumulative Codebook*, National Opinion Research Center, 2007. National Data Program for the Social Sciences Series, no. 18.

24. Cathleen Kaveny, "Long Goodbye: Why Some Catholics Are Leaving the Church," *Commonweal* 137, no. 18 (October 22, 2010): 8.

25. Thomas Reese, SJ, "The Hidden Exodus: Catholics Becoming Protestants," *National Catholic Reporter*, April 18, 2011.

26. Peter Steinfels, "Further Adrift: The American Church's Crisis of Attrition," *Commonweal* 137, no. 18 (October 22, 2010): 16-19

27. Suzanne Sataline, "The Changing Faiths of America: Study Shows Big

Declines among Major Denominations; a Boon for Evangelicals," *New York Times*, February 26, 2008.

28. Neela Banerjee, "A Fluid Religious Life Is Seen in U.S., with Switches Common," *New York Times*, February 26, 2008. For the study, see http://religons.pew forum.org/experience.

29. Smith and Snell, *Souls in Transition*, 96, 105, 108.

30. John Flynn, LC, "Religion in America: New Book Examines the Diversity of Faith," http://www.zenit.org/article-30812?I=english.

31. Smith and Snell, *Souls in Transition*, 295.

32. Ibid., 297.

33. Gabriele Garcia, "Letter to Father Crosby," 3 February, 2007. In file of the author. I must add, however, that this response was the only one I received from my other letters of comments and concerns to Cardinal Joseph Ratzinger (as well as to other cardinals based in Rome), Pope John Paul II, and Pope Benedict XVI in the past. To these I never received any indication of their reception, much less their contents.

34. Michael H. Crosby, OFMCap., Letter to His Holiness Pope Benedict XVI, December 10, 2006, with a copy to Archbishop Timothy Dolan (of Milwaukee). Letter in file of the author.

35. Reese, "Hidden Exodus," 24.

36. Michael J. Buckley, SJ, "Experience and Culture: A Point of Departure for American Atheism," *Theological Studies* 50 (1989): 453.

37. Paul Froese and Christopher Bader, *America's Four Gods: What We Say about God—and What That Says about Us* (Oxford/New York: Oxford University Press, 2010). A related piece (unscientific) served as the cover story in *USA Weekend*: Cathy Lynn Grossman, "How Americans Imagine God," *USA Weekend*, December 17-19, 2010, 6-7.

38. Unsigned editorial, "Economic Focus: The Beautiful and the Damned," *The Economist*, January 22, 2011. *The Economist* points to similar patterns in England. See "Reversing Inequality: For He That Hath," January 30, 2010.

39. Mark Whitehouse, "Number of the Week: 364%," *Wall Street Journal*, February 19, 2011.

40. Nicole Neroulias, "Poll: Americans See Clash between Values of Christianity, Capitalism," Religious News Tracking Poll (http://www.publicreligon.org/research/?id=554).

41. David Brooks, "The Triumph of Hope over Self-Interest," *New York Times*, January 12, 2003.

42. For more on this notion, see my comments on my website: www.michael-crosby.net.

43. David Gelernter, "Americanism—and Its Enemies," *Commentary* 119, no. 1 (January, 2005), 41. For an application of some of the negative notions around "The New 'Americanism'" to Catholics, see "The New 'Americanism,'" editorial, *America* 205, no. 3, August 1-8, 2011, 5.

44. John J. DiIulio, Jr., "Blending In," *America* 203, no. 16, November 29, 2010, 11.

45. Alan Jacobs, "Too Much Faith in Faith," Houses of Worship column, *Wall Street Journal*, June 6, 2008.

2. Imbalance in Church Governance
Based on a Misuse of Scripture

1. Most Reverend Donald W. Wuerl, "Reflections on Governance and Accountability in the Church," in Francis Oakley and Bruce Russett, eds., *Governance, Accountability and the Future of the Catholic Church* (New York: Continuum, 2003), 13-24.

2. Peter Steinfels, "Necessary but Not Sufficient: A Response to Bishop Wuerl's Reflections," in Oakley and Russett, *Governance,* esp. 26-29.

3. For more of my reflections on this subject, see my "Doing Moral Theology in Light of an Ecclesiological Reflection on Matthew 16 and 18," in Eileen P. Flynn, Seminar on Moral Theology, *The Catholic Theological Society of America Proceedings of the Forty-Eighth Annual Convention* 48, pp. 156-58, and Michael H. Crosby, *The Dysfunctional Church: Addiction and Codependency in the Family of Catholicism* (Eugene, OR: Wipf & Stock, 2011), 49-52.

4. Pontifical Biblical Commission, September 21, 1993, "The Interpretation of the Bible in the Church [IBC]," *Origins* 23, no. 29, January 6, 1994, 500.

5. IBC, 513.

6. Ibid., 500.

7. Joseph Ratzinger (Pope Benedict XVI), *Jesus of Nazareth: From the Baptism in the Jordan to the Transfiguration,* trans. Adrian J. Walker (New York: Doubleday, 1997), xii-xix.

8. IBC, 501.

9. Ibid., 510.

10. Ibid., 509.

11. Ibid., 510.

12. John P. Meier, *The Vision of Matthew: Christ, Church and Morality in the First Gospel* (New York: Paulist Press, 1977), 132.

13. Donald Senior, 161.

14. IBC, 515.

15. If the recalcitrant member of the community does not convert after the threefold process, traditional interpretation indicates the community can then excommunicate by the words: "if he refuses to listen even to the church, let him be to you as a Gentile and a tax collector" (Matt. 18:17). It will be clear from my interpretation of Peter's response that this does not refer to the power to excommunicate as much as it reflects Jesus' pattern of unconditioned forgiveness.

16. IBC, 509-10.

17. Ulrich Luz, "The Primacy Text (Matt. 16:18)," *Princeton Seminary Bulletin* 12 (1991): 55.

18. James Hanvey, "Tradition as Subversion," *International Journal of Systematic Theology* 6, no. 1 (January, 2004): 50.

19. Hanvey, "Tradition as Subversion," 59. Here he references Hannah Arendt, *The Origins of Totalitarianism* (New York: Harcourt, 1973), 167.

3. Catholicism's Crisis as Organizational

1. Michael H. Crosby, *The Dysfunctional Church: Addiction and Codependency in the Catholic Church* (Eugene, OR: Wipf & Stock, 2011), 1991; Michael H. Crosby, *Rethinking Celibacy, Reclaiming the Church* (Eugene, OR: Wipf & Stock, 2003). While another book does not directly address aberrations around power in the Roman Church, the notions can be applied, along with those times it is explicitly mentioned. See Michael H. Crosby, *The Paradox of Power: From Control to Compassion* (New York: Crossroad, 2008).

2. Dominic Doyle, "Post-Traumatic Ecclesiology and the Restoration of Hope," *Theological Studies* 72, no. 2 (June, 2011): 275-95.

3. Pierre Hegy, *Wake Up, Lazarus! On Catholic Renewal* (Bloomington, IN: iUniverse, Inc., 2011). Besides sources quoted in this book, Hegy relies heavily on the General Social Surveys (GSS) on religious affiliation and practice which are taken periodically. He also uses the findings and insights of William D'Antonio, James D. Davidson, Dean R. Hoge, and Mary L. Gautier, *American Catholics Today: New Realities of Their Faith and Their Church* (New York: Rowman & Littlefield, 2007).

4. James D. Davidson, "Generations of American Catholics," Keynote Address, in *Proceedings of the Sixty-Third Annual Convention of the Catholic Theological Society of America* 63 (2008), 1-17. Davidson's sources for his presentation are covered in his first footnote on page 1. His data do not reference but do echo similar findings covering a broader field of young people, including younger Catholics who are the least affiliated with the institution of Catholicism. See Christian Smith, with Patricia Snell, *Souls in Transition: The Religious and Spiritual Lives of Emerging Adults* (Oxford/New York: Oxford University Press, 2009).

5. Davidson, "Generations of American Catholics," 2.

6. This phrasing was first popularized by Eugene Kennedy, *Tomorrow's Catholics, Yesterday's Church* (San Francisco: Harper & Row, 1988).

7. Davidson, "Generations of American Catholics," 5.

8. Robert D. Putnam and David E. Campbell, *American Grace: How Religion Divides and Unites Us* (New York: Simon & Schuster, 2010).

9. Olivier Roy, *Holy Ignorance: When Religion and Culture Part Ways* (New York: Columbia University Press, 2010), 5.

10. Roy, *Holy Ignorance*, 9ff.

11. Ken Wilber, *A Brief History of Everything* (Boston: Shambala, 2007), 39.

12. For more on the nature of power and its expressions in our personal, group, and institutional relationships, see my *The Paradox of Power: From Control to Compassion* (New York: Crossroad, 2008). Also my DVD series, *Choosing Compassion: The Paradox of Power* (www.choosing compassion.net).

13. Joseph Ratzinger, *Das neue Volk Gottes: Entwuerfe zur Ekklesiologie* (Düsseldorf: Patmos, 1969), 144.

14. As I was writing this chapter a news item noted a *fatwa* that declared it was God's will that canonized the practice of fathers arranging marriages for their daughters "even if they are in the cradle." Sheik Saleh al-Fawzan, one of Saudi Arabia's "most important clerics," stated: "Those who are calling for a minimum age for marriage

should fear God and not violate his laws or try to legislate things God did not permit." This followed a previous *fatwa* by the Grand Mufti, the nation's highest religious
leader, against women working "as supermarket cashiers." Angus McDowall and
Summer Said, "Influential Saudi Cleric Backs Child Marriages," *Wall Street Journal*,
July 29, 2011.

15. When one investigates the statements of Pope Benedict XVI, both theological and political (such as those dealing with the European Union and who constitute it), the notion clearly involves a high primacy given the Western culture, despite
affirmations of the value of all cultures to the contrary. These sentiments are noted in
the words of Olivier Roy: "Pope Benedict XVI has returned to a more ethnocentrist
standpoint, or, to be more exact, one which favours the religious culture of the period
before the Second Vatican Council . . . ; he thus automatically promotes the Western
dimension of Christianity" (*Holy Ignorance*, 63-64).

16. Michael H. Crosby, OFMCap, "Letter to His Holiness Pope Benedict XVI,"
March 26, 2006. My first letter in this vein to Cardinal Joseph Ratzinger was sent in
1996. Because I did not receive a response to either letter I feel no loyalty has been
broken by my keeping it confidential. In the 2006 letter I added: "Again, your Holiness, I write this from a desire to be faithful in this church, to be honest in my sincere
and theologically-grounded disagreement in those matters that have not been officially been declared infallible and for my own integrity and sense of solidarity with
those people whom the leaders of the institutional church do not deem acceptable
for ordination." I also asked for "the possibility of such a dialogue that would find us
'practicing the truth in charity in order to build up the body of Christ' (Eph. 4:15)."

17. The origin of the model I use was inspired by a workshop I attended that was
led by Anthony Gittins, CSSp.

18. The notion of holarchy is a scientific explanation of the cosmic order; its origin
is the "holon." A holon is any whole in itself, such as a cell; however, it is embedded
within another holon which is a larger whole, such as an organ. Each holon is self-
contained and has its own self-interest but is embedded within the reality and self-
interest of the larger holon that contains it. This dynamic, from the smallest quark or
packet of energy-creating matter up to the universe, forms a holarchy. Because everything is part of the whole or holarchy, any hierarchy is not separate from but at the
service of the holarchy.

19. Pope Benedict XVI, "On Christian Unity in 2009," January 20, 2010, http://
www.zenit.org/article-28108?I=english. A few lines later the pope quoted from the
Second Vatican Council's *Unitatis redintegratio* (#1) which affirmed "the division
between the disciples of Jesus 'openly contradicts the will of Christ, scandalizes the
world, and damages the holy cause of preaching the Gospel to every creature.'"

20. Pope Benedict XVI, "Lay People in the Church: From Collaboration to 'Co-
Responsibility,'" May 26, 2009. In *L'Osservatore Romano*, June 3, 2009.

21. Hugh Heclo, *On Thinking Institutionally* (Boulder, CO: Paradigm, 2008).

22. George Lakoff, *Moral Politics: How Liberals and Conservatives Think*, 2nd edition (Chicago/London: University of Chicago Press, 2002), 245-62.

23. For more on this, see the findings of Dan Kahan of Yale Law School (http://

www.law.yale.edu/faculty/DKahan.htm) and a more popular version of these find-ings in https://motherjones.com/files/kahan_paper_cultural_cognition_of scientific _consensus.pdf.

24. William R. Hosmer, e-mail message to author, September 2, 2011.

25. Lakoff, *Moral Politics*, 35. Jonathan Kay shows how, since September 11, 2001, in the United States, these two positions have become more pronounced in the parti-sanship that has come to color political discourse in the nation. "Like an earthquake, 9/11 produced a great fissure through the heart of America's political center," he notes. Pointing to the deeper issue raised by the likes of Lakoff, he adds: "It is not just politics that separates these two camps, but the very manner by which they answer fundamental questions about the world" (Jonathan Kay, *Among the Truthers* [New York: HarperCollins, 2011]).

26. Enda Kenny, quoted in Eamonn Quinn and Stacy Meichtry, "Vatican Recalls Ireland Envoy after Dublin's Criticism," *Wall Street Journal*, July 26, 2011, A11.

27. Janet Ruffing, RSM, Sunday Plenary Session, CD 2, Spiritual Directors Inter-national, April 31, 2011 (Berkeley, CA: Conference Recording Service, 2011), SDI11-330.

28. Lakoff, *Moral Politics*, 31.

29. Francis of Assisi, *Earlier Rule* 22.33, in Regis J. Armstrong, OFMCap, J. A. Wayne Hellmann, OFMConv, and William J. Short, OFM, eds., *Francis of Assisi: Early Documents* I (New York: New City Press 1999), 80.

30. In both the earlier and later Rules, the brothers' way of relating to one another was to be based on the pattern of a nurturing Mother to whom one might confidently make known his needs. Also, in his Rule for Hermitages, Francis's form of relating among the brothers involved was based on a nurturing model. The relationship was not "father" and "son" but "mothers" and "sons." See "A Rule for Hermitages," in Arm-strong et al., *Francis of Assisi: Early Documents* I, 61-62.

31. In his "Prayer Inspired by the Our Father," Francis wrote: "O *Our Father* most holy: Our Creator, Redeemer, Consoler, and Savior," 1. In Armstrong et al., *Francis of Assisi: Early Documents* I, 158. It is generally accepted by Franciscan scholars that Francis's whole approach to each person of the Blessed Trinity was always inclusive of the other persons.

32. *Legend of the Three Companions*, 20, in Regis J. Armstrong, OFMCap, J. A. Wayne Hellmann, OFMConv, and William J. Short, OFM, eds., *Francis of Assisi: Early Documents* II (New York: New City Press, 2000), 80.

33. Davidson, "Generations of American Catholics," 3.

34. The most likely group of emerging adults who will be dropping their religious affiliation in the future are Jews and Catholics. See Smith and Snell, *Souls in Transi-tion*, 108.

35. The lack of any support for this position by the millennials begs for further evidence, especially when it is known that some of its members are staunchly anti-abortion. The difference could be that they too find the locus for their position coming from their own informed conscience rather than outside themselves, in statements of the hierarchy.

36. Mark Pattison, "Poll Shows 'Dramatic' Loss of Confidence in Pope, U.S. Bishops," Catholic News Service, May 8, 2010 (http://www.americancatholic.org/news/news2print/news report.aspx?id=2573).

37. This insight of Diarmuid Martin regards Irish Catholics. See Barb Fraze, "Dublin Archbishop Says Catholics Not Passing on Faith to Young People," Catholic News Service, May 11, 2011 (http://www.catholicnews.com/data/stories/cns/1101942.htm).

38. John C. Haughey, "Church-ianity and Christ-ianity: Why Are Catholics Slow to Profess Their Faith?" *America* 190, no. 18 (May 24-31, 2004): 8.

39. Cardinal Joseph Ratzinger, Conclave Homily, April 18, 2005. Zenit News Service.

40. Pope Benedict XVI, Spontaneous Remarks, July 25, 2005. ZE05072909.

41. Otto Neubauer, "Reflections on Evangelization Shared with Ratzinger Students," August 28, 2011 (http://www.zenit.org/article-33325?I=english).

42. Bishop John A. Quinn, "A Looming Crisis of Faith," *America* (July 7, 2002): 14.

43. Enda Kenny, quoted in AP story, "Ireland: Parliament Blames Vatican for Covering Up Pedophile Cases," *New York Times*, July 21, 2011 (http://www.zenit.org/article-33129?l=english). Roberto Lombardi, SJ, of the Vatican Press Office defended the actions of the Vatican and said all statements must be considered.

44. Archbishop Timothy Dolan, in Laurie Goodstein, "A New Leader Confronts Catholics' Disaffection," *New York Times*, November 22, 2010.

45. Bob Dixon, Head of Pastoral Research Office, Australian Conference of Catholic Bishops, in "Mass Discontent," *[Melbourne] Age*, March 16, 2011.

46. An evidence of the clericalized nature of the Vatican was abundantly clear when its Zenit News Service touted a headline stating that a "Uruguayan Takes Highest Curia Post Ever Given Layman." This was to be the Secretary of the Pontifical Commission for Latin America "which depends on the Congregation for Bishops" (http://www.zenit.org/article-32597?I=english).

47. Archbishop Diarmuid Martin, "Archbishop Martin's Analysis of Church in Ireland," February 22, 2011, in Zenit 11022602 (http://www.zenit.org/article-31862?I=english).

48. Archbishop Diarmuid Martin, Marquette University, April 5, 2011 (http://www.cathnews.com/article.aspx?aeid=25752).

49. Pope Benedict XVI, December 19, 2010, in Rachel Donadio, "Pope Says Sex Scandal Has Hit Unimaginable Dimension," *New York Times*, December 20, 2010.

50. Sharon Daloz Parks, *The Critical Years: The Young Adult Search for a Faith to Live By* (San Francisco: Harper & Row, 1986), 13-14.

51. I am sharing a part of this longer letter now here because of the fact that this and other letters to Cardinal Ratzinger and Pope Benedict XVI privately addressing issues now shared publicly in this book, such as this discussion here, never received any real acknowledgment. These letters began in 1996, so it cannot be said that I did not try "to work within the system."

52. Drew Christiansen, "A Conspiracy of Bishops and Faithful: Reading Newman's *On Consulting the Faithful* Today," *America* 203, no. 7 (September 9, 2010): 24.

53. Michael H. Crosby, *The Paradox of Power: From Control to Compassion* (New York: Crossroad, 2008).

54. The psychological phrase "the paradox of power" refers to the phenomenon of people whose "very traits that helped leaders accumulate control in the first place all but disappear once they rise to power." Their exercise of "authority undermines the very talents that got them there." See Jonah Lehrer, "The Power Trip," *Wall Street Journal,* August 14, 2010.

55. Dacher Kelnter (a psychologist at the University of California, Berkeley), quoted in Jonah Lehrer, "The Power Trip."

56. Christiansen, "A Conspiracy of Bishops and Faithful."

57. Pope John Paul II, *Redemptoris Missio,* On the Permanent Validity of the Church's Missionary Mandate, 54, quoting *Lumen Gentium,* 17 (Washington DC: United States Catholic Conference, 1990), 93.

58. Langdon Gilkey, "Evolution, Culture, and Sin," *Zygon* 30 (1995): 305.

59. Ilia Delio, OSF, *The Emergent Christ: Exploring the Meaning of Catholic in an Evolutionary Universe* (Maryknoll, NY: Orbis, 2011), 118.

60. Tony Schwartz, quoted in "Being More Productive," *Harvard Business Review,* May, 2011, 87.

61. The second law of thermodynamics states that whenever energy is transformed, some energy is lost in the process. In 1868 the German physicist Rudolf Clausius called this loss of energy "entropy." Entropy involves the extent to which available energy in any subsystem of the universe becomes no longer available. "Entropy is an inverse measure of a system's capacity for change. The more entropy there is, the less the system is capable of changing" (Margaret J. Wheatley, *Leadership and the New Science: Learning about Organization from an Orderly Universe* [San Francisco: Berrett Koehler Publishers, 1994], 76).

4. Finding a New Model of Meaning

1. See especially, Max Weber, *The Sociology of Religion,* trans. Ephraim Fischoff (Boston: Beacon, 1963).

2. I showed how Weber's pattern is replicated in the church and the Franciscan Order in my *Franciscan Charism: A Sociological Investigation* (Pulaski, WI: Franciscan Publishers, 1969).

3. Stephen V. Doughty, "Mystery and Institutional Rebirth," *Weavings* 21, no. 1 (January/February, 2006), 27-28.

4. Thomas Berry, *The Sacred Universe: Earth, Spirituality, and Religion in the Twenty-first Century,* ed. Mary Evelyn Tucker (New York: Columbia University Press, 2009), 54-55.

5. Joseph Campbell, *The Inner Reaches of Outer Space: Metaphor as Myth and as Religion* (New York: Harper & Row, 1986), 12.

6. Joan Chittister, OSB, "Foreword," in Angela Iadavaia, ed., *Common Sense Spirituality: The Essential Wisdom of David Steindl-Rast* (New York: Crossroad, 2008), 8.

7. Thomas Petzinger, Jr., interview with Edward O. Wilson, *Wall Street Journal,* January 1, 2000.

8. Karen Armstrong, *The Case for God* (New York: Random House Anchor Books, 2010), xi.

9. Armstrong, *The Case for God*, 318.

10. Joseph Campbell, referenced in Edwin M. McMahon and Peter A. Campbell, *Rediscovering the Lost Body-Connection within Christian Spirituality: The Missing Link for Experiencing Yourself in the Body of the Whole Christ Is a Changing Relationship to Your Own Body* (Minneapolis: Tasora Books, 2010), xix.

11. Armstrong, *The Case for God*, xi.

12. For more on quantum theory and its implications for life today, see Jeremy Bernstein, *Quantum Leaps* (Cambridge, MA/London: Belknap Press of Harvard University Press, 2009). See also his review of Jim Baggott's *The Quantum Story* (Oxford: Oxford University Press, 2011) in "A Portrait of the Subatomic World," *Wall Street Journal*, April 16, 2011.

13. For a more recent summary of her thinking on the subject, see Sandra M. Schneiders, "Spirituality and the God Question," *Spiritus* 10, no. 2 (2010): 243-50.

14. Pope Benedict XVI, "Lay People in the Church: From Collaboration to 'Co-Responsibility,'" 26 May 2009 in *L'Osservatore Romano*, June 3, 2009.

15. For a deeper development of this dynamic see Gordon Allport, *The Individual and His Religion* (New York: Macmillan, 1950).

16. For more on this, see my *The Dysfunctional Church: Addiction and Codependency in the Family of Catholicism* (Eugene, OR: Wipf & Stock, 2011 [1991]) and my *Rethinking Celibacy, Reclaiming the Church* (Eugene, OR: Wipf & Stock, 2003), 42-46, esp. 133-68.

17. Charles Taylor, *A Secular Age* (Cambridge, MA: Belknapp Press of Harvard University, 2007), esp. 171, 323.

18. Sam Harris, *The End of Faith: Religion, Terror, and the Future of Reason* (New York/London: W. W. Norton, 2004), 15.

19. Karl Rahner, *Concern for the Church*, trans. Edward Quinn (Theological Investigations 20; New York: Crossroad, 1981).

20. Harris, *The End of Faith*, 43.

21. Günther Bornkamm, "*Mystērion, Mueō*," in Gerhard Kittel, *Theological Dictionary of the New Testament*, IV, trans. and ed. Geoffrey W. Bromiley (Grand Rapids, MI: Wm. B. Eerdmans, 1973), 802-28.

22. Ibid., 805.

23. James W. Fowler, *Stages of Faith: The Psychology of Human Development and the Quest for Meaning* (San Francisco: Harper & Row, 1981).

24. Pierre Hegy, *Wake Up, Lazarus! On Catholic Renewal* (Bloomington, IN: iUniverse, Inc., 2011), 188.

25. For the need to understand Jesus' flesh and blood as risen and, therefore, transubstantiated, see my *"Do You Love Me?" Jesus Questions the Church* (Maryknoll, NY: Orbis Books, 2004), 40-56.

26. For more on the different levels of belief in transubstantiation among U.S. Catholics (ranging from practicing Catholics to non-practicing Catholics), see http://cara.georgetown.edu/masseucharist.pdf. This data shows there was a drop in belief in the Real Presence of Christ in the Eucharist from 2007 (63%) to 2008 (57%).

27. I base this model on Juan Luis Segundo's *The Liberation of Theology* (Mary-

knoll, NY: Orbis Books, 1976), 9. See my adaptation of this in *Spirituality of the Beatitudes: Matthew's Vision for the Church in an Unjust World*, new rev. ed. (Maryknoll, NY: Orbis Books, 2005), 16-20.

28. Harris, *The End of Faith*, 221. See also http://www.vatican.va/holy_father/john_paul_ii/encyclicals/documents/hf_jp-ii_enc_30121987_sollicitudo-rei-socialis_en.html

29. Joseph Campbell, *Thou Art That: Transforming Religious Metaphor*, ed. Eugene Kennedy (Novato, CA: New World Library, 2001), 1.

5. The Apocalypse Facing Catholicism

1. Kenneth Ewart Boulding, *The Meaning of the Twentieth Century: The Great Transition* (New York: Harper & Row, 1964), 199.

2. Unsigned lead editorial for its cover feature, "Welcome to the Anthropocene," *The Economist*, May 28, 2011, 11. In an accompanying piece, it was noted that the "prominent use of the term" Anthropocene was now being made by the Pontifical Academy of Sciences. See "A Man-Made World," *The Economist*, May 28, 2011, 81.

3. It can be argued that this reality, with its sustaining by false Christian consciousness, was articulated years ago by Lynn White in his "The Historical Roots of our Ecologic Crisis," *Nature* (1967).

4. "Welcome to the Anthropocene." For a more conservative approach to the subject of how we should respond to the Anthropocene era, see Mark Lynas, *The God Species: Saving the Planet in the Age of Humans* (Washington, DC: National Geographic, 2011).

5. For more on this, see his website: http://www.familyradio.com/graphical/literature/judgment/judgment.html.

6. "Notable and Quotable" (Karol Cardinal Wojtyla), *Wall Street Journal*, November, 1978. My own search did not arrive at a credible source for this alleged statement of the then-Cardinal Wojtyla. However, the fact that it is on these websites indicates that such attributions often become part of the urban legends surrounding viewpoints like those on such websites.

7. Robert Corin Morris, "Apocalypse Fever: The Perennial Return of the End Times, *Weavings* 21, no. 6 (November/December, 2006): 40.

8. Catherine Cory, "Seeing God's Back and Beholding God's Face: Violence in the Book of Revelation," *The Bible Today* 46 (May, June, 2008): 163.

9. Pope Benedict XVI, "Lord: Help Us Be Converted," October 2, 2005. ZE05100207.

10. The talks took place over a period of years. They were condensed in written form by Regina Shulte. See Michael H. Crosby, OFMCap, "Developing a Spirituality of Exile," *Corpus Reports* 31, no. 3 (2005): 4-11.

11. Edward Hays, *Letters to Exodus Christians: Comfort and Hope for Those Who Have Trouble Going to Church* (Notre Dame, IN: Forest of Peace Publishing, 2008).

12. Walter Brueggemann, *Cadences of Home: Preaching among Exiles* (Louisville, KY: Westminster John Knox Press, 1997), 1.

13. Sharon Daloz Parks, "Home and Pilgrimage: Companion Metaphors for Personal and Social Transformation," *Soundings* 72, nos. 2-3 (Summer/Fall, 1989): 301.

14. Parks, "Home and Pilgrimage," 300.

15. Gary Macy, "Impasse Passé: Conjugating a Tense Past," Opening Address, in Jonathan Y. Tan, ed., *Proceedings of the Sixty-fourth Annual Convention*, Catholic Theological Society of America 64 (2009), 17.

16. Macy, "Impasse Passé," 17-18.

17. Ibid., 18.

18. Brueggemann, *Cadences of Home*, 2.

19. Ibid., 1.

20. David Brooks, citing data related to perceptual bias, in "The Behavioral Revolution," *New York Times*, October 28, 2008.

21. Brueggemann, *Cadences of Home*, 3.

22. Thomas of Celano, *The Life of St. Francis*, 4.8, in Regis J. Armstrong, OFMCap, J. A. Wayne Hellmann, OFMConv, and William J. Short, OFM, eds., *Francis of Assisi: Early Documents* I (New York: New City Press, 1999), 188.

23. For an application of addiction theory, following a "family systems model," see my *The Dysfunctional Church: Addiction and Codependency in the Family of Catholicism* (Eugene, OR: Wipf & Stock, 2011 [1991]).

24. Macy, "Impasse Passé," 18.

25. Deidre Mullen, RSM, personal correspondence with the author.

26. My own benefits from the Roman Church's institutional dysfunction have come from the money I received from speeches and a book on the topic (Crosby, *The Dysfunctional Church*).

27. I am indebted to my cousin Suzanne Tamiesie for this insight. She gained it from her own experience of having many close friends die, including some who died of HIV/AIDS.

28. Brueggemann, *Cadences of Home*, 16.

29. Therese A. Rando, *Treatment of Complicated Mourning* (Champaign, IL: Research Press, 1993), 22.

30. Bradford E. Hinze, "Ecclesial Impasse: What Can We Learn from Our Laments?," *Theological Studies* 72 (September, 2011): 471.

Part II. Jesus' *Dao* of the Kingdom

1. I describe some of these dynamics in Chapter 2 ("In What Do We Believe: 'One, Holy, Catholic and Apostolic Church' or One-half, Roman, Curial and Apodictic Clique") of my book *Rethinking Celibacy, Reclaiming the Church* (Eugene, OR: Wipf & Stock, 2003), 37-63.

6. The "Gospel" of the Historical Jesus

1. Avery Dulles, *Models of the Church* (New York: Doubleday Image Books, 1978).

2. Cardinal Francis George, interview with John Allen, "Cardinal George's Plan to Evangelize America," *National Catholic Reporter*, October 7, 2009 (http://ncronline.org/print/15222).

3. Robert L. Short, *The Gospel according to Peanuts*. Foreword by Martin E. Marty (Louisville, KY: Westminster John Knox Press, 1965).

4. Vikas Bajaj, "Household Wealth Falls by Trillions," *New York Times*, March 13, 2008, B1.

5. Wealth is the sum of such assets as a home, cars, stocks, bank and retirement accounts, minus the sum of debt. Income refers to wages, interest, profits, and other earnings. The main difference between wealth and income is that wealth can be passed on.

6. Miriam Jordan, "White-Minority Wealth Gulf Widens," *Wall Street Journal*, July 26, 2011.

7. "What's Your True Calling? An Easy-Does-It Guide to Finding (and Fulfilling) Your Life's Purpose," *O: The Oprah Magazine*, November, 2010. Cover and article: "Everyone Has a Calling. What's Yours?" pp. 170ff.

8. See www.choosingcompassion.net.

9. Jena McGregor, "Ladies and Gents . . . Marcus Buckingham! The Business Sage Is Spreading His Gospel via a Bus Tour—and Eyeing Wider Audiences," *BusinessWeek*, March 26, 2007, 44.

10. In a 2010 Pew Center survey on religious literacy by its Forum on Religion & Public Life, the data showed that in response to thirty-two questions about the "basics" of religion, atheists and agnostics were the most-informed (20.9 questions answered correctly). White Catholics knew half (16 questions answered correctly); Hispanic Catholics ranked at the bottom with 11.6 of the questions answered correctly). For more, see http://pewresearch.org/pubs/1745/religious-knowledge-in-america-survey-atheists-agnostics-score-highest

11. Theodore Jennings, Jr., *Good News to the Poor: John Wesley's Evangelical Economics* (Nashville: Abingdon, 1990), 186, 187.

12. John P. Dickson, "Gospel as News: εὐαγγελ- from Aristophanes to the Apostle Paul," *New Testament Studies* 51 (2005), 214.

13. Lizette Alvarez, "Where the British May Reign but the Monkeys Rule," *New York Times*, June 28, 2005.

14. "Q" is the name given to the second common source (= "*Quelle*") that was shared by Matthew and Luke, in addition to their reliance on the first source, Mark, for their Gospels. The understanding of this kind of effort to bring about equality comes from an examination of the texts in Matthew and Luke related to debt forgiveness in "The Lord's Prayer." See Giovanni Battista Bazzana, "*Basileia* and Debt Relief: The Forgiveness of Debts in the Lord's Prayer in the Light of Documentary Papyri," *Catholic Biblical Quarterly* 73, no. 3 (2011): 525. Bazzana is indebted to the work on "Q" and the papyri of Melanie Johnson-DeBaurfre, *Jesus among Her Children: Q, Eschatology, and the Construction of Christian Origins* (Harvard Theological Studies 55; Cambridge, MA: Harvard University Press, 2005), 197.

15. For more discussion on the consequences of viewing the Trinity in connection to the household from a more hierarchical or egalitarian perspective, see Brian T. Trainor, "The Trinity and Male Headship of the Family," *Heythrop Journal* 52, no. 5 (September, 2011), 724-38.

16. For more on this, see my paper given at the Washington Theological Union. The notion of "domestic asceticism" in Mark comes from Leif E. Vaage, "An Other Home:

Discipleship in Mark as Domestic Asceticism," *Catholic Biblical Quarterly* 71 (2009): 741-61. The connection between discipline and discipleship is not made but seems to be implied in LaCugna's statement that the "*achievement of personhood requires ascesis.*" See Catherine Mowry La Cugna, *God for Us* (San Francisco: Harper, 1973), 291.

17. David Brooks, "The Gospel of Wealth," *New York Times,* September 6, 2010, quoting David Platt, *Radical: Taking Back Your Faith from the American Dream.*

18. Sabrina Tavernise, "Poverty Reaches a 52-Year Peak, Government Says," *New York Times,* September 14, 2011, A1. See also Conor Dougherty, "Income Slides to 1996 Levels," *Wall Street Journal,* September 14, 2011.

19. Much of this data comes from Thomas Piketty and Emmanuel Saez whose specialty, according to the *Wall Street Journal,* is "earnings inequality" and "wealth concentration." See Daniel Henninger, "The Obama Rosetta Stone," March 12, 2010. See also Gerald F. Seib, "Malaise Casts Shadow on '12 Vote," *Wall Street Journal,* July 7, 2011.

20. Tyler Cown, "The Inequality That Matters," *The American Interest* 6, no. 3 (January-February, 2011), 29-38. Richard Wilkinson and Kate Pickett have argued convincingly that gross inequities damage the whole fabric of society. See their *The Spirit Level: Why More Equal Societies Almost Always Do Better* (New York: Penguin Books, 2009). For a more condensed analysis, outlining the professions that find their members in the top, see Peter Whoriskey, "With Executive Pay, Rich Pull Away from Rest of American," *The Washington Post,* June 18, 2011. For an analysis by the esteemed economist Joseph E. Stiglitz, see his "Inequality: Of the 1%, by the 1%, for the 1%," *Vanity Fair,* May 2011.

21. Tom Kertscher, "Inequality Claim Checks Out," *Milwaukee Journal Sentinel,* March 13, 2011, 2A. Two months later a *New York Times* piece showed that, in 2007, "the average income tax rate paid by the richest 400 taxpayers in the country was 16.62 percent—according to figures from the Internal Revenue Service" (Eduardo Porter, "A Budget without Core Purposes, Taxation without Compassion," *New York Times,* May 23, 2011).

22. Such "gradualism" is belied, again, by Internal Revenue Service findings. Its 2010 data shows that "the 400 highest-earning households in the United States made nearly $345 million in 2007, up 31 percent from a year earlier." Furthermore, "each of the top 400 earning households paid an average tax rate of 16.6 percent, the lowest since the IRS began tracking the data in 1992" (Bloomberg News, "Top-Earning U.S. Households Averaged $345 Million in '07," *New York Times,* February 18, 2010).

23. Jacob Hacker and Paul Pierson, *Winner-Take-All Politics: How Washington Made the Rich Richer—and Turned Its Back on the Middle Class* (New York: Simon & Schuster, 2010), 151.

24. David Books, "Who Is James Johnson?" *New York Times,* June 17, 2011, A31.

25. Drake Bennett, using the findings of Dan Ariely and Marshal I. Norton, "Commentary: The Inequality Delusion," *Bloomberg Business Week,* October 25-31, 2010.

7. Economics, the Economic Trinity, and the Economy of Salvation

1. John Polkinghorne, *Science and the Trinity: The Christian Encounter with Reality* (New Haven/London: Yale University Press, 2004), 61. If we look to science for models

that would resonate with approaches to the trinitarian challenge between the one and the many we can find these discussed in Colin Gunton's Brampton Lectures found in *The One, The Three and the Many* (Cambridge: Cambridge University Press, 1993 [2002]) and Joseph A. Bracken, *Subjectivity, Objectivity and Intersubjectivity: A New Paradigm for Science and Religion* (Philadelphia: Templeton Press, 2009).

2. Francis S. Collins, *The Language of God: A Scientist Presents Evidence for Belief* (New York: Free Press, 2006).

3. Elizabeth A. Johnson, *She Who Is: The Mystery of God in Feminist Theological Discourse* (New York: Crossroad, 1996), 221; idem, *Quest for the Living God: Mapping Frontiers in the Theology of God* (New York/London: Continuum, 2007), 220.

4. Robert D. Hughes III, "Dust and DNA: The Intertwining of Word and Spirit in History and the Trinitarian Life," The Sixth Annual Holy Spirit Lecture and Colloquium, September 17, 2010 (Pittsburgh: Duquesne University, 2011), 9.

5. Since this book is written for a more general audience and because tomes have been written on the Trinity for centuries, I will not approach the Trinity ontologically (who God is) but from what we know from revelation about God through Jesus Christ and our tradition (what God has done). Neither will I discuss any supposed differences between the "Immanent Trinity" (who God is in God's self) and the "Economic Trinity" (how we have come to know about this God), believing, with Karl Rahner that "The 'economic' Trinity is the 'immanent' Trinity, and the 'immanent' Trinity is the 'economic' Trinity"; Karl Rahner, *The Trinity*, trans. Joseph Donceel (New York: Crossroad, 1998), 22.

6. Russ Roberts, "Is the Dismal Science Really a Science?" *Wall Street Journal*, February 27-28, 2010.

7. Denis Edwards, *The God of Evolution* (New York/Mahwah, NJ: Paulist, 1999), 28.

8. For more on the biblical background related to words and dynamics associated with *oikia* and *oikos* and their role as metaphor for one's individual body, the group, and the whole social order of the nation and creation itself (as well as God's reign and God's family), see Rudolf Bultmann's entry in Gerhard Friedrich, ed., *Theological Dictionary of the New Testament* V, trans. and ed. Geoffrey W. Bromiley (Grand Rapids, MI: Wm. B. Eerdmans, 1973), 119-61.

9. Michael H. Crosby, *House of Disciples: Church, Economics in Matthew* (Eugene, OR: Wipf & Stock, 2004), 10-12, *passim*.

10. Sharon Daloz Parks argues that the notion of house is one of two underlying metaphors (along with pilgrimage) for life itself. See her "Home and Pilgrimage: Companion Metaphors for Personal and Social Transformation," *Soundings* 72, nos. 2-3 (1989): 297-315.

11. M. Douglas Meeks, *God as Economist: The Doctrine of God and Political Economy* (Minneapolis: Fortress, 1989), 2.

12. Catherine M. LaCugna, *God for Us: The Trinity and Christian Life* (New York: HarperSanFrancisco, 1991), 221-24.

13. LaCugna, *God for Us*, 411. It is not my purpose here to discuss LaCugna's differences with Rahner over the (dis)value of his equation of the notions of the immanent and Economic Trinity or her contention that "*theologia* is fully revealed and bestowed in *oikonomia*, and *oikonomia* truly expresses the ineffable mystery of *theologia*" (221). This has already been done. See for instance, Elizabeth T. Groppe, "Catherine Mowry

LaCugna's Contribution to Trinitarian Theology," *Theological Studies* 63 (2002): 730-63.

14. St. Bonaventure was basically Cappadocian in his trinitarian theology. Like them, as he evidenced in his "The Soul's Journey into God," the reality of the Trinity is grounded in cosmology. This connection of the Cappadocians is made by Jeffrey C. Pugh and serves as the basic thesis of his book: "For the Cappadocians, Trinity and cosmology were correlative doctrines." See Jeffrey C. Pugh, *Entertaining the Triune Mystery: God, Science, and the Space Between* (Harrisburg, PA: Trinity Press International, 2003), 34.

15. St. Bonaventure, *Itinerarium mentis in Deum*, in *Works of St. Bonaventure* II.6.2, trans. Zachary Hayes, OFM (Saint Bonaventure, NY: Franciscan Institute Publications, 2002), 123, 125.

16. Ibid., 5.2, quoting John Damascene, *De fide orthodoxa*, I.9 and Dionysius, *De divinis nominibus*, III.1.113.

17. Ibid. 6.2, in Hayes, trans., *Works of St. Bonaventure* II, pp. 123-25. For more on this, see Ilia Delio, OSF, *Crucified Love: Bonaventure's Mysticism of the Crucified Christ* (Quincy, IL: Franciscan Press, 1998), 97.

18. Given the monadic nature of the Divine Name as "I am" and Jesus' use of that reference to himself, which elicited the charge of blasphemy, I believe we can move from the traditional male-oriented categories of God to those inclusive of male and female images of God if we adapt Heribert Mühlen's trinitarian application of Martin Buber's I/Thou categories to include *Ich/Du/Wir* (I/Thou/We). For more on this, see his *Der Heilige Geist als Person in der Trinität, bei der Inkarnation und im Gnadenbund: Ich-Du-Wir* (Münster: Verlag Aschendorff, 1966). Unfortunately neither Mühlen nor his trinitarian approach has received much attention in English. His virtual absence in English-language trinitarian studies is evidenced starkly in such survey books as Samuel M. Powell, *The Trinity in German Thought* (Cambridge: Cambridge University Press, 2001), Stanley J. Grenz, *Rediscovering the Triune God: The Trinity in Contemporary Theology* (Minneapolis: Fortress Press, 2004), and Anne Hunt, *Nexus of the Mysteries of Christian Faith* (Theology in Global Perspectives; Maryknoll, NY: Orbis Books, 2005). LaCugna relegates him to her footnotes.

19. Delio, *Crucified Love*, 76.

20. Crosby, *House of Disciple, passim.* I, in turn, relied on the writings of Marshal D. Sahlins to describe the three forms of reciprocity.

21. Pope Benedict XVI, "Love Alone Makes Us Happy." General Audience Reflections on Hugh and Richard, of the Abbey of St. Victor, November 25, 2009 (http://www.zenit.org/article-27665?I=english). This notion is wonderfully summarized in Maria Calisi's book, *Trinitarian Perspectives in the Franciscan Tradition*: "If we believe that God is three-in-one, what does it mean to be 'made in God's image'? If we recognize that the social nature of God is foundational to our own quest for happiness, what structures can we create so as to anticipate this celestial economy of exchange *in via*? If we are to practice what we believe, how can we recommit ourselves to the creation of loving ecclesial relationships, to the treasuring of the revelation of God's relational being in all of creation?" (Olean, NY: St. Bonaventure University, 2008), 8.

22. Pope Benedict XVI, *Caritas in veritate*, 54 (emphasis in original). Quoting *Lumen Gentium*, 1 (Washington, DC: USCCB Publishing, 2009), 61-62.

8. Jesus' Call to Asceticism

1. The actual day I wrote this part of the chapter the Vatican news service, Zenit, published the full address of Pope Benedict XVI's "Address to Representatives of the Worlds of Culture, Art and the Economy" (May 8, 2011) in Venice. He said, "The Gospel is the greatest power for transformation in the world, but it is neither a utopia nor an ideology. The first Christian generations were called rather the 'way,' that is, the way of living that Christ practiced first and invites us to follow" (http://www.zenit.org/article-32521?I=english).

2. Pope Benedict XVI, ibid.

3. A critically acclaimed history of the papacy, which appeared while I was writing this book, was John Julius Norwich's *Absolute Monarchs* (New York: Random House, 2011). According to the cover-feature review of the book by Bill Keller in the *New York Times Book Review*, "the truly great popes were outnumbered by the corrupt, the inept, the venal, the lecherous and the mediocre" (July 9, 2011).

4. Pope Benedict XVI, Trinity Sunday Homily, June 7, 2009 (http://www.zenit.org.article-26113?I=english).

5. John Zizioulas, *Being as Communion: Studies in Personhood and the Church* (Crestwood, NY: St. Vladimir's Seminary Press, 1993), 17.

6. Jürgen Moltmann, *The Trinity and the Kingdom: The Doctrine of God*, trans. Margaret Kohl (San Francisco: Harper & Row, 1981), 197.

7. Catherine Mowry LaCugna, *God for Us: The Trinity and Christian Life* (New York: HarperSanFrancisco, 1991), 380.

8. LaCugna, *God for Us*, 391.

9. *Catechism of the Catholic Church*, 966, 974 (New York: Catholic Book Publishing Company, 1994), 252, 254.

10. Gretchen Morgenson and Joshua Rosner, *Reckless Endangerment: How Outsized Ambition, Greed, and Corruption Led to Economic Armageddon* (New York: Times Books, 2011).

11. Leif E. Vaage, "Ascetic Moods, Hermeneutics, and Bodily Deconstruction: Response to the Three Preceding Papers," in Vincent L. Wimbush and Richard Valantasis, eds., *Asceticism* (New York: Oxford University Press, 1997), 250-51.

12. Richard Valantasis, "Constructions of Power in Asceticism," *Journal of the American Academy of Religion* 63 (1995): 797.

13. Ibid., 799.

14. Ibid.

15. Leif E. Vaage and Vincent L. Wimbush, eds., *Asceticism and the New Testament* (New York/London: Routledge, 1999).

16. Leif E. Vaage, "An Other Home: Discipleship in Mark as Domestic Asceticism," *Catholic Biblical Quarterly* 71 (2009): 744.

17. Ibid.

18. Mary Ann Tolbert, "Asceticism and Mark's Gospel," in Vaage and Wimbush, *Asceticism*, 43.

19. See website of the Catholic Bishops' Conference of England and Wales (http://

www.catholicchurch.org.uk/Catholic-Church/Events/Bishops-Conference-May-2011.
Plenary-resolutions-May2011 [1]pdf).

Part III. The *Dao* of Being a "Kindom" Catholic

1. In discussing the elements and practice of a "Catholic *dao*," I am well aware of the tendency to do a disservice to one tradition by trying to show its relevance for another. The consequences can be very detrimental as well as dishonest and, in a case of taking an Eastern concept like the *dao* and applying it to a Western reality like Catholicism, can be a form of subtle disrespect for the integrity of the former. For more on this, see Rick Fields, "Divided Dharma: White Buddhists, Ethnic Buddhists, and Racism," in Charles S. Prebish and Kenneth T. Tanaaka, eds., *The Faces of Buddhism in America* (Los Angeles: University of California Press, 1998), 196-206.

2. Michael H. Crosby, *Celibacy: Means of Control* or *Mandate of the Heart?* (Notre Dame, IN: Ave Maria Press, 1996). This book received first place in its category from the Catholic Press Association of Canada and the United States.

See also Michael H. Crosby, *Rethinking Celibacy, Reclaiming the Church* (Eugene, OR: Wipf & Stock, 2003).

3. Adrian Piper, "The Meaning of Brahmacharya," in Valerie Jeremijenko, *How We Live Our Yoga* (Boston: Beacon Press, 2001), 36-56.

4. See books noted above as well as Michael H. Crosby, "Celibacy: A Main Reason for the Lack of Vocations?" *Human Development* 32, no. 2 (Summer, 2011): 30-33.

5. My ideas here and throughout this book related to the *dao* are distilled from Willard G. Oxtoby and Roy C. Amore, eds., *World Religions: Eastern Traditions*, 3rd ed. (New York: Oxford University Press, 2010).

6. I am indebted to Doctors Jake and Rosemary Carbine for giving me insights that have helped sculpt the thoughts in this section.

9. The Cosmic Way

1. St. Thomas Aquinas, *Summa Contra Gentiles* II.3.3; trans. James F. Anderson (Garden City, NY: Hanover House, 1956), 33.

2. I am not going to discuss the semantic issue of the "fact" of scientific "truths" vs. the hypotheses that these often entail. For me this can be a smokescreen that keeps honest dialogue about differences between science and religion from taking place. A good example is stressing evolution as a "theory" that disallows an honest discussion of it and the appropriate religious response to it.

3. Cornelia Dean, "Believing Scripture but Playing by Science's Rules," *New York Times*, February 12, 2007, 1A.

4. For a review of recent books on the subject, see Clive Cookson, "Worlds without End," *Financial Times*, April 23-24, 2011. Cookson is science editor for the *Financial Times*.

5. Terrence J. Moran, CSsR, "Spiritual Direction and the New Cosmology," *Presence* 15, no. 3 (September, 2009), 11.

6. Pope Benedict XVI, "Technology Should Help Nature Develop along the

Lines Envisioned by the Creator," June 9, 2011 (http://www.zenit.org/article-32804?I=english).

7. Michael Dowd, *Thank God for Evolution: How the Marriage of Science and Religion Will Transform Your Life and Our World* (New York: Viking, 2007).

8. Denis Edwards, *The God of Evolution: A Trinitarian Theology* (New York/Mahwah, NJ: Paulist, 1999), 15.

9. Thomas Berry, "The Earth: A New Context for Religious Unity," in Anne Lonergan and Caroline Richards, eds., *Thomas Berry and the New Cosmology* (Mystic, CT: Twenty-Third Publications, 1987) 37.

10. Thomas Berry, *The Sacred Universe: Earth, Spirituality, and Religion in the Twenty-first Century* (New York: Columbia University Press, 2010).

11. St. Bonaventure, *Collations on the Six Days* 12.3, *The Works of St. Bonaventure,* V, trans. José de Vinck (Patterson, NJ: St. Anthony Guild, 1970), 174.

12. Ilia Delio, *Christ in Evolution* (Maryknoll, NY: Orbis Books, 2008), 59. She shows that this is accomplished in the Word Incarnate, the revelation of God's inner trinitarian reality.

13. Thomas Berry, CP, in Thomas Berry, CP, in dialogue with Thomas Clarke, SJ, Stephen Dunn, CP, and Anne Lonergan, eds., *Befriending the Earth: A Theology of Reconciliation between Humans and the Earth* (Mystic, CT: Twenty-Third Publications, 1995), 10.

14. Pope Benedict XVI, "No Opposition between Faith's Understanding of Creation and the Evidence of the Empirical Sciences," October 31, 2008, Zenit News Service (http://www.zenit.org/article-24120?I=english).

15. Berry, "The Earth," 37-38.

16. Jennifer (Jinks) Hoffman, "Our Stories" © 2011. Heard by Michael Crosby at Spiritual Directors International Conference, Atlanta. Reprinted with permission of Spiritual Directors International, www.sdiworld.org.

17. Margaret J. Wheatley, *Leadership and the New Science: Learning about Organization from an Orderly Universe* (San Francisco: Barrett-Koehler Publishers, 1994), 104.

18. See *L'Osservatore Romano*'s report on the speech (September 21, 1978).

19. *Catechism of the Catholic Church,* 370 (2nd ed.; Washington DC: United States Catholic Conference, 2003), 94.

20. Committee on Doctrine, United States Conference of Catholic Bishops, "Statement on *Quest for the Living God: Mapping Frontiers in the Theology of God,* by Sister Elizabeth A. Johnson, 7.

21. Committee on Doctrine, "Statement," 16.

22. Alice Walker, *The Color Purple* (New York: Washington Square Press, 1982), 177.

23. Edward O. Wilson, to Thomas Petzinger Jr., "Edward O. Wilson," Talking about Tomorrow, *Wall Street Journal,* January 1, 2000, R16.

24. Thomas of Celano, *The Remembrance of the Desire of a Soul,* CXXIV.165, in Regis J. Armstrong, OFMCap, J. A. Wayne Hellmann, OFMConv, and William J. Short, OFM, trans. and eds., *Francis of Assisi: Early Documents* II (New York: New City Press, 2000), 353.

25. For a connection to the themes of this book, see Berry, *Sacred Universe.*

26. Brian Swimme, *The Universe Is a Green Dragon: A Cosmic Creation Story* (Santa Fe, NM: Bear & Co., 1984).

27. Ilia Delio, OSF, *The Emergent Christ: Exploring the Meaning of Catholic in an Evolutionary Universe* (Maryknoll, NY: Orbis Books, 2011); idem, *Christ in Evolution* (Maryknoll, NY: Orbis Books, 2008).

28. Judy Cannato, *Radical Amazement: Contemplative Lessons from Black Holes, Supernovas, and Other Wonders of the Universe* (Notre Dame, IN: Sorin Books, 2006). A less insightful, but still helpful book is her *Field of Compassion: How the New Cosmology Is Transforming Spiritual Life* (Notre Dame, IN: Sorin Books, 2010).

29. Pope Benedict XVI, "Humans Have Love in Their Genes," June 7, 2009 (http://www.zenit.org/article-26113?I=english).

30. This is the same David Gelernter we discussed regarding his views on "Americanism" in Chapter 1.

31. David Gelernter, "Does the Universe Have a Purpose?" personal reflections in an ad by that name from the John Templeton Foundation in the *New York Times*, October 7, 2007, 8.

32. St. Francis of Assisi, "A Salutation of the Virtues," 14, in Regis J. Armstrong, OFMCap, J. A. Wayne Hellmann, OFMConv, and William J. Short, OFM, trans. and eds., *Francis of Assisi: Early Documents*, I (New York: New City Press, 1999), 165.

33. Ignatius of Loyola, *The Spiritual Exercises of St. Ignatius*, 233, trans and commentary by Louis J. Puhl, SJ (Chicago: University of Loyola Press, 1951), 101.

10. The Christic Way

1. Ilia Delio, OSF, *Christ in Evolution* (Maryknoll, NY: Orbis Books, 2008), 55-56.

2. Delio, *Christ in Evolution*, 56.

3. Catherine Mowry LaCugna, "Problems with a Trinitarian Reformulation," *Louvain Studies* 10 (1985): 324.

4. Barbara Brown Taylor, "Truth to Tell," in *Bread and Wine: Readings for Lent and Easter* (Maryknoll, NY: Orbis Books, 2005), 89.

5. St. Ignatius of Loyola, *The Spiritual Exercises of St. Ignatius*, 102, trans. and commentary by Louis J. Puhl, SJ (Chicago: Loyola University Press, 1951), 49.

6. Michael H. Crosby, Retreat Notes, Los Altos, CA, January 8, 2010.

7. Delio, *Christ in Evolution*, 7.

8. Bonaventure, *Breviloquium* 2.12, V.230., trans. Dominic V. Monti, in *Breviloquium. Works of St. Bonaventure*, 9, ed. Robert J. Karris (St. Bonaventure, NY: Franciscan Institute Publications, 2005), 96.

9. In the 1800s nobody captured this notion of how our *haecceitas* is that by which we become icons of God better than the Jesuit Gerard Manley Hopkins. Captured by this notion, he tried to articulate its power in his various poems through the notion of "inscape" and other images. In my mind, his *As Kingfishers Catch Fire* captures this sense better than anything else.

10. Michael H. Crosby, "Be-ing about the Business," Retreat Notes, January, 2010.

11. Anne Dawson, *Freedom as Liberating Power: A Socio-Political Reading of the Exousia Texts in the Gospel of Mark* (Göttingen: Vandenhoeck & Ruprecht, 2000), 138.

12. Dawson, *Freedom as Liberating Power*, 221.

13. Pope Benedict XVI, Weekly Audience, January 14, 2009 (www.zenit.org/article-24787?l=english).

14. Pope Benedict XVI, November 24, 2005 (www.catholic.org/featured/headline.php? ID=2783).

15. Pope Benedict XVI, "On St. Bonaventure," March 3, 2010. Pope Benedict quoted from Pope John Paul II's *Tertio millennio ineunte*, no. 29.

16. Pope John XXIII, *Mater et magistra*, 65, in Joseph Gremillion, presenter, *The Gospel of Peace and Justice: Catholic Social Teaching since Pope John* (Maryknoll, NY: Orbis Books, 1976), 157.

17. The image of illumination was wonderfully articulated by Pope Benedict XVI in an address to the youth of San Marino/Montefeltro, June 19, 2011. He urged them, "Let the mystery of Christ illumine your whole person" (http://www.zenit.org/article-32907?I=english).

18. Pope Benedict XVI, Address to the Delegates of the Annual Meeting of the Archdiocese of Rome, May 26, 2009 , *L'Osservatore Romano,* June 3, 2009.

19. Delio, *Christ in Evolution,* 63.

20. Daniel Pink, *Drive: The Surprising Truth about What Motivates Us* (New York: Riverhead, 2009).

11. The Way of Consciousness

1. Margaret J. Wheatley, *Leadership and the New Science: Learning about Organization from an Orderly Universe* (San Francisco: Berrett-Koehler, 1994), 104.

2. Wheatley, *Leadership and the New Science,* 106.

3. For a good review of recent books on this topic, see Stephen Cave, "Being Human: Can Behaviour and Consciousness Be Reduced to the Workings of Genes and Brain Cells?" *Financial Times,* June 25-26, 2011.

4. David Eagleman, *Incognito: The Secret Lives of the Mind* (New York: Pantheon, 2011).

5. David Brooks, "The Neural Buddhists," *New York Times,* May 13, 2008, A23.

6. Brooks, "The Neural Buddhists."

7. Nick Humphrey, *Soul Dust: The Magic of Consciousness* (Princeton, NJ: Princeton University Press, 2011).

8. Brooks, "The Neural Buddhists."

9. Ibid.

10. For a deeper examination of what he believes to be a connection between a Buddhist and Christian approach to mindfulness, see Aloysius Pieris, SJ, "Spirituality as Mindfulness: Biblical and Buddhist Approaches," *Spiritus* 10, no. 1 (2010): 38-51.

11. Antonio Damasio, *Self Comes to Mind: Constructing the Conscious Brain* (New York: Pantheon, 2010).

12. 1971 Synod of Bishops, "The Ministerial Priesthood," *The Pope Speaks* 16, no. 4 (1972), 238.

13. Jonah Lehrer, "When We See What We Want," *Wall Street Journal,* June 25-26, 2011.

14. For more on confirmation bias, see Cordelia Fine, *A Mind of Its Own: How Your Brain Distorts and Deceives* (New York: W. W. Norton, 2008). See also, her "Biased but Brilliant," *New York Times*, July 31, 2011.

15. Dan Sperber and Hugo Mercier, "Why Do Humans Reason? Arguments for an Argumentative Theory," *Behavioral and Brain Science* 34 (2011), 57. An insightful blog discussing their arguments is Gary Gutting, "Argument, Truth and the Social Side of Reasoning," The Stone Forum, *New York Times* blog, June 29, 2011.

16. Margaret Heffernan, *Willful Blindness: Why We Ignore the Obvious at Our Peril* (New York: Walker, 2011).

17. Benedict Cary, "Why All Indiscretions Appear Youthful," Science section, *New York Times*, October 5, 2010.

18. David Gal and Derek D. Rucker, "When in Doubt, Shout!: Paradoxical Influences of Doubt on Proselytizing," *Psychological Science*, October 13, 2010 (http://pss.sagepub.com/content/early/2010/10/12/0956797610385953).

19. Thomas J. DeLong and Sara DeLong, "The Paradox of Excellence," *Harvard Business Review* (June 2011), 119-23.

20. Shirley S. Wang, "Researchers Study What Gives Social Norms Their Power," *Wall Street Journal*, May 3, 2011.

21. Daniel H. Pink, *A Whole New Mind: Why Right-Brainers Will Rule the Future* (New York: Riverhead Penguin Books, 2006), 3.

22. Wheatley, *Leadership and the New Science*, 106-7.

23. Ibid., 64.

24. Ibid., 91ff.

25. Philip Chard, "Deep Probe Inward Dissolves Sense of Self," in Out of My Mind Column, *Milwaukee Journal Sentinel*, March 15, 2005, 2F.

26. Eleanor M. Godway, "Faith *and* Knowledge in Crisis: Towards an Epistemology of the Cross," *Listening, Journal of Religion and Culture* 27, no. 2 (1992): 102. To develop this kenotic "unknowing," Godway highlights the notion of conversion developed by Kurt H. Wolff in his image of "Surrender and Catch." I applied Wolff's model to that of Francis of Assisi in my *Finding Francis, Following Christ* (Maryknoll, NY: Orbis Books, 2007), 93-99.

27. Godway, "Faith *and* Knowledge," 103.

28. Andrew Cohen, "The Interdynamics of Culture and Consciousness," in The Guru & the Pundit, Dialogue XXI, *EnlightenNext* (December 2008–February 2009), 43.

29. Philip Chard, "Don't Let Emotions Take the Breath Right out of You," *The Milwaukee Journal Sentinel*, October 5, 1999.

30. John Donohue, *Anam Ċara: A Book of Celtic Wisdom* (New York: Cliff Street Books, 1997), 70.

12. The Way of Connectedness

1. Richard Feynman, quoted in Carl Rollyson, "A Curious Mind," book review of Lawrence M. Krauss, *Quantum Man: Richard Fenyman's Life in Science* (New York: Norton, 2011), *Wall Street Journal*, April 2-3, 2011.

2. Erich Jantsch, *The Self-Organizing Universe* (Oxford: Pergamon, 1980), 196. I am indebted to Margaret Wheatley for this quote.

3. Margaret J. Wheatley, *Leadership and the New Science: Learning about Organization from an Orderly Universe* (San Francisco: Berret-Koehler, 1994), 38.

4. John Tierney, "A Generation's Vanity, Heard through Lyrics," Findings, *New York Times*, April 26, 2011.

5. Ross Douthat, "The Online Looking Glass," *New York Times*, June 13, 2011.

6. Sherry Turkle, *Alone Together: Why We Expect More from Technology and Less from Each Other* (New York: Basic Books, 2010).

7. Ilia Delio, OSF, *The Emergent Christ: Exploring the Meaning of Catholic in an Evolutionary Universe* (Maryknoll, NY: Orbis Books, 2011), 90.

8. Paul Krugman, "A Tale of Two Moralities," *New York Times*, January 14, 2011.

9. John: 1:32, 33, 38, 39; 2:12; 3:36; 4:40 (2x); 5:38; 6:27, 56; 7:9; 8:31 35 (2x); 9:41; 10:40; 11:6, 54; 12:24, 34, 46; 14:10, 17, 25; 15:4 (3x), 5, 6, 7 (2x), 9, 10, 16; 19:31; 21:22, 23.

10. For more on this, see my *"Do You Love Me?" Jesus Questions the Church* (Maryknoll, NY: Orbis Books, 2000), especially 199-222.

11. Pope Benedict XVI, "The Risen Lord Gives Us a Place of Refuge, a Place of Light," September 22, 2011 (http://www.zenit.org/article-33498I=english).

12. John D. Zizioulas, *Being as Communion: Studies in Personhood and the Church* (Crestwood, NY: St. Vladimir's Seminary Press, 1973), 17.

13. Robert Barron, "Evangelizing the American Culture," in Ronald Rolheiser, ed., *Secularity and the Gospel: Being Missionaries to Our Children* (New York: Crossroad, 2006), 172.

13. The Contemplative Way

1. Alice Walker, *The Color Purple* (New York: Washington Square Press, 1982), 178.

2. Thomas Merton, *Conjectures of a Guilty Bystander* (Garden City, NY: Doubleday, 1966), 142.

3. Sam Harris, *The End of Faith: Religion, Terror, and the Future of Reason* (New York/London: W. W. Norton, 2004), 205. I do not equate the terms "spirituality" and "mysticism." I equate mysticism with the experience of contemplation, and I describe spirituality as the experience of something transcendent that becomes the foundation of one's life from which one desires to construct a world to match that experience (within a community of like-minded people).

4. Harris, *The End of Faith*, 207.

5. Angela of Foligno, *The Book of Blessed Angela of Foligno* VI, in *Angela of Foligno: Complete Works*, trans. Paul Lachance, OFM (Classics of Western Spirituality; New York/Mahwah, NJ: Paulist Press, 1993), 169-70.

6. Constance Fitzgerald, "From Impasse to Prophetic Hope: Crisis of Memory," *Proceedings of the 64th Annual Convention*, Catholic Theological Society of America 64 (2009), 34.

7. Evelyn Underhill, *Mystics in the Church* (New York: Schocken Books, 1971), 32-33.

8. This has been an underlying theme of this book.

9. Bonaventure of Bagnoregio, "Sermon I: Concerning the Threefold Testimony of the Most Holy Trinity," 7, trans. Zachary Hayes, OFM, *Greyfriars Review* 20, no. 2 (2006): 134.

10. Fitzgerald, "From Impasse to Prophetic Hope," 23.

11. Ibid., 31.

12. Abraham Heschel, *The Prophets* (New York: Harper Torchbooks, 1962), 202.

13. J. D. Salinger, *Franny and Zooey* (New York/Boston: Little, Brown, 1989), 36-37.

14. Pope Benedict XVI, Reflections on St. Teresa of Avila, February 2, 2011 (http:// www. vatican.va/holy_father/benedict_xvi/audiences/2011/documents/hf_ben-xvi_ aud_20110202 _en.html).

15. I have outlined an evangelically based approach to such prayer, based on Psalm 24 and Matthew 6:19-34, in the chapter "Blessed Are the Pure of Heart; They Will See God," in my *Spirituality of the Beatitudes: Matthew's Vision for the Church in an Unjust World* (rev. ed.; Maryknoll, NY: Orbis Books, 2005), 140-58.

16. St. Clare of Assisi, Third Letter to Agnes of Prague, 12-13, in Regis J. Armstrong, OFMCap, and Ignatius C. Brady, OFM, *Francis and Clare: The Complete Works* (The Classics of Western Spirituality; New York: Paulist Press, 1982), 200.

17. St. Clare of Assisi, Fourth Letter to Agnes of Prague, 24-25, in Armstrong and Brady, *Francis and Clare*, 205.

18. St. Clare of Assisi, First Letter to Agnes of Prague, 8, in Armstrong and Brady, *Francis and Clare*, 191.

19. St. Clare of Assisi, Second Letter to Agnes of Prague, 4, 7, in Armstrong and Brady, *Francis and Clare*, 195.

20. St. Clare of Assisi, Third Letter to Agnes of Prague, 12-13, in Armstrong and Brady, *Francis and Clare*.

21. 1971 Synod of Bishops, "The Ministerial Priesthood," *The Pope Speaks* 16, no. 4 (1972), 368.

22. St. Francis of Assisi, *Earlier Rule* (1221), 7.2, in Regis J. Armstrong, OFMCap, J. A. Wayne Hellmann, OFMConv, and William J. Short, OFM, eds., *Francis of Assisi: Early Documents* I, *The Saint* (New York: New City Press, 1999), 68.

23. St. Francis of Assisi, Testament 19, in Armstrong et al., *Francis of Assisi: Early Documents* I, 125.

24. St. Francis of Assisi, Earlier Rule (1221), 16.6, in Armstrong et al., *Francis of Assisi: Early Documents* I, 74. This passage is in the section of his Earlier Rule outlining how the brothers were to go among the Muslims and other unbelievers.

25. St. Francis of Assisi, Second Letter to the Faithful, 47, in Armstrong et al., *Francis of Assisi: Early Documents* I, 48.

26. For more on the connection between the approach to God and creation of Francis and Ignatius, see Ewert H. Cousins, "Franciscan Roots of Ignatian Meditation," paper shared with the author by Regis Armstrong, OFMCap.

27. St. Ignatius of Loyola, *The Spiritual Exercises*, 233. The actual wording in this last section of the *Exercises*, entitled "Contemplation to Attain the Love of God," is that "I may in all things love and serve the Divine Majesty" (trans. Louis J. Puhl, SJ; Chicago: Loyola University Press, 1951), 101.

28. See United States Catholic Bishops, "When I Cry for Help: A Pastoral Response to Domestic Violence against Women," 10th Anniversary Edition, November 12, 2002 (http://www.usccb.org/issues-and-action/marriage-and-family/marriage/domestic-violence/when-i-call-for-help.cfm).

14. The Compassionate Way

1. Tenzin Gyatso (14th Dalai Lama), "Many Faiths, One Truth," *New York Times,* May 24, 2010.

2. Natalie Angier, "The Biology behind the Milk of Human Kindness," Science section, *New York Times,* November 23, 2009.

3. Michael H. Crosby, *The Paradox of Power: From Control to Compassion* (New York: Crossroad, 2008).

4. Frans de Waal, *The Age of Empathy: Nature's Lessons for a Kinder Society* (New York: Three Rivers Press/Random House, 2009).

5. A good summary of some of this research can be found in Jean Decety and Philip L. Jackson, "A Social-Neuroscience Perspective on Empathy," *Current Directions in Psychological Science* 15, no. 2 (2006): 54-58.

6. David Brooks, commenting on the research of Jonathan Haidt for a book to be published in 2012 (tentatively called *The Righteous Mind*), "Nice Guys Finish First," *New York Times,* May 17, 2011.

7. Vince Beiser, "Save the Poor. Sell Them Stuff. Cheap!" *Miller-McCune* (May/June 2011), 48.

8. Beiser, "Save the Poor," 50.

9. Jeremy Rifkin, *The Empathic Civilization: The Race to Global Consciousness in a World in Crisis* (New York: Jeremy P. Tarcher/Penguin, 2010), 223.

10. Rifkin, *The Empathic Civilization*, 121.

11. The rejection of women throughout history (with its concomitant shaming), including that which has taken place and continues to take place in the church, seems to have been acknowledged as wrong by Pope John Paul II in his 1995 "Letter to Women." There he said, "Unfortunately, we are heirs to a history which has *conditioned* us to a remarkable extent. In every time and place, this conditioning has been an obstacle to the progress of women. Women's dignity has often been unacknowledged and their prerogatives misrepresented; they have often been relegated to the margins of society and even reduced to servitude. This has prevented women from truly being themselves and it has resulted in a spiritual impoverishment of humanity. Certainly it is no easy task to assign the blame for this, considering the many kinds of cultural conditioning which down the centuries have shaped ways of thinking and acting. And if objective blame, especially in particular historical contexts, has belonged to not just a few members of the Church, for this I am truly sorry. May this regret be transformed, on the part of the whole Church, into a renewed commitment of fidelity to the Gospel vision. When it comes to setting women free from every kind of exploitation and domination, the Gospel contains an ever relevant message which goes back to the *attitude of Jesus Christ himself.* Transcending the established norms of his own culture, Jesus treated women with openness, respect,

acceptance and tenderness. In this way he honoured the dignity which women have always possessed according to God's plan and in his love. As we look to Christ at the end of this Second Millennium, it is natural to ask ourselves: how much of his message has been heard and acted upon?" ("Letter of Pope John Paul II to Women," 3, June 29, 1995, http://www.vatican.va/holy_father/john_paul_ii/letters/documents/hf_jp-ii_let_29061995_women_en.html).

12. Rifkin, *The Empathic Civilization*, 350.

13. Ibid., 350.

14. An exception to this is the significant statement by Pope Benedict XVI that the "tender compassion of God" serves as "the hallmark of every movement, action and expression of the Church in all of her sacramental, charitable, educational and social endeavors, so that in everything her members may strive to make the Triune God known and loved through Jesus Christ" ("Address to Bishops of Indonesia," October 7, 2011 [http://www.zenit.org/article-33621?l=English]).

15. Marcus J. Borg, *Meeting Jesus Again for the First Time: The Historical Jesus and the Heart of Contemporary Faith* (San Francisco: HarperSanFrancisco, 1994), 50.

16. Bruce J. Malina and Richard I. Rohrbaugh, *Social-Science Commentary on the Synoptic Gospels* (Minneapolis: Fortress, 1992), 59.

17. Max Weber, *The Theory of Social and Economic Organization*, trans. A. M. Henderson and Talcott Parsons (Glencoe, IL: Free Press, 1947), 369.

18. This is particularly evident in at least one of our major political parties. In a debate among the Republican candidates for president of the United States, September 12, 2011, a good number in the audience "erupted in cheers" at the notion of allowing someone without health care to die. This led Nobel Prize winner (economics) Paul Krugman to write: "American politics is fundamentally about different moral visions." He suggested such a response attests to the fact that "compassion is out of fashion—indeed, lack of compassion has become a matter of principle, at least among the G.O.P.'s base" ("Free to Die: When Lack of Compassion Becomes a Principle," *New York Times*, September 16, 2011).

19. Maureen H. O'Connell, *Compassion: Loving Our Neighbor in an Age of Globalization* (Maryknoll, NY: Orbis Books, 2009).

20. O'Connell, *Compassion*, 29, 30.

21. George W. Bush, First Inaugural Address, January 20, 2001 (http://www.bartleby.com/124/pres66.html).

22. Daniel Henninger, "The Numbing Down of America," *Wall Street Journal*, April 7, 2007. A similar sentiment around the same time in another *Wall Street Journal* piece came from another conservative writer, Peggy Noonan. See her "Cold Standard: Virginia Tech and the Heartlessness of Our Media and Therapy Culture," *Wall Street Journal*, April 20, 2007.

23. Joseph Goldbrunner, *Holiness Is Wholeness* (Notre Dame, IN: University of Notre Dame Press, 1967).

24. Michael E. Cavanagh, "Rediscovering Compassion," *Journal of Religion and Health* 34, no. 4 (1995): 318.

25. Tenzin Gyatso, *The Compassionate Life* (Somerville, MA: Wisdom Publications, 2003).

26. Pope Benedict XVI, Address to the 37th Conference of the United Nations Food and Agriculture Organization, 3, July 1, 2011 (http://www.zenit.org/article-32993?l=english).

27. Pope Benedict XVI, Food and Agriculture Organization Talk, 3 (http://www.zenit.org/article-32993?l=english).

28. O'Connell, *Compassion*, 34, 71, *passim*. Surprisingly, since she uses the story of the Good Samaritan throughout her book, O'Connell does not address the systemic obstacles to compassion that were endemic in the religious leaders' interpretation of the "holiness codes" that Jesus was challenging. When I raised this issue with her in a private conversation she acknowledged her lack of development of this dimension of the story. In my mind this supports my thoughts on how deep our culturally received blinders regarding holiness can be when someone as insightful as O'Connell would not have recognized the deeper issue at stake.

15. The Way of Community

1. I have written about these patterns for over twenty years. Since my original writing, the number of members of the Catholic family "in the West" who no longer call it "home" has only increased. See Michael H. Crosby, *The Dysfunctional Church: Addiction and Codependency in the Family of Catholicism* (Eugene, OR: Wipf & Stock, 2011 [1991]). A later book expanded the familial dynamics around addiction to the notion of abuse as defined by the U.S. bishops ("any way one uses to control another through fear and intimidation") and applied it to the institutional dynamics of the Roman Church. See Michael H. Crosby, *Rethinking Celibacy, Reclaiming the Church* (Eugene, OR: Wipf & Stock, 2003).

2. These would be found in the classical writings of such theorists as Max Weber, *The Sociology of Religion*, trans. Ephraim Fischoff (Boston: Beacon Press, 1963); Emile Durkheim, *The Elementary Forms of the Religious* Life, trans. Joseph Ward Swain (Glencoe, IL: Free Press, 1947); Ernst Troeltsch, *The Social Teaching of the Christian Churches* II, trans. Olive Wyon (London: George Allen & Unwin, 1949); and Anthony F. C. Wallace, "Revitalization Movements," *American Anthropologist* 58, no. 2 (1956), 264-81. I have applied their theories to the role of alternative communities in my *Franciscan Charism: A Sociological Investigation* (Pulaski, WI: Franciscan Publishers, 1969).

3. Pope Benedict XVI, "In Our Affluent Western World, Much Is Lacking," September 24, 2011; ZE11092404 (http://www.zenit.org/article-33516?I=English). It seems that Pope Benedict XVI has put more trust in such small faith communities than his predecessor, who resisted their development, especially in Latin America.

4. Greg Esty and Mary Testin, "Pastoral Practice in a Postmodern Church," *Pastoral Practice* 20, no. 3 (2005): 5.

5. Ilia Delio, *Crucified Love: Bonaventure's Mysticism of the Crucified Christ* (Quincy, IL: Franciscan Press, 1998), 138.

6. Robert Christian Smith, Karl Christofferson, Hilary Davidson, and Patricia Snell Herzog, *Lost in Transition: The Dark Side of Emerging Adulthood* (Oxford/New York: Oxford University Press, 2011).

7. Robert Christian Smith, N. Bellah, Richard Madsen, William M. Sullivan, Ann

Swindler, and Steven M. Tipton, *Habits of the Heart: Individualism and Commitment in American Life* (Berkeley: University of California Press, 1985), 221.

8. Thomas Berry, CP, in Thomas Berry, CP, with Thomas Clarke, SJ, *Befriending the Earth: A Theology of Reconciliation between Humans and the Earth,* ed. Stephen Dunn, CP, and Anne Lonergan (Mystic, CT: Twenty-Third Publications, 1995), 14-15.

9. Donald W. Winnicott, *Human Nature* (Philadelphia: Brunner/Mazel, 1988), 131.

10. Thomas Moore, "Transmute Narcissism into Community," *Spirituality and Health* 8 (November/December 2005): 10-11.

11. David Brooks, "The Social Animal," *New York Times,* September 12, 2008.

12. Pope Benedict XVI, "Sagrada Familia," November 7, 2010 (http://www.zenit.org/article-30881?l=english).

13. Pope John Paul II, Post-Synodal Apostolic Exhortation *Ecclesia in Africa*, 43, I, in Maura Browne, SND, *The African Synod: Documents, Reflections, Perspectives* (Maryknoll, NY: Orbis Books, 1996), 245.

14. Pope John Paul II, *Ecclesia in Africa*, 63, quoting Proposition 8, in Browne, *The African Synod*, 251.

15. Michael Battle, *Ubuntu: I in You and You in Me* (New York: Seabury Books, 2009), 88.

16. Benson Kumbukani Makileni, conversation with author, North Richland Hills, TX, June 28, 2011.

17. Desmond Mpilo Tutu, *No Future without Forgiveness* (New York: Doubleday Image Book, 1999), 265.

18. First African Synod, "Message of the Synod," nos. 27-31, in Browne, *The African Synod*, 78-79.

19. Avery Dulles, SJ, *Models of the Church,* expanded ed. (New York: Doubleday, 1999), 204-26.

20. Joseph Bracken, SJ, "The Trinity as a Community of Persons," Seminar on the Doctrine of the Trinity, *Catholic Theological Society of America* 35 (1980), 180.

21. Donald W. Winnicott, *The Maturational Process and the Facilitating Environment: Studies in the Theory of Emotional Development* (New York: International Universities Press, 1965).

22. For a feminist approach to Winnicott's "holding environment," see Mary Baird Carlsen, *Meaning-Making: Therapeutic Processes in Adult Development* (New York/London: W. W. Norton, 1988), 51ff.

23. Wendell Berry, *Sex, Economy, Freedom and* Community (New York/San Francisco: Pantheon, 1993), 143.

24. Hubert Dreyfus and Sean Dorrance Kelly, *All Things Shining: Reading the Western Classics to Find Meaning in a Secular Age* (New York: Free Press, 2010).

25. Elizabeth A. Johnson, "Women, Earth, and Creator Spirit" (1993 Madeleva Lecture), in *Spirituality* (New York/Mahwah, NJ: Paulist Press, 1993), 30-31.

26. Tutu, *No Future without Forgiveness*, 31.

27. Attributed to Albert Einstein. While widely identified with Einstein, I have not been able to find a solid citation from anything he said or wrote with this wonderful reflection.

Index